DRUGS & CRIME

Jill Taylor: lost while writing this book but lovingly remembered forever

KEY APPROACHES TO CRIMINOLOGY

DRUGS & CRIME

TAMMY AYRES & STUART TAYLOR

Sage

1 Oliver's Yard
55 City Road
London EC1Y 1SP

2455 Teller Road
Thousand Oaks
California 91320

Unit No 323-333, Third Floor, F-Block
International Trade Tower
Nehru Place, New Delhi 110 019

8 Marina View Suite 43-053
Asia Square Tower 1
Singapore 018960

Editor: Rhoda Toweh
Editorial assistant: Pippa Wills
Production editor: Sarah Sewell
Copyeditor: Raxshana Ravindraraj
Proofreader: Girish Sharma
Indexer: TNQ Tech Pvt. Ltd.
Cover design: Bhairvi Vyas
Typeset by: TNQ Tech Pvt. Ltd.
Printed and bound by CPI Group (UK) Ltd, Croydon, CR0 4YY

Library of Congress Control Number: 2024941409

British Library Cataloguing in Publication data

A catalogue record for this book is available from the British Library

ISBN 978-1-5264-8684-4
ISBN 978-1-5264-8683-7 (pbk)

CONTENTS

AUTHOR BIOS

Tammy Ayres is an Associate Professor of Criminology at the University of Leicester. She has spent her entire career working in the area of drugs and prisons as a researcher and academic.

Stuart Taylor is a Staff Tutor in Social Policy and Criminology at the Open University. He has worked within the field of drugs and crime for his whole career, initially as a practitioner and latterly as a researcher and academic.

ACKNOWLEDGEMENTS

This book took a little longer to write than expected. Our thanks must therefore go to all those at Sage who have showed patience and support in equal measure: Natalie Aguilera, Sarah Moorhouse, Pippa Wills and Rhoda Ola-Said.

As co-authors, we love working together (well, most of the time), and so need to thank the wonderful human being and fantastic drugs scholar who brought us together: Julian Buchanan. We are forever thankful and you will always have a special place in our hearts. You created a dream team.

On the home front, we also need to acknowledge the assistance and tolerance that we have received. Stuart would like to therefore thank Bill, Gaby, Lennie and Stan for their unwavering support, warm hugs and continuous love. Meanwhile, Tammy would like to thank Colleen and William, Nelroy, Leroy, Sereta, Dexter, Elliott and Tommy for their continued love and support.

On the academic front, we would like to acknowledge friends and colleagues who have helped and supported us and our work along the way: Simon Winlow, Avi Brisman, Nigel South, Travis Linnemann, James Treadwell, Oliver Smith, Rowland Atkinson, Mark Hamm, Steve Hall, Craig Kelly, Corina Medley, Keith Hayward, Alex Hall, Jo Large, Ross Coomber, Jeff Ferrell, Eamonn Carrabine, Eddy Green, Dan Briggs, Craig Ancrum, Yvonne Jewkes, Matthew Millings, Reece Walters, Clare Anderson, Kellie Moss, Lol Burke, Ester Ragonese, Helen Beckett Wilson, Anne Rees, Emma Murray, Helena Gosling, Chris Allen and George Mair.

INTRODUCTION

As a global society, we are consistently alerted to matters of drug use, drug dependency, drug dealing, drug trafficking, drug cartels, drugs in prison, drug testing and drug treatment. What do all these issues have in common? They all relate aspects of drugs to aspects of crime. Whether that be drugs as a crime, drug-related crime, the policing of drugs, the criminal justice systems' processing of drug offences and offenders or the delivery of court-mandated drug services to treat those whose crimes are associated with their drug use. The media reporting of such issues feeds into the *simmering panic* (Taylor, 2008) surrounding drugs and crime, which prompts societal and indeed political concern due to the associated damaging and destructive outcomes. Despite continuous attempts by the authorities to respond to drugs and crime, they remain omnipresent in every jurisdiction across the globe. As a result, drugs and crime have become inextricably linked around the world In this sense, the year prior to the publication of this book was a typical one in the world of drugs and crime.

The United Kingdom prohibited nitrous oxide. The Netherlands began piloting the legal production of cannabis. The Bolivian government questioned why the coca leaf is outlawed. Globally, more drugs were said to have been produced than ever before. In Spain, a narco submarine was found carrying £120 million worth of cocaine from South America. In Sri Lanka, more than 29,000 individuals were arrested over a monthlong drive against drug traffickers. In London, two Metropolitan police officers were dismissed for gross misconduct having stopped, searched, detained and handcuffed two Black people after lying that they had smelled cannabis. In England and Wales, record numbers of drug-related deaths were reported. In the United States, over 80,000 people lost their lives due to the ongoing opioid crisis. We could go on.

Drugs and crime are therefore a ubiquitous societal feature. They are also in a constant state of flux. Yet the issues that drugs and crime present are rarely novel, with emerging issues and patterns often matching those of the past due to the perpetual dance between illegal drug market actors and those authorities attempting to police them, which sees both sides utilising different strategies and innovative technologies in an everlasting game of cat and mouse. Certain trends remain consistent, however, and these underline the importance of this field – drugs and crime – to academics, practitioners and policymakers alike. For example, the global prison population consistently shows that almost a fifth of people imprisoned are incarcerated for drug offences, with these often being low-level offenders, such as people who use drugs or small-scale suppliers, with the proportion of women imprisoned for drug-related offences being almost double that of men (UN, 2021). At least 467 people were executed in 2023 for drug offences, which represents a 44% increase from 2022, and a staggering 1450%

increase from 2020 (HRI, 2023). Meanwhile, in jurisdictions like the United States and United Kingdom, minority ethnic groups continue to be disproportionately stopped by the police, arrested and sentenced to custody for drug offences. All of this means that issues of drugs and crime are a criminological, sociological and psychological mainstay. This continues a century-long trend of drugs and crime being a pervasive social, political and economic feature. It is also, for many people, a deeply personal issue that effects, influences and fascinates us. The authors included.

Growing up in the United Kingdom during the 1990s saw us witness firsthand several drug- and crime-related phenomena. Firstly, there was an ongoing rise in the use of heroin whereby we saw friends and acquaintances progress into heroin use, many trying it for the first time during the summer of 1994 when a cannabis drought led to heroin being offered as a substitute via the illegal drug marketplace. Some of these individuals enjoyed and controlled their use, some developed a dependency, some paid for their drugs through legitimate means, others committed crime to fund their use, some entered treatment and some lost their lives. The response by the UK government was to move drugs policy from a health orientated approach to one firmly rooted in criminal justice, with those heroin users who committed crime being coerced into treatment, meaning the way people with drug dependencies were framed moved from them being perceived as needing care to being criminal. As such these so-called problematic drug users became the focus of drug policy, which saw the introduction of invasive processes including the monitoring of their movements via electronic tagging, targeted surveillance of their behaviours by the police, the scrutiny of what they were putting into their bodies via drug testing, and being coerced into drug treatment.

Secondly, the outside free party (or 'rave') scene was buoyant in the early 1990s. At these events, people came together to dance and often take illegal drugs. Initially, these parties would only conclude when the police arrived, an end was negotiated, and all partiers made their way home. Yet this changed with the 1994 Criminal Justice and Public Order Act, which afforded authorities new powers to remove persons attending or preparing a rave. This represented a watershed moment where a cultural lifestyle and indeed a specific type of music were in essence criminalised due to their association with specific types of drugs and their use. All of this took place at a time when levels of self-reported drug use among young people were at their highest and the use of illegal drugs was said to be attaining a normalised status (Parker et al., 1998), meaning that whether one used illegal drugs or not, they were now part and parcel of everyday life (South, 1999), particularly for adolescents and young adults.

Thirdly, the 1990s saw continued efforts by the police to destabilise drug markets and make arrests for drug offences. In 1995, an 18-year-old male friend, working as a glass collector in a nightclub was approached by a female looking to acquire drugs. He informed her that he did not sell them but would ask around (as he was keen to get her phone number for a date). Later, he saw someone he knew to be involved in the drugs trade, checked that he could tell the woman to approach him, and returned to pass on the information. It would transpire that this woman was an undercover police officer.

The following morning his family home was raided by the police (no drugs were found). The day after, the local newspaper named him as one member of a 'drugs ring'. The police began pulling his car over as a known 'criminal' face. A ban on overseas travel during the investigation saw him miss out on a long-awaited summer holiday to celebrate the completion of his college exams. With little life experience or money for legal advice, he was convicted of supplying a Class B drug. With it went his ambition of becoming a teacher. Here, the criminalisation of drugs altered someone's life course in their first year of adulthood – in this instance, someone who had never taken illegal drugs, let alone sold them, had their life irreparably altered because of drugs.

What these examples show us are that issues of drugs and crime can affect society in many ways and that social, legal and political constructions of illegal drugs, illegal drug users and illegal drug market actors lead to a variety of outcomes through the process of their criminalisation. They also highlight the importance of recognising that drug laws outlaw certain substances, consumption practices and behaviours, with certain substances being construed as inherently criminal and harmful, and that frameworks of legal regulation can shape people's life experiences. Although the examples may have changed, all continue to be crucially important in the drugs and crime landscape of the 2020s as they were three decades ago. Many of you may be thinking, well drugs are illegal for a reason – they are bad, they cause crime, we should 'just say no' to them. Yet we have to ask how much of what we think and know about drugs is based on fact or fiction?

What this book will show is that much of what we are told about drugs are mythological illusions that have been constructed to serve the interests of those in power, whether it was the early colonisers or contemporary politicians, drugs and crime win votes, manufacture consent and serve as 'opium for the people' (Debord, 1969). Drugs and crime have become society's spectacles that shape people's perceptions and experiences, creating a reality dominated by appearances. Drugs and crime are society's scapegoats as are the actors that participate in them. While we are not saying substances cannot be harmful or everyone should rush out and use drugs, what this book aims to do is separate fact from fiction, and instead offer a critical overview of drugs and crime, and why they have become inextricably linked in contemporary society.

THE VOLUME

So, a book on drugs and crime: where to start? That was the initial thought facing us when we began conceptualising this text. The scope of the subjects encapsulated within this field is considerable. So much so, that many writers before us have distilled their discussions down to a core of subjects, which are replicated in the contents of most textbooks on the topic. We, however, were keen to break from the normative mould. Whilst on one level, drugs and crime are intrinsically linked, there is also a need to highlight how the criminalisation of drug use is equally important to consider – and how, in effect, this relationship could be labelled 'crime and drugs'. Undoubtedly, a consideration of factors, such as how drugs and crime are related, how the criminal justice system (and wider authorities) processes drug offences/offenders and what the outcomes of these are, is essential. But so is a more critical exploration of these phenomena, as this affords a more nuanced picture of the drugs and crime relationship to emerge, which offers differential ways of thinking about, conceptualising and investigating these topics.

In this sense, we encourage readers to expand their thinking around those drug laws that lie at the heart of so many issues within the drugs and crime sphere. One way that this book attempts this is by exploring such issues in relation to Steven Box's five-point framework of crime and criminalisation. In this, Box (1983) maps out the outcomes of the criminalisation process, whereby underprivileged/powerless people are disproportionately criminalised, creating a problematic population that is consequently engineered to be seen as morally defective and warranting of punishment, which in turn renders invisible the greater harms caused by the privileged/powerful, which then frames 'justice' as legitimate and above refute, and resultantly, this enhances reliance on the state to protect us from the apparent problem, despite the state being the fundamental problem. Clearly, the law is central to Box's argument, but in relation to drugs and crime, there is a need to think more widely, to recognise the multitude of sociolegal factors – including drug laws, drug prohibition, drug policy and the wider historical and contemporary context of consumer capitalism – that have come to define which drugs, drug manufacturers, suppliers and users are seen as illegitimate and harmful, leading to their criminalisation and ultimately to the study of drugs and crime.

Throughout this book then, we attempt to outline mainstream understandings around drugs and crime but offer alternative ways of thinking about these. This is perhaps a necessity given that much of what is known about drugs and crime is grounded in mythical notions and untruths (Saper, 1974), perpetuated by a reductionist discourse that provides only a half-formed picture of the status quo. As Toby Seddon (2007a:154) argues, we must ask whether the demonisation of certain drugs is 'serving not only to exacerbate rather than minimise human misery but also to obscure some of the more significant questions of social and legal policy with which it has become entangled' as we 'force the facts of social life through the sieve of dominant ideology' (Reinarman and Duskin, 1992:15). As Box (1983:15) observes 'for too long too many people have been socialised to see crime and criminals through the eyes of the state', meaning that there is much more to the issue of drugs and crime than first meets the eye, 'but most people cannot see it'. As such, this book seeks to identify the bigger drugs and crime picture through a series of discussion points focused on the juxtapositions, contradictions and dichotomies evident within this field.

Before embarking on any such analysis, however, it is imperative to define the two key terms that fuse this book together – those of drugs and crime. In relation to the former, this book focuses predominantly on those illegal drugs that are prohibited internationally via the 1961 UN Convention of Narcotic Drugs and domestically in the United Kingdom via the 1971 Misuse of Drugs Act. This includes substances such as heroin, cocaine, ecstasy, cannabis and LSD. Importantly, however, this conceptualisation of drugs is questioned throughout the book, as such a narrow definition can be problematic. This is because it accepts the state-defined legal status of certain drugs and therefore the division between those substances that are classified as illicit and those which are legally produced, sold and used. We therefore argue that a much more encompassing definition of a drug is 'a medicine or other substance which has a physiological effect when ingested or otherwise introduced into the body' – a definition closely aligned to Brownstein's (2013:87) definition of a drug being 'any chemical you take that affects the way the body works'. This allows us to explore both the links between illegal drugs and crime and the links between legal drugs and crime, as well the burgeoning grey area that exists in between these.

In relation to the latter term, this book again predominantly focuses on the crimes of drug offences and drug-related offences. This in effect means we concentrate on the activities of illegal drug market actors who manufacture, traffic, supply and use illegal substances or on the criminal behaviours of those dependent on illegal drugs. Again, however, this surface level definition is limiting. This is because for some, the reasons underpinning why drug use and/or supply are crimes are opaque and should therefore be critically questioned from both a historical and contemporary perspective. Meanwhile this also restricts the focus of the discussion onto actions and behaviours that are illegal rather than similar activities that are not and so again fails to incorporate discussions of the grey areas that sit between these. We therefore employ the definition of crime as not just comprising statues of criminal law but as including a consideration of the criminalisation process which leads to such laws being implemented in the first instance. It is hoped that this expansion of these normative definitions leads to a more encompassing and insightful exploration of drugs and crime. Instead of just focusing on crime, this book adopts a Zemiological twist, by also looking at social harm – the social harm arising from drug policy and legislation, including the harms that are disavowed and ignored, as well as the lives lost and/or ruined because of it.

Although this book centres predominantly on issues presented as drugs and crime within England and Wales, it continually considers these in a comparative fashion with wider experiences from around the globe. In doing so, it highlights how drugs and crime represent an international issue, crucial to the global criminological field as the key themes, trends and evidence presented have worldwide significance due to the scale of drug markets impacting every jurisdiction around the world.

The book begins with Chapter 1 providing a synoptic overview of the different theoretical lens that can be employed to look at issues of drugs and crime. This represents a crucial starting point for anyone wishing to study drugs and crime because how we view such issues is influenced, whether consciously or not, by our theoretical beliefs. So, for example, whilst those favouring classicist, biological or sociological explanations of drugs and crime may take illegal drug possession as a crime at face value, critical criminologists might question why such substances were made illegal in the first place, drawing attention to how cultural and social contexts relate to their criminalisation.

Employing different lens also influences the perceived solutions we might envisage to different drug- and crime-related issues. Those following a psychological approach to drug dependency and the committal of crime to finance this might see cognitive behavioural therapy as one way of addressing both an individual's drug use and their offending behaviour. Alternatively, labelling theorists may argue that unless we address the wider stigmatisation of drug use, addiction and crime in society, certain individuals will continue to use drugs and commit crime regardless of any such treatment interventions. This chapter seeks to act as a toolkit for readers to use, by illustrating how theory can be used to explain and understand issues of drugs and crime, using illustrative examples to show how they are used to influence and underpin policy and practice. The theories covered in this chapter can be applied to the topics being discussed in the subsequent chapters giving you a theoretical toolkit to utilise throughout the remainder of the book.

Chapters 2 and 3 offer an equally important footing on which to build our understanding of drugs and crime by exploring the historical backdrop to modern-day drugs and their prohibition and therefore the emergence and evolution of drug laws. In doing so, they encourages readers to make connections between how issues of colonialism, indentured labour, slavery and the emergence of capitalism with its differential hierarchies of wealth and privilege have influenced the development of modern-day systems of drug control. They show why some drugs are legal and privileged, while others are not. History is often pushed aside by scholars of drugs and crime in favour of a focus on the contemporary, but this belies that the roots of drug prohibition and the framing of certain substances and their use are sewn into the social, political and economic landscapes of the past. An understanding of how these historical processes influenced thinking around different drugs and their producers and users has led to their differential social positioning today and is therefore crucial. Chapter 2 begins this analysis by exploring the development of drug policy up until the 1960s with Chapter 3 then considering more recent historical developments in this field.

Building on these historical foundations, Chapter 4 explores drugs, crime and criminalisation in the era of drug prohibition, offering specific insight into how we arrived at the status quo, whereby certain drugs are illegal with those who break the law punished for their actions, whilst other drugs enjoy a position of legal privilege. In doing so, it critically analyses the two central tenants of drug prohibition – that illegal drugs represent the most harmful drugs and that drug prohibition protects society from harms. This leads to an exploration of whether the inverse of these central tenants is equally permissible – that illegal drugs are no more harmful than currently legal drugs and that drug prohibition proliferates rather than mitigates drug-related harms, through the processes of criminalisation engineered by what is referred to as a drug apartheid.

Chapter 5 turns attention towards a central concern of this book, that of the relationship between drugs and crime. This involves breaking down oversimplified understandings of how drugs and crime are linked by considering the different ways and frameworks which connect these phenomena, including drugs as a crime in their own right but also wider crimes that are seemingly prompted by and as politicians might have us believe 'caused by drug use'. Within this discussion, we identify which drugs and which drug market actors are associated with which crimes – including a consideration of how aspects of age, gender, race and social class sit alongside factors such as family background, peer groups, education, prior experiences of abuse and/or trauma and socio-economic circumstances. The chapter focuses on the root sources of drugs and crime as both having a common aetiology, rather than focusing on the mono-causal relationships that often dominate understandings in this field, especially that drug use causes crime – a mainstay of UK drug policy and its subsequent strategies.

Stemming from these discussions, Chapters 6 and 7 consider the contemporary landscape of drug offences and drug-related offences. These two chapters aim to provide insight into the existing trends and patterns evident in the England and Wales criminal justice systems. Chapter 6 focuses on drug possession and supply offences and how these are policed. This includes an analysis of the use of stop and search and its disproportionate deployment upon minority ethnic groups, especially young Black males. We also look at how those guilty of drug offences are responded to via both out-of-court disposals and more formal sentencing practices.

Chapter 7 then focuses on the combined issues of drug-related offences and so-called problematic drug users – those people who have a dependency on heroin/crack cocaine and who seemingly commit waves of property crime to fund this. This leads to an analysis of the bespoke criminal justice system that has emerged since the 1990s, which aims to break the cycle of drug addiction and crime through court-mandated sentences which include elements of drug treatment. We explore the efficacy of these interventions whilst questioning whether such strategies are appropriate and/or ethical.

One of the key responses to both drug offences and drug-related offences are custodial sentences. Chapter 8 therefore seeks to develop understanding around the positioning of drugs in a prison system which sees a significant element of its population serving sentences for drug offences alongside a significant population who are drug users. The result is that drugs are freely available in the custodial estate and rates of self-reported drug use are considerable despite attempts by authorities to stem the supply of drugs into prisons. Yet prisons also provide an opportunity for those who might use drugs to access services to address their drug using behaviour. An overview of how drug treatment in prisons operates is offered, including an evaluation of its utility, and its issues.

Those individuals who are imprisoned for drug offences are often sentenced for incidents of supply. Chapter 9 therefore maps out the evolution and contemporary positioning of drug production and supply, considering the shape and form of global drug markets and the actors associated with these. This includes an analysis of drug dealing as a form of work and indeed illegal entrepreneurship, which allows us to place those who supply drugs within the wider context of consumer capitalism. This affords insight into why people, whether entering the trade in a voluntary or coerced manner, engage in this activity and how aspects of gender, ethnicity and class interlink with this.

Given the extensive global drug supply network and the persistence of drug production, trafficking and distribution, illegal drug markets present a perpetual problem for those authorities tasked with policing them. They are also associated with a variety of other issues, which critics of drug prohibition have identified as prompting a range of problems and harms (Taylor et al., 2016). Chapter 10 therefore offers an overview and explanation of alternative ways of approaching drug policy by considering drug policy reform and how this may affect matters of drugs and crime. This includes an overview of reforms within the currently dominant system of drug prohibition as well as how more radical policies of drug decriminalisation and legalisation might impact on the status quo and alleviate drug-related harm and crime.

Chapter 11 draws the various elements of the book together with a concluding chapter that focuses on drugs and crime moving forwards. In doing so, it provides an overview of key emerging and/or contemporary issues within the drugs and crime field, including the challenges presented by evolving types and patterns of drugs, developing drug markets and the advancement of responses to these. Yet it also offers a blueprint for how we might expand our thinking about drugs and crime, enabling a more nuanced understanding of associated issues in the future.

1

THEORISING DRUGS AND CRIME

Overview

This chapter aims to provide you with:

- A critical understanding of theories explaining drugs and crime.
- A critical overview of each theory, particularly in the contemporary context and how it helps to understand, explain, prevent and respond to drugs and crime.
- An overview of the main criticisms and limitations of each theory.
- An understanding of how each theory provides an evidence base for policy and practice.

You will be introduced to the key terms:

- Theory
- Prevention
- Normalisation
- Policy

INTRODUCTION

Whatever your discipline, theory has a role to play. This is because theories provide us with frameworks through which we can understand and interpret different social issues. This chapter draws on a variety of different theoretical perspectives from a spectrum of disciplines (sociology, psychology, philosophy and cultural studies) to make sense of drugs and crime from a criminological perspective. It should be noted that whilst certain theories align and complement each other, some theories fundamentally disagree and contradict each other, but all have their limitations. In short, theory can be a messy business, but the good news is that it offers us a variety of different lenses, which we can use to understand and interpret issues of drugs and crime. This chapter therefore aims to provide you with a theoretical toolkit, which you can utilise throughout the remainder of this book, to independently analyse relevant policy, practice and developments within the field in a more analytical and critical fashion. This is crucial as when we consider drugs and crime, the different theoretical lens that we employ very much influences our understanding of different phenomena, what we might see as problematic and what we might see as being the best way of responding to/resolving different issues. But what is theory?

What Is Theory?

- Theories provide a theoretical framework that organises the concepts of crime, criminality, drug use and dependence/addiction into a set of basic principles.
- Theoretical frameworks provide a lens through which to explore, explain and understand complex social issues and multifaceted human behaviours.
- Theories permit its advocates to identify and prioritise problems, to search for and discover solutions within the context or boundary of the theory.
- Theories can be used to explain crime and/or drugs on an individual level (micro), societal/group level (meso) and wider global and nation state level (macro).
- Different theoretical perspectives make different assumptions about the nature of society.
- Theories have commonalities, but differences also exist between them, which results in contradictory perspectives that purport to explain drugs and crime.
- Each theory provides a unique perspective and understanding.

CRIMINOLOGY

Criminology is a rendezvous subject (Downes, 1988) that incorporates a wide range of theories that span multiple disciplines. Criminology brings together scholars from a variety of disciplinary origins, who meet in the territory called crime and criminal justice. Therefore, theories used in criminology cover the making and the breaking of the law, criminal and deviant behaviour, patterns of criminal activity, the criminal justice system, its agents and society's response to crime (e.g. how to control, prevent and reduce it). In this sense, criminological theory is not abstract and has real-world application as they are often used to guide policymaking and legislation, including drug policy and drug laws.

The theoretical perspectives discussed here illustrate the evolution of criminological thinking and indeed the development of understandings of drugs and crime (see Chapters 2 and 3). Initial theorising (including classicist and positivist perspectives) tended to focus on explaining why certain people used/became dependent on drugs and committed crime. Such thinking often took for granted that 'drug users' were somehow different from non-drug users whilst accepting drug laws at face value and therefore drugs as being intrinsically related to crime. As we move through the theories, however, we see the emergence of more critical perspectives, which fundamentally questioned whether illegal drug-taking should be seen as a deviant/criminal activity, critique the legitimacy of drug laws and differential processes of criminalisation, whilst drawing attention to the contradictory positioning of different drugs within the wider socio-political economy.

CLASSICAL THEORIES

The Classical School (Classicism) is often regarded as the philosophical birthplace of criminology. Its origins lie in the reaction (by white male intellectuals) to the broader political economy during the Enlightenment period and the cruel forms of punishment dominant at the time (see Reiner, 2016). Classicism proposed two key intellectual foundations: social contract theories and utilitarianism. Social contract theory explains why societies need laws/rules. It is based on the view that a persons' moral and/or political obligations are dependent upon an actual or hypothetical compact/agreement between the ruled and their rulers (Rousseau, 1978). Utilitarianism believes that a morally right action is the one that produces the most happiness for the most people.

Classicism sees people as rational actors – free moral agents who exercise their will without restrictions and enter into social contracts with the state/government that enact laws and policies, which ensure the greatest happiness of the greatest number (Bentham, 1988) (see the Box below). Therefore, the mischief of crime (and drugs) is prohibited as it is seen to breach this social contract and interfere/conflict with the happiness of the greatest number. The law is hence used to reduce harmful acts to society, which maximises the happiness (utility) of the majority by utilising the pleasure-pain principle (Hopkins-Burke, 2018; Reiner, 2016). Utilitarian's recognise the importance of hedonism. Whilst certain drug use may therefore elicit pleasure, its use is prohibited in contemporary society through a belief that it is also harmful – we all therefore forego the right to use illegal drugs as this means that the majority are protected from the harmful outcomes associated with this.

Classicists Bentham, Beccaria and Mill proposed that hedonism was a basic human trait and every individual is governed and motivated by the pleasure-pain principal.

Recognising people are rational actors it purports they make a cost–benefit analysis when deciding whether to commit crime and/or use drugs based on whether the pleasures/benefits outweigh the potential pains/punishment. Thus, they will seek pleasure while trying to avoid pain (Hopkins-Burke, 2018). For Bentham, crime was committed to gain pleasure/excitement, money and any other benefits. Although omitted from the official discourse, it is widely recognised that people commit crime and/or drugs for pleasure as there is pleasure from transgression (Presdee, 2000). Therefore, the punishment/pain must outweigh any pleasure derived from drugs and/or crime meaning laws are based on the punitive logic of deterrence – individual and general – that uses the threat of punishment/pain to control people's behaviour. In short, the pain of punishment associated with breaking drug laws should persuade people not to use or supply these substances.

According to classical theorists, punishment must be swift, severe, certain and proportionate to the crime to act as a deterrent to individuals and society (Beccaria, 1986). Premised on this logic, increasing the punishments for drugs and/or crime should deter people; however, evidence suggests that this is not the case. In fact, the empirical evidence underpinning deterrence and its effectiveness is severely lacking, even if tougher sanctions are introduced (Rosmarin and Eastwood, 2012). In fact, evidence shows that pleasurable 'drug use cannot be legislated out of existence' (Measham and Shiner 2009: 6) and seemingly nor can drug supply. This is of crucial importance as the war on drugs (see Chapter 3) has seen ever increasing punitive responses to drug law infractions across the globe. Despite this, people continue to both use and supply illegal substances. This means that rates of use/supply remain relatively consistent but greater numbers of people have been engulfed in the criminal justice system.

Free Will/Rational Choices?

A central tenant of classicism is that humans have free will and rationally weigh up the pros and cons of committing crime (e.g. breaking drug laws before deciding on their actions). This thinking has, however, been criticised:

- It is contended that not everyone is capable of thinking rationally whether that is due to substance use/intoxication or mental illness, which are both high among offender populations. It also ignores other mediating factors and for many entrepreneurial career offenders, including drug dealers, punishment (prison) is a hazard of the job and does not outweigh the benefits (e.g. money, lifestyle, identity and status).
- If human beings are driven by natural instincts – pleasure and pain – then claiming they have free will is contradictory. Utilitarianism also fails to account for how contemporary consumer culture manipulates people to bypass 'the rational calculation of consequences and risk the high costs... associated with illegal expressive and acquisitive activities' and goods (see Hall and Winlow, 2015).

- It is argued that humans do not always make rational decisions or assess the potential risk of punishment before committing crime and/or using/supplying drugs. Conversely, offenders often think they will not be caught, let alone punished, illustrating that deterrence being an influence on decision-making is problematic as the odds of apprehension are low (Hopkins-Burke, 2018).
- Also, if 'people act due to principles of rationality and free will then why is it that the poor are predominating in the criminal justice system?' (Hopkins-Burke, 2018); this point also applies to certain minority ethnic groups. Not everyone has the same access to choices as choices are structured – choices might be constrained by structure – but they are not determined by structure as everyone responds differently to their situation (Seddon, 2006).
- Although classicism may explain drug use, can it explain drug addiction? Are people addicted to drugs rational? While some argue that addiction is a rational choice (leading to the moral model of addiction), others argue this is associated with a lack of free will due to physical addiction and the way drugs change the brain, thus fostering compulsion (neuroadaption), leading to the disease model of addiction.

The Classical School argued that the law must apply equally to all citizens, not be so harsh/severe as to reduce the greatest happiness for the majority and not be open to interpretation and be efficacious in preventing mischief if it restricts an individual's autonomy (Bentham, 1988). Punishment is justified only if it excludes some greater evil and if it is regulated by the rule of law (Bentham, 1988). If punishment causes harm to the offender that outweighs the advantage to society, it cannot be justified. When it comes to drug laws, however, the punishments often exceed the crime (e.g. drug supply/trafficking), they are not equitable or efficacious in preventing the mischief and they may actually be more harmful – including imprisonment – than the substances they purport to protect us from, meaning drug laws are potentially illegitimate and unjust. The illegitimacy of drug controls has serious implications since they inevitably constrain behaviour (Beetham 1991; Bentham, 1990) and thus individual sovereignty.

A Legal/Human Right to Use Drugs?

Szasz (1992:122) contends that 'in a free society it is none of the government's business what ideas a man puts into his head; likewise, it should be none of its business what drugs he puts into his body'. Consider this point in relation to:

- How this applies to classicism and its justification of drug laws.
- Whether people should have a legal/human right to use illegal drugs.

Read the Box on page 254 of Chapter 10 to see how this relates to drug laws and their reformation.

In fact, the utilitarian harm principle proposed by Mill's (1910:4) states, 'the only purpose, for which power can be rightfully exercised...is to prevent harm to others. His own good, either physical or moral, is not sufficient warrant'. Since all drug possession offences are victimless crimes, or at least crimes where the victim consents to the harm inflicted on them, it is questionable/debatable whether drug laws are legitimate especially since the majority of drug users, particularly recreational users, regulate their own drug use (irrespective of drug) using informal rules and boundaries (see Shewan and Dalgarno, 2005) and cause harm only to themselves. Therefore, state intervention appears morally reprehensible and an illegitimate use of state power. Even if the harm principle was extended to include indirect remote harms inflicted on the state (i.e. health costs) and other citizens (e.g. crime), the subsidiary effect of drugs on wider society remains negligible, particularly when compared to the societal costs of legal drugs like alcohol and tobacco (see Chapter 4). Consequently, the justification underpinning the use of the criminal law to control drug use is missing, especially since drug laws are not premised on evidence (Nutt et al., 2010), especially since drugs have become normalised (Parker et al., 1998) (see sociological explanations).

PRACTICAL IMPLICATIONS – POLICY AND PRACTICE

- Classical theories are extensively used to underpin/justify crime prevention strategies that include the rationale for the use of CCTV and policing initiatives/operations (e.g. policing hotspots – see Jacobson, 1999; Weisburd and Mazerolle, 2000).
- Classicism informs the moral model of addiction (see Chapter 2).

Routine Activities Theory

- Routine activities theory (RAT) explains how crime occurs based on everyday patterns and activities of individuals and can be applied to preventing crime including drug dealing.
- RAT looks at circumstances and environmental factors that make crime more/less likely to occur.
- For a crime to take place, three elements must converge: (1) a motivated offender (drug dealer), (2) a suitable target (buyer) and (3) the absence of a capable guardian (police or CCTV).
- Remove one of the three elements and it should prevent the crime taking place (see Cohen and Felson, 1979); however, think about this in relation to the section on deterrence.

Example

1) **Motivated Offender:** Drug dealers looking to sell.
2) **Suitable Target:** Individuals seeking to buy drugs, in a particular area.
3) **Absence of Capable Guardians:** Lack of law enforcement presence.

Outcome

1) **Deterrence of Motivated Offenders:** Increased police presence and/or CCTV increases the likelihood that drug dealers would be caught, thus deterring them from engaging in drug dealing in those areas.
2) **Reduction of Suitable Targets:** The visibility of police patrols and/or a CCTV camera should discourage potential buyers from seeking drugs in those areas, as the risk of being caught increases.
3) **Creation of Capable Guardians:** Regular police patrols and/or installation of CCTV act as capable guardians, disrupting the convergence of offenders and targets.

- Rationale choice theory and utilitarianism provide the evidence base for the harsh punishments imposed for drug use and dealing, where the punishment – pain – should outweigh the pleasure. Although, the evidence base underpinning this is somewhat lacking (see above section on deterrence), some studies suggest that severe punishments can deter crime (Nagin, 1998). Others, however, argue severe punishment has limited impact on reducing drug-related offences and may lead to negative social consequences (e.g. increased incarceration rates without significant reductions in drug use) (Tonry, 1994).

CLASSICISM: LIMITATIONS AND CRITICISMS

Classicism has received much academic criticism as the evidence base underpinning it is weak. Classicism ignores the aetiology of crime and/or drugs, and instead just assumes these factors exist. It cannot account for and tackle expressive crimes (e.g. anger) and ignores how contemporary consumer culture manipulates people to bypass 'the rational calculation of consequences and risk the high costs [and often debt] associated with illegal expressive and acquisitive activities' (Hall and Winlow, 2015:7; Hayward, 2007). Humans do not always make rational decisions or assess the potential risk of punishment before committing crime and/or using/dealing drugs. In fact, research shows that often offenders do not think they will be caught, let alone punished, illustrating that deterrence being an influence in decision making is problematic (Hopkins-Burke, 2018).

Critical Thought – Think About

Although classicism may explain drug use, it is questionable whether it explains drug addiction – are problematic drug users and/or drug addicts rational?

Hopkins-Burke (2018) also highlights that 'if people act due to principles of rationality and free will then why is it that the poor are predominating in the criminal justice system?'

(Continued)

(Continued)

Does drug legislation (prohibition) undermine the principles set out in the moral (legal) philosophy of utilitarianism, thus making it illegitimate (see MacCoun and Reuter, 2001; and Chapter 4)?

While some may argue that yes problematic drug users and/or addicts make a rational choice leading to the moral model of addiction others argue that addicts lack free will due to physical addiction and the way drugs change the brain, thus fostering compulsion (neuroadaption), particularly if addiction is seen as a disease and/or a mental illness (Volkow, 2001; cf. Heather, 2017) (see also biological and genetic theories below).

BIOLOGICAL AND GENETIC THEORIES

Similar to classicism, biological and genetic theories ignore the aetiology of crime, drugs and laws and instead just assume these factors exist. In taking these for granted, biological and genetic theories focus on what it is about certain people that make them more likely to use/become addicted to or supply illegal substances.

Biological and genetic theories are positivistic in nature, meaning that they are deterministic and located in the predestined actor model. Unlike classicism, which sees crime and/or drugs as a rational choice, positivism sees them as determined by factors (e.g. biological, psychological, neurological, pathological or social) beyond the individuals control. These factors can be either internal or external to the human being, which cause (although see Chapter 5 for problems associated with establishing causation in relation to drugs and crime) people to act in a way over which they have little or no control. In effect, such theories attempt to identify commonalities among those who take drugs and break the law in order to explain their seemingly abnormal behaviour. Drug users and/or criminals are thus seen as different from non-drug users/criminals.

Early biological criminologists like Lombroso, Ferri and Garofalo focused on the scientific study of criminals and saw them as evolutionary throwbacks, genetically abnormal and inferior to non-criminals. These atavistic explanations of crime suggested that criminals were born with primitive characteristics, which were indicators of their unlawful disposition (see Chapter 2 for examples and how these were indoctrinated/legitimised in drug policy/legislation). Although these biological/genetic explanations of criminality have been heavily criticised and largely discredited – there has more recently been an increased focus on neurodiversity as an explanation of crime and/or substance use (see HMICFRS, 2021) – they are still often used to explain drug use and addiction. This is because drugs are said to alter the body's biochemistry, which can impact on behaviour and continued drug use/addiction.

Biological explanations for drug use are harder to discredit than those for criminality, as substances affect biochemistry and act upon the reward systems in the brain, which it is argued can lead to neurochemical adaption. For some, drug use and addiction are a brain disease (Volkow et al., 2016), a metabolic (pharmacodynamic) disease (Dole and Nyswander, 1967) or a disease of learning and memory (Hyman, 2005). Others still claim to have found an 'addictive gene' (Ducci and Goldman, 2012). To provide empirical support for these theories, family (Goddard, 1914), adoption (as it separates genetic/biological influences from environmental/social factors) and twin studies,which indicate a genetic/hereditary component, are often used to support these suppositions (e.g. Hopkins-Burke, 2018; Kendler et al., 2003; Verhulst et al., 2015). These biological/genetic theories have also been used to explain gender differences in crime/criminality, substance use and addiction (Anker and Carroll, 2011; Lynch, et al., 2002) (see also Ruiz and Strain, 2014).

'Research suggests alcohol addiction is about 50 percent heritable, while addiction to other drugs is as much as 70 percent heritable' (Dick, 2022:1). Some even talk about having an addictive personality, although this has little empirical support (Ruiz and Strain, 2014), and there has also been a criminal personality (Yochelson and Samenow, 1976). While many of these theories have been heavily contested and criticised (e.g. Hammer et al., 2013; Levy, 2013), research does show that certain personality traits increase the risk of substance use and criminality (e.g. impulsivity, IQ). For example, those with a personality disorder are said to be 2.5 times more likely than those without to be dependent/addicted to substances and are also more likely to commit crime and be in prison (Mundt and Baranyi, 2020; Ruiz and Strain, 2014).

Life-course criminology (which aims to establish the connection between patterns in life events and human behaviour) and the intergenerational transmission of drugs and crime have lent further support to the biological and genetic explanations (Farrington et al., 2009), although it has also shown that both can be attributed to other factors (e.g. parenting, socialisation/social learning, abuse/maltreatment, disrupted families, socio-economic circumstance, family size, criminal/drug using parents and siblings) (see Farrington, 2011). This highlights how biological and genetic factors may have a limited role explaining human behaviour on their own, whether referring to drugs and/or crime. A reason being that it (partially) ignores human agency and factors that interact with and influence the development of drugs and/or crime like upbringing, socialisation, family, socio-economic circumstances (nurture) and social bonds, which can affect individual factors that can be linked to crime and/or drug use like impulsivity and self-control (Gottfredson and Hirschi, 1990). By integrating genetic and biological factors with social and environmental influences, life-course criminology attempts to provide a more holistic understanding of criminal behaviour, allowing for more effective prevention and intervention strategies.

A key outcome of this swathe of biological and genetic perspectives of drug use/addiction and crime is that they frame drug users and/or criminals as being abnormal and that drug use and addiction are therefore viewed as problematic and in need of treatment – a historical legacy (see Chapter 2). Addiction (substance use disorder (SUD)) is seen as a disease/illness under the medical model and is classified in the American Diagnostic and Statistical Manual of Mental Disorders (DSM)/World

Health Organization's International Classification of Diseases (ICD) as a mental disorder (Hasin et al., 2013) meaning drug users and criminals are innately different from non-drug users and non-criminals. Addiction or SUD is conceptualised as a disease or illness under the medical model due to its chronic nature, biological basis and classification in diagnostic systems like the DSM and the ICD. This perspective has evolved to reflect advancements in neuroscience, genetics and psychiatry. Addiction is often considered a chronic condition, with cycles of relapse and remission similar to other chronic diseases like diabetes or hypertension (McLellan et al., 2000), which some argue alters brain structure and function, particularly in the reward, motivation and memory systems, reinforcing the cycle of addiction (Volkow et al., 2003). As a result, drug users (and/or criminals) are seen as sick, biologically inferior and thus in need of treatment in order to be cured of the predisposing condition that causes their drug use and/or criminality, which has influenced prevention, treatment and rehabilitation.

PRACTICAL IMPLICATIONS – POLICY AND PRACTICE

As Hopkins-Burke (2018:27) highlights 'for most of the twentieth-century crime control was dominated by the "treatment model" prescribed by the predestined actor model of crime and criminal behaviour and closely aligned to the benevolent state, which was obliged to intervene in the lives of offenders and seek to diagnose and cure their criminal behaviour'. This also applies to drug use and addiction (see Chapters 4 and 7). This has materialised in a variety of different treatment practices, which have been influenced by biological/genetic theories. For example, the framing of drug use as a disease, which underpins drug treatments (e.g. the 12-step model implemented in Alcoholics Anonymous and Narcotics Anonymous whereby abstinence from drugs is the goal) (see Chapter 2). Yet such thinking has also led to the development of some ethically dubious processes, such as advocating brain surgery and the death penalty, to protect society from those understood to be untreatable. Similarly, it has seen treatments emerge, which seek to stem the spread of drug use/addiction through practices such as sterilisation (see the Box below).

Sterilisation of Drug Addicts: Ethical or a Contemporary Form of Eugenics?

Project Prevention is a non-profit organisation established in 1997 by Barbara Harris in the United States. It operates predominantly across the United States but also in the United Kingdom. Project Prevention:

- offers cash incentives to those addicted to drugs/alcohol to use birth control to prevent child abuse.

- payments of between £200/$200 and £300/$300 are made to those who agree to take long-term contraception and/or be sterilised to ensure they do not get pregnant and have children while they are using drugs/alcohol.
- as of 2024, has 'treated' approximately 8000 individuals with birth control such as tubal ligations, contraceptive implants and vasectomies.
- has been heavily criticised for targeting poor, non-white women and has been compared to the Nazis' eugenics programme and described as unethical (Derkas, 2011, 2012; Monroe and Alexander, 2005).

The framing of drug users as somehow different – or in need of curing – has led over the decades to the medicalisation of social, economic, cultural and criminal justice issues, which can be seen as a form of social control with the potential for misuse by governments and its agencies, which discriminates – sexism, racism and immoral eugenic policies – against different social groups based on the presence of biological risk factors (Hopkins-Burke, 2018; Wright and Miller, 1998), which has led to much criticism.

LIMITATIONS AND CRITICISMS

Many early biological theories of criminality, and to a lesser extent drug use, have been called 'reductive, individualistic, decontextualized, misleading and politically dangerous' (Hall and Winlow, 2015:19; Nutt, 2012; Reinarman, 2005), and in the past have been used as a form of social control of supposedly undesirable populations by governments and its agencies, which is often discriminatory (see Chapter 2). Such thinking – that there is something fundamentally different between a drug user and a non-drug user meaning that interventions with the former are a necessity – also overlooks that most people mature out of drugs and/or crime as they progress into adulthood (Moffit, 1993, 2003; Parker et al., 1998). Also, what constitutes a crime and/or a drug is socially constructed and thus transient meaning that biological/genetic explanations may become outdated. Subsequently, genetic and biological factors have a limited role explaining human behaviour on their own whether referring to drugs and/or crime (Reinarman, 2005).

(SOCIAL)PSYCHOLOGICAL THEORIES

Despite their different focal points – biological theories emphasise physiological and genetic factors, while psychological theories concentrate on mental processes and personality traits – biological and psychological theories of crime and drug use also share similarities in their focus on individual factors, the recognition of the role of internal processes and developmental influences and the implications this has for treatment. These theories often complement each other, providing a more complete picture of the complex interplay between biology, psychology and behaviour in drugs and crime (see Chapter 5).

Psychological explanations of drugs and crime tend to fall into three main categories that overlap with sociological theories to create social psychological theories like general strain theory or differential association (Hopkins-Burke, 2018). Many psychological theories fall into the positivist paradigm and the predestined actor model as they locate the explanations for drugs and crime within the individual (see the Box below). Individual factors interact with social influences to shape individual experiences (e.g. individuals with poor emotional regulation may be more likely to observe and adopt drug use as a coping mechanism, which if seen as a way to manage emotional difficulties may become a learnt behaviour) as reflected in social learning theories.

Psychological Theories

- **Psychodynamic/Psychoanalytical Theories (Freud, Lacan, Klein):** psychodynamic explanations of drug use/addiction and criminality can be linked/attributed to biological drives, innate desires and the unconscious mind meaning that drug use/addiction is a symptom of underlying psychopathology (see Loose, 2002). Psychodynamic principles underpin some therapeutic communities, some forms of counselling and the 12-step programme.
- **Attachment Theories (Bowlby, Harlow):** show that maternal deprivation can increase the likelihood of crime (Bowlby, 1951; Harlow, 1958), drug use and addiction in adulthood (Delavari et al., 2016). The research supporting this in relation to drugs, however, tends to focus on animal studies (e.g. Vazquez et al., 2006). If a child is deprived of mother–infant emotional bonds before the age of five, it has a negative effect of the child's emotional and behavioural development (e.g. they become cold, affectionless and delinquent). More recent research has shown that maternal deprivation can remodel the brain and child's brain, which leads to 'long-term effects on learning and cognition, the development of mental disorders, aggression, and an increased tendency for the drug abuse' (Čater and Majdič, 2022:2058).
- **Personality Traits (e.g. impulsivity, personality disorders) (Eysenck):** certain personalities (e.g. extroverts, neurotics and psychotics) and their traits (e.g. impulsivity) predict drug use, addiction and crime (see Hammersley, 2008) with certain personality traits linked to certain crimes (e.g. violent offenders have lower scores on neuroticism) (Eysenck and Eysenck, 1977) and drug use/addiction (e.g. cocaine-dependent users scored high on neuroticism and psychoticism) (Prisciandaro et al., 2011).

Social learning theories can be applied to drugs and/or crime:

- **Social (Behavioural and Cognitive) Learning Theories:** can be used to understand as well as explain and treat drugs and crime. Behavioural learning theory focuses on how human learning and behaviour is a result of stimulus associated with a reward or punishment, while cognitive learning theory examines the way humans speak, think and resolve problems. Drugs and/or crime are merely behaviours people so learn (Becker, 1963; Smith, 2021). Prior learning influences behaviour, which can be learnt through observation and imitation as outlined below.

- **Classical Conditioning (Pavlov):** illustrates how behaviours can be learnt to occur in response to stimuli, so a conditioned response (salivation) normally produced by one stimulus (the unconditioned stimulus – giving dog food) comes to be controlled by another stimulus (the conditioned stimulus – ringing bell) as well. Dopamine would usually be released into the brain when the dog is shown the food and salivation occurs, but over time, learning the association between ringing the bell and food means dopamine will be released into the brain at just the sound of ringing the bell.
- **Operant Learning/Conditioning (Skinner, [1938] 1971):** involves active learning when behaviour is determined by the consequences it produces for the individual. Behaviour that is positively reinforced (rewarded) will continue and often increase, while behaviours that lead to non-reinforcement and/or negative consequences (pain) will decrease/stop. The system of rewards and punishments eventually become anticipated by the individual. Drugs provide both negative (e.g. avoid withdrawal) and positive reinforcement (e.g. getting high/euphoria), and according to Skinner, reinforcement is preferable to punishment.

Needle Fixation: An Example

A good example of conditioning in relation to drug use/addiction is needle fixation, which occurs when injecting becomes as or more important than the actual act of injecting drugs with users in some instances injecting inert substances like water (McBride et al., 2001; Pates et al., 2001). Conditioning creates the triggers and cues associated with problematic/addictive substance use. Triggers/cues are environmental stimuli associated with drug-taking that can induce physiological responses (e.g. sweating, increased heart rate, nausea) that are specific to the individual.

- **Cognitive Social Learning (Bandura, 1977):** focuses on what goes on between the stimulus and the response to show that behaviour may be reinforced not only through actual rewards and punishments but also through expectations that are learnt by watching what happens to other people. Through the process of behaviour modelling, people learn through the observation of others from three main sources: (1) family interaction, (2) environmental experiences and (3) and role models (e.g. mass media via symbolic modelling) (Bandura, 1986). Thus, drugs and crime are learnt at a cognitive level by observing and imitating/modelling the behaviour of others (see Becker, 1963). Through observation, people learn at a cognitive level how to perform certain behaviours, how to get rewards/pleasure and avoid distress/pain and how to use and appreciate drugs and/or commit crime.

- **Differential Association (Social Psychological Theory) (Sutherland, 1947):** describes the social conditions and the process by which individuals become a criminal and/or a drug user as a result of different interactions and patterns of learning that occur through association with close personal groups, not necessarily criminals and/or drug users per se, just people with favourable definitions/attitudes towards crime and/or drugs. Sutherland argued that through these differential associations, techniques (e.g. how to commit crime, how to use and appreciate drugs) and definitions favourable to breaking the law are learnt (e.g. attitudes, rationalisations, values, beliefs and norms). It has been tested empirically by research on crime and/or substance use (Alarid et al., 2000; Grey et al., 2015; Rebellon, 2012). Sutherland also claimed that subcultures in the 'higher echelons of society could also adopt and reproduce criminal values and practices', being one of the first to recognise and make 'an inaugural and seminal contribution to the study of the "crimes of the powerful"' (Hall and Winlow, 2015) (see the Box below).

Crimes of the Powerful: Big Pharma

- Sutherland (1949:9) also coined the term 'white-collar crime' that he defined as 'a crime committed by a person of respectability and high social status in the course of [their] occupation' and argued that powerful people, businesses and professionals all routinely commit crime and inflict social harm.
- Organisational (corporate) crime are crimes committed by organisations via their CEOs, board of directors and managers.
- Sutherland also highlighted the unequal application of the criminal law, meaning that crimes committed by powerful people/organisations are rarely prosecuted as a crime, which has led to calls for looking at social harm instead – zemiology.
- Examples include the recent opioid crisis (Vadivelu et al., 2018 – see Chapters 2 and 11) or the environmental harm arising from the cannabis industry (Zheng et al., 2021).

- **Differential Reinforcement/General Social Learning Theory/Social Structure Social Learning (Akers, 2009):** Akers went on to develop social learning theory (SLT) further by retaining the key principles of differential association, and combining it with classical and operant conditioning so that it included rewards and punishments. An individual's rewards and punishments in the past, present and future will determine and explain the likelihood of these behaviour – drugs and/or crime – occurring again. It has been applied to a range of crimes as well as substance use (Akers and Lee, 1996; Akers and Silverman, 2004; Kruis et al., 2020).

Outsiders: An Example

Becker's (1953/1963) iconic study of cannabis users showed how 'people learn through social interaction to interpret their own physical experience' and illustrated how drug use is socially learnt, which includes how drug users learn to respond to, experience and enjoy the effects (pleasures) of drugs as well as learning the techniques of how to use/smoke drugs and the right dosage. Therefore, drug-taking is learnt via 'observation and imitation' between experienced and novice users. Continued drug use is a result of positive experiences learnt from members of (usually positive) drug subcultures. Drug use is therefore embedded in a set of cultural practices that give the pharmacological process meaning, where users can learn to appreciate and enjoy its effects.

There is an increasing body of evidence, which shows individuals may engage in drug use/dealing and/or criminal behaviour as coping mechanisms or learnt responses to traumatic experiences in their life. Individuals who experience trauma may observe or experience drug use or criminal behaviour as a coping strategy through direct exposure to substance use in a household where those actions are perceived as rewarding, effective (even if only temporary) and/or normal in addressing problems and may learn to use drugs and/or crime as a coping mechanism when faced with their own emotional distress or trauma. Consequently, SLT provides a framework for understanding how individuals may turn to drugs and/or crime as coping mechanisms in response to trauma (Ayres, 2020c; Hammersley and Delgarno, 2013; Hirschi, 1969).

Trauma can occur anytime during a person's life, including childhood, and is also known as negative life events (NLEs) and adverse childhood events/experiences (ACEs) in the literature. Research shows that NLEs/ACEs contribute to an increased risk of deviance, juvenile delinquency, violence, mental ill health, offending and drug use, particularly problematic and intravenous drug use in adulthood (Ayres, 2020c; Grella et al., 2005; Hammersley et al., 2016; Winlow, 2014; for a review, see Evans et al., 2013) (see Figure 1.1: ACE pyramid). The prevalence of NLEs/ACEs is also higher among offenders and drug users (Reavis et al., 2013; Swogger et al., 2011), with over 90% of drug users reporting at least one traumatic event in their lifetime (Reynolds et al., 2005). These individuals also experience more NLEs/ACEs, with cumulative levels of childhood trauma being high among drug-using offenders (Grella et al., 2005; Swogger et al., 2011), which also predicts early onset of offending and life-course persistent offending – meaning delinquency continues from childhood to adulthood – and can lead to an escalation in drug use and offending (Hoffman and Cerbone, 1999; Wills et al., 1992). The research, however, shows the relationship varies by gender, with some research showing a consistently strong relationship among women (Lansford et al., 2010; Min et al., 2007; Widom et al., 2006) and men (Messina et al., 2007) although this was not always as strong for men (Englund and Egeland, 2009 cited in Lansford et al., 2010).

This might be attributable to studies that show boys and girls are exposed to different NLEs/ACEs (risk factors) (e.g. boys have higher rates of physical abuse, while girls have higher rates of sexual abuse) (Baglivio et al., 2014; Teague et al., 2008) and that they also respond differently. Different pathways between NLEs/ACEs exist for boys and girls (Leban and Gibson, 2020).

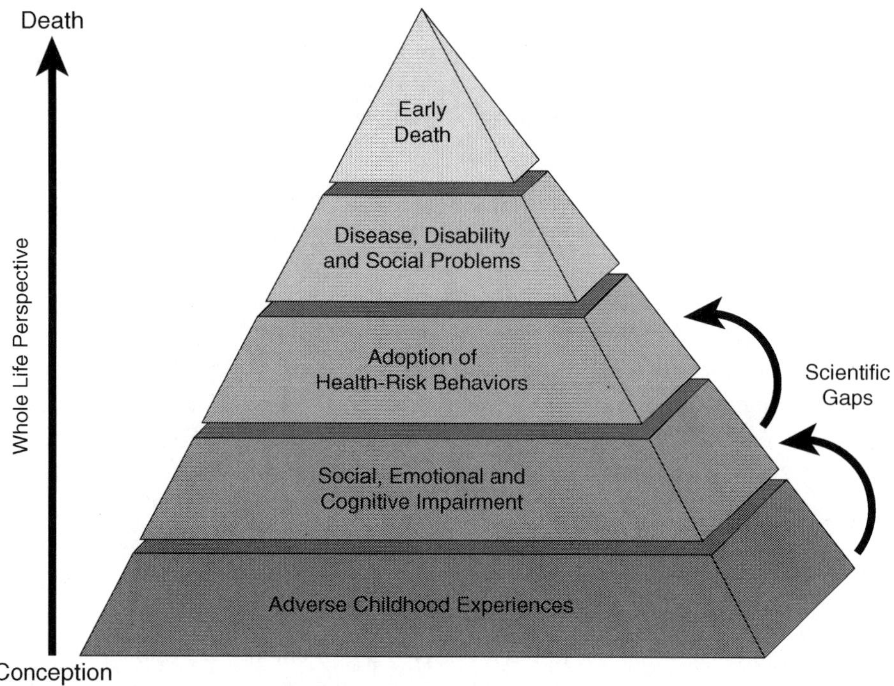

Figure 1.1 Trauma-Informed Care Pyramid

Girls are more likely to respond with internalising behaviours (e.g. depression and anxiety that leads to substance use) and boys with externalising behaviours (e.g. aggression and violence) (Muniz et al., 2020). These different pathways also explain why ACEs may uniquely be associated with delinquency for boys and substance use for girls (Leban and Gibson, 2020). However, specific types of NLEs may also be linked to specific – internalising and externalising – behaviours. For example, Muniz and colleagues (2019) found sexual abuse was uniquely related to internalising outcomes. Individuals who experience physical, sexual or emotional abuse during childhood are at a significantly higher risk of entering sex work (see Chapter 5).

To complicate the relationship further, NLEs/ACEs also have an impact on other factors linked to crime and/or drug use (e.g. self-control) and the relationship is also mediated by other factors (e.g. the stressfulness of the event, coping strategies; Ayres, 2020c; Min et al., 2007), self-control (Wills et al., 2011) and impulsivity (Hayaki et al., 2005) (see Chapter 5). Childhood trauma has also been examined through the lens of general strain theory (e.g. Carson et al., 2009) and has been identified as a criminogenic risk factor, which has been used to inform policy and practice.

PRACTICAL IMPLICATIONS – POLICY AND PRACTICE

- SLT has been very influential in terms of treatment programmes for both crime and drugs (Andrews and Bonta, 2024), which involves modifying behaviour and/or cognitions.
- Cognitive behavioural therapy (CBT) has been widely used with offenders where they have proved to be effective, reducing recidivism by 20–35% (Blattman et al., 2023; Harper and Chitty, 2005; Landenberger and Lipsey, 2004) and the treatment of offenders with substance use and/or dependence/addiction (Boness et al., 2023; Pearson and Lipton, 1999).
- Trauma-informed care has also become the new buzzword in treatment and rehabilitation in and out of the criminal justice system for drug users and/or offenders (Willmot and Jones, 2022) (see Figure 1.1).
- Most offender behaviour programmes, including those for substance use, are premised on the 'what works' principles, which is based on personality theory and cognitive SLT (Andrews and Bonta, 2024), with varying degrees of effectiveness (Hollin, 1999). Identified as a criminogenic need, substance use is a dynamic risk factor amenable to change, which means tackling it reduces the likelihood of a person reoffending, although not all programmes are effective in this respect (e.g. Addressing Substance-Related Offending (ASRO), see Palmer et al., 2011) and may cause more harm than good (see the Box below).

Ineffective (Harmful) Programmes

Scared Straight: was a cognitive behavioural therapy (CBT) programme from the US designed to deter juvenile delinquency and prevent crime in adulthood. Research shows, however, that it increased delinquency and was worse than if they had done nothing at all (Petrosino et al., 2013).

Tranquility Bay: was a behaviour modification centre based on operant conditioning in Jamaica where 250 children, mostly from the United States, were sent by their parents against their will to learn how to be respectful, polite and obedient enough to rejoin their families. At the cost of $25,000-$40,000 a year, it was just one of many such schools (e.g. CASA by the Sea in Mexico or Teen Mentor in Costa Rica), run by WWASPS (the World Wide Association of Speciality Programs and Schools) that inflicted physical and sexual abuse, which has resulted in a WWASPS survivors' group (Aitkenhead, 2003; Hopkins-Burke, 2018).

DARE (Drug Abuse Resistance Education): aimed at young people, police officers went into schools to warn children of the harmful effect of drugs so as to

(Continued)

(Continued)

prevent peer pressure to use drugs, join a gang and be violent. Unfortunately, the programme was ineffective, with those completing it having higher rates of drug use than those not exposed to the programme. This was often attributed to increasing their knowledge and awareness of drugs, which resulted in them trying drugs at a much younger age (Evans and Bosworth, 1997; Hamilton, 1997; Rosenbaum and Hanson, 1998). Others found it had little to no effect (Ennett et al., 1994; Lynam et al., 1999).

- Cognitive behavioural principals and SLT underpin the bio-psychosocial model of addiction (Wanberg and Milkman, 1998) that uses developmental risk factors to describe aspects of a person's life that trigger involvement in substance use and/or crime, as well as the stages of change model (Prochaska and DiClemente, 1983) that underpin treatment programmes.

LIMITATIONS AND CRITICISMS

Despite being widely used, socio-psychological theories have been heavily criticised. For example, operant conditioning, cognitive theory and social learning have been described as overly simplistic as they do not explain the aetiology of drug use/supply and/or crime, while differential association has been described as 'cultural reductionism' as it cannot explain opportunistic and spontaneous crimes or those 'crimes committed by solitary individuals' (Hall and Winlow, 2015:16–17; Hopkins-Burke, 2018). In fact, the research underpinning some psychological theories is lacking or has led to skewed results and unreliable theories. Similar criticisms can be applied to the research on drugs and crime (see Chapter 5) and drug dealing (see Chapter 9). CBT is widely utilised in the criminal justice system in offender and drug treatment programmes (Dolan and Hamilton, 2016; Shaw, 2015). Although, its widespread use has been driven by its efficacy in addressing both issues, the research is mixed, particularly when it comes to assessing the long-term benefits/changes; this could be attributable to poor implementation (Weissman et al., 2006). CBT has also been criticised as being 'too mechanistic' failing 'to address the concerns of the whole patient' and needs modifying as it was conceptualised in the 1970s meaning 'the theoretical basis of CBT [is]...not well connected to the emerging science of human cognition' (Gaudiano, 2008:3). Regardless of the theoretical underpinnings, however, evidence shows drug treatment is mostly ineffective, particularly over the long term (e.g. all types of cocaine treatment were only 2% more effective at reducing heavy use than no treatment at all according to Bovard et al., 1998).

SOCIOLOGICAL EXPLANATIONS

Sociological explanations consider factors external to the individual that impact on drugs and crime, including the environment, neighbourhood (see the Box below), culture and ideology, which will be the focus of the ensuing section.

Social Disorganisation

Shaw and McKay (1972:14) concluded that disorganised neighbourhoods help produce and sustain 'criminal traditions' that compete with conventional values and can be 'transmitted down through successive generations of boys, much the same way that language and other social forms are transmitted'. Thus, young people growing up in socially disorganised inner-city slum areas, characterised by the existence of a value system that condones criminal behaviour, could readily learn these values in their daily interactions with older adolescents.

STRAIN

Mertonian Strain (1938) – anomie: explains drugs and crime as a response to social structures and cultures. Merton acknowledged that despite society advocating meritocracy, not everyone is equally placed to achieve culturally approved success/goals (e.g. wealth, success, status, material possessions) through legitimate means (e.g. school, university and employment) as society is stratified. Merton (1938:672) was interested 'in discovering how some social structures exert a definite pressure upon certain persons in the society to engage in nonconformist rather than conformist conduct'. Nonconformist – criminal – behaviour occurs when society's cultural goals are accepted, but access to the legitimate/institutional means to achieve them is limited by the position of a person in the social structure. When this occurs, Merton identified five responses to this lack of fit – strain:

1) Conformity: is the acceptance of cultural goals and the legitimate/institutional means to achieve them.
2) Innovation: is the acceptance of cultural goals, but a rejection and/or lack of access to the legitimate/institutional means to achieve them. Innovators are not always criminal, but some are (e.g. drug dealers, sex workers, burglars, robbers) as they find alternate ways – sometimes through illegitimate means – to achieve the culturally approved goals.
3) Ritualism: is the rejection of cultural goals but an acceptance of the legitimate/institutional means to achieve them (e.g. someone that gives up on and/or does not want to buy a house but goes to work every day anyway).
4) Retreatism: is the rejection of cultural goals and a rejection and/or lack of access to the legitimate/institutional means to achieve them. This group includes the homeless and addicts/problematic drug users (alcohol and drugs).
5) Rebellion: is where the cultural goals and legitimate/institutional means to achieve them are rejected and substituted with news goals and standards as they seek to change the existing social system.

Thus, criminals like drug dealers are innovators, while Merton (1938:677) considered drug addicts as retreatists alongside 'vagrants, vagabonds, tramps and chronic drunkards' as 'in the society but not of it'.

Agnew's General Strain Theory (1992, 2006): developed Merton's theory, and although Agnew agreed strain came from an inability to achieve cultural goals, he believed there were two more types of strain to accompany it. Agnew (1992) identified three categories of strain: the failure to achieve valued goals, the anticipated or actual exposure to negative (toxic) stimuli/treatment (e.g. bullying, violence, abuse) and/or individuals as well as the anticipated or actual loss of positively valued stimuli (e.g. divorce, theft of property, death of a loved one) both of which include a wide range of stressful – often negative – life events (see NLEs section). The greater the strain resulting from this experience, the more likely the reaction is to be deviant. Agnew (1992, 2006) identified objective strain (disliked by most people) and subjective strain (disliked by the person experiencing it), which he believed was a stronger predictor of crime as subjective strains were significant/important – severe, frequent, of long duration – to the individual. Drugs and/or crime alleviate the strain associated with these actual and/or anticipated experiences (Agnew, 2006), which varies according to gender (Broidy and Agnew, 1997; Grothoff et al., 2014) and race/ethnicity (Peck et al., 2018; Piquero and Sealock, 2010).

Cohen (1955) also sought to develop Mertonian strain placing emphasis on the pursuit of status and respect rather than monetary success, which led to his work on subcultures.

SUBCULTURES

In the 1940s–1950s, subcultural explanations for crime and drug use became popular. Cohen (1955) observed that previous criminological research largely ignored the existence and role of deviant subcultures or gangs when it came to explaining deviance. Instead, he argued that gang members committed crime for fun and to acquire a reputation for being tough, which would earn them status and respect in their gang/subculture since they were never going to achieve the middle-class norms promoted in society. Although not all subcultures are deviant, certain drugs have always been associated with youth subcultures (see Chapter 3).

Examples: Counter-Cultures/Subcultures

Northern Soul was associated with amphetamines (see Wilson, 2008).
Jazz music with amphetamines and opiates (see Singer and Mirhej, 2006).
Hippies used psychedelics and cannabis (see Wesson, 2011; Young, 1971).
Rave music and the chemical generation used MDMA mostly alongside other stimulants (e.g. amphetamines) (Hammersley, 2001) and more recently ketamine (Moore and Measham, 2008).

A subculture can be defined as a 'culture within a culture' that is often a smaller group within larger mainstream culture – also referred to as counter-cultures in the literature (Duncan, 2013; Frood, 2008) – with its own norms and values. This often legitimises all the things the dominant culture rejects (e.g. hedonism, aggression, deviance), which may include crime and/or drug use but not always. As such, subcultures have their own distinct symbols/cultures that can include music, fashion and other signs (e.g. scooters, glow sticks) that can include drugs. In fact, Blackman (1996) states that drug use has become an integral element of youth subculture (see Chapter 3).

There is, however, much debate about subcultures and whether they still apply in contemporary society or if we live in post-subcultural world (Muggleton, 2000; Muggleton and Weinzierl, 2003; Redhead, 1997). Golub, Johnson and Dunlap (2005) found that individuals are often members of multiple subcultures and engage with more than one subculture at a time that can be deviant and/or non-deviant/decent, which are usually based around their interests (e.g. drugs, ethnicity, religion, music, hobbies or sport). New terms have been offered that include scenes and tribes/neo-tribe (Bennett, 1999, 2005; Hesmondhalgh, 2005). However, there are those that continue to defend subcultures (Blackman, 2005). Drugs – use and supply – are also no longer confined to these counter-cultures/subcultures, but some would argue that they have entered and been accommodated into the mainstream, making them normalised (Aldridge et al., 2011; Parker et al., 1998) and functional (see the Box below).

Functionality of Drug Use

Annabel Boys and colleagues (1999, 2000, 2001) have explored the functionality of drug use, particularly in the context of young people. Her research emphasises understanding why individuals use drugs, focusing on the roles that drugs play in their lives in the four areas – recreation, self-identity, lifestyle and emotional control – rather than solely viewing it as deviant or problematic behaviour. The more functions a drug plays, the more likely the person is to use it showing how functions are associated with whether drug use remains recreational or becomes problematic. The functions reflect a person's lifestyle at a specific moment in time and are therefore susceptible to change. While Boys' work touches on the normalisation of drug use, this perspective is connected to social learning theories, which explain how behaviours are adopted through interactions with others.

The conceptual framework of drug normalisation developed by Parker and colleagues (1998:26) asserts that there has been a 'demise of youth cultures and subcultures' and that drugs had entered mainstream youth cultures. Normalisation not only represents a shift in the beliefs and norms of society (as already discussed) but demonstrates an unwillingness to conform and consent to the norms imposed on them by legislation as large sections of society use drugs despite their prohibition.

NORMALISATION

Parker and colleague's (1998:29) conceptual framework aimed to explain why drug use had become a widespread feature of young adulthood and how drugs related to young people's lifestyles and leisure activities by explaining 'how an illegal activity, recreational drug use, has spread into mainstream adolescent pursuits – youth culture has accommodated a drugs culture'. It was a longitudinal study that started with nearly 800 young people in their early teens (aged 13–14) and was undertaken annually. A recapture analysis was done in 2000/2001, when the participants were aged 22–23 and again when they were aged 27 (see Aldridge et al., 2011). Initially the study only focused on the use of cannabis, poppers, amphetamines, LSD and ecstasy/MDMA. Heroin and cocaine were not included, although as the participants aged and by the recapture analysis, some of the respondents were using cocaine (Aldridge et al., 2011; Parker, 2005; Parker et al., 1998). In fact, the availability of cocaine doubled from age 18 (23%) to age 22 (47%) as did its use (4%–16%), which remained the same when the cohort was revisited again at age 27 (16%) (Aldridge et al., 2011).

Originally it had six key areas. These were (1) drug availability; (2) drug trying; (3) drug use; (4) being drug wise (social accommodation, where all young people – even abstainers – had knowledge of drugs and their use); (5) cultural accommodation (a blurring of licit and illicit substances as young people rationally choose their recreational activities by implementing a pick-n-mix approach according to the night out they want – a deviant activity has entered mainstream culture); and (6) future intentions (an open-mindedness and acceptance about trying/reusing drugs in the future). It also incorporated a social re-construction of a serious criminal offence – drug dealing/supply – as friends were supplying drugs to each other – user–dealers – but did not do it for profit/money and nor did they see it as a criminal offence, merely that they were helping their friends out (see Chapter 9). Social supply (sometimes involving large amounts of drugs/money) has to some extent seen the normalisation of drug dealing, which has become accepted among this group 'as something closer to gift-giving or friendship exchanges' rather than drug dealing (Coomber et al., 2016:255) (see the Box on page 213–214 of Chapter 9).

The research showed that drug availability, trying and use all increased with age until early twenties (age 22) where it levelled out before it began to decline except for a group of core users where drug use remained fairly stable (Aldridge et al., 2011; Parker, 2005; Parker et al., 1998). Cannabis use dominated, but cocaine use increased with age and alcohol was central throughout. The majority had been drinking alcohol the last time they also used a drug illustrating a blurring between illicit and licit substances (indicative of cultural accommodation). Using this framework, drugs can be fully or partially normalised (Parker, 2005; Pilkington, 2006) and has been used for different substances (e.g. heroin, Pilkington, 2006 and cannabis, Hathaway et al., 2011, 2016) around the world (e.g. America, Europe, New Zealand, Australia) (Pennay and Measham, 2016). There is some evidence to suggest slippage from controlled recreational use of drugs to more problematic patterns (see the Box below).

Slippage: Recreational to Problematic Use?

- Research is increasingly suggesting that the boundaries – the Rubicon – dividing recreational drug use and more problematic patterns of use is being bridged (McDonald and Marsh, 2002, 2005; Pilkington, 2006).
- As McDonald and Marsh (2002:27) highlight 'normative, cultural barriers between "recreational" and "problematic" drug use may be being eroded and that increasing proportions of "socially excluded" youth are "crossing the Rubicon" in drug careers that extend to heroin use'.
- Is this attributable to a slippage of recreational drug users into more problematic patterns of drug use or the recreational use of more problematic and addictive drugs like cocaine?

The findings from 20 years of studies show different results (see Pennay and Measham 2016 for a review). Normalisation has also been heavily contested (e.g. Blackman, 2007; Shiner and Newburn, 1997), which led to the concept of differentiated (relative) normalisation (O'Gorman, 2016; Shildrick, 2002).

Key Term

Differentiated Normalisation: allows for the ways in which different types of drugs and different types of drug use may be normalised for different groups of young people (Shildrick, 2002:36).

The normalisation thesis indicates a shift in social norms, where drug use is no longer seen as deviant but rather as a common and integrated aspect of mainstream youth culture, although this may not be the case more widely as the official discourse promotes drug abstinence, which is disseminated via traditional institutions (e.g. school, family, church, job) and government policy. As recreational drug use becomes more normalised, the bonds drug users have with society and its norms are weakening, which can lead to an increase in drug use as strong bonds can prevent deviance, crime and drug use (see the Box below).

Control Theories

- **Social Control Theories:** explain why people obey the law (conform) and refrain/desist from committing crime and/or getting involved with drugs, which according to Hirschi (1969) relies on the bonds an individual has with society. Hirschi (1969) argues that human conformity rests on the internalisation of societal norms and values through attachment, commitment, involvement and

(Continued)

(Continued)

belief in the norms of society. The weaker the bonds, the higher the deviance/criminality/drugs.

- **Techniques of Neutralisation:** are used by offenders to justify and/or excuse their delinquent/criminal behaviour. Sykes and Matza (1957) provide five types of neutralisation: the denial of responsibility, denial of injury, denial of the victim, the condemnation of the condemners and the appeal to high loyalties.
- **Drift:** in life, people drift between non-criminal, conventional and criminal/deviant behaviour, existing 'in limbo between convention and crime' (Matza, 1964:28), involving affinity (proximity to criminal opportunities), affiliation (social relations and learning processes) and signification, which they justify through techniques of neutralisation.

Drug users and dealers implement techniques of neutralisation and drift in and out of both behaviours (Coomber et al., 2016; Mohamed and Fritsvold, 2010; Murphy et al., 1990).

- **Subterranean Values:** of hedonism, excess and excitement exist alongside mainstream values (not only in deviant subcultures). Without rejecting mainstream values people also participate in hedonism, excitement and excess, which they seek to justify (e.g. worked hard all week) (Matza and Sykes, 1961). Drugs and crime are part of a work-hard-play-hard lifestyle (Stevens, 2011a).
- **General Theory of Crime:** 'is meant to explain all crime, at all times' (Gottfredson and Hirschi, 1990:117), including gender/sex and racial/ethnic differences (De Li, 2005; Higgins, 2004; Higgins and Rickets, 2005; Vazsonyi et al., 2001). It argues that people with low self-control tend to have weaker bonds, be impulsive, take risks and pursue immediate gratification/pleasure increasing their propensity for drugs and crime (Ford and Blumenstein, 2013). Arising from poor parenting, those with poor self-control are less likely to see the negative consequences (pains) arising from their actions and are more likely to value the rewards/pleasures of deviance over the punishments.

SYMBOLIC INTERACTIONISM AND LABELLING

Labelling individuals as criminals and/or drug users is value-laden even though it is a social construct that is transient and varies over time, meaning deviance/crime and/or drug use are merely those things we describe and label as such. Therefore, these behaviours are only considered criminal when the label is officially applied, meaning labelling theory focuses on society's reaction to the act, rather than the act itself (no act is inherently criminal), as actions are invested with meaning and a reaction depends on the basis of this meaning. As Becker (1963:4) highlights:

> social groups create deviance by making the rules whose infraction constitutes deviance, and by applying those rules to particular people and labelling them as outsiders. . .the deviant is one whom the label has been successfully applied; deviant behaviour is behaviour people so label.

Sitting in phenomenology, ethnomethodology and symbolic interactionism (George Herbert Mead) 'suggests individuals acquire their sense of self through interacting with others' (Treadwell, 2013:56). Labelling has three main concerns (see Hopkins-Burke, 2018:193):

1) Why and how do some acts come to be defined as criminal when others are not?
2) The differential application of laws and labels to certain individuals/groups that are more likely to attract deviant and criminal labels than others.
3) The experience of being labelled, which can actually reinforce and create criminality and/or drug use.

Becker (1963) argued that the rules/laws and subsequent labels arising from breaking these rules/laws are created by the powerful and imposed on the powerless and that no act is inherently deviant/criminal, it only becomes deviant/criminal when it is so labelled. Instead, these labels are created and applied to certain people/groups who are then labelled as the outsiders. The labels are usually negative and pejorative, which leads to stigmatisation, marginalisation and eventually exclusion (e.g. from housing, employment, healthcare, education). The label separates the individual out from the rest of society, it categorises and stereotypes them, permitting/facilitating their removal from mainstream society, which may lead to punishment (e.g. drug dealers) and/or treatment (e.g. drug addicts); they become the outsiders. Drug addicts, some drug users (not all) and drug dealers are the outsiders. Thus, deviance, crime and drug use/supply are simply those things we label as such. Drugs and crime/deviance are merely the successful application of labels rather than the breaking of rules.

Key Thinker

Frank Tannenbaum (1938) proposed the dramatisation of evil hypothesis, whereby the community defines actions of the individual as evil, but eventually goes on to define and see the individual as evil (e.g. drug dealers/pushers, Myra Hindley). This is further dramatised by separating the individual from their group and administering treatment and/or punishment to cure the evil, which leads to further isolation and internalisation of their new label, which redefines their self-image in line with the label that feeds into popular opinion and discourse.

Once applied, these labels can determine an individual's identity and it may become their master status (e.g. junkie, murderer). Labels can also create self-fulfiling prophecies where the public react to them based on the stereotype associated with the label that may lead to discrimination (e.g. in law enforcement, employment) that the labelled individuals then live up to. This can lead to them adopting the label as their master status as well as deviance amplification (e.g. they are labelled as a no good junkie, so behave like a no good junkie) (see Becker, 1963). The label, particularly psychiatric labels, according to Szasz not only controls deviant behaviours and (undesirable) populations, thus enforcing societal norms, but is also stigmatising, emphasising the role of power in the process of labelling and the anti-psychiatrists highlight the authority of the medical profession in imposing labels.

Key Thinkers

Anti-Psychiatrists

- The anti-psychiatrists Laing (1964) and Szasz (1961)) are critical of the medical model and the idea that criminals and/or drug users are sick and only treatment can cure them. Instead, they argue that we have seen the medicalisation of social problems that allows society to label and control undesirable/disapproved behaviour either via punishment and/or treatment, thus legitimising their removal from society.
- The anti-psychiatrists show the power labelling has on how drugs, crime and mental illness is represented and viewed by both patients and wider society.
- They describe mental illness and drug addiction as myths; people have problems with living, which are then labelled as medical conditions – illnesses. This results in the medicalisation of social problems that are labelled as diseases so they can be controlled because they do not fit society's definition of normal.
- The label ensures conformity through social stigmatisation and exclusion that can only be cured via punishment and/or treatment.
- Medicine is seen as a form of social control. The medical profession controls the definition of drugs (therapeutic or toxic), their legitimate and illegitimate uses, their availability (prescriptions) and the diagnosis and treatment of drug addiction.

REALISM

Realist criminology sees crime and its subsequent statistics as real and not just a social construct. Realism can be politically aligned to the right or left.

Left Realism (Currie, 1985; Lea and Young, 1984; Young and Matthews, 1992): was about taking crime seriously by addressing crime and the causes of crime via societal intervention(s) (Hopkins-Burke, 2018; Treadwell, 2011). Left realists largely focused on street crime, but left realism has also been applied to drugs (Mugford and O'Malley, 1991). Politically aligned with the left and arising out of an era of critical/radical criminology, left realists advocated the square of crime, and acknowledged that crime and/or drug use were a result of four factors and their interaction/

relationship: the criminal justice system (the state and its agencies like the police), society (the public), the offender and the victim. Left realists believe the main causes of crime are relative deprivation, marginalisation/social exclusion and subcultures (Lea and Young, 1984). Crime prevention involves some relationship between the corners of the square.

Right Realism (Murray, 1990; Wilson, 1975): focuses on street crimes that include drug use and dealing, particularly of the poor/socio-economically deprived people, which Murray (1990) has called the underclass who are welfare dependent and often socially excluded (e.g. homeless vagabonds, drunks, addicts and the mentally ill). Right realists recognise that crime tends to be concentrated in certain socio-economically deprived areas/estates and disproportionately impacts the poor as both the perpetrators and victims of crime come from the same communities (Hopkins-Burke, 2018). Placing an emphasis on upholding public order and morality, they argue for more rigorous control of street offences – sex work, drug use/dealing and graffiti – as these signal crimes create fear and act as a precursor to more serious crime. This is illustrated in Wilson and Kelling's (1982) broken windows thesis, which emphasises that physical and social disorder exerts a causal effect on criminal behaviour as it 'signals' to criminals the local community's indifference to crime. Indirectly disorder thus encourages more disorder to take place as social control declines. Signal crimes are those that indicate (act as a warning) to people (e.g. street drinking, harassment, graffiti, vandalism, litter and noise), illustrating an increased risk of crime and being victimised, which has a disproportionate impact on their fear of crime (Innes and Fielding, 2002). Right realists believe the individual is at fault, not society, and the solution is to clamp down on the individual behaviour of those posing risk by restoring order through policing (e.g. identifying hotspots, problem-orientated policing) to reduce behaviour that is not necessarily criminal, just undesirable (Braga et al., 1999; Clarke, 1995; Weisburd and Mazerolle, 2000). Therefore, situational crime prevention initiatives aim to reduce the opportunity for crime by reducing the rewards and increasing the punishments. It influences policing and that crime can be designed out of an area – crime prevention through environmental design (CPTED) (Clarke, 1995).

To add to the realisms, there is also **Critical Realism** (Bhaskar, 2008), which Matthews (2014) argues could be used to develop left realism further.

PRACTICAL IMPLICATIONS – POLICY AND PRACTICE

- The sociological aspect of gateway theory underpins the cannabis cafes in the Netherlands (see the Box on page 244–245 of Chapter 9), since it stops young people from going to illicit dealers to buy cannabis – dealers who often sell other substances that these young people might buy and use (see the Box below).

Gateway Theory

Gateway theory proposes that the use of 'soft drugs' like cannabis leads to an increased risk of using more harmful substances – 'hard drugs' – and becoming involved in crime in two ways:

1) Risk Assessment: young people use the drug they perceive to be the safest first, which tends to be cannabis. Since cannabis use does not cause the harms attributed to it by official discourse, the user's expectations of other drugs' effects and risks are lowered, making them more likely to try and use them.
2) Sociological Factor: people who have bought illegal 'soft drugs' like cannabis have made connections to illicit drug dealers who may also sell illegal 'hard drugs', making them more likely to buy and use more harmful substances as they are available to buy.

There is little evidence supporting gateway theory (Secades-Villa et al., 2015), which has been heavily criticised and largely discredited (see Pudney, 2002 and criticisms below).

- Left realism influenced Tony Blair and New Labour's (1994) 'tough on crime, tough on the causes of crime' approach, which targeted the individual and structural factors that led to crime and/or drugs. Initiatives included supporting families, education and employment schemes (e.g. New Start and New Deal) (Hopkins-Burke, 2018) alongside a new drug strategy 'Tackling Drugs to Build a Better Britain' (see Chapter 3) that advocated a multi-agency approach, which is also advocated by left realists. According to Matthews (2014), antisocial behaviour orders also embodied left realist principles, although the influence of left realism on New Labour's policies has been contested by Lea (2010).
- Right realism and situational crime prevention initiatives influence policing and the design of buildings and spaces (e.g. CPTED) that has included benches – the Camden Bench – that prevent drug dealing and blue lights in toilets to deter intravenous drug use in public toilets (Crabtree et al., 2013). While the evidence around the effectiveness of situational crime prevention initiatives is mixed, there is increasing evidence that it may have a 'diffusion of benefits effect', which means it has an impact on other crimes not directly targeted in the initiative (see Jacobson, 1999).

LIMITATIONS AND CRITICISMS

Over the years, sociological theories have received much criticism:

- Subcultural theory has been heavily criticised (e.g. Cohen did not base his theory on empirical data) (Hopkins-Burke, 2018) and is often seen as outdated in contemporary society (Hall and Winlow, 2015).

- Left realism has been heavily criticised (e.g. it has never been empirically tested, for being more idealistic than realistic, for being overly deterministic and for relying too heavily on victim surveys), thus confusing the reality of crime and drugs (Akers and Sellers, 2008; Walklate, 2007).
- Gateway theory has been heavily criticised since most cannabis users, and most recreational drug users, will not go on to use drugs like heroin and crack or develop more problematic patterns of use (Aldridge et al., 2011), and actually, legal substances such as alcohol and tobacco are nearly always used before cannabis as are volatile substances such as glue. In fact, young people with a history of inhalant use by age 16 are over nine times more likely to begin heroin use by age 32, even when other risk factors were held constant. So, ***is solvent/inhalant use a gateway to heroin use and is legal substance use a gateway to illicit substance use?*** In fact, if cannabis is a gateway, it is a very small gateway.
- Situational crime prevention has also been heavily criticised (see Hayward, 2007), as it often displaces rather than eradicates the issue, and many of the crime prevention initiatives incorporated into environmental design have been shown to increase harm (Crabtree et al., 2013; Parkin and Coomber, 2010).

CRITICAL AND CONTEMPORARY THEORIES

Recently, there has been a call for the creation of more contemporary theories to explain crime and drugs in contemporary society. Many criminological theories still used today originate from the 1930s–1970s, when society and the world were very different, meaning they are no longer applicable. As a result, a range of new critical theories have been developed that challenge mainstream criminology, which include cultural criminology, zemiology, queer theory, critical race theory (CRT), ultra-realism and deviant leisure to name a few.

CRT (Bell): argues that racial bias/prejudice is ingrained/inherent in legislation and institutions that include the criminal justice system and its agents (e.g. the police), all of which are structured to maintain White privilege. CRT has been applied to crime and the criminal justice system (Delgado and Stefancic, 2007), drug couriers (Gonçalves 2020) and the war on drugs (Fornili, 2018). It has been criticised for seeing and looking for racism in every aspect of life/relationships in contemporary society, even when it does not exist, while Bell's interest convergence thesis makes it impossible for anyone with racial privilege to do anything for anyone of a different race without it being in their own self-interests and/or exploitative/extractive (Lindsay, 2022). Recently, arguments have arisen against the use CRT (see Greenberg and Sherman, 2021; Sawchuk, 2021).

Critical Realism (Bhaskar, 1997): the three pillars of critical realism are epistemological fallibilism (empirical), ontological realism (real) and judgemental rationality (actual), and the framework argues that the real is not observable at the deeper level as causes are complex structures and processes that are not directly observable; therefore, they require sophisticated conceptualisation. It provides a framework for understanding the complexity of the world and guides how we make sense of the relationship between observable phenomena, the unobservable mechanisms behind them, and our interpretations of both. Critical realism has recently been applied to substance use (Bower et al., 2020), addiction (Selbekk et al., 2015), recovery (Edwards and Burton, 2021) and drug policy (Stevens, 2020).

Ultra-Realism (Hall and Winlow, 2015): draws from an array of disciplines – philosophy, history, neuroscience, psychoanalysis and moral philosophy – 'to return criminology to its fundamental question: why do some individuals and groups risk harm to others as they pursue their instrumental and expressive interests rather than seek solidarity with one another?' (Hall and Winlow, 2018:1976). Ultra-realism has been used to explain drug use/addiction (Ayres, 2023), crime, including drug dealing (Hall et al., 2008) and human enhancement drugs (Hall, 2019).

Zemiology (Hillyard and Tombs, 2007; Raymen, 2022): is the study of social harms, arising from crime and/or drugs, which offers an alternative framework to traditional criminology by focusing on the broader concept of harm rather than just on the law and legal definitions of crime and/or drugs. When applied to drugs, Zemiology emphasises the social, economic and health-related harms caused by drug use, production and policy (e.g. Detadian and Askew, 2024), rather than solely focusing on the criminal aspects of drugs. It assumes the powerful have co-opted the legal system to protect their interests and power. Zemiology argues that focusing on harm can help us better understand and respond to social problems, including crimes committed by the powerful.

Deviant Leisure (Raymen and Smith, 2019): adopts a zemiological focus on social harm to consider the harms that are embedded within some of the most popular and familiar forms of commodified leisure. Also drawing on ultra-realism, zemiology and green criminology, Raymen and Smiths conceptualisation of deviant leisure inverts the traditional conception of deviance as the contravention of (non-existent) social norms, values and ethical standards, and instead explains the normalised harms that emanate from the relationship between commodified leisure and consumer capitalism, and includes drugs and alcohol in the NTE (e.g. Raymen and Smith, 2019).

Green Criminology (South and Brisman, 2020): considers environmental harms, laws, regulations and crimes against the environment and focuses on the impact of human activities on ecosystems and non-human species. When relating green criminology to drugs, the primary concerns involve the environmental impacts of drug production, distribution and consumption (see Ayres, 2020b).

Cultural Criminology (Ferrell, Hayward, Young and Presdee, 2000): explaining drug use, supply and crime, cultural criminologists emphasise the role of subcultures, symbolic meanings, emotions (e.g. excitement, pleasure and fear) and the socio-cultural context in shaping individuals' engagement with drugs and crime, as both are performative acts of carnival (Presdee, 2000) (see Chapter 3). They also emphasise the role of the media, as media representations play a significant part in constructing societal perceptions of drug use and crime, which can influence public opinion and policy responses.

CONCLUSION

This chapter has offered a critical overview of the main theoretical perspectives, which are used to explain drugs and crime as well as provide an evidence base for policy and practice. Showing how drugs and crime can be conceptualised – positively and negatively – depending on the theoretical perspective being adopted provides a theoretical toolkit, which you can apply to drugs – use, production and supply – and crime, or even policy and practice, to independently analyse relevant developments within the field, although theories are often characteristic of the epoch and as such some have been described as old, outdated and no longer applicable to contemporary consumer society (e.g. subcultures). The origins of these theories can be traced back through history and the socio-economic and political context of the time, which is the focus of the next chapter.

SUMMARY

- **Theories help to simplify and explain complex human behaviours that include drugs and crime, and each theory offers a unique perspective.**
- **Theories often ignore the interaction between factors and the complex interplay of events impacting on and factors underpinning drugs/addiction and crime (e.g. a lack of self-control is linked to intelligence – higher levels of intelligence are correlated with higher levels of self-control).**
- **Research is constantly testing academic theory and will often compare theories (e.g. see Meneses and Akers, 2011) to ascertain their validity.**
- **Each theory is often highly critical of the other theories.**
- **Theory and research provide the evidence base for policy, practice, treatment and rehabilitation.**
- **Only by combing micro, meso and macro theories can multifaceted behaviours like drugs and crime be understood (see Chapter 5).**

Here are some points and questions for you to consider after reading this chapter:

1) Are criminals and/or drug users born (nature) or made (nurture)?
2) Should drug addicts and/or criminals be paid and/or coerced/forced to be sterilised?
3) Which theory best explains crime and/or drug use?

(Continued)

(Continued)

Here are some useful resources for those wanting to further explore the issues raised in this chapter:

- Hopkins-Burke, R. (2018) *An Introduction to Criminological Theory*. London: Routledge. This book provides a comprehensive but general overview of criminological theories, but does not necessarily apply them to drugs, which was the main focus of this chapter.
- Lilienfeld, S.O. (2007) Psychological Treatments that Cause Harm. *Perspectives on Psychological Science*, 2:53–70.
  This paper explores the concept of iatrogenic effects, where certain psychological treatments may cause more harm than good, highlighting harmful psychological treatments and therapies, which have been shown to result in negative outcomes. The article stresses the need for evidence-based approaches and rigorous scientific scrutiny to avoid harmful interventions.
- Shiner, M. (2009) *Drug Use and Social Change*. Basingstoke: Palgrave-Macmillan.
  Investigating the relationship between drug use and social change, particularly in the United Kingdom, this book examines how drug use has evolved in response to broader shifts in society, culture and political economy, considering the role of social class, inequality and marginalisation in shaping patterns of drug consumption and the changing social meanings of drug use.

2

THE HISTORICAL DEVELOPMENT OF DRUG POLICY AND PROHIBITION – UP UNTIL THE 1960s

Overview

This chapter aims to provide you with:

- A historical overview of drugs (production, supply and use) and their control and regulation through key periods in history up until the 1960s.
- An overview of drug use not only through history, but in different countries and cultures up until the 1960s.
- A comprehensive overview of the key drug legislation and policies – international and domestic up until the 1960s.

You will be introduced to the key terms:

- Colonialism
- Prohibition
- Narcotics
- Psychotropic

INTRODUCTION

The previous chapter outlined the theories relevant to understanding and explaining drugs and crime, some of which are representative of the historical era in which they were conceptualised. This chapter builds on this understanding of drugs and crime by exploring the historical backdrop to modern-day drugs and their prohibition via the emergence and evolution of drug laws. It will show how colonialism has shaped drug policies and practices and how and why controls have been implemented throughout history. This chapter encourages readers to make connections between how issues of colonialism and the emergence of capitalism with its differential hierarchies of wealth and privilege have influenced the development of modern-day systems of drug control (see Chapter 3).

Although this chapter largely focuses on the history of drug control in the United Kingdom, and to a lesser extent America, examples from around the world are also covered since a lot of drug legislation and the foundations of prohibition are a result of international treaties and conventions. Writing about the origins and use of drugs, particularly from the dawn of time to now or from continents like Africa or Asia where records have been destroyed or there is a paucity of evidence (written or visual), must be acknowledged before reading this chapter, which is based on available historical evidence.

HISTORICAL SUBSTANCES: FLORA AND FAUNA

Whether obtained from plants (e.g. coca, cannabis, mushrooms) or fermenting fruits and/or cane sugar (e.g. alcohol), humans and animals have always sought out intoxicating substances to get high and as a form of medication (Jay, 2010). For example, migrating birds eat fermented fruits to get drunk (e.g. Australia has drunken parrot season), reindeer and Siberian bears like the mind-altering effects of fly agaric mushrooms and cats go crazy for catnip (Jay, 2010; Muller, 2011). Animals seek out and consume psychedelic substances and, like humans, consume them for a variety of reasons. In fact, there is evidence to show humans learnt about plant-derived drugs from watching and copying animals (e.g. goats eating coffee in Ethiopia led priests who watched them to roast and boil coffee beans to stay awake through nights of prayer) (Crocq, 2007; Jay, 2010). It is difficult to verify when humans started using substances as there are no records available to verify this.

The records that do exist however show that psychotropic substances in plants were discovered by hunter-gathers before the Neolithic period with pipes containing the shrub *Anadenanthera* (a source of dimethyltryptamine) found dating from 2000BC in the Andes (Barton, 2011; Guerra-Doce, 2015; Jay, 2010). Cannabis – referred to as *ganja* or *gaja* – is mentioned in the Rig Vedas of India – one of the oldest sacred books of Hinduism – prior to 1000BC as a favourite drink of the God Indra which he gave to people so that they might 'attain elevated states of consciousness, delight in worldly joy, and freedom from fear', a concept later vocalised in Rastafarian ideology (see the Box on page 41(Emboden, 1990:225 as cited in Benard, 2007:95). Hemp was cultivated in China from 4000BC, while alcohol has also been traced to an Early Neolithic village in China in 7000–6600BC. Poppy heads/extracts were mentioned in Sumerian texts and in Egyptian hieroglyphics from third BC, including using it to sedate children and to prevent babies screaming, before making their way to Europe, including England, between the tenth and thirteenth centuries (Barton, 2011; Crocq, 2007; Guerra-Doce, 2015; Jay, 2010). Opium was used extensively in Greek and Roman cultures and was a staple drug for physicians (e.g. like paracetamol today), including its use in the widespread practice of assisted suicide. In fact, opium use was so widespread in Roman society that the state fixed the price. There were no concerns about opium addiction (and no Latin word for it either), but alcohol addiction was widely recognised (Barton, 2011) and among some, condemned.

Alcohol is one of the most extensively used substances throughout history, embedded in a diverse array of cultures around the world. Whether that is natural forms of alcohol (e.g. fermented fruit, roots and plants) or distilled alcoholic beverages, alcohol in all its various forms has been culturally defined (e.g. form, use and meaning) and largely accepted (Mandelbaum, 1965). From traditional drinks like kava (a narcotic drink) from Fiji, to the sweet liquors created and sold in Paris in 1332 (Courtwright, 2001; Jay, 2010), alcohol has not only been a stable in the diet of many cultures (e.g. Greeks and Egyptians) but has also traditionally been used in religious and spiritual practices (e.g. the Nigerian Kofyar believed that 'a man's way to god is with a beer in hand' (Netting, 1963:1–5 as cited in Mandelbaum, 1965). Religion and cultural practices, however, have also defined acceptable and unacceptable consumption practices as illustrated in early religious teachings (e.g. early Christians saw alcohol as a gift from God but drinking too much was a sin), some of which still define acceptable consumption practices today. These cultural boundaries of acceptable and unacceptable use led to alcohol prohibition in the US , while in other cultures, excessive use is considered symbolic (e.g. among the Aztecs not getting drunk would displease the Gods) and has continually been shown not to result in addiction (Mandelbaum, 1965). Excessive consumption of substances was often celebrated (e.g. Egyptian men smoked excessive amounts of hashish to increase their sexual potency), but also led to more formal controls being imposed as expressed by Plato (1952b:3 as cited in Nencini, 1997): 'sobriety, therefore, was to be imposed by law...no children under eighteen may touch wine...young man under thirty may take wine in moderation, but that he must entirely abstain from intoxication, and heavy drinking', while drinking unmixed wine without a physician's prescription was punishable by death. Other substances were also routinely mixed with alcohol (e.g. green cannabis seeds soaked in wine were used to treat ear ache in ancient Rome and Greece) (Courtwright, 2001; Jay, 2010). Apothecaries emerged, which were early practitioners of pharmacy that prepared and sold medicinal substances, herbs and potions in ancient civilisations (e.g. Mesopotamia, Egypt, Greece, Rome, Baghdad (eighth century) and Europe (twelfth century)) (Gootenberg, 2022). In fact, many medicines used to treat conditions today originated from historical traditional cures (e.g. Chinese medicine introduced ephedrine to treat asthma and the

Quechua people of Peru introduced quinine to treat malaria) (Thompson, 2014). Substances have always been mixed to create medicines to treat physical and psychiatric illnesses.

It is believed, like humans, animals consume psychoactive substances for the chemical rewards, but in more contemporary laboratory experiments, environment also plays a part, as animals (e.g. rats) are more inclined to take drugs if in captivity, particularly if they are bored with nothing to do (Jay, 2010). Drug use in humans is also influenced by the person and the environment (set and setting) (see Zinberg, 1984 – in the Box below). The dose/concentration of the substance being used also reflects the different uses (e.g. Native Americans used thorn apple – *Datura Stramonium* – as a local anaesthetic, but in higher doses, it was used in religious rituals as it induced delirium and hallucinations) (Thompson, 2014). Altered states of consciousness have also been shown to facilitate, enhance and inspire creativity both now and in the past (e.g. Paleolithic times it was linked to cave paintings) (Kedar et al., 2021). Traditionally, different cultures have certain substances embedded in them as part of their traditions (e.g. kola nuts in Sudan, betel nuts or quids – a mixture of spices, the areca nut and slaked lime wrapped in betel vine leaves – in Asia, India and China, khat chewing in Somalia and cocoa leaf chewing among Amazonian tribes).

In addition to religious and spiritual practices, the preparation and consumption of substances historically has been about socialising, building communities and creating solidarity, but substances have also been divisive, stratifying societies on the basis of gender and respectability (class) (Jay, 2010; Mandelbaum, 1965). In Rome, no 'slave nor a free-born woman could drink wine' (Athenaeus, 1969b as cited in Nencini, 1997), while the use of kava in most South Pacific cultures is the preserve of men as the ground where kava is prepared is taboo to women (Jay, 2010). Similar gender divisions are seen elsewhere, such as smoking in Arabia, the use of ayahuasca in the Amazon or drinking alcohol in egalitarian India, where these practices were considered the preserve of men (Jay, 2010; Mandelbaum, 1965). Substances have always been an indication of respectability and class, with 'elegant betal habits' being a sign of refinement as young women were 'judged on how neatly they roll their leaf into a quid' (Jay, 2010:31), while hashish was often a drug of the lower classes (Gootenberg, 2022), although this varied across countries and cultures.

Zinberg (1984) argues that substance use is related to three factors:

1) **The Substance** – the pharmacology and its physiological effects;
2) **The Set** – the individual user (e.g. personality, mood); and
3) **The Setting** – the environment – physical and social context – in which use occurred.

Becker's (1963, also see Chapter 1) work also illustrates how users of drugs learn to expect, experience and enjoy certain effects when they consume substances, which is supported by research. For example, use of magic mushrooms, which leads to hallucinations, mind-expending colourful trips and enhancement of bright colours and music, is in stark contrast to historical accounts of accidental ingestion where none of these effects were expected but the painful onset of poisoning/toxicity was recorded (Jay, 2010).

Throughout history, substances have been used medicinally, spiritually and for religious purposes among ancient tribes, witch doctors and shamanic communities around the world. There is evidence to suggest hallucinogens – from mushrooms and cacti – heavily influenced the major religions of India, Americas, China/Middle East and Europe, including Christianity, and were used in ritual practices to communicate with the spirit world (Guerra-Doce, 2015). In fact, many cultures have developed around the use of substances – hallucinogens facilitate shapeshifting into animals or communing with the ancestors, while cannabis seeds were part of the Scythian's death ritual (Gootenberg, 2022; Jay, 2010; Mandelbaum, 1965). Many early Christian groups partook in heavy drinking and feasting as part of their celebrations, but this became largely symbolic, with only the priest using bread and wine. While there were no formal controls on drugs at this time, there is evidence to suggest that certain drugs – hallucinogens – were (informally) controlled by the shamans and religious leaders confining their use to certain rituals, while the Roman state controlled the price of opium (Barton, 2011). While medical treatment was provided by some institutions in Greece and Rome, the first hospitals came from Christianity. Religion was also a factor in the control and prohibition of many intoxicating substances at this time, particularly alcohol, which was officially banned in Christian and Islamic societies (Courtwright, 2001; Mandelbaum, 1965).

Despite its long tradition, Christian religions (e.g. Protestantism) attacked and morally condemned the use of substances in religious ceremonies as well as for recreational use, particularly opium, attacking the age-old practice of suicide on religious ground, in fact, opium was declared the work of Satan (Barton, 2011; Courtwright, 2001). Substances became demonised as ruinous vices, particularly recreational non-medical – pleasurable – use, which was said 'to lead to slavery, as manifested in addiction, and to ruin, as manifested in disease, pauperism and depravity' (Courtwright, 2019:125).

FROM THE MIDDLE AGES TO THE MIDDLE PASSAGE AND COLONIALISM

Not much changed in the mediaeval ages, as alcohol, opium and cannabis remained in use medicinally, recreationally, spiritually and religiously, but it was also an era that heralded new controls on these substances, which varied across countries and cultures. In the twelfth-thirteenth century, hashish (*kaif*) became one of the most prominent recreational drugs in mediaeval Muslim societies, where it was consumed (mostly eaten) in various solid preparations (Gootenberg, 2022), while alcohol was a key feature of mediaeval life, including a regular part of meals (e.g. beer soup for breakfast) (Schivelbusch, 1992). In fact, at this time, beer was seen as the second main source of nourishment after bread, with 'about three litres of beer per person daily, children included' (Schivelbusch, 1992:22). Combining/mixing substances also continued with alcohol and opium to produce a tincture called laudanum in the 1600s, a new smoking mixture madak (tobacco mixed with opium) appeared in China in the 1700s, sugar was added to coffee, tea and tobacco 'to preserve, flavour and colour', while molasses was used to preserve tobacco leaves (Courtwright, 2001:30; Dasgupta, 2019). Many substances considered drug foods during this time were still being used religiously/spiritually and medicinally also.

Medicine and treatment in the middle ages were a mixture of religion (e.g. priests exorcising evil spirits that were seen to cause mental illness), traditional herbal remedies (e.g. henbane/hemlock) and superstition (e.g. magic charms). Priests, nuns and monks ran hospitals in their monasteries, barber surgeons performed minor surgical procedures (e.g. bloodletting, removing bones/teeth) and local wise women administered traditional cures/treatments. Wise women who used herbs/plants mixed with superstition and religion were also known as botanists and later witches. Witches used willow bark for treating inflammation and psychotropic/psychedelic plant compounds called 'flying ointments' whose psychedelic properties became attributed to Satan/Devil (Hatsis, 2015; Thompson, 2014). Hallucinogens were also connected to European witchcraft in mediaeval and early modern times. There were also concerns about sexual activity and the morality of these women in relation to substance use (Barton, 2011); they were persecuted for corrupting Christian society and blamed for the black death/plague (alongside the Jews), which the Church said 'was God's punishment for the sinfulness of humankind' (Hajar, 2012). The *Malleus Maleficarum* (1487), a treatise on witchcraft, played a significant role in linking women's medical practices and certain substances with witchcraft. This was partly driven by the increasing professionalisation of medicine that sought to standardise treatments and eliminate the use of unregulated remedies, which began to dominate in the sixteenth and seventeenth centuries, often sidelining traditional female healers. Many women who practised traditional healing methods and midwifery were often accused of witchcraft and tried as witches – a few for illegally practising medicine. Accusations of witchcraft were often influenced by social, economic and religious factors, which reflected wider European class struggles and the continuing domination of the Christian church as widows, unmarried women and those who were socially marginalised were more likely to be accused of witchcraft (Hatsis, 2015; Thompson, 2014).

As the witch hunts burnt many of the local wise women, controls on the use and distribution of substances were also starting to be introduced by the merchant classes confining them to emerging apothecaries that were attached to grocers and were largely based on superstitions, the supernatural and humoral medicine (Barton, 2011). The witch hunts also extended to the colonies, and accusations of devil worship were a key function of slavery and the colonisation of indigenous populations (Sutherland et al., 2013; Voeks,

1997). The perception was 'almost all negroes that leave their country are sorcerers or at least they are able to use magic, witchcraft and poison' (Voeks, 1997:46), which was called Obeah. Obeah was brought to the colonies by enslaved Africans. It used plants and herbs to heal and harm and was associated with evil, devil worship, curses, suspicious disappearances and poisonings, which allowed the colonisers to prohibit it, especially since it was deemed irrational to the modern scientific worldview of emerging European Enlightenment. The real reason Obeah was prohibited, however, was the colonisers' fear of slave uprisings and its role in slave revolts as these healers had great power and influence over the enslaved (Sheridan, 1985; Sutherland et al., 2013; Voeks, 1997).

Term

The word '**Drug** emerged in the late mediaeval period from the Middle Dutch term droge vate (dry vat): a container for non-perishable goods. By the sixteenth century, "drug" and its cognates had become incorporated into English, French, Italian, Portuguese, and Spanish, among other languages' (Gootenberg, 2022:114).

Colonialism developed and spread globally from the fifteenth to the mid-twentieth century with Europeans conquering 35% of the world by 1800, and even more by World War I (Hoffman, 2015). Substances were an integral part of colonialism and the building and binding of empires (Ayres et al., 2024). Colonialism and the plantation system were based around the commerce and consumption of substances. Trade routes were established and large trading companies dominated (e.g. East India Trading Company) the triangular (slave) trade, particularly the trade in luxurious and addictive substances like tea, coffee, tobacco, opium, cocaine, sugar and distilled liquor, which left their countries of origin and spread around the globe where they became popular (Ayres et al., 2024; Crocq 2007; Schivelbusch, 1992). Sugar was the only one of these substances to escape religious prescription (Mintz, 1985). Under colonial regimes, these luxurious substances became cash crops that commanded high prices reflecting the long and arduous trade routes. In this epoch, the new luxurious substances were used as food/drink (e.g. coffee, alcohol and sugar), socially (e.g. coffee houses), religiously (e.g. tea) and medicinally (e.g. coffee and sugar were viewed as a panacea for everything, rose sugar was used to break a fever, soothe hoarseness and pains in the breast, while coffee dried out the bodies phlegm and mucus and improved blood circulation) (Mintz, 1985; Schivelbusch, 1992).

Deliberate disregard for health and well-being by the colonial masters, coupled with the high cost of limited medical resources, exposed the enslaved and later the indentured labourers – after slavery was abolished in 1845 – to the full violence of disease, thereby forcing them to tend to their own healthcare needs using traditional healing (Sutherland et al., 2013; Voeks, 1997). During the Middle Passage, an array of traditional substances were used on the slave ships to treat illness, injuries and wounds, while also helping those on board to cope with the traumatic, squalid and cramped conditions. Once they arrived, these same substances were used on the plantations where conditions were equally as bad (Ayres et al., 2024; Sheridan, 1985; Sutherland et al., 2013). During this time, traditional healing was most critical in the treatment of psychological distress. As a result, enslaved Africans and indentured labourers from India and China imported new substances into the colonies (e.g. bhang, ganja and opium). The cultivation and use of psychoactive substances in their countries of origin, including fermented and distilled alcoholic drinks, opium and cannabis, were widespread and culturally accepted. Among the enslaved and indentured labourers, these substances were used unproblematically, even opium, which became known for alleviating boredom and anxiety (Dikötter et al., 2007; Sutherland et al., 2013).

The use of traditional substances and healing dominated as enslaved Africans and indentured Asians did not trust White doctors and their harmful – often fatal – treatment methods (e.g. bloodletting, purging and the use of toxic mercury and antimony). Although more prevalent among doctors in the colonies, doctors in North America and Europe often overdosed their patients with drugs (e.g. opium, mercury) as the sale of imported medicines made up a large part of a doctor's income (Sheridan, 1985). According to Sheridan (1985:331), the reason why overdosing was so prevalent among the enslaved was 'the belief that tropical diseases needed to be arrested quickly with strong remedies and the racist myth that blacks were less sensitive than Whites to strong medicines'. Alongside other tropes constructed by Western powers, substances became tied to colonial Western ways of knowing that created racialised regimes of truth that had no scientific evidence base but created 'the colonial imaginary' (Ayres et al., 2024), which was used by the colonisers to justify their treatment of the workers and as a form of social control as migrants were ascribed certain traits (e.g. servile, crafty, idle, uncivilised and immoral) that warranted their control/regulation (Ayres et al., 2024; Berridge, 1999). As such, traditional healers became referred to as 'witch doctors' who perpetuated traditional healing practices as evil magic – Obeah – thereby justifying its prohibition and the forced conversion to Christianity (Sheridan, 1985). These views were supported by a growing temperance movement that sought to control the poor working classes and uncivilised racialised others through religion (Berridge, 1999; Courtwright, 2001). Furthermore, the consumption of intoxicating substances was increasingly believed by missionaries to accentuate these 'problem' traits of each race. This connection soon led to the racialisation of certain substances, which determined which drugs were acceptable, alongside appropriate consumption practices (e.g. controlled, medical use), and the drugs that needed prohibiting (Ayres et al., 2024; Courtwright, 2001).

Key Term

Racialisation of drugs refers to the process by which certain drugs become associated with specific racial and/or ethnic groups, often leading to racialised stereotypes, discriminatory policies and unequal enforcement of drug laws. This process has deep historical roots and continues to influence contemporary drug policy and law enforcement today. The racialisation of drugs during colonial times was a tool used by European powers to assert control over colonised populations and justify their imperial endeavours. By associating certain drugs with specific racial/ethnic groups and traits, colonial authorities could implement discriminatory policies and reinforce social hierarchies. Understanding this history is crucial for recognising the long-lasting impact of colonialism on contemporary drug policies and racial attitudes, many of which are still prevalent today.

The plantation system and slavery were premised on the commercial production and trade of drug foods like sugar, rum and tobacco, which transformed the production, consumption and regulation of substances/drugs. The enslaved and indentured migrants routinely used drugs like opium and cannabis to deal with the anxiety and stress created by familial separation, to cope with the harsh conditions, long hours, boredom, stress and anxiety as well as the social stimulus and camaraderie it provided in group settings. Even the plantation owners recognised the ability of intoxicating substances to keep the migrants subdued and to alleviate the debilitating effects of the plantation permitting their use (Ayres et al., 2024; Jankowiak and Bradburd, 2003). Psychoactive substances, especially opium and cannabis, rendered its users docile – 'someone dreaming opium dreams is not going to formulate anti-colonial thoughts, much less act' (Schivelbusch, 1992:222) – which also applied to the stupefaction and exploitation of workers on the domestic front as drugs were freely available and widely used (Berridge, 1999; Courtwright, 2001). As a result, many indigenous populations (e.g. Native Americans), enslaved plantation workers and later indentured labourers were dependent on these – addictive – substances, which was encouraged and promoted by the colonisers/planters (Ayres et al., 2024; Gootenberg, 2022; Jankowiak and Bradburd, 2003). In the Caribbean, the colonisers paid their workers in rum and set up liquor shops – they owned – next to the plantations, often locating them near the pay office with extended opening hours to create a captive group of consumers who demanded substances, particularly substances they produced (e.g. rum). Rum and other spirits (e.g. whiskey, brandy and gin) provided a means for the colonisers to not only make money but also buy, retain, pay and control their workers. Gradually, the use of traditional migrant drugs like opium and cannabis became linked to undesirable – and often racialised – activities, such as idleness, crime, promiscuity, violence, gambling, poor health, (in)efficiency and poor productivity, which led to colonial substances (e.g. rum) being introduced as a preferable 'more wholesome' alternative (Aaron and Musto, 1981; Ayres et al., 2024). In fact, 'substances of the colony' (Ayres et al., 2024) were routinely introduced and used by the colonisers to pacify and coerce labourers and indigenous populations to perform their bidding/services/tow the line across the globe, which they also directly profited from. Introducing these addictive substances also created a physiologically dependent and indebted population of captive consumers, which was constantly being replenished, transforming drug production and consumption.

Substances like sugar, tobacco, coffee and alcohol became integral to everyday life, as substances became commodified and 'emerged as global items of consumption and exchange' (Gootenberg, 2022:114).

During the colonial era, substances were a staple part of people's diets for all classes (e.g. beer soup, wine and sugar for breakfast) and were a popular substitute for water as they provide stamina and good health. Colonialism, the sugar trade and the importation of molasses fuelled the distillation of alcohol and its commercial exploitation, which created stronger alcoholic drinks. Strong alcohol like distilled and fermented liquors were considered not only healthy but also medicinal 'with curative and preventative properties' as well as being 'important and invigorating foods' 'whose restorative powers were a natural blessing' as the 'ascribed benefits corresponded to the strength of the drink' (Aaron and Musto, 1981:2). Alcohol at this time also 'played an essential part in rituals of conviviality and collective activity', including social gatherings, as taverns and liquor shops were central to social life in colonial towns and cities, with alcohol and intoxication/drunkenness providing a temporary escape from the hardships of poverty (Aaron and Musto, 1981:2). Other substances were also used socially. Tobacco was smoked or chewed as a form of relaxation and social interaction, whereas coffee was a sober beverage drank in the coffee houses (e.g. Lloyds), which soon evolved as a meeting place for people, conducting business, socialising or just to read newspapers (Schivelbusch, 1992:19). The widespread use of food substances, to pay wages, as medicines and for leisure and recreation, led to excessive consumption and addiction that justified – racialised – legislation restricting consumption, which was increasingly linked to antisocial behaviour, immorality, crime, a lack of productivity and absences from work (Berridge, 1999; Courtwright, 2001; Dikötter et al., 2007). For example, in China, the Jiaqing Emperor issued laws banning the importation, production and sale of opium in 1799 (Dasgupta, 2019) and Australia prohibited the supply of opium to Aboriginals via the Aboriginals Protection and Restriction of the Sale of Opium Act 1897. Laws prohibiting drunkenness also pervaded America, Europe and Britain as well as their colonies as part of broader efforts to maintain public order and morality (e.g. to prevent sin), which was largely influenced by religion. Public drunkenness was punished via public shaming (e.g. stocks or whippings), fines, banishment and/or imprisonment (Aaron and Musto, 1981; Berridge, 2013; Warner, 2003). Even the large trading companies controlled/regulated drunkenness (e.g. the East India Company regulations punished drunkenness among its employees with fines and dismissal for those caught drunk on duty). These laws also extended to the illegal production of substances, particularly alcohol, as regulations and licences were introduced (e.g. Alehouse Act 1604; Gin Act 1743 and 1751 in Britain) that criminalised illicit production and trade (Nicholls, 2009). This ensured that the trading companies, merchants and the state benefited economically from the production and sale of these substances, which were heavily taxed, thus minimising their losses as they criminalised the illicit production and sale of alcohol and other substances that they did not make money from.

Acceptable modes of production and consumption – non-medical/recreational and excessive/uncontrolled use – was linked to undesirable behaviours (e.g. gambling, promiscuity, disorderly antisocial behaviour), and controls on certain substances were introduced in many colonies in an attempt to retain power over the migrants and avoid a decline in labour and productivity (Aaron and Musto, 1981). Composed of orientalist tropes regarding race, substance use and moral degeneracy, unacceptable substance use was increasingly distinguished from acceptable use, views that were supported by a growing temperance movement that sought to control the poor working classes and uncivilised racialised others alongside a growing medical profession and pharmaceutical industry (Berridge, 1999; Courtwright, 2001). Subsequently, substances became further racialised and used as a tool of control and oppression, as particular races/ethnicities premised on colonisers' atavistic explanations and vulnerability to intoxication were mentioned in the legislation (see also above). For example, Native Americans and other indigenous populations (e.g. Amerindians in Guyana or Aboriginals in Australia) were often prohibited from buying or consuming substances (e.g. alcohol and opiates), which were often framed as being for their own protection (Ayres et al., 2024; Bauvais, 1998; Kidd, 1997).

Apothecaries, Colonialism and the Commodification of Drugs

- Colonial expansion had a profound impact on the development and practice of pharmacy. This period saw the extraction of botanical knowledge, medicinal substances and pharmaceutical practices between Europe and its colonies, leading to the globalisation of medicine and the establishment of regulatory frameworks.
- European apothecaries set up shops in colonial territories, serving both European settlers and indigenous populations. Colonisers relied on the extensive botanical and medicinal knowledge of indigenous people, which they adapted and integrated with their own European practices.
- In England, in 1617, the Society of Apothecaries was established that marked the emergence of the pharmacy and 'by 1780 sales of medication in England stood at £187,500 per annum' (around £12 million in today's prices) (Holloway, 1995:86 as cited in Barton, 2011).
- Apothecaries transformed 'traditional botanicals' into marketable global commodities (Gootenberg, 2022:117).
- European companies began to manufacture medicines on a large scale, often using substances sourced from the colonies, which led to the growth of the pharmaceutical industry and the creation of commodified 'compound medicines with exotic – and vague – names'. This meant apothecaries could not only charge more money but also defraud their customers by using cheaper substances in place of more valuable ones as adulteration and profit were prioritised over their efficacy and safety (Gootenberg, 2022:117).

The sixteenth to eighteenth centuries saw significant growth in apothecaries (see the Box above), pharmacies and the medical profession. Advancements in medical knowledge, the establishment of formal training institutions, technological advancements and the development of regulatory frameworks for the practice of medicine revolutionised the categorisation, production, distribution and consumption of drugs. Licenced apothecaries in the sixteenth and seventeenth centuries used distilling alongside other advancements in technology to process the drugs that they sold (e.g. refining, purifying, pulverising, fermenting, powdering, sugaring and macerating), which not only contributed to the marketability of these substances and their commodification but also created the new medical marketplace and 'the emergence of the modern shop', making them more lucrative/profitable (Gootenberg, 2022:117). Consequently, the number of recipes and cures containing opium – like laudanum – increased exponentially alongside patent medicines as cure-alls for an array of ailments (e.g. Daffy's Elixir and Godfrey's Cordial). They gained widespread popularity in the eighteenth century as American and British patent medicines were distributed around the world. This marked a significant development in the commercial and medical landscapes of the time despite the fact that their ingredients were usually kept secret, the products unregulated and largely ineffective (Berridge, 1999). The establishment of the medical profession, pharmacists and apothecaries saw the state starting to take control of the manufacture and supply/sale of certain substances controlling how they were used, which was profitable for the merchant classes as people in urban areas were increasingly forced to buy plants/remedies/medicines from these outlets/providers (Barton, 2011).

Key Term

Laudanum was created by Paracelsus in the sixteenth century. In the seventeenth century (1660s), the English physician Thomas Sydenham refined the formula and called it Sydenham's Laudanum, although it differed substantially from the laudanum of Paracelsus. Laudanum was standardised with the use of Sydenham's recipe and commodified. Although not originally a patent medicine, it was sold commercially by various manufacturers with some manufacturers of patent medicines including laudanum as an ingredient in their products (e.g. Dover's Powder for colds and fevers). (see Davenport-Hines, 2004)

Coupled with the industrial and intellectual revolution (e.g. emergence of Adam Smith in 1759 and Jeremy Bentham in 1776 – founder of utilitarianism – see Chapter 1) at this time opened up free trade markets and commerce with mercantile exports and the imports of exotic foreign goods (and people) that led to their expansion. This relied on work and productivity, which had been deemed incompatible with intoxication, particularly of certain substances, further justifying their prohibition, that discriminated along the lines of gender, class and race/ethnicity (Ayres et al., 2024; Barton, 2011; Berridge, 1999) (see the Box below).

Middle Ages to Colonialism: Drugs and Stratification

Gender

- As the apothecaries and male-dominated medical and pharmaceutical industries emerged, traditional female healers were sidelined, vilified and criminalised, with some being burnt as witches. Many of those accused of witchcraft were already poor or marginalised individuals (e.g. widows or those without male protectors as they were often among the poorest in their communities and thus more likely to be accused). Women were disproportionately targeted in witch hunts, partly because of societal views that associated women with moral and physical weakness, making them more susceptible to the devil's influence (Hatsis, 2015; Thompson, 2014).
- Women were integral to the manufacture and processing of substances. In mediaeval times, women often worked as alewives, brewing and selling ale from their homes or in small alehouses, while in China, they became integral to processing opium to make paste (Gootenberg, 2022).
- Many women became early opium smokers, as opium was integral to the recreational sex industry in many countries (e.g. China, Britain), which provided pleasure for the high-ranking officials and wealthy merchants who were mostly men (see the Box on page 132 of Chapter 5).

Respectability/Class

- Substances, particularly exotic and luxurious ones brought from the colonies, were a status symbol, an emblem of power and wealth – a form of conspicuous consumption – particularly among the ruling classes.
- Substance use reflected class (e.g. the working class in Britain largely consumed laudanum because it was cheaper than gin or wine, since it escaped taxation (Crocq, 2007)), but this varied by country and was influenced by local availability, cultural practices and economic conditions.
- Some substances were consumed by all classes: rich and poor alike (e.g. opium, sugar, alcohol, tobacco) (Berridge, 1999; Gottenberg, 2022; Schivelbusch, 1992). Affiliating substances with disorderly, criminal and immoral behaviour among the lower classes justified the introduction of regulations that began controlling the substances of the poor and the migrants (e.g. opium, cannabis) in the colonies and coloniser countries. The substance use of the merchants/professionals and upper aristocratic classes was largely ignored (Berridge, 1999; Courtwright, 2001).

Race/Ethnicity

- Throughout this period, drugs were racialised, legacies that remain embedded in current drug policy and legislation around the world.

The history of drug control from the Middle Ages to the period of colonialism reflects a transition from largely unregulated production and unrestricted use of substances to more formalised and regulated practices. This period saw the influence of exploration, trade and colonialism in shaping attitudes towards drugs, leading to the development of early regulatory frameworks (formal and informal). Colonialism, slavery and indentured labour opened up the world to free trade, dominated by companies that acted more like states and were key drivers of emerging global capitalism, which stitched colonies and their inhabitants into an economic system that opened them up to extraction, oppression, exploitation and eventually global capitalist markets, which continues today. Trading companies established a monopoly on the production and exportation of substances (e.g. cinchona bark and opium were dominated by the British East India Trading Company) as part of broader efforts by the company to dominate various lucrative trades in the colonies under its influence (Ayres et al., 2024; Berridge, 1999).

During this period, there was a significant shift from superstition and religious explanations for illnesses and their cures towards more scientific and medical explanations, which saw medical knowledge and practices standardised alongside drugs/medicines. This transition marked the early stages of the Enlightenment, a period characterised by a growing emphasis on reason, empirical evidence and scientific enquiry, and the start of the Industrial Revolution, which continued into the nineteenth century and the Victorian era alongside the commodification and further prohibition of drugs. Colonialism played a significant role in introducing new drugs, medical knowledge and practice and in controlling their trade/consumption, further shaping the medical landscape of the time. Only the controlled consumption of 'substances of the colony' was permitted (e.g. tobacco, alcohol, sugar), while everything else was slowly controlled and criminalised (e.g. opium, cocaine, cannabis), particularly substances seen as coming from and being used by foreigners, other often barbaric, uncivilised orientalist cultures (see Ayres et al., 2024:6), which continued into the Victorian era.

THE VICTORIAN ERA TO THE 1950s

The intersection of colonialism with the Victorian era (spanning the late nineteenth and twentieth centuries) is a period marked by significant expansion of European empires, the consolidation of colonial rule and industrialisation marked by the Industrial Revolution. During this time, colonisers extended their control over large parts of Africa, Asia and the Americas, profoundly influencing global trade, culture and politics, including those surrounding substances/drugs. This period also saw the establishment of more formalised systems of colonial administration and control, exploitation of resources and the imposition of European cultural values on colonised societies. During the Victorian era, there was a significant shift in attitudes towards drug use and an increase in drug legislation and control globally largely driven by concerns over public health, morality and social order. Substances once freely available and widely consumed started being formerly regulated and prohibited, based on prejudices, morality and religion that differentiated substances and their use based on race/ethnicity, class and gender (Ayres et al., 2024; Barton, 2011; Berridge, 1999), although this was never officially acknowledged.

The use and sale of drugs/substances during this period was practically unrestricted, and they could be bought like any other commodity from grocers' shops, apothecaries and street vendors. There was also no professional body to oversee the production and dispensing of substances (Barton, 2011). This lack of oversight and regulation led to the prevalence of patent medicines, many of which contained potentially harmful substances. They often contained high levels of alcohol, opium and cocaine (Berridge, 1999). As a result, opium was the most widely used substance during this time, but cocaine and cannabis were also widely available in a variety of products (e.g. opium poppy tea and plasters, cocaine tooth drops, Vin Mariani and Dr James' extract of cannabis indica). These drugs were aggressively marketed in pills, potions, tinctures, teas, soaps and lozenges, which were widely used and socially acceptable (Barton, 2011; Berridge, 1999; Courtwright, 2001). Gin was seen as more of a problem at this time than many now illicit drugs (Berridge, 2013; Warner, 2003). Using drugs like opium at this time was normalised and demand across the globe was high. As such, the British developed a profitable monopoly over the trade in opium, and despite the 1799 ban (to control domestic use), British merchants continued to illegally smuggle opium into China, which led to two opium wars (1839–1842 and 1856–1860) that resulted in China's defeat and the imposition of unequal treaties favouring British trade interests being implemented (see the Box below) (Dasgupta, 2019). The British government and the East India Trading Company became the biggest drug dealers in the world, forcing opium on China, even though they did not want it.

Chinese Opium Wars

- **1839–1842:** was about the amount of opium entering China. Britain demanded free trade and diplomatic equality which led to this first war. It concluded with the Treaty on Nanjing, which not only opened up five ports but also controlled Chinese customs, so the British could continue importing opium to China without restraint, and required the cession of Hong Kong to Britain.
- **1856–1860:** increasingly dissatisfied with the terms of their treaties with China, and the Qing Government's failure to adhere to them, Britain and France went to war again. The Second Opium War further entrenched the opium trade in China, resulting in more treaties that expanded Western influence and legalised opium trade under certain conditions. It was brought to an end with the Treaty of Tientsin/Tianjin, which opened more ports to Western trade and residence (e.g. in Beijing for foreign envoys and the right of foreign travel in the interior of China), including the freedom of movement for Christian missionaries.

Opium was in high demand globally, as it was a key ingredient of many patent medicines alongside other substances (e.g. cocaine, cannabis and alcohol). The widespread use of patent medicines and the use of multiple products containing the same and/or different combinations of these substances, however, led to an increase in addiction, overdose, death and various health issues that led the emerging medical profession to advocate against their unregulated sale. The increase in drug-related deaths, particularly from opium and among infants, alongside addiction led to a public outcry and prompted the medical profession to advocate for more regulation. In Britain, this led to the Arsenic Act 1851, followed by the 1868 Pharmacy Act (see the Box below) and the Pure Food and Drug Act of 1906 in the US (Berridge, 1999, 2013; Musto, 1999).

The 1868 Pharmacy Act: attempted to control the sale and supply of poisons (e.g. cyanide) and opium by ensuring that they could only be sold by registered pharmacists and were clearly labelled. This was largely ineffective, as there was no limit on the amount the chemist could sell. Patent medicines were also excluded meaning opium-based products remained available and were not subject to the same strict regulations as poisons and dangerous drugs. The 1868 Pharmacy Act was a pivotal moment in the regulation of drugs and poisons, setting a precedent for the controlled sale of dangerous substances and the professionalisation of pharmacy and the pharmaceutical industry as the Act mandated the creation of a register for pharmacists, setting standards and ensuring that only qualified individuals could dispense drugs and poisons. The new controls aimed to enhance public health and safety as clear labelling and proper documentation helped prevent accidental poisonings and overdoses. The 1868 Pharmacy Act laid the groundwork for all subsequent legislation in the United Kingdom and other countries (Barton, 2011; Berridge, 1999, 2013).

The Victorian attitude to drugs at this time was complex and largely dependent on race and class. The middle and upper classes often viewed drug use among the lower classes, particularly heavy non-medical (recreational) use, through a lens of moral judgement and social control, associating it with immorality, depravity, disorder, disease and poor public health. In fact, the furore around infant doping and the number of deaths among children from opiates ignored the dosing of children among the middle and upper classes, focusing solely on the poorer working classes. The middle classes actually saw drug use and addiction as both a root cause and a symptom of poverty. However, the middle and upper classes saw their own drug use, particularly recreational drug use, as acceptable – a habit – which allowed them to luxuriate, enhance their creativity and facilitate deep philosophical thinking as famous poets and writers (e.g. Charles Dickens) were users of laudanum and opium (Berridge, 1999, 2013; Schivelbusch, 1992).

Public health reformers, often from the middle classes, alongside the growing temperance movement sought to kerb alcohol consumption, and to a lesser extent drug use, among the working classes in the UK, US, Europe and their colonies (e.g. Anglo-Indian Temperance Society, 1885) as a form of social control (Berridge, 1999, 2013). Alongside the temperance movement, there was a growth in labour movements. Both movements sought to improve the living conditions of the working classes and saw substance use as major obstacles to achieving social and economic progress as intoxication and the use of substances were also becoming a concern when it came to labour and production. Although previously substance use had been seen to facilitate hard work, intoxication was increasingly seen as incompatible with labour and productivity as workers were too stupefied to work, sometimes falling asleep on the job. The practice of infant doping (the use of opiates to sedate children) by women working in factories was also a result of the severe economic and social conditions of the time, but caused public outrage and medical concern. Faced with long hours and the need to work, women were compelled to bring their children to work, with some mothers doping their children with laudanum so they could fulfil their daily labour obligations (Berridge, 1999).

The Industrial Revolution and accompanying technological advancements of the epoch brought about significant changes in the global production, distribution and consumption of substances, while economic and social changes increased the demand for drugs, particularly among the working classes (Barton, 2011; Berridge, 1999). Mechanisation of distilleries increased the production and strength of alcohol, while medical advancements like the hypodermic needle and synthesis of new, more addictive drugs like heroin intensified the rewards (high) from drugs quickening the onset of addiction (Barton, 2011; Courtwright, 2019; Crocq, 2007). Interestingly, heroin was considered a non-addictive drug and marketed as a better alternative to opium and morphine, despite the reality. Drug addiction was not recognised as a problem until the mid-to-late nineteenth century where it was seen as an effect of the drug itself with emerging medical texts discussing the concept of opium habituation and morphinomania/morphinism (addiction to morphine) as inebriation became a growing concern, although this still focused mostly on alcohol as opium addiction was excluded from the 1888 Inebriates Act (Barton, 2011; Berridge, 1999; Courtwright, 2001; Gootenberg, 2022).

Inebriation and addiction were often exacerbated as physicians supported the use of substances to treat addiction to other substances (e.g. opium was used to treat alcohol addiction as well as cocaine and conversely alcohol and cocaine were used to treat opium addiction), and despite a growing awareness of the adverse effects habitual use of these substances might have, one addiction was merely swapped for another. Polydrug use also emerged. Combining drugs like morphine/heroin and cocaine in a hypodermic needle – speedballing – became popular among the American underworld and then showbusiness types (Berridge, 1999; Courtwright, 2001, 2019; Musto, 1999). The way addiction seen was also largely determined by social standing – class, gender and race/ethnicity – of the addict, as addiction was seen as a moral failing and personal weakness due to the strong influence of religious and social attitudes, which emphasised personal responsibility and moral integrity. Subsequently, addicts were often stigmatised and marginalised. Smoking of opium for pleasure at this time was also racialised and largely seen as a vice practised by the Chinese – Orientals – as the establishment of opium dens became focal points of racialised fears. These dens were often depicted in the media as dangerous corrupting influences (e.g. places where Chinese men lured White women into addiction and moral decay), which resulted in several laws being enacted (e.g. the 1875 San Francisco Opium Den Ordinance and Chinese Exclusion Act of 1882 in the US). Despite these dominant moralistic views, some medical professionals in the Victorian era began to recognise addiction as a medical condition and began to study the human body and develop medical science, which influenced the rise of biological positivism and its theories (see Chapter 1). They observed that addiction could affect individuals regardless of their moral character and that it had physiological and psychological components. Early treatments for addiction, however, were still influenced by moralistic attitudes, implementing methods aimed at instilling discipline and moral fortitude (e.g. confinement in asylums or forced abstinence). The establishment of asylums for inebriates in the mid-nineteenth century reflects a growing recognition of addiction as a condition requiring specialised medical treatment (Berridge, 1999; Musto, 1999). This led to the medicalisation of addiction that was tantamount to medicalised social control of the poor, working class and ethnic minority's consumption practices, particularly of psychoactive substances (Szasz, 2003). Addiction became seen as a disease (see the Box below).

Addiction: From Morality to a Disease

- In the early nineteenth century, addiction was seen through a moralistic lens, which was reinforced by the temperance movement.
- Addiction was a result of moral weakness, lack of willpower and/or a character flaw, and responsibility for addiction was placed on the individual, suggesting they had the power to overcome their addiction if they choose to do so through self-discipline and moral effort.
- The moral model continued to dominate in the late-nineteenth century, although there were emerging scientific perspectives on addiction as medical professionals began to study addiction more (e.g. as a disease requiring treatment), but the moral model still heavily influenced public perception and policy.
- Towards the mid-to-late nineteenth century, medical science started to challenge the purely moralistic view of addiction and the disease model of addiction began to gain popularity, which continued into the twentieth century.
- The disease model of addiction gained significant traction with the establishment of Alcoholics Anonymous (AA) in the US in 1935, which recognised addiction as a disease and advocated for a therapeutic approach based on abstinence and peer support. In Britain, similar shifts occurred with the establishment of treatment centres and the influence of AA, although the disease model was slower to be fully embraced in the UK compared to the US.

The racialisation of popular drugs like opium and particularly its association with Chinese immigrants significantly influenced public attitudes and led to calls for prohibition and control in the late nineteenth and early twentieth centuries that resulted in legislation being enacted in some countries (e.g. America, Canada and Australia), which also influenced international drug policy. Opium addiction had spread to other parts of the world, prompting international concern that resulted in the Shanghai Convention (1909), which was the first international conference to discuss and confront this burgeoning global issue. It recommended measures to gradually regulate and control the opium trade and restrict the use of opium to medical and scientific purposes. The commission marked the beginning of international drug control policies and resulted in the first concerted international effort to regulate and eventually eradicate the non-medical use of opium and its derivatives, namely heroin, which was even more addictive than morphine (Davenport-Hines, 2004). The main weakness about the Shanghai Commission was it did not create legally binding agreements, rather it merely set forth thirteen recommendations that laid the groundwork for future international drug control efforts and for the first international drug control treaty, which was binding. The 1912 Hague Convention was the first binding international effort to introduce global restrictions on drug supply and outline that all drug control policies should be uniform across the world.

The Hague Convention required signatory countries to enact domestic legislation to regulate the manufacture, sale and distribution of narcotics and to report their actions to an international body, while agreeing to repress opium use. It established a framework for national drug control legislation and international cooperation to monitor and restrict the production and distribution of drugs, laying the foundation for subsequent international drug control treaties and the establishment of global drug control organisations. Britain, however, was reluctant to ratify the convention due to its economic interests in the opium trade leading to two more conferences (1913 and 1914) before Britain finally ratified the convention in 1914. The outbreak of World War I in 1914 interrupted the implementation and enforcement of the Hague Convention as nations focused on the war effort (Barton, 2011; Berridge, 1999).

Shortly after the outbreak of World War I, Britain introduced legislation to grant the government extensive powers to control many aspects of daily life to support the war effort, which included the control of drugs. The Defence of the Realm Act (DORA) 1914 was implemented in Britain during World War I for three reasons. The first related to the efficiency of the workforce, particularly in industries relating to wartime production (e.g. munition workers) as the regulation of drugs was seen as necessary to prevent absenteeism, accidents and a decrease in productivity caused by inebriation and intoxication. The second was driven by the need to maintain public health and morale by reducing the availability and use of drugs to maintain a healthy and productive population, which related to the third rationale. The final reason related to the troops – British and allied soldiers – using cocaine while visiting sex workers. Berridge (1999) refers to it as the 'so-called cocaine "epidemic" of 1916' that brought fears about recreational drug use spreading in the army, which could impair soldiers' performance and discipline, making regulation appear essential for the military's effectiveness. DORA made 'the sale or gift of intoxicants to a member of the armed forces with the intent to make him drunk or incapable...an offence' (Barton, 2011:15). The Act included measures to control the supply and consumption of alcohol (e.g. reducing pub opening hours and the strength of alcoholic beverages) and other narcotics, mostly opium and cocaine, by restricting non-medical sales (e.g. to those with medical prescriptions) and mandating sellers (e.g. pharmacies) to keep detailed records of all narcotic sales, including the names and addresses of purchasers. DORA 40B prohibited the importation of opium and cocaine unless under a Home Office licence and made it an offence for anyone bar doctors, pharmacists and vets to be in possession of cocaine, to sell it or give it away (Berridge, 1999). The war put the Home Office in charge of the country, which included enforcing narcotic restrictions that criminalised 'all unauthorised supply and all unauthorised possession' (Barton, 2011:16). The Treaty of Versailles, 1919 signed at the end of the war established the League of Nations and requested all nation states formulate domestic drug legislation to address their respective drug problems. It called on signatory nations to implement measures to restrict the importation, sale and use of opium and other narcotics, which laid the foundations of contemporary international drug control policies (see Chapter 7). In Britain, this led to the Dangerous Drugs Act 1920 (DDA20), which was introduced to regulate the control and distribution of certain dangerous drugs, reflecting the country's commitment to international drug control agreements (Barton, 2011; Berridge, 1999).

The Harrison Act

The Harrison Act was partly a response to international calls for more stringent drug regulations and helped the US align with international standards and treaties outlined in the Hague Opium Convention of 1912. It was framed as a tax law rather than outright prohibition and by imposing taxes and requiring registration, the government could regulate the distribution of narcotics. The Act also required detailed record-keeping and registration, which facilitated government oversight and enforcement (Musto, 1999).

The DDA20 was a penal reaction in response to the growing number of addicts, particularly among veterans, who had been exposed to drugs during the war. It put the Home Office in charge of drugs, despite the newly created Ministry for Health (1919), thus setting in motion the long-standing and still unresolved dichotomy: **is illicit drug use a medical or criminal justice issue?** Emulating the Harrison Act in the US (see the Box above) that regulated the medical profession and a doctors' ability to prescribe narcotics in the US, the Home Office sought to impose more stringent controls over the dispensing and prescribing practices of British doctors (e.g. elimination of addicts and maintenance prescriptions), which caused outrage among the medical profession as non-medical use and supply was criminalised. The DDA20 was followed by subsequent regulations in 1921 and 1922 and an amendment in 1923, which saw continued attempts by the Home Office to impose a penal approach to drugs (e.g. increased police powers, higher fines and longer sentences) aimed at imposing even more stringent measures on medical professionals and pharmacists. The development of drug policy during this period was characterised by a battle for control between the Home Office (penal criminalisation and punishment) and the Ministry for Health (public health-medicalised treatment), which led to the establishment of the Rolleston Committee (Barton, 2011; Berridge, 1999).

The Rolleston Committee was convened by the UK government in response to growing concerns about the use of morphine and heroin, particularly in relation to addiction/dependent use, and as a response to interference from the Home Office on the autonomy of doctors and pharmacists. Due to the content of the DDA20, its regulations and amendments, doctors faced 'the ever-present threat of prosecution', which led some to refuse 'to prescribe or dispense cocaine or opiates' at all (Barton, 2011:17). As a result, the main objectives of Rolleston were to investigate the nature of addiction, determine what constituted legitimate prescribing practices and recommend appropriate measures for controlling the use of these drugs, while ensuring the medical profession could still use them for therapeutic purposes. The Rolleston Report (1926) concluded that addiction should be treated as a medical condition rather than solely a criminal issue. It also recognised the need to control non-medical use to prevent abuse and illicit trafficking. The report recommended that doctors be allowed to prescribe morphine and heroin to addicts in controlled quantities to manage withdrawal symptoms and maintain their health, a practice that became known as the 'British System' of addiction treatment. This approach to supervised drug provision differed significantly from the inflexible prohibition adopted in the US under the Harrison Act (Barton, 2011; Berridge, 1999).

Key Term

The British System: medical control over drug addiction and treatment operating within a penal framework of national and international controls that punish unauthorised – non-medical – production, possession, use and sale.

After 1926, there was very little change to drug policy and legislation – the British System remained until the 1960s – although the rest of the era in the UK and US did see new substances emerge, and used recreationally, which led to further legislation/regulations as outlined below:

1920s Britain: Post-War Trauma and Opium Use – In Britain, the aftermath of World War I saw many soldiers returning home with physical and psychological injuries, leading to the widespread use of opiates – morphine and heroin – for pain management as well as recreationally. This contributed to an increase in addiction.

1920s America: The Prohibition era (1920–1933) – Several factors contributed to the onset of the prohibition era – the Volstead Act 1919 – including social (e.g. religion/temperance movement), political (e.g. the Anti-Saloon League and World War I) and economic (e.g. industrialisation and urbanisation) influences. This led to the illegal production and sale of alcohol (bootlegging), with speakeasies becoming popular. The bootlegging industry also spurred a growth in organised crime and cannabis use as the government's focus on enforcing alcohol prohibition sometimes diverted attention from other substances (e.g. cannabis). With alcohol prohibited, cannabis became a more popular recreational substance, particularly in jazz circles, where it was seen as socially acceptable and normal. Jazz musicians and their audiences embraced cannabis as an alternative to alcohol, contributing to its cultural prominence and illustrating how alcohol prohibition inadvertently facilitated the rise of cannabis use.

The 1920s saw a dramatic rise in recreational drug use (e.g. opium, heroin, morphine and cocaine) in the US and UK, leading to widespread addiction and social issues that became a global concern. This led to the DDA20 in Britain (see above). International concerns about the social and health impacts of narcotics, the rising tide of addiction and the recognition of the need for global cooperation to control the drug trade led to the 1925 Geneva Opium Conventions (see the Box below).

The Geneva Opium Conventions

- 1925 Geneva Opium Conventions established stringent controls on the manufacture, trade and use of opium and other narcotic drugs (e.g. morphine, cocaine and heroin). They sought to kerb the illicit drug trade and promote the medical and scientific use of narcotics. Signatories were required to submit detailed reports on the production, distribution and consumption of narcotic drugs to the Permanent Central Opium Board (PCOB), a body established to oversee its implementation.
- The Conventions had significant implications for global drug control policy and legislation: by emphasising the importance of international cooperation in addressing the drug problem, requiring signatories to align their national drug laws with the international standards set forth in the agreements, create supervisory bodies such as the Permanent Central Opium Board (PCOB) and the Supervisory Body for the Limitation of Manufacture and lay the groundwork for the development of more comprehensive agreements (e.g. 1961 Single Convention).
- The 1925 Dangerous Drugs Act in Britain was a response to this Convention while the Narcotic Drugs Import and Export Act 1922 was introduced in the US.

1930s Britain and America: Rise of Amphetamines and the Jazz Scene – The 1930s saw the introduction and growing use of amphetamines in both countries, initially for medical purposes, but also recreationally as well as in the military. Amphetamines were linked to the American jazz scene alongside heroin and cannabis. The ban on alcohol pushed people towards other intoxicants, creating a vibrant underground market for illicit substances, which were used for both recreational and performance-enhancing purposes (e.g. jazz musicians used amphetamines to enhance their creativity and performance during long hours of playing), which was racialised, as Black and White youth socialised together. In Britain, the connection between music and amphetamines did not become prominent until later (1940s). Amphetamines were not as widely recognised or used recreationally in Britain during the 1930s as they were in the United States. The emergence of jazz as an African American musical form resonated with the themes of resistance and empowerment, particularly of African Americans, as the Harlem Renaissance, a cultural, social and artistic explosion among African Americans in the 1920s and 1930s, shared an emphasis on African heritage and pride advocated by Marcus Garvey. Jazz was a significant part of this renaissance, parallelling the rise of Rastafarianism in its quest for identity and liberation (see the Box below). In the United Kingdom, the 1930s was marked by increasing immigration from the Caribbean, which laid the groundwork for later cultural exchanges and the spread of Rastafarianism outside Jamaica.

Rastafarianism and Cannabis: The Holy Herb

- Rastafarianism began in Kingston, Jamaica, in the 1930s and was born out of White oppression of Black people (racial and classist), the Black movement, which espoused Black consciousness and identity, including the sacred nature of Mother Africa and the restoration of its cultural traditions.
- Rastafarian ideology believes in Haile Selassie as Jah (God), Zion (Ethiopia) as heaven on earth, the spiritual use of cannabis, a restricted diet (vegetarian or vegan, no salt, no alcohol, cigarettes or drugs), a natural way of life (your body is a temple), wearing dreadlocks (incorporated in the 1940–1950s) and unique rituals (Nyabingi/Bingi) that involve drumming, singing, smoking the holy herb cannabis and prayers, which were all 'assigned Biblical correlates and became sanctified' (Benard, 2007:92).
- Cannabis initially provided poor Black Jamaicans with money as they grew and sold it. It was also a medicine and a symbol of resistance to colonial oppression. They believed the bible sanctioned its use as a 'holy herb' that induces a meditative state bringing them closer to god as 'ganja is a plant that is termed the healing of a nation' (Morgan, 2013:170). Smoking cannabis is not a mandatory practice of all Rastas.

1930s America: Reefer Madness and Anti-Drug Campaigns – The Federal Bureau of Narcotics (FBN) was established in 1930 headed by Harry Anslinger – an early propagandist for the war on drugs – who pushed for federal regulation of cannabis, leveraging public fear and racial prejudices as the justification. Cannabis in the US was commonly associated with Mexican immigrants and African Americans, who were often portrayed as dangerous and immoral. These racial stereotypes were used to justify stricter drug laws. It also led to sensationalist journalism that played a significant role in spreading anti-cannabis sentiment, which was also accompanied by the 1936 film *Reefer Madness* (originally titled *Tell Your Children*) that depicted the supposed dangers of cannabis use linking it to violence, insanity, crime and moral degradation. The anti-drug campaigns and *Reefer Madness* of the 1930s led to the criminalisation of cannabis (Marihuana Tax Act 1937) and reinforced negative stereotypes about drug use (e.g. causes crime and moral decay) and minority communities. Despite these campaigns, cannabis remained popular, particularly with jazz musicians and bohemian communities.

The 1931 Convention: Limiting the Manufacture and Regulating the Distribution of Narcotic Drugs – was an international treaty established under the League of Nations. The convention aimed to control the manufacture and distribution of narcotic drugs more strictly by limiting their production to the amounts needed for medical and scientific purposes. It was introduced as previous conventions were seen as inadequate in addressing the scale of the problem. In the US , the Narcotic Drugs Import and Export Act (amended in 1931) implemented its provisions, while in Britain, it was the 1932 amendment to the DDA20.

1940s Britain (and America): Drug Use in the Jazz Scene – The British jazz scene was influenced by America and brought with it a more relaxed attitude towards certain drugs. Whereas heroin and cannabis were significant in the American scene, amphetamines and cannabis were more prominent in Britain. Both scenes were marked by drug use and interracial socialisation that emphasised interactions between Black and White youth framing them as dangerous and morally suspect, which drew media attention and societal concern that fuelled racial tensions and led to calls for stricter legal controls on drug use and nightlife activities.

1940s Britain and America: Wartime Amphetamine Use – The most significant use of amphetamines in Britain came during World War II, when the military used them to keep soldiers awake and to combat battle fatigue. Both the British and American armed forces distributed amphetamines to their troops to enhance performance and endurance during long missions. After the war, these substances found their way into civilian life, particularly among those seeking to enhance productivity or cope with stress.

1953 Opium Protocol: formally known as the 'Protocol for Limiting and Regulating the Cultivation of the Poppy Plant, the Production of, International and Wholesale Trade in, and Use of Opium', it was an international treaty established under the auspices of the United Nations. Its primary objectives were to limit the production and trade of opium to medical and scientific needs, and to kerb the illicit production and trafficking of opium and its derivatives. The Permanent Central Opium Board was authorised to take corrective action against states not complying with the provisions of the protocol or becoming sources of illicit opium. The Narcotic Control Act of 1956 implemented provisions of the 1953 Protocol in America, while the 1951 Dangerous Drugs Act implemented it in Britain.

1950s Britain and America: Emergence of Youth Subcultures/Counter-cultures – The 1950s saw the emergence of youth subcultures, which were associated with drug use and led to academic research and theories on counter-cultures/subcultures (see Chapter 1). For example, the Teddy Boys in Britain – associated with rock and roll music, alcohol and cannabis use – and the Beat Generation in America – a literary movement that embraced alternative lifestyles and was often associated with cannabis and Benzedrine use. The influence of American culture (e.g. Hollywood movies and jazz) played a role in shaping attitudes towards drugs in the United Kingdom.

The 1950s and the 1960s in the United Kingdom and United States reflects a significant period in the history of prescription drug use, particularly amphetamines marketed under various brand names (e.g. Benzedrine and Dexedrine), which was part of a broader cultural shift during the post-war period that saw an increasing reliance on pharmaceutical solutions for mental health and well-being. Amphetamines were widely prescribed for conditions such as depression, fatigue and weight control, making them the perfect solution for women who were struggling with the monotony and exhaustion of suburban housewife life. Advertisements often targeted housewives, promoting amphetamines as a way to stay slim, energetic and happy. Advertising was more aggressive in the US than in the UK as pharmaceutical companies capitalised on the idea of the perfect housewife to sell drugs. The social pressure on women to maintain an idealised version of domestic life contributed to the normalisation of amphetamine use among housewives and mothers. Amphetamines helped them to cope with the demands of daily life, including managing household duties, child-rearing and societal expectations of maintaining a cheerful demeanour, which led to them being called 'mothers' little helpers' which was also the name of a Rolling Stones song (Rasmussen, 2008).

CONCLUSION

This period saw new substances brought from the colonies being incorporated into the colonisers' medical, social and cultural practices, as they developed a monopoly over some substances (e.g. Britain monopolised cinchona bark, tea and opium), whilst stealing, standardising, commodifying and selling the extensive botanical and medicinal knowledge of the indigenous people they colonised. Alongside the Industrial Revolution, technological advancements and war, which led to an increase in addiction, drug-related deaths and a significant shift in attitudes towards drug use, came the introduction of formal regulations over narcotics both internationally and domestically. Most domestic legislation was enacted due to international treaties and the obligations it imposed on signatories, which were largely driven by concerns over public health, morality and social order as drugs were racialised and gendered throughout this period, alongside issues of class and respectability that were also used to justify introducing controls and regulations.

Addiction, once seen as an inherent effect of the drug itself, became linked to morality and then a condition – disease – requiring specialised medical treatment as the addict was brought under the medical gaze, even though most of these early controls were actually about exclusion, exploitation, labour, production and capital. Throughout this period in Britain, there was a wrangling for power between the Home Office that advocated for a penal, law enforcement approach to drugs and the newly established Ministry for Health, which focused on drugs as a public health issue. This period saw the medicalisation and criminalisation of drugs, which saw a distinction made between substances (e.g. legal/uncontrolled versus illegal/controlled) and modes of consumption (medical versus non-medical) that determined whether the person received treatment or punishment, which continued into the 1960s and onwards.

SUMMARY

Throughout History

- **Humans have always used psychoactive compounds to alter their experiences of the world, whether it is for recreational, social, medical, religious or practical purposes.**
- **Historically, substances have been integral to the building and binding of empire, and now capitalism.**
- **The sale and prescribing of medicines, regardless of their harmfulness (e.g. overdosing, addiction), was practised by colonial doctors as substances became commodified and medicalised.**
- **Substances stratify populations and societies on the basis of race/ethnicity, gender and respectability (class). Racial stereotyping, gendered anxieties and cultural discrimination have routinely been the source of drug panics, addiction threats and prohibitions.**

Here are some points and questions for you to consider after reading this chapter:

1) What colonial reasons are used to justify the control/regulation of substances?
2) How might the theories in Chapter 1 explain some of the issues discussed in this chapter?
3) What patterns/themes can you see across this period?

Here are some useful resources for those wanting to further explore the issues raised in this chapter:

- Barton, A. (2011) *Illicit Drugs* (Second Edition) London: Routledge.
  This book provides a comprehensive overview of the history, criminalisation and policy surrounding illicit drugs, examining how laws and law enforcement have shaped the contemporary drug landscape.
- Berridge, V. (1999) *Opium and the People*, London: Free Association.
  This seminal text examines the role of opium in British society during the nineteenth century, exploring how it was consumed, regulated and perceived, tracing the transition of opium from a normalised everyday substance widely accepted and consumed to a medicinal substance subject to control and prohibition.
- Courtwright, D. (2001) *Forces of Habit: Drugs and the Making of the Modern World.* Cambridge: HUP.
  Offering a global history of drugs, this book traces the role of psychoactive substances, including how the use and control of drugs like alcohol, tobacco, opium and caffeine have influenced economic and cultural developments across different societies, as well as their commercialisation and how governments responded with policies of regulation and prohibition.

3

THE HISTORICAL DEVELOPMENT OF DRUG POLICY AND PROHIBITION – THE 1960s ONWARDS

Overview

This chapter aims to provide you with:

- The control and regulation of drugs from the 1960s onwards.
- A critical look at how colonial legacies surrounding drugs are still present in contemporary drug policy and legislation.
- An overview of drug use and the key drug legislation and policies – international and domestic – from the 1960s onwards.

You will be introduced to the key terms:

- Strategy
- Policy
- Conventions
- Treaties

INTRODUCTION

Following on from where the previous chapter left off, this chapter focuses on drugs, drug policies and practices and how controls have been implemented from the 1960s onwards. It will show how drugs, drug users and drug policy continue to develop. Finally, this chapter will illustrate how issues of colonialism (see Chapter 2) have influenced the development of modern-day systems of drug control, showing how colonial legacies linger in the present. Although this chapter largely focuses on drug control in the United Kingdom, and to a lesser extent the United States, examples from around the world are also covered illustrating drugs are a global issue.

THE 1960s–1980s

Drug use and addiction increased into the early 1960s, particularly the recreational use of drugs like heroin and cocaine, particularly among young counter-culture/subcultural movements (e.g. Northern Soul). This increase raised concerns about public health, safety and social order, prompting the need for a thorough investigation and effective policy response. In Britain, the government recognised there was a need for a comprehensive understanding of the effectiveness of existing control measures, the impact drug use was having on society, patterns of drug addiction and the importance of having expert advice and evidence-based recommendations to help inform policy and legislation, which led to the Brain Committee being set up in 1961. In the United States, the President's Commission on Law Enforcement and Administration of Justice (President's Crime Commission) played a significant role in examining issues related to drug abuse and control and was tasked with studying the entire criminal justice system, including the growing problem of drug use, which was seen as a significant factor contributing to crime and social issues (Barton, 2011; Berridge, 1999; Musto, 1999).

In Britain, the first report published by the Brain Committee in 1961 focused on the use of drugs and the need for better control mechanisms. The committee was reconvened in 1965 due to an increase in drug use alongside changing patterns and an increase in non-therapeutic addicts. Its second report recommended stricter controls and better treatment options. These reports influenced the development of the Dangerous Drugs Act 1964, the Dangerous Drugs (Prevention of Misuse) Act 1964 and the Dangerous Drugs Act 1967, which collectively tightened controls on the production, distribution and use of dangerous drugs, introduced stricter penalties for drug-related offences and aimed to prevent the misuse of both narcotic and psychotropic substances. The Brain Committee's findings helped the United Kingdom align its drug policies with international standards and address the growing problem of drug use in a more systematic and informed manner. In the United States meanwhile, the President's Crime Commission's report, published in 1967, highlighted the need for a balanced approach to drug control that included law enforcement, prevention and treatment. The establishment of the Brain Committee and President's Crime Commission also reflected broader international concerns about drug addiction alongside efforts to comply with international treaties and conventions. While not directly a legislative response to the 1960s drug scene, the Single Convention on Narcotic Drugs of 1961 was introduced to unify and streamline international drug control efforts – previously governed by multiple treaties – into one comprehensive framework, simplifying and strengthening international drug control measures (see the Box below) (Barton, 2011; Berridge, 1999; Musto, 1999).

International Conventions: 1960s–1970s

- **The 1961 UN Single Convention on Narcotic Drugs:** focused on prohibiting the production, supply and transportation of narcotic drugs (opiates, cannabis and cocaine) for non-medical and non-scientific purposes, which it supposedly ranked according to their harmfulness (see Chapter 4) and enhanced cooperation among nations, and it established the Commission on Narcotic Drugs (CND) responsible for global policy and the International Narcotics Control Board (INCB) to monitor the implementation of the treaty. In the United Kingdom, the 1964 Dangerous Drug Act implemented the Convention, followed by the Misuse of Drugs Act (MDA) 1971, while the United States introduced the 1970 Controlled Substances Act (CSA), which created a framework for regulating the manufacture, distribution and use of controlled substances with stricter penalties, and created the Drug Enforcement Administration (DEA) in 1973.
- Psychotropic substances were becoming a global issue, but the 1961 Single Convention primarily focused on narcotic drugs and did not adequately cover psychotropic substances, illustrating the need for an international framework to regulate these substances and ensure their availability for medical and scientific purposes, while preventing abuse and illicit trafficking, which led to the 1971 Convention.
- **The 1971 UN Convention on Psychotropic Substances:** established a drug scheduling framework to control stimulant drugs and psychedelics (e.g. amphetamines, LSD and barbiturates), which were increasingly popular, but had not been adequately covered in the 1961 Convention. The Convention established a system to classify psychotropic substances into four schedules based on their potential for abuse, therapeutic value and risk to public health. It restricted some dugs (e.g. cannabinol) so much that they could not be used even with a prescription.
- In Britain, the MDA provided a comprehensive framework for drug control in line with the Convention as it categorised drugs based on their harmfulness whilst also establishing penalties for related offences. In America, the Psychotropic Substances Act of 1978 amended the CSA to comply with the 1971 Convention, by extending the scheduling system to include a broader range of psychotropic substances.

The domestic legislation introduced in Britain in the 1960s was largely a result of the 1961 Single Convention and the changing drug scene. The 1960s saw a significant increase in the use of psychotropic substances (e.g. amphetamines, barbiturates and hallucinogens/LSD) largely related to the increase in the counter-culture movements (see below and Chapter 1 page 36 subcultures/counter-culture Box), which raised public health concerns globally. The increase in the recreational use of amphetamines, which were previously only available through prescriptions for conditions such as obesity and depression, raised concerns about addiction, psychosis and social disturbances, which led to the 1964 Dangerous Drugs (Prevention of Misuse) Act in the United Kindom . The Act replaced restrictions on the possession, supply and production of amphetamines, introduced harsher penalties and provided the Home Secretary with the power to classify substances and regulate their use based on emerging patterns of use. In the United States, the Drug Abuse Control Amendments of 1965 and the Psychotropic Substances Act of 1978 were introduced to control psychotropic substances (e.g. depressants, stimulants and hallucinogens). In Britain, the 1967 Dangerous Drugs Act also expanded the range of substances under control (e.g. LSD) to reflect the changing patterns of drug use. It tightened regulations around the prescribing and dispensing of controlled drugs to prevent their diversion onto the illegal market. The 1967 Act also retained the British System of prescribing, but required doctors to be licensed by the Home Office. It also established Drug Dependency Units across England to provide specialist treatment. Both acts represented a shift towards a more regulated and punitive approach to drug use in Britain and laid the groundwork for later legislation, including the MDA (see the Box below), which further consolidated and expanded drug control measures and remains the main piece of legislation controlling drugs today. These Acts were influenced by a growing recognition of the need to treat rather than solely punish those with substance use disorders (Barton, 2011 Berridge, 1999; Musto, 1999).

Counter-Cultures/Subcultures

The counter-cultural movements of the 1960s in the United States, Europe and the United Kingdom used drugs as symbols of rebellion, self-exploration and social experimentation. The United States saw the rise of the hippie movement, which was characterised by its opposition to the Vietnam War, its embrace of civil rights and its desire for social and personal liberation, which deeply connected to the use of cannabis and hallucinogens/LSD. The hippie movement was also prominent in the United Kingdom, alongside mods with their distinctive fashion, love of scooters and their appreciation for modern jazz, R&B, soul and early rock and roll. Mods used amphetamines (speed) to enhance energy and stamina for dancing and socialising through the night. Emerging out of the Mod scene, early skinheads were influenced by Jamaican rude boy culture and ska music that was characterised by heavy drinking and amphetamine. Organised crime groups (OCGs) expanded their operations to meet the increased demand.

Misuse of Drugs Act, 1971

Possession Offences: Possession with intent to supply (s.5(3)).

Supply Offences: Supply a controlled drug and offering to supply (s.4(3)(a)); Being concerned with supply (s.4(3)(b)); Being concerned in offer to supply (s.4(3)(c)).

Production Offences: Production of a controlled drug (s.4(2)(a)); Being concerned in the production (s.4(2)(b)); Cultivation of the cannabis plant (s.6(2)).

Occupier Offences: Permitting premises to be used for producing (s.8(a)); Permitting premises to be used for supplying (s.8(b)); Permitting premises to be used for smoking cannabis (s.8(d)).

Importation and Exportation Offences: The importation (s.3(1)(a)) or exportation (s.3(1)(b)) of any controlled drug is prohibited unless in accordance with the terms of a licence granted by the Secretary of State (s.3(2)).

Class A: Maximum: Life imprisonment. Offence range: High level community order to 16 years' custody

Class B: Maximum: 14 years' imprisonment and/or unlimited fine or both. Offence range: A fine to 10 years' custody

Class C: Maximum: 14 years' imprisonment and/or unlimited fine or both. Offence range: A fine to eight years' custody

The 1970s saw the continuation of the drug culture that emerged in the 1950–1960s, particularly among the youth counter-culture movements in Britain and America. In America, as a response to growing public concern over drug use and its perceived impact on society, President Richard Nixon declared a 'War on Drugs' in 1971 (see Chapter 4). He saw drugs as public enemy number one, which led to increased law enforcement efforts, including the 1970 CSA and the establishment of the DEA in 1973. The focus was part of Nixon's broader political strategy to portray himself as tough on crime and decisive in addressing social issues. He framed the war on drugs as a national security and crime control issue as drugs threatened public safety, undermined social order and contributed to rising crime rates. Over the years, the war on drugs has evolved into a comprehensive and controversial (penal) policy framework that disproportionately targets minority communities, contributes to mass incarceration and has not effectively addressed the underlying issues of addiction and public health, which has turned into a war on (certain) drug users (Buchanan and Young, 2000; Wacquant, 2009) (see Chapter 4).

In Britain, the MDA replaced the Drugs (Prevention of Misuse) Act 1964 and the Dangerous Drugs Acts of 1965 and 1967. The 1971 Act distinguished between supply and possession offences and varied punishments/sanctions based on the harmfulness of the substances with Class A drugs receiving the harshest penalties (see the Box above). The Act also introduced 'a new system of licensing doctors to prescribe heroin and cocaine to addicts; the requirement for all doctors to notify addicts to the Home Office; regulations on the safe custody of drugs; and national stop and search powers for the police'. It also established the first statutory advisory body, the Advisory Council on the

Misuse of Drugs (ACMD), which was to monitor drug trends, conduct research and review scientific evidence and 'to advise government ministers on the measures to be taken for preventing the misuse of drugs or for dealing with the social problems connected with their misuse' (Runciman, 2000:15). The ACMD was established to provide independent and evidence-based recommendations from professionals with expertise in medicine, pharmacology, sociology and law enforcement. This multidisciplinary perspective was intended to respond to new challenges and create and update policies based on the latest information that not only addressed criminal activities but also supported public health and social welfare (Barton, 2011; Runciman, 2000). The MDA has been amended several times to reflect changing drug trends and new substances (e.g. the introduction of temporary class drug orders (TCDOs)), which is done via the passing of regulations and modifications (e.g. the MDA (Modification) Order 1986, the MDA (Amendment) Order 1989). It remains the cornerstone of UK drug policy, providing the basis for law enforcement against drug offences and influencing public health approaches to drug use. Alongside the MDA, the Medicines Act 1968 also regulates substances with the potential for abuse, ensuring they are handled in a manner that minimises risk to public health and safety. Under the Medicines Act, certain substances are legal if prescribed to the user (e.g. heroin, benzodiazepines), but if there is no prescription, then they become illegal to possess or supply as they fall under the MDA.

The MDA has however been heavily criticised even when it was first proposed. Referring to the Bill, Jock Young (1971:204) predicted the impact of the Act when he said 'it has little to do with empirical reality of drug use in Britain, and its effects are likely to be unfortunate in the extreme...the hippie is more like to be apprehended for marijuana offences than his working fellow smoker...other groups, especially immigrants, will also feel the brunt of such *selective* reactions'. Criticisms of the 1971 Act have amplified in recent years as it has failed to achieve many of its objectives (e.g. to reduce use, production or supply). It has been described as being out of date and no longer fit for purpose as it does not reflect contemporary drugs; there is no evidence that criminal sanctions act as an effective deterrent; it is discriminatory, even racist, harmful, unscientific, unclear and confusing as it contains no information that would enable it to function satisfactorily as an indicator of the relative harms associated with different drugs; and it offers no explanation why particular substances are in particular classes (see Runciman, 2000; Transform, 2022). Despite the criticisms and its failure to meet any of its aims, the MDA remains the main piece of legislation through which illicit drugs are controlled in the United Kingdom. Despite calls for the Act to be reviewed and reformed, the government recently said 'it has no plans to review the Misuse of Drugs Act 1971' (House of Commons, 2021:2). The Act led to a significant increase in the criminalisation of drug users as penalties for drug offences became more severe, and the number of arrests and incarcerations for drug-related crimes increased, and by the 1980s, Britain saw a sharp increase in drug-related imprisonments, contributing to overcrowded prisons and raising concerns about the effectiveness of punitive approaches.

The 1973 Misuse of Drugs (Notification and Supply to Addicts) Regulations: were introduced in the United Kingdom as part of broader efforts to address drug addiction and improve the management of controlled substances. The regulations were introduced to establish a system for supplying certain drugs to addicts, which aimed to manage the distribution of addictive substances more effectively and reduce their use. The regulations sought to integrate drug treatment and rehabilitation into the broader framework of drug control. Providing controlled access to drugs was seen as a way to facilitate treatment and support recovery among addicts and represented a shift towards a more structured and regulated approach to managing drug addiction in the United Kingdom. By integrating supply reduction with treatment initiatives, the regulations aimed to reduce the harms associated with drug addiction and promote public health, whilst also aligning with international drug control standards.

The 1970s also saw the emergence of powerful drug cartels, which demonstrated the significant role of OCGs in the drug trade (also see Chapter 9). The Medellín and Cali cartels, based in Colombia, played a crucial role in the crack epidemic. They used sophisticated networks and violence to control trade and were instrumental in the production, distribution and proliferation of crack cocaine, which had devastating social and economic impacts on urban communities across the united States. Cocaine was imported into America in powder form as the process of converting powder cocaine into crack (a cheaper, smokable form of cocaine) was developed to maximise profits. Crack could be sold in smaller, more affordable quantities, making it accessible to a broader and often poorer demographic, which fuelled its rapid spread. As a result, America enacted the 1986 Anti-Drug Abuse Act, which introduced harsh mandatory minimum sentences for crack cocaine offences, which disproportionately affected African American communities. This legislation aimed to deter drug trafficking and crack use and also contributed to mass incarceration, particularly of African Americans (Alexander, 2010; Wacquant, 2009).

By the late 1970s and early 1980s, crack cocaine had emerged in the United States as a significant public health and law enforcement issue, particularly in urban areas alongside heroin, which had also become an issue in Britain (Dorn and South, 1987; Johnson and Golub, 2007; Musto, 1999; Pearson, 1987; Taylor and Bennet, 1999). The cheap price and addictive nature of heroin and crack contributed to widespread use and an array of associated social problems that were exacerbated by the economic climate as both countries were in an economic recession. The 1980s heroin epidemic that emerged in both countries was due to a convergence of factors that had seen the availability of heroin increase significantly, partly due to changes in international drug trafficking routes and the emergence of new heroin sources (e.g. Afghanistan and the Golden Triangle), which made the drug more accessible and affordable to a broader range of users. In America, the crack epidemic largely overshadowed the increase in heroin use but both were closely linked to socio-economic factors, including inner-city poverty, unemployment and social disintegration. Urban areas, particularly African American communities, were disproportionately affected by crack due to economic decline and lack of opportunities. Its low cost, ease of production and intense euphoric effects led to widespread use and addiction, but it was also associated with increased levels of violence, crime and social unrest in affected communities, which led to legislation being passed to tackle the issue (e.g. the Anti-Drug Abuse Act of 1986, also known as the crack house statute because its primary purpose was to outlaw the operation of houses and buildings where crack and other drugs were made or used). It also led to the 1980s 'crack babies' myth that children born to mothers who used crack cocaine during pregnancy would suffer severe, irreversible physical and cognitive impairments. This myth gained significant media attention and influenced public perception and policy, despite lacking substantial scientific evidence to support the most extreme claims, which some might describe as a moral panic, but which has been shown to deter women from seeking drug treatment and/or prenatal care (see the Box below).

The Crack Baby Myth

The increase in crack cocaine use led to media outlets reporting on a supposed epidemic of 'crack babies' being born to crack addicted – largely African American – women who were doomed to lives of severe disability, behavioural problems and lower intelligence due to their prenatal exposure to crack cocaine. In 1985, *The New York Times* described crack babies as 'biological throwaways' contributing to widespread fear and stigma. Although early studies did report some developmental issues among infants exposed to crack cocaine in utero, these studies failed to account for other factors (e.g. poverty, lack of prenatal care and additional substance use), which have also been shown to have a detrimental impact. In 1992, the National Institute on Drug Abuse (NIDA) (1996) found no consistent negative effect of prenatal crack exposure on infants' developmental outcomes compared to other risk factors like socioeconomic status and maternal education. This myth, however, has contributed to punitive approaches towards pregnant women who use drugs in America, including increased surveillance, state control of women's bodies, removal of children and criminalisation, although evidence suggests that criminal prosecution in this area relies on questionable procedures, is unevenly applied and may act as a barrier to treatment and healthcare (Coles, 1992; Frank et al., 2001).

In Britain, high unemployment rates and social deprivation created environments where heroin could flourish as a coping mechanism for young people trying to escape from bleak economic prospects. The increase in heroin also corresponded to an increase in crime, particularly acquisitive crime and a flurry of research (e.g. Hammersley et al., 1989, 1990; Hammersley and Morrison, 1987; Jarvis and Parker, 1989; Mott, 1986; Parker and Newcombe, 1987; Pearson, 1987), that firmly established a link between problematic heroin use and criminality (see Chapter 7). In fact, Goldstein's (1985) tripartite framework advocating drugs cause crime was premised on research he undertook at this time, which showed crack-related violence often stemmed from disputes over drug territory (systemic), addiction-driven behaviour (psychopharmacological) and the economic desperation of users (economic compulsive), which has also led to many of its limitations and criticisms (see Chapter 5).

Heroin addiction rates soared during this period in Britain (e.g. London, Glasgow and Liverpool) and America (e.g. New York City, Baltimore and Los Angeles), which was accompanied by a shift towards injecting heroin use, driven by factors such as the purity of available heroin and social norms within drug-using communities. Many heroin users transitioned to injecting the drug, which provided a quicker and more intense high, which increased the practice of sharing needles increasing the transmission of HIV/AIDS. The spread of HIV/AIDS led to serious public health concerns, which provoked a public health response that included the introduction of harm reduction measures (e.g. needle exchange programmes and methadone maintenance treatment) as the threat of the spread of HIV/AIDS into the general population justified attracting drug users into treatment services to minimise this threat. Public health campaigns were also launched to raise awareness about the risks of injecting drug use and the transmission of HIV/AIDS (e.g. heroin screws you up or just say No). At this time, 'AIDS was more of a threat than drug use' (ACMD, 1988). The heroin epidemic and the HIV/AIDS crisis led to a gradual shift in drug policy, towards more health-centred approaches, which also led to an increase in funding for treatment services and a greater focus on harm reduction strategies as part of drug policy (ACMD, 1988; Berridge, 1996; Stimson, 1990; Strang and Gossop, 2005). Up until this point, there had been an absence of any real drug strategy, but this changed in 1985 when the Conservative Party created 'Tackling Drug Misuse' as a response to the growing drug problem. This strategy marked the first comprehensive national drug strategy in the United Kingdom, signalling a significant shift towards a more co-ordinated and strategic approach to addressing drug use. Although the initial implementation faced challenges, including insufficient funding, lack of co-ordination and varying levels of commitment across different regions and agencies, this strategy laid the foundations for future drug strategies.

It was led by then Prime Minister Margaret Thatcher who aimed to demonstrate strong leadership and responsiveness to public concerns. While Thatcher did not declare a 'War on Drugs' in the same explicit manner as Nixon, her government adopted a more hard line law and order stance on drugs. Although Thatcher's government did not emphasise drug policy, rising concerns about drug use, particularly heroin, led to a shift and introducing a national drug strategy suddenly became part of the Conservatives broader crime and social order agenda. The strategy aimed to provide a co-ordinated framework for addressing drug use, incorporating law enforcement, education, prevention and treatment measures. The policy had five areas:

1) Reducing supply from abroad;
2) Making enforcement more effective;
3) Maintaining effective deterrents and tighter domestic controls;
4) Developing prevention;
5) Improving treatment and rehabilitation.

(Barton, 2011:144)

It was underpinned by a flurry of legislation (e.g. Controlled Drugs (Penalties) Act 1985, the Prevention of Misuse Act 1986; Drug Trafficking Offences Act 1986), which 'placed the police, customs, courts and prisons at the forefront of control policy and practice' (South 1995:31 as cited in Barton, 2011:145). The enforcement approach was evident not only in Britain but also in America as the war on drugs escalated during the Reagan administration. Its focus on stringent law enforcement, heavy penalties and significant federal funding for anti-drug programmes, which included military and paramilitary efforts to combat drug production and trafficking, particularly from Latin America, was embodied in the legislation passed at this time. The Anti-Drug Abuse Acts of 1986 and 1988 were introduced, establishing mandatory minimum sentences for drug offences and significantly increasing funding for drug law enforcement. These laws also created the Office of National Drug Control Policy (ONDCP). In both countries, however, the link between intravenous drug use and the spread of HIV/AIDS led to public health initiatives aimed at reducing transmission, although it also incited criticism. Governments were accused of being soft on drugs and encouraging drug use as they were giving out free drugs (methadone) and the means to use them (syringes).

The late 1980s saw the globalisation of drug use, which continued to rise, and a dramatic increase in global drug trafficking, which had expanded into a multi-billion pound/dollar industry that justified an enhanced law enforcement-led approach, with a particular focus on organised crime as drugs and the illicit drug cartels became seen as a threat to national security. During this period, drugs and crime had become an important factor in the evolution of terrorism as the word narcoterrorism emerged, which also became linked to OCGs (see Chapter 5). Existing international drug control treaties were not sufficiently comprehensive to address the complexities of modern drug trafficking (e.g. money laundering and precursor chemicals) indicating a need for a stronger international legal framework and improved international cooperation to effectively combat the global drug trade. This led to the 1988 United Nations Convention against Illicit Traffic in Narcotic Drugs and Psychotropic Substances (see the Box below).

International Conventions: 1980s

The 1988 UN Convention against Illicit Traffic in Narcotic Drugs and Psychotropic Substances (Vienna Convention): specifically required countries to adopt *criminal* sanctions for the production, supply, trafficking and use of drugs (although non-criminal sanctions for minor offences specified in the 1961 treaty still applied) and related activities (e.g. money laundering). It enhanced international cooperation in law enforcement (e.g. to confiscate proceeds of drug-related crime, while facilitating extradition for drug-related offences). It also created new controls restricting the manufacture and distribution of precursor chemicals, used to produce drugs scheduled under the 1961 and 1971 conventions. It also emphasised the importance of demand reduction (e.g. treatment).

Culminating in the 1988 United Nations Convention against Illicit Traffic in Narcotic Drugs and Psychotropic Substances, the international treaties and laws passed during this period created the 'Global Drug Prohibition Regime' (Andreas and Nadelmann, 2006:37–46), which could also be termed the 'Global Drug Apartheid' (see Taylor et al., 2016) (see Chapter 4). The 1988 convention also addressed the loopholes in the 1961 and 1971 convention as they 'lacked clarity in relation to the offence of possession, cultivation and purchase in relation to personal use' (Barton, 2011:45). In fact, Transform argue that 'the 1971 Convention controls "psychotropic" drugs and the 1961 Convention controls "narcotic" drugs, yet neither term has a coherent scientific meaning' or basis (UNODC as cited in Transform, n.d.). These conventions, however, remain the cornerstone of the international drug control system and continue to guide actions aimed at supposedly safeguarding health and well-being from the evil menace of drugs. Many would argue, however, that the conventions still stand as a major obstacle to the introduction of pragmatic approaches to drug use at a national level and are inhumane and harmful, particularly since they prioritise punitive measures over harm reduction and public health strategies. In fact, international drug control treaties have led to mass incarceration, particularly of minority ethnic groups, human rights abuses and significant public health issues (Nadelmann, 1992). Yet they continue to shape drug policies worldwide, influencing how governments regulate and control substances deemed to be addictive or harmful to public health, despite the evidence base showing that many legal substances are more harmful than those prohibited and controlled under these now old and outdated conventions (see Chapters 4 and 10).

The late 1980s also started to see the emergence of acid house and rave music. The use of drugs (amphetamines, ecstasy and LSD) transitioned and increased in popularity in the 1990s. This period, often referred to as the 'Chemical Generation', also saw the proliferation of substances such as MDMA (ecstasy), amphetamine, LSD and other synthetic hallucinogens and stimulants. Events like the United Kingdom's 'Summer of Love' in 1988–1989 laid the groundwork for the proliferation of rave culture in the 1990s (see Hammersley, 2001) (see the Box below).

The Chemical Generation

- Rave culture was characterised by the widespread use of synthetic drugs, particularly MDMA (ecstasy), and the formation of a youth subculture centred around electronic dance music (EDM) and dance events. The burgeoning rave scene began in the United Kingdom and quickly spread to other parts of Europe and America.
- Rave culture promoted values of peace, love, unity and respect (often abbreviated as PLUR). This ethos was reflected in the inclusive and communal nature of rave events, which brought together people from diverse backgrounds. The subculture

(Continued)

(Continued)

(see Chapter 1) also had a significant impact on fashion, with distinctive styles such as bright colours, baggy clothes and rave accessories (e.g. glow sticks and whistles), which emphasises the body and its adornment.

- Ravers partook in hedonistic consumption in pursuit of pharmacological pleasure and leisure as they concentrated on the ecstatic out-of-mind experience that placed the hedonism of the body before the logic of the mind as they escaped into sensation (Presdee, 2000).
- Presdee (2000) used the concept of the 'carnival of rave' to describe the subversive and liberating nature of rave culture to highlight how raves function as spaces where traditional social orders are temporarily overturned, allowing for new forms of social interaction and personal freedom. Acts of carnival have become a daily need for social survival – reflecting the rationality of modern-day life and the work hard, play hard lifestyle.
- MDMA (ecstasy) became the drug of choice for many ravers due to its euphoric and empathogenic effects, which enhanced the communal and emotional aspects of the rave experience. Other drugs commonly associated with the rave scene included LSD, amphetamines and, later, ketamine. The use of these substances was seen as a way to enhance the sensory experience of the music and the environment, and to provide the energy to dance all night.
- Implementing a pick-n-mix approach to substance use according to the night out they want, drugs were commodities to be bought and sold – branded and sought out like designer clothes.
- The rise of rave culture and its association with drug use led to increased scrutiny and regulation by authorities and the regulation and criminalisation of youth (sub) cultures and clubbing. In the United Kingdom, the Criminal Justice and Public Order Act 1994 gave police greater powers to shut down illegal raves and prosecute organisers where 'music includes sounds wholly or predominantly characterised by the emission of a succession of repetitive beats'. In the United States, the RAVE Act (Reducing Americans' Vulnerability to Ecstasy Act) of 2003 aimed to kerb the use of MDMA and other club drugs by holding event organisers accountable for drug-related activities. In both countries, the regulation and criminalisation of youth culture and clubbing are evident through police raids in clubs, the use of drug-sniffing dogs, searches in the queues and arrest or refusal of entry to clubbers found with traces of drugs like cocaine on their hands.

1990s ONWARDS

House music began to gain mainstream success in the early 1990s and the rave scene also exploded as massive raves and dance festivals became common, with EDM as a central soundtrack. The mid-to-late 1990s saw the rise of progressive house, which incorporated elements of trance and techno, and was characterised by a more expansive, melodic sound as superclubs like Ministry of Sound in London and Pacha in Ibiza emerged and rave became commercialised. Within the context of the rave scene, drug use was viewed as a normative behaviour, which has extended into the night-time economy (NTE) (see the Box below) as drugs have been accommodated into the mainstream, particularly mainstream youth cultures, making them normalised (Aldridge et al., 2011; Parker et al., 1998–see Chapter 1). One indicator of normalisation was the blurring of licit (alcohol) and illicit (ecstasy) as people adopted a pick-n-mix approach to clubbing, leisure and pleasure (Parker et al., 1998).

Alcohol, Drugs and the Night-Time Economy

- The rise of binge drinking has been linked to the development of the NTE and its commercialisation of nightlife, with its emphasis on bars, clubs and late-night entertainment, which has created spaces where binge drinking is not only facilitated but also encouraged.
- Most people who frequent the NTE are polydrug consumers, although polydrug using repertoires have been associated with specific venues, activities and genres of EDM.
- The NTE is characterised by excessive determined intoxication/determined drunkenness, which often involves risky patterns of planned inebriation, like pre-loading and binge drinking.
- The increased use of drugs in the NTE illustrates how drugs have been accommodated into the mainstream, making them normalised (see Chapter 1).
- Alcohol and drug use in the NTE are linked to incidents of violence, anti-social behaviour, sexual assault and crime, posing challenges for law enforcement and public safety.

(see Ayres, 2019; Hadfield, 2006; Hayward and Hobbs, 2007; Hutton, 2006; Measham, 2002, 2004; Measham and Moore, 2009; Redhead, 1997; Smith, 2014)

The change in drugs and their increased popularity among ravers/clubbers led to legislation in the United Kingdom being passed to tackle illegal raves, as they were associated with the use of illicit drugs, although so were the more mainstream clubs, but the legislation passed focused exclusively on illegal raves, in the form of the Criminal Justice and Public Order Act 1994. It aimed to kerb the rave culture and associated drug use by criminalising unlicensed outdoor events. America was much slower at passing legislation related to raving, which did not appear until 2003 in the form of the RAVE Act. It aimed to hold event organisers accountable if they knowingly allowed drug use on their premises by modifying the existing 'crack house' statute (introduced as part of the 1986 Anti-Drug Abuse Act) to include temporary venues like rave parties. It was controversial and criticised for potentially discouraging harm reduction measures at events (e.g. providing water and cool-down spaces), which also became an issue with the commercialised night club industry. Commercialised raves/clubs have been criticised for implementing measures that prioritise profits but potentially risk the health and well-being of their patrons (e.g. switching the cold water off in the toilets so that people buy bottled water that they charge exorbitant prices for), especially as many clubs and rave events used alcohol promotions (e.g. cheap drink offers and happy hours), which encouraged heavy drinking. As rave and clubbing cultures became more commercialised, the focus on profit led to environments where alcohol consumption was a central part of the experience. This commercialisation contributed to the growth of binge drinking as clubs aimed to maximise their revenue as these promotions were designed to attract patrons and increase sales. In many rave and nightclub environments, binge drinking became a normalised part of the party experience, although these experiences were often gendered (see the Box below).

Women's Gendered Experiences of Clubbing and Drug Use

- The rise of raving and club culture shows that gender dynamics influence drug use, experiences in clubs and the portrayal of women within this context.
- Not only do women use different drugs when clubbing, but they also use them for different reasons (e.g. to fit in, enhance their confidence, meet perceived standards of behaviour within the clubbing environment) as drug use is gendered, meaning that men and women experience and engage in drug use differently due to societal gender norms and expectations.
- Women's experience of risk and pleasure in drug use is also gendered as they often have to negotiate their use in ways that balance enjoyment and safety, which can involve moderating their intake, choosing particular substances over others and relying on peer support networks to manage the risks.
- Women will often take specific precautions to manage their safety and drug use when out clubbing, including staying in groups and monitoring each other's consumption of alcohol and/or drugs. This is because women are often subject to sexualisation and objectification and are more likely to be sexually assaulted in clubs/NTE than men.
- Hutton (2006) refers to club babes to describe young women who are heavily involved in the clubbing scene who use fashion, behaviour and drug use to assert their presence and agency as they navigate their identities within the male-dominated environment of the club.
- In the club, women sometimes engaged in behaviours traditionally associated with men and masculinity to fit in and assert their presence. This included behaviours like heavy drinking, drug use and engaging in risk-taking activities, which helped them to gain respect and social capital within the club scene. Women performed gender to fit into and challenge the norms of club cultures (see Hutton, 2006; Measham, 2002).

Binge drinking also increased, finally emerging as a major public health issue, in both America (e.g. among college students and young adults) (Wechsler and Nelson, 2001) and the United Kingdom (Hayward and Hobbs, 2007; Measham and Brain, 2005).

The United Kingdom's response included public health campaigns, legislative measures (e.g. Licensing Act 2003) and integration into broader alcohol strategies (e.g. 2004 Alcohol Harm Reduction Strategy for England, the 2007 Safe. Sensible. Social. The Next Steps in the National Alcohol Strategy, culminating in the 2012 Government's Alcohol Strategy) and drug strategies. The 1995 'Tackling Drugs Together' (TDT) white paper built on the 1985 strategy 'Tackling Drug Misuse' mentioned the need to address alcohol abuse alongside illicit drug use, recognising the overlap in social and health issues arising from both.

Key Term

Binge drinking refers to the consumption of an excessive amount of alcohol in a short period, leading to a blood alcohol concentration of 0.08% or higher. For men, this typically involves consuming five or more drinks within about two hours, and for women, it involves consuming four or more drinks within the same time frame. The 1980s and 1990s saw a rise in binge drinking, particularly among young adults and college students. This period coincided with increased marketing of alcohol to younger demographics and the normalisation of heavy drinking in social contexts (e.g. the NTE – see the Box on page 81). Binge drinking is a significant aspect of youth culture. It is often a ritualistic and collective activity, serving as a means of social bonding and identity formation among youth.

TDT represented a shift in policy, as it recognised the need to reduce the demand for drugs via education, prevention and treatment, alongside the traditional focus on supply reduction via law enforcement, which still took priority. It focused on three strands – prevention, education and treatment – and identified three areas 'crime, young people and public health' that laid 'the foundations and framework for a new approach to drug policy in England' (Barton, 2011:147–149). It has been described as 'the first genuinely strategic response in England to the complexities of the drugs problem' (Home Office, 1998:10). The overriding innovations of TDT were to establish new structures and set out clear goals and objectives for a co-ordinated strategy. Although the Conservative government never got to implement the strategy as they were not re-elected, New Labour, who won the elections, introduced 'Tackling Drugs to Build a Better Britain' that closely resembled the TDT white paper. The 1998 Tackling Drugs to Build a Better Britain had four specific areas – young people, communities, treatment and availability – which have been the basis of drug strategy ever since. Subsequent strategies have retained the four pillars merely adding to them over the years as new issues have emerged (e.g. the 2008 strategy added families while the 2010 one added recovery and abstinence) (see Table 3.1). The National Drug Control Strategy in the United States often includes similar themes, focusing on prevention, law enforcement and treatment/recovery support.

Table 3.1 Drug Strategy in Britain

Year	Name of Drug Strategy	Legislation Accompanying and Implementing the Strategy
1998	Tackling Drugs to Build a Better Britain	Crime and Disorder Act 1998; Youth Justice and Criminal Evidence Act 1999; Powers of Criminal Courts (Sentencing) Act 2000; Health Act 1999; Proceeds of Crime Act 2002
2002	2002 Updated Drug Strategy 2002 Tackling Crack: A National Plan	Criminal Justice and Police Act 2001; Police Reform Act 2002; Proceeds of Crime Act 2002; Criminal Justice Act 2003; Anti-Social Behaviour Act 2003; Drugs Act, 2005
2008	Drugs: Protecting Families and Communities	Serious Crime Act 2007; Criminal Justice and Immigration Act 2008; Health and Social Care Act 2008; Policing and Crime Act 2009
2010	Reducing Demand, Restricting Supply, Building Recovery	Police Reform and Social Responsibility Act 2011; The Health and Social Care Act 2012; The Crime and Courts Act 2013; The Anti-social Behaviour, Crime and Policing Act 2014
2017	2017 Drug Strategy	Serious Crime Act 2015; Policing and Crime Act 2017; Criminal Finances Act 2017
2021	From Harm to Hope: A 10-year drugs plan to cut crime and save lives	The Police, Crime, Sentencing and Courts Act 2022; The Health and Care Act 2022

The transition from 'Tackling Drugs Together' to 'Tackling Drugs to Build a Better Britain' represented a significant shift in the United Kingdom's drug policy, moving towards a more comprehensive and integrated approach that addressed not only the immediate issues of drug use but also the underlying social factors. This evolution was driven by the need to respond to emerging drug trends and to improve the effectiveness of drug prevention, treatment and enforcement strategies. The 1995 strategy also marked a fundamental shift towards the discourses of crime, enforcement and punishment, with greater involvement of the criminal justice system in drug issues and drug treatment. The 'drugs problem' started being framed and managed as a 'crime problem', whilst the so-called 'drugs–crime link' had become the driving force behind policy development, which was maintained in the 1998 strategy (Duke, 2006:409) and remains a key focus today (see Chapter 6). The focus on crime also brought heroin and/or crack users – problematic drug users – to the forefront of drug policy as they became reframed as the drug problem, particularly in relation to crime and the increasing drug-related crime rates (see Chapters 5 and 8). This focus on problematic drug users was epitomised in the 2002 strategy, Tackling Crack.

The 1998 strategy was updated in 2002. The 2002 Updated Drug Strategy had a tighter focus, which has led some to argue was a result of the unrealistic targets set in the 1998 strategy that were never met (e.g. to reduce the availability Class A drugs by 25% by 2005 and 50% by 2008), especially since they were abandoned in the 2002 update (see Parker, 2006). The updated strategy also addressed new and emerging challenges (e.g. a tougher focus on Class A drugs), incorporated the latest research and tried to create a more effective and integrated approach to tackling drug use that was implemented by the Drug Intervention Programme (DIP) (see Figure 3.1 and the Box below), which was enforced by the Tough Choices Agenda that basically made drug testing for individuals arrested for trigger offences (e.g. theft, robbery, drug offences) mandatory and if drugs were detected, they were required to undergo an assessment with a drugs worker which was reinforced with legal sanctions (e.g. bail conditions/breaches) (see Chapter 7). In fact, the use of crack in Britain had increased so much by the early 2000s that a crack specific strategy was also implemented (Tackling Crack) to address the specific and severe challenges it posed, which created a need for targeted law enforcement and community safety strategies. The aim was to reduce drug-related crime as

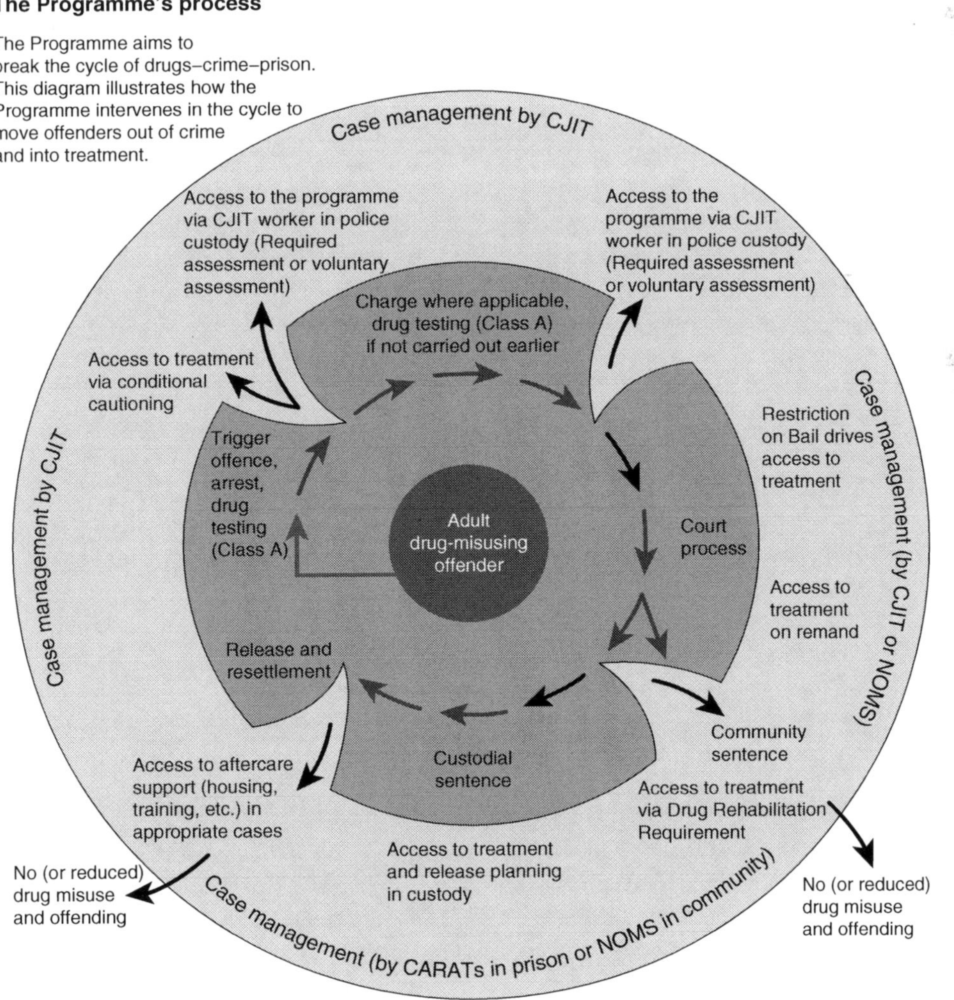

Figure 3.1 Diagram of the Drug Intervention Programme

crack cocaine had been closely linked to an increase in violent crime and drug-related offences. As a result, the focus switched to reducing the crime associated with problematic drug use as they were some of the most persistent offenders, which reinforced and embedded the drug–crime link even further, placing it at the centre of British drug strategy (Barton, 2011–see Chapter 5). This focus on reducing crime was evidenced in the 2001 Home Office report 'Reducing Crime: A New Approach' and still dominates contemporary drug strategies in Britain but has often been criticised for potentially undermining treatment and public health approaches, which has led to negative outcomes for individuals with substance use disorders (e.g. by diverting funding and resources away from treatment services, impacting their availability and quality) (Nutt, 2012; Stevens, 2011a). Although others have argued that framing drug issues in terms of crime and criminal justice often attracts more funding and political attention than framing them in terms of health or social care, thereby securing continued funding for these sectors, it often leads to punitive measures rather than effective public health strategies that could better address the underlying issues of drug use and dependency/addiction (see Stevens, 2011b).

The Drug Intervention Programme

- The Drug Intervention Programme (DIP) was a key part of the UK government's 2002 strategy to tackle drug-related crime. Introduced in 2003, the programme aimed to engage drug-using offenders who used Class A drugs (heroin and crack/cocaine) out of crime and into treatment.
- It operated at every stage of the criminal justice system to break the cycle of drug use, crime and prison by offering a beginning-to-end support system – a wraparound service – which involved multi-agency working and a joined-up approach to stop people slipping through the next.
- **Arrest Referral:** drug users who were arrested were referred to drug workers who could assess their needs and direct them to appropriate treatment services.
- **Drug Testing on Charge:** offenders arrested for trigger offences (e.g. theft and burglary) were subject to mandatory drug testing.
- **Court Orders:** could mandate treatment as part of sentencing, which included Drug Rehabilitation Requirements and Drug Treatment and Testing Orders (see Chapter 7).
- **Post-Sentencing Support:** continued support and monitoring for offenders after they were released from custody or completed their sentence.
- **Case Management:** each offender had a dedicated case manager who co-ordinated their treatment and support services.
- Studies showed that DIP had some success in reducing drug-related reoffending rates. For instance, a Home Office evaluation found that offenders who engaged with DIP were less likely to reoffend compared to those who did not engage. The Home Secretary claimed that the DIP's case management and coercion contributed to a 20% reduction in recorded acquisitive crime, which had fallen by

32% in England and Wales since 2003. However, the effectiveness varied significantly across different regions and depended on the quality and availability of local services.

- One major challenge was resource constraints and funding cuts over time that undermined the programme's capacity to deliver consistent and comprehensive services.
- Some critics argued that DIP was overly focused on coercion and compulsion, potentially undermining the voluntary nature of treatment and rehabilitation. Others pointed out that the programme did not sufficiently address the broader social determinants of drug use, such as poverty, unemployment and housing.

Drug use in many Western countries, including the United Kingdom and the United States, saw the highest levels during the 1990s, which peaked in the mid-to-late 1990s/ early 2000s, before beginning to decline. According to the British Crime Survey (now called the Crime Survey for England and Wales), the highest levels of drug use among young adults (aged 16–24) were recorded in 1998, with about 30% reporting having used drugs in the last year. From 2000 onwards, drug use, supply and policy in the United Kingdom and United States have been marked by significant shifts as both countries have grappled with the rise of new substances (e.g. crystal meth in America – see the Box below), evolving public health crises (e.g. opioid epidemic and opioid related deaths, crystal meth epidemic) and changing legal landscapes around cannabis (see Chapter 11).

America's Crystal Meth Epidemic

The late and early 1990s began to see methamphetamine, particularly crystal meth use (the cooked-up form), rise sharply in the United States, which was driven by its availability, low cost and the ease of production using over-the-counter pseudoephedrine and other household items that led to widespread social anxieties over home-cooked methamphetamine. The increase in small-scale meth labs in people's homes contributed to fuelling this panic. Framed as a rural, poor white trash problem, the dangers and prevalence of meth use were over-exaggerated. This justified draconian, militarised, zero-tolerance policing, increased surveillance and control alongside aggressive, punitive measures to be introduced to combat meth use, rather than addressing the root causes. As a result, the Combat Methamphetamine Epidemic Act of 2005 was passed (as part of the Patriot Act reauthorisation), which regulated the sale of meths key ingredient requiring it to be sold behind the counter and limiting the amount an individual could purchase. Anti-meth campaigns were also launched, 'Not Even Once' and the 'Faces of Meth'. Following this legislation, the production of methamphetamine shifted from small domestic labs to larger, more sophisticated

(Continued)

(Continued)

operations primarily based in Mexico that could produce larger quantities of more potent methamphetamine, which was then sold on the US market. By 2010, meth-amphetamine use and meth-related deaths began to rise, and despite its use being low and concentrated in certain rural areas, it continues to be framed as a significant issue as the meth imaginary dominates (see Linnemann, 2016).

Cannabis: the legal landscape around cannabis began to shift, first in the United States and then the United Kingdom. In 1996, California's decision to legalise cannabis for medical use through Proposition 215, also known as the Compassionate Use Act, was driven by advocacy by medical professionals and patients who highlighted the thera-peutic benefits of cannabis for various medical conditions (e.g. cancer, AIDS, chronic pain and glaucoma). The 1980s AIDS epidemic in particular galvanised activists who saw cannabis as a critical treatment for alleviating symptoms and improving the quality of life for patients. The legalisation of medical cannabis in California was part of a broader national trend towards more lenient attitudes on drug policy (e.g. Oregon, Washington and Alaska followed suit with similar laws in the late 1990s and early 2000s). Despite state-level reforms, cannabis remained illegal under federal law. This created a complex legal landscape and ongoing tension between state and federal authorities (Bock, 2000). Like America, there was a growing perception in the United Kingdom that cannabis was less harmful and posed a lower risk than other Class B drugs, which was confirmed by the ACMD in their 2002 report. As such, cannabis was reclassified to a Class C drug in 2004. The reclassification was also aimed at freeing up police resources to focus on more serious crimes and reduce the burden on the criminal justice system. After growing health concerns about stronger strains – skunk – and mental ill health, particularly psychosis and schizophrenia, and despite the ACMD assessing the evidence and advising against reclassification, the government decided to proceed with upgrading cannabis to Class B. This decision was controversial and led to the resignation of several ACMD members (see Chapter 4). From 2000, the United Kingdom started to see the emergence of cannabis farms (see the Box on page 217–218 of Chapter 9).

Opioids: from 2000 onwards, the United States faced a severe opioid crisis, with a dramatic rise in opioid prescriptions, heroin use and synthetic opioids (e.g. fentanyl) that were accompanied by a corresponding increase in opiate-related deaths (see Chapter 11). The crisis emerged due to aggressive marketing by pharmaceutical companies (e.g. Purdue Pharma) to physicians, claiming opioid painkillers (e.g. hydrocodone, OxyContin) were a safe and effective treatment for chronic pain with a low risk of addiction. This led to a significant increase in over-prescribing by doctors. 'Purdue Pharma, expended $200 million promoting the drug in 2001, which resulted in an increase in the prescription of Oxycontin by almost 10-fold to nearly 6.2 million annual prescriptions the following year' (Vadivelu et al., 2018:2). As a result, various measures have been enacted that include prescription monitoring programmes, stricter regulations on opioid prescribing and initiatives to increase access to addiction treatment and overdose-reversal drugs like naloxone. Efforts to kerb opioid prescriptions, however, have led prescription opioids to become more difficult to obtain and more expensive, leaving many addicted individuals to turn to heroin (as it is cheaper and more widely available) and synthetic opioids (e.g. fentanyl) instead, exacerbating the crisis further and leading to more deaths. The rise in fentanyl production, primarily in clandestine labs in China and Mexico, has also increased availability of these stronger synthetic substances exacerbating the opioid crisis. The crisis has also imposed substantial economic burdens on the healthcare system, law enforcement and social services that has led to some inhumane practices. For example, one state introduced a three-strikes-style policy for people who repeatedly overdose, which meant those who had received overdose treatment twice in the past would not have an ambulance sent to resuscitate them or receive life-saving medication on the third time (Wootson, 2017). Although some states have adopted needle exchange programmes and supervised injection sites, many areas still lack these critical harm reduction services due to legal and political barriers, which explicitly criminalise the distribution and possession of drug paraphernalia (e.g. syringes and needles), creating a confusing regulatory environment that undermines harm reduction (see Des Jarlais et al., 2009). It has also seen legislation passed – SUPPORT for Patients and Communities Act, 2018 – aimed at addressing the opioid crisis, which focuses on treatment, prevention and recovery. While not as severe as in the United States, the United Kingdom has also seen increasing concerns about prescription opioid use and associated deaths. Drug-related deaths in England have been increasing steadily reaching their highest recorded levels, with 2022 seeing the highest number since records began in 1993 (ONS, 2023) representing a public health crisis. The reasons behind the high numbers of drug-related deaths are multifaceted, but socio-economic changes, including increasing deprivation, changes in the availability and purity of heroin on the street alongside budget cuts and reduced access to drug treatment and harm reduction services, have left many users without adequate support.

Human Enhancement (HED)/Performance and Image Enhancing Drugs (PIEDS): substances have been used to enhance performance throughout history (e.g. 1950s–1970s saw the anabolic steroids became popular among athletes), but the emergence of HED/PIEDS (e.g. cognitive enhancers, slimming and tanning pills, growth hormones) has increased in popularity in the 2000s and 2010s, with use increasingly being reported among diverse groups of users (e.g. adolescents, students, non-athlete adults and the elderly seeking anti-ageing products). As a result, both the United Kingdom and United States have strengthened regulations to combat the non-medical use of these substances, although they are still widely available to buy on the internet (Evans-Brown et al., 2012; McVeigh, 2020).

Psychoactive Substances: from 2000 onwards, the United Kingdom and United States saw an increase in legal highs, also known as new/novel psychoactive substances (NPS), which were substances designed to mimic the effects of traditional illicit drugs but fell outside of the law making them legal due to their constantly evolving chemical structure. They gained popularity due to their availability online and in head shops, they were convenient, of high purity, cheap and perceived as safer than illicit drugs because they were legal (see Chapter 11). In fact, some argued that the prohibition of illegal drugs fuelled the NPS market in the first place (Rolles and Kushlick, 2014). Initially, all first- and second-generation NPS were brought under the MDA via TCDOs, which were introduced through the Police Reform and Social Responsibility Act 2011. Like most drug legislation/policy, these orders were reactive and designed to address the rapid emergence of NPS as they allowed for the temporary banning of these substances while a permanent classification was considered. Their temporary nature, however, meant that there was a constant need to renew or replace these orders (most only lasted for 12 months), which led to the Psychoactive Substances Act 2016. Rather than waiting for harm to be demonstrated before taking action, the 2016 Act was proactive, making it an offence to produce, supply or possess with the intent to supply any psychoactive substances, except for those specifically exempted (e.g. alcohol, tobacco, caffeine and medicinal products). The Act did not criminalise possession for personal use (except in custodial settings – see Chapter 8).

Psychoactive Substances Act, 2016

- Producing a psychoactive substance (s.4). Maximum: seven years' imprisonment. Offence range: Fine to six years' custody
- Supply of a psychoactive substance and offering to supply a psychoactive substance (s.5). Maximum: seven years' imprisonment. Offence range: Fine to six years' custody
- Possession with intent to supply psychoactive substances (s.7). Maximum: seven years' imprisonment. Offence range: Fine to six years' custody
- Importing or exporting a psychoactive substance (s.8). Maximum: seven years' imprisonment. Offence range: Discharge to six years' custody.
- Supply and conveyance of psychoactive substances in a custodial institution

Like most drug legislation, the Act has been heavily criticised however. There has been little evidence that it has reduced the availability or use of psychoactive substances and has actually led to a displacement effect, where users switch from one banned substance to another that is not yet banned or to more harmful substances, potentially increasing health risks. The definition of psychoactive substance has also been described as being overly broad and vague, making the law difficult to enforce and leading to potential legal ambiguities (e.g. nitrous oxide – Box below) (Home Office, 2014; Stevens and Measham, 2014; Winstock and Barratt, 2013).

Nitrous Oxide

Nitrous oxide, commonly known as laughing gas, presents a contentious issue in relation to the Psychoactive Substances Act 2016 due to its dual use for legitimate medical (e.g. aesthetic in dentistry), industrial purposes and the food industry (e.g. in whipped cream dispensers) as well as (illicit) recreational use, due to its euphoric and dissociative effects when inhaled, which has raised public health and safety concerns, particularly related to its widespread availability and potential for abuse. Nitrous oxide then is exempt due to its legitimate uses, but this exemption creates a loophole that can be exploited for recreational use, complicating enforcement and regulation. Retailers selling nitrous oxide for recreational use often exploit its exemption by marketing it under the guise of its legitimate uses. Nitrous oxide now falls under the MDA where it is a Class C drug.

The implementation of the Psychoactive Substances Act 2016 led to a shift in the trade of NPS on cryptomarkets, as suppliers and users moved onto these platforms to continue their activities in a less regulated environment, thereby increasing the role of cryptomarkets in the distribution of NPS as well as illicit drugs, which from their emergence in 2010 marked a significant development in the online drug trade. The most notable early cryptomarket was Silk Road, which was launched in February 2011 and operated until it was shut down by law enforcement in October 2013. These online marketplaces facilitated the anonymous buying and selling of various goods, including illegal drugs, using cryptocurrencies like Bitcoin, providing both buyers and sellers anonymity (Martin, 2014, 2023; Mounteney et al., 2018) (see Chapter 8).

CONCLUSION

Many of the issues highlighted in Chapter 2 continue to haunt contemporary society as outlined in this chapter, as the opium epidemic rages in the United States and drug-related deaths continue to rise exponentially in the United Kingdom. Drug use despite an overall downward trend has seen an increase in the use of cocaine and cannabis in the United Kingdom and a resurgence of methamphetamine use in America. Cannabis reform continues unabated in the United States (see Chapter 11), while in the United Kingdom legalised cannabis-based products for medicinal purposes following high-profile cases of children with severe epilepsy benefiting from cannabis oil (see BBC, 2018), but both countries face ongoing debates between harm reduction approaches, treatment and public health compared to more traditional punitive law and order measures that criminalise, stigmatise and marginalise. What is clear from this chapter, however, is how colonial legacies from Chapter 2 continue to haunt contemporary perceptions of drugs and their users, as well as drug policy and legislation as outlined below.

DRUG POLICY: COLONIAL CONTINUITIES

The impact of colonialism on contemporary drugs, drug policy and legislation can be observed through various continuities from the colonial period to the present day. These colonial continuities manifest in five areas and although there are many more, not everything can be covered here:

Drug Policy: There has been a historical reproduction of drug policy and strategy that has been described as contradictory (e.g. twin-track approach that combines prohibition and harm reduction, punishment and treatment) and counter-productive, which has weakened it and led to it failing to meet its aims. Despite calls for reform, little has changed and the evidence base is still lacking (see Chapter 10). The historical reproduction of drug policy has also meant the reproduction of its problems, failures and harms, including its focus on making money/profit for those in power – colonisers/ capitalists – and (supposedly) reducing crime.

Stratification and Racialisation of Drugs: Colonial powers used drug laws as tools of racial and social control, targeting indigenous populations, suppressing resistance and encouraging work/productivity. Many of the colony's regulations on substances were racially motivated and disproportionately discriminated against ethnic minorities, which continues in contemporary society (e.g. Yardie gun wielding crack dealers) so much so that drug legislation has been described as the new Jim Crow laws (Alexander, 2010). Drugs have not only been racialised but also gendered and used by the upper-middle classes to control poor people. Contemporary drug policies continue to disproportionately impact racial minorities, poor people and other marginalised groups (e.g. women, LGBT+), reflecting these historical practices of dominance, control and suppression.

Substances of the Colony/Capitalism: From the early substances of the colony to the substances of capitalism not much has changed. The substances largely stay the same (e.g. tea/coffee, sugar, alcohol and tobacco) and remain legal despite evidence showing that some are more harmful (e.g. alcohol, tobacco and sugar) than many prohibited drugs. Colonial authorities frequently stigmatised traditional drug use and its practices, imposing Western norms and substances, while criminalising indigenous ones, legacies that remain today (e.g. see street heroin versus prescription opioids). A similar stigmatisation of drug use continues today, often rooted in these colonial attitudes and the dichotomy of legal versus illegal, which is erroneous and unscientific, but ensures we only buy and use substances that capitalism produces and profits from.

Sex Work and Drugs: Throughout history, drugs – use and supply – have been associated with sex work around the world – India, France, the United States, England, China and Japan. During the Victorian Era, the vast majority only practised the trade occasionally, most likely when they were in between jobs or needed to supplement their normal salary or were newly arrived immigrants. Substances and sex work have always been closely intertwined. To relax the client and sex worker beforehand and remove inhibitions, drinking and/or drug use was often a prerequisite for sex; they were often paid in drugs; sometimes they sold/supplied drugs to their clients; substances were used not only to enhance the experience but also to blot out and cope with not only sex work and the occupational anxieties that arose from it but also their meagre lives; substances were also used to spike clients so they were easy to rob; and these were used by the sex workers to relieve pain and lift their mood when they were feeling low (see the box on page 132–133 of Chapter 5).

Cannabis and Madness: From the slaves and indentured labourers in the eighteenth-nineteenth century to the reefer madness of the twentieth-century, cannabis has always been associated with mental ill health, often also alongside race/ethnicity. The link with psychosis was also the reason given for reclassifying cannabis and moving it back up to a Class B drug in 2009 (see Chapter 4).

SUMMARY

- **Humans have always used psychoactive substances and continue to do so for recreational, social, medical, religious or practical purposes, although the compounds being used have changed alongside technology.**
- **The same substances – production, supply and use – alongside modes of consumption (e.g. excessive, non-medical use) remain prohibited while others are widely accepted and encouraged, despite them sometimes being more harmful and a lack of evidence underpinning these distinctions.**
- **Substances remain medicalised and criminalised, which decides whether punishment or treatment is received, despite a lack of evidence underpinning drug policy and prohibition.**
- **Overprescribing has always been blamed for fuelling drug use, which is reflected in the legislation.**
- **Substances stratify populations and societies on the basis of race/ethnicity, gender and respectability (class) and the prohibitions as substances disproportionately discriminate along these lines (gender, race/ethnicity, class).**
- **Drug policy cannot keep up with the transient and ever-changing nature of drugs and cannot contend with the complexity of drug use, production and supply.**
- **Drug policy and prohibition are discriminatory, unjust, inhumane and cause harm (e.g. to the environment, countries, users).**

Here are some points and questions for you to consider after reading this chapter:

1) Is drug policy about reducing drug use or reducing crime?
2) Should drugs and their users be a public health or criminal justice issue?

(Continued)

(Continued)

3) What patterns/themes can you see across this period, and how do they compare to those you identified in Chapter 2?

Here are some useful resources for those wanting to further explore the issues raised in this chapter:

- South, N. (1999) *Drugs: Cultures, Controls and Everyday Life*. London: SAGE.
  This seminal text explores the complex and multifaceted relationship between drug use and society, focusing on how drugs shape, and are shaped by, cultural norms, social practices and everyday life.
- Musto, D.F. (1999) *The American Disease*. Oxford: OUP.
  Providing a historical examination of drug control policies in the United States, from the nineteenth-twentieth century, Musto argues that racial prejudice, moral panic and shifting political agendas played significant roles in shaping American drug policy, leading to the American disease, which is the idea that drug use is inherently deviant and dangerous.
- Duke, K. (2006) Out of crime and into treatment? The criminalisation of contemporary drug policy since Tackling Drugs Together. *Drugs: Education, Prevention and Policy*, 13(5):409–415.
  This article critiques the shift in UK drug policy after the Tackling Drugs Together strategy, which aimed to reduce drug use through both crime control and treatment programmes, to show that although it emphasised treatment and rehabilitation, it ultimately resulted in the increased criminalisation of drug users.
- Transform Drug Policy Foundation: Drug Policy Timeline (Available: https://transformdrugs.org/timeline).
  This online resource provides a historical and analytical timeline on drug policies, illustrating how these policies have evolved over time globally.

4

DRUGS, CRIME, CRIMINALISATION: PROHIBITION AND HARM

Overview

This chapter aims to provide you with:

- An overview of drug prohibition.
- An understanding of drug-related harm.
- A critical insight into the links between drug policy and harm.
- An introduction to the drug apartheid.

You will be introduced to the key terms:

- Drug prohibition
- War on drugs
- Drug-related harm
- Drug apartheid

INTRODUCTION

The previous chapters provide a critical insight into the historical background and development of drug policy, highlighting how colonialism and capitalism have played influential roles in determining how we, as a global society, govern the manufacture, supply, possession and use of different substances. Resultantly, it explains how certain drugs are legal and either freely available or accessible via regulatory restrictions, whilst other drugs are illegal and outlawed. This chapter further explores this framework, through a consideration of drug prohibition – providing an assessment of its foundations, rationale and outcomes. In doing so, it critically considers the two central pillars on which prohibition is built: that illegal drugs represent the most dangerous drugs in society, and that drug prohibition protects people from harm. Finally, the chapter highlights how drug prohibition and those drug policies implemented under its pretext can be viewed as both inconsistent and contradictory – to the point that they may be seen as proliferating rather than mitigating drug-related harms.

PROHIBITING THE MOST DANGEROUS DRUGS

Drug prohibition refers to those policies that make the manufacture, supply and possession of specific substances illegal – policies evident, albeit in different guises, in every country across the globe. The origin of this system lies within the 1919 Treaty of Versailles' stipulation that nation states formulate domestic drug legislation to address their respective 'drug problems' (Barton, 2011:16) – the background to which we explain in Chapter 2. Yet it was not until the 1961 United Nations Single Convention on Narcotic Drugs (UN Convention) that drug policy was globally unified. The UN Convention achieving this by providing a definitive list of those drugs deemed the most dangerous to society, requiring all member states enact legislation to prohibit these.

Importantly, the UN Convention defines 'drugs' as simply being those listed within its schedules. No explanation is provided as to why certain substances are regarded as 'drugs' and appear in its schedules whilst other substances do not. Whilst lacking in definition, the underpinning reason for inclusion/exclusion appears to be harm – with the substances listed representing the most dangerous drugs. Yet the UN Convention fails to substantiate why these drugs are considered harmful in their own right, or comparatively to those not listed. It would seem, therefore, that the drugs listed in the UN Convention appear because they are *understood*, rather than *proven*, to be dangerous. Hence, global drug policy is formulated on the *assumption* that these substances are the most dangerous.

On a domestic level, the 1971 Misuse of Drugs Act (MDA) satisfies the UN Convention by prohibiting the substances it lists under UK law. In doing so, it categorises each substance as being a Class A, B or C drug – a classification again guided by the principle of harm. Those listed as Class A represent the most harmful drugs, Class B the next most harmful and Class C the least. This classification system is significant as it governs the sentencing thresholds for infractions of the law, with the most punitive responses reserved for Class A substances due to the greater harms associated with these (see Table 4.1).

Table 4.1 Misuse of Drugs Act 1971: Drug Classification Framework

Classification	Drug	Possession	Dealing
Class A	Ecstasy, LSD, heroin, cocaine, crack, magic mushrooms, methamphetamines	Up to 7 years in prison or an unlimited fine or both	Up to life in prison or an unlimited fine or both
Class B	Amphetamines, barbiturates, cannabis, mephedrone, ketamine, spice	Up to 5 years in prison or an unlimited fine or both	Up to 14 years in prison or an unlimited fine or both
Class C	Anabolic steroids, tranquilisers, GHB, khat, nitrous oxide	Up to 2 years in prison or an unlimited fine or both	Up to 14 years in prison or an unlimited fine or both

When conceived, the MDA was envisaged as a fluid framework. In theory, this meant that drugs would change classification in line with emergent evidence around their harm. In practice, however, most drugs have rigidly maintained their original classifications. Aside from the prominent example of cannabis (which moved from Class B to Class C in 2004 but returned to Class B in 2009), few other drugs have been downgraded (or indeed legalised). The only evident direction of travel has been upgrading, for example, ketamine (which moved from a Class C to a Class B in 2014) and methamphetamine (which moved from Class B to Class A in 2007), whilst other, previously legal drugs have been added to the classification structure and therefore made illegal, for example, khat, spice, mephedrone and nitrous oxide.

Assessing the level of harm that an individual substance presents is a difficult task, as a spectrum of variables may influence this. This is why the UK government professes to a reliance on the best/latest evidence (Home Office, 2010, 2017) to guide the MDA classification system. This includes referring to the Advisory Council on the Misuse of Drugs (ACMD), a dedicated statutory body, to advise them on such matters. It has been argued, however, that the drug classification process (and in effect therefore the measuring of harm itself) is rooted in political rather than empirical reason (see the Box below). This critique is born from two apparent contradictions of the MDA. Firstly, that evidence suggests that prohibited drugs are no more/less harmful than legal ones. Secondly, that evidence indicates that the MDA classification structure does not reflect the comparative harms of individual substances.

The Politics of Harm – The Advisory Council on the Misuse of Drugs

The 2017 drugs strategy for England and Wales noted that the UK government is committed to grounding drug policy in the 'latest available evidence' and that the 'advice of the Advisory Council on the Misuse of Drugs (ACMD) is fundamental to informing our approach and we will continue to seek their valuable input and advice' (Home Office, 2017:7). Whilst the UK government outwardly promotes its evidence-based credentials, how it responds to evidence and advice provided by the ACMD indicates a process that is as political as it is pragmatic. For example:

> In the last decade their [ACMDs] scientific assessments of cannabis, MDMA and khat led to recommendations that these substances should remain in their current classification band, be downgraded or remain legal respectively... all of which were ignored by government. Contrastingly, the ACMDs review of ketamine... led to a recommendation that the drug should be upgraded (enabling a more punitive response to its use and supply) and therefore fitted the UK government's principle of only ratcheting drugs up the UK classification system... this resulted in legislative change. (Taylor, 2016:104)

The uneasy relationship between the government and the ACMD – and the role of evidence within this – has been illustrated by the departures of two prominent AMCD panel members from their respective positions. Professor David Nutt was sacked as Chair of the ACMD in 2009 after expressing that people were statistically more at risk of harm when horse riding than when taking ecstasy and that certain illegal drugs were less harmful than alcohol (Nutt, 2012). Furthermore, Professor Alex Stevens resigned from the ACMD in 2019 over the political vetting of ACMD panel members by the government, claiming that this 'fundamentally undermines the independence of the council' which is 'supposed to be protected by the working protocol between the home secretary and the ACMD. This does not seem compatible if ministers exclude those who disagree with them' (Busby, 2019:1).

A leading figure in this critique is David Nutt, who, alongside colleagues, has facilitated several studies (Nutt et al., 2007, 2010; van Amsterdam et al., 2015), which calculate the levels of harm related to individual substances. Their findings illustrate some apparent contradictions within the MDA. Firstly, they question whether prohibited drugs represent the most dangerous drugs. Nutt and colleagues (2010 – see Figure 4.1) identify that the legal substance alcohol presents a greater risk of harm (when one considers the harm it represents to users alongside the harm it represents to others in society) than all illegal drugs. Simultaneously, the legal drug tobacco carries a greater risk than several illegal drugs, including cannabis and amphetamine. Secondly, in relation to the comparative classification of illegal drugs based on harm within the MDA, they identify that whilst certain Class A drugs, for example, heroin, crack cocaine and cocaine, score relatively highly, and therefore seem accurately classified, other Class A drugs, for example, ecstasy, LSD and magic mushrooms present a much lower risk of harm. These latter substances appear to be misplaced within the MDA, as they carry comparatively less harm than not only other Class A drugs but also the majority of Class B and Class C drugs.

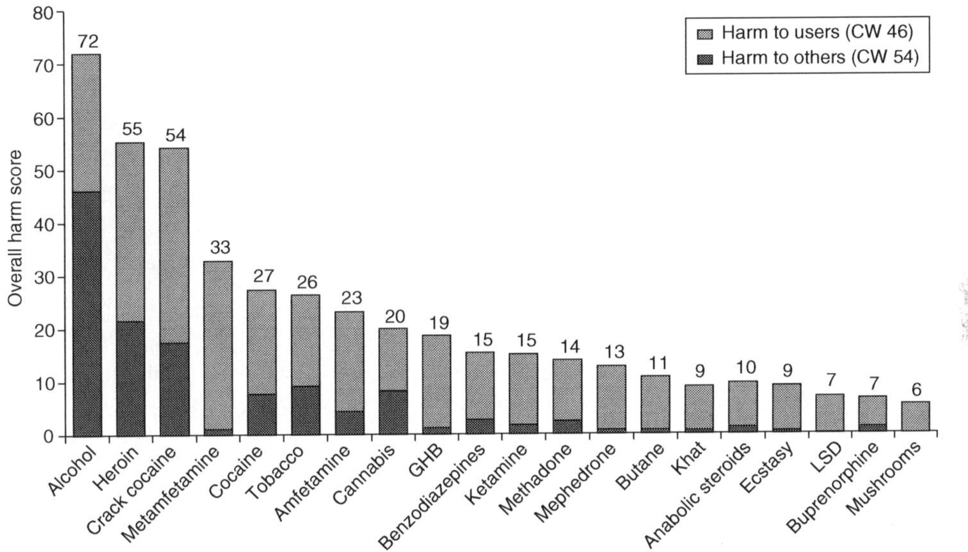

Figure 4.1 Drugs Ordered by Their Overall Harm Scores, Showing the Separate Contributions to the Overall Scores of Harms to Users and Harm to Others
Source: Nutt et al. (2010:1561).

These findings infer that at both the global and national level, the premise that evidenced notions of harm guide drug prohibition is disputed. In the first instance, they frame the current division between legal and illegal drugs as arbitrary rather than rooted in an evidence base of harm, therefore questioning why certain substance use is permitted, whilst other substance use is outlawed. Simultaneously, the contradictions they highlight in the MDA's classification system point towards a potential injustice. This is because drug-related harm depicts the classification of each specific drug listed in the MDA. This in turn acts as a framework for the sentencing of drug offences (see Figure 4.1) with the level of punitive response to such infractions aligning with the position of a drug in the classification system. This means that those arrested for the manufacture, supply or use of ecstasy ostensibly face the same levels of punishment as someone arrested for the same offence relating to heroin – yet this belies Nutt and colleagues (2010) findings that ecstasy is a drug carrying a disproportionately lower risk of harm. If calculations of harm are therefore inaccurate with drugs erroneously classified, this jeopardises the fairness and proportionality of the criminal justice system's response.

Furthermore, the MDA's sentencing framework can also be questioned in relation to harm using the case study of cannabis. When cannabis was downgraded to a Class C substance in 2004, as evidence suggested it was less harmful than previously considered, it contradictorily prompted a change in the MDA sentencing framework for all Class C substances. Hence, the maximum sentence for supplying a Class C substance was increased at this time from five to 14 years' imprisonment (the same as for Class B substances). Yet when cannabis was again reclassified to a Class B drug in 2009, the new sentencing threshold for Class C substances remained.

Crucially, when we consider the potential harm of any substance, we must recognise that this is not solely attributable to the chemical makeup of a specific substance. Equally as important in shaping such harm is the wider context of the drug user and the drug-using environment (Zinberg, 1984). It is imperative to therefore recognise that the contents of a drug, the mindset of drug users and the spatial context in which drug use takes place are influenced by the (non)conventions imposed by respective drug policies. Consequently, structures of legal governance – whether they relate to the unrestricted supply of caffeine, the regulation of e-numbers in food, the licensing of alcohol and the laws governing tobacco packaging – have inferences for the outcomes of legal drug use on both an individual and societal level. Thus construed, drug policy plays a pivotal role in shaping drug-related harm and sequentially in mitigating or indeed proliferating such harms. Rolles and Measham (2011:245) illustrate how the policy environment affects issues of harm by painting contrasting pictures of two injecting heroin users:

> [T]he first is committing high volumes of crime to fund their illicit habit, using 'street' heroin (of unknown strength and purity) with dirty, possibly shared needles in unsupervised and unsanitary environments. Their supplies are purchased from a criminal dealing/trafficking infrastructure that can be traced back to illicit production in Afghanistan. They have HIV, Hepatitis C and a long, and growing, criminal record. The second uses legally manufactured and prescribed pharmaceutical diamorphine of known strength and purity in a supervised, clinical setting, with clean injecting paraphernalia. There is no link to failing drug producer states; no criminality, profiteering or violence involved at any stage of the drug's production, supply or use; no blood borne disease transmission risk; a near zero risk of overdose death; and no offending to fund use.

Hence, when we consider the harm of illegal drugs, we cannot simply associate this with the innate toxicity of these apparently dangerous drugs – we instead must consider the inferences of drug prohibition upon this – a crucial facet given prohibition's second key premise – that it protects society from drug-related harm.

PROTECTING SOCIETY FROM DRUG-RELATED HARM

Historically, a central argument among anti-prohibition drug policy campaigners was that citizens should be at liberty to put whatever substances they wished into their own body. Whilst the popularity of this argument has waned, it still represents a useful starting point to consider how drug laws retain legitimacy. According to John Stuart Mill's (1910) utilitarian argument, restrictions to a citizen's liberty, for example, the right to use all drugs, are only justified if they are proven to be for the betterment of wider society. In this sense, drug prohibition is vindicated by its purported ability to afford the majority of society protection from drug-related harms – and if it does not, should be seen as lacking legitimacy.

In 1998, the United Nations general assembly asserted their allegiance to drug prohibition via their slogan 'a drug free world – we can do it'. In doing so, they re-emphasised the utopian ideal of prohibition, whereby illegal drugs become obsolete – an outcome that in essence should be relatively straightforward. Citizens, having agreed to give up a degree of individual freedom (the right to use illegal drugs), in order to protect wider society (from illegal drug-related harm), obey the law. At the same time, the threat of legal reprisal ensures that anyone tempted to produce, sell or use illegal drugs is deterred from doing so. Hence, a drug-free world emerges. Whilst the United Nations may have thought this possible even as late as the turn of the twenty-first century, the reality is that six decades after the UN Convention, a considerable body of people remain involved with illegal drug markets, where consistent demand is met by ever willing suppliers. Yet this apparent failing has done little to diminish the appetite for prohibition. A key reason being that despite this pitfall, prohibition is construed as successful. For whilst a significant minority of citizens are involved in illegal drug markets, the *majority* are not – and are seemingly therefore protected from its harms – reinforcing drug law legitimacy.

If we consider official statistics of drug use in England and Wales, we see that illegal drug users represent a noteworthy but minority proportion of the population, with around a third of adults reporting such use during their lifetime. When one drills down into these statistics, however, we see that just over 9% report using illegal drugs in the last year and 5% in the previous month (ONS, 2022a). It would seem, therefore, that the definitive aim of prohibition – to protect society from the harms of illegal drugs – has been achieved, as the majority do not use them. If we consider this comparatively with non-prohibited substances, we see that a drug's legal status appears important. For example, 90% of the US population use the legal drug caffeine on a regular basis (Frary et al., 2005), whilst 79% of over 16-year-olds in England and Wales report past year alcohol use including 49% who drink at least once a week (NHS, 2024). On the surface, therefore, prohibiting a drug appears to limit its use and therefore the scope of its harm.

However, whilst the majority of society are not actively engaged in manufacturing, supplying or using illegal drugs, it is impossible to claim that they are deterred from doing so due to the drugs' legal position. In terms of tobacco, for example, the majority of society are not involved in its manufacture or supply, whilst just 12% of UK adults self-report to be smokers (NHS, 2024). This indicates that legal status does not necessarily equate to proportionally high rates of drug use, especially when a substance is sufficiently researched progressively regulated and adequate advice around its use is disseminated. Whilst prohibition undoubtedly plays a role in rates of illegal drug use, evidence from those countries where drug policy reform has removed or lessened criminal penalties indicates that rates of use have remained relatively stable (Drug Policy Alliance, 2018; Transform, 2014). It would appear, therefore, that rates of drug use are not simply related to the punitive level of drug policy (Stevens, 2019). Admittedly, such research is unable to predict the long-term implications of policy reform – as liberalising drug policy does not immediately remove the stigmatisation and rhetoric of fear that surrounds the use of illegal drugs (Taylor, 2008). Yet this evidence pours light on the value of drug prohibition as a deterrent tool, which is of crucial importance as this is the primary method through which prohibition attempts to protect society. If prohibition has little deterrent value (and therefore effect upon rates of drug use), its utility must be questioned.

The mechanisms of drug prohibition, however, are not solely restricted to legal deterrence, with a variety of additional techniques employed to minimise drug-related harms. That such methods even exist implies failure on one level, as they would not be necessary if prohibition effectively deterred involvement with illegal drugs in the first instance. Such mechanisms fall into two broad (and indeed, contrasting) categories. Firstly, they relate to the protection of society through war, which includes attempts to stifle drug demand and supply and to identify, criminalise and punish those who break the law. Secondly, they relate to the management of harm via techniques of harm reduction, which seek to lessen the potential harms of illegal drug taking. As such, these require further consideration.

PROTECTION THROUGH WAR

Despite drug prohibition threatening criminalisation for those who manufacture, supply or use illegal drugs, a body of people continue to be involved with such drug markets. Hence, relevant authorities employ both proactive and reactive responses to drug law infractions. Such measures see a spectrum of international, national and local practices employed by a multitude of organisations to enforce prohibition, seeking to destabilise the supply of illicit drugs and to apprehend those involved in illegal markets. These approaches align with the slogan that is synonymous with drug prohibition – *the war on drugs* – a term first used by US President Richard Nixon to indicate the country's aggressive response to the emerging drug markets of the 1970s. The *war on drugs* has subsequently become a normative element of drug policy discourse, employed by world leaders, policymakers, reformists and academic researchers alike to describe the get-tough drug policies enacted under the guise of drug probation, which have seen ever expanding, pervasive, and punitive measures employed to 'do battle' with illegal drug marketeers.

The term *war on drugs* in itself indicates an inherent contradiction of prohibitionist drug policy – that it aims to protect society via war, with war by its very nature intended to cause harm. Whilst the war on drugs indicates a war on illegal substances, it is not so much the substances that are warred against, than the people who produce, traffic, distribute and use them. The war on drugs therefore seeks to harm those minorities who transcend the boundaries of drug laws in order to protect the majority. In doing so, it emphasises the misnomer that prohibitionist governance structures only allow for punitive responses to drug use and users and has consequently motivated a spectrum of get-tough drug approaches, stretching from macro level policies of economic sanctions through to the micro level policing of individual drug users. At the top of this spectrum sit efforts to eradicate the manufacture and supply of illegal substances at source, for example, governmental sanctions (e.g. economic sanctions imposed by the United States on Venezuela) and crop eradication (e.g. the chemical spraying of cocaine crops in Colombia and opium crops in Afghanistan). In the middle, we see efforts to disrupt organised supply networks, which sees armed forces and law enforcement attempt to identify, detect and arrest those involved in drug trafficking/supply whether that be in a drug's country of origin, in transit or on the streets. At the bottom, we have localised policing of drug use (e.g. police drug dogs at music festivals, the stop and search of those suspected of possessing drugs). Most of these techniques see war waged through the medium of criminalisation. Hence, whilst criminalisation is used as a deterrent to discourage engagement with drug markets/use, it also represents a tool through which to respond, punish and therefore control those subpopulations who break the law.

On a domestic level, the sum of these efforts is illustrated by approximately 16% of the sentenced prison population and 24% of the untried prison population in England and Wales being incarcerated for drug offences (Ministry of Justice, 2022a). Yet the justice system's process of criminalisation is most frequently applied to those possessing rather than supplying drugs, adding credence to the claim that the war on drugs has cascaded to a micro level war on drug users (Buchanan and Young, 2000). For example, in the year 2022–23 (ONS, 2023b), there were a total of 179,874 drug offences recorded by police in England and Wales with 47,646 of these being for trafficking and the remaining 132,228 being for possession (of which 98,452 were for possession of cannabis). Yet drug possession itself has not historically been a priority for UK police forces. In essence, if you use drugs in a way that does not bring you to the attention of the authorities, your use will likely go unnoticed (Askew and Salinas, 2019). This is illustrated by the fact that despite the 132,228 possession offences noted above, during the same time period in England and Wales, an estimated 3.1 million people used an illegal drug (ONS, 2023a). Instead, the police (and indeed the wider criminal justice system) focus attention on a specific subpopulation whose wider pattern of criminal behaviour is the key concern – the *problematic drug user*.

The catalyst for this realignment of the war on drugs onto a war on drug users can be found in the increased rates of heroin (and to a lesser extent crack cocaine) use, addiction and crime recorded during the 1980s and 1990s in the United Kingdom. At this time, a number of government-funded research studies identified a relationship between heroin/crack use and the committal of high rates of property crime (see e.g. Bennett, 1998). This cemented a belief that drug use caused crime, attributing the bulk of street crime to those who funded their drug dependency through criminality. Whilst the causal link between drugs and crime is far from clear (see Chapter 5) and the scale and cost of drug-related crime seemingly overestimated (Stevens, 2007), this evidence base mirrored the wider socio-cultural framing of problematic drug users as social pariahs (Taylor, 2008). The problematic drug user, therefore, was presented as a risk to themselves, but perhaps more importantly, to wider society. As Stimson (2000) identifies, this resulted in a paradigm shift in UK drug policy in the mid-1990s, from a health-centred to criminal justice-orientated system. Instead of seeing problematic drug users as victims *of* the drug problem, this group was reframed *as* the drug problem. As such, the war on drugs extended to a war on problematic drug users.

This expanded remit is evident in the successive drug strategies for England and Wales published since the mid-1990s (Home Office, 1998, 2008, 2010, 2017, 2021), which share three consistent ambitions. The first of these being to reduce the demand for drugs. The second being to reduce the supply of drugs. The third being to identify problematic drug users and to address the issues they present. In line with what we discuss above, the first two aims are in essence redundant, as history teaches us that demand and supply continue regardless of governmental efforts to lessen them. In essence, the pursuit of these aims is merely symbolic, acting as a rhetorical reminder of the United Kingdom's continued allegiance to drug prohibition. Hence, the only realistically achievable aim within these drug strategies has been to develop a process whereby problematic drug users could be detected and their behaviours managed – allowing their drug use and therefore their wider criminality to be addressed. Stop drug use, stop crime, simple. To achieve this, a bifurcated criminal justice system was developed, whereby drug-using offenders were/are processed differentially than others, with drug interventions delivered at every stage of this process (see Chapter 7). At the centre of this model is a carrot-and-stick approach whereby drug-using offenders are offered the opportunity to overcome their addiction (and therefore wider criminal behaviour) via expedient court-mandated access to treatment and support services coupled with punitive aspects of sentencing, and indeed, punitive responses to non-compliance.

This hybrid approach of mixing treatment with punishment serves a dual protective purpose – it offers an individual help to move beyond their harmful drug use whilst simultaneously managing the risk they represent to wider society (in terms of their problematic, criminal behaviour). It therefore fits drug prohibition's mantra of protecting the majority from drug-related harm. It also, despite extending the reach of state control (through the medium of coerced drug treatment with penalties for failure) appears benevolent, as on the surface it attempts to help drug users overcome their dependency. The implications of this process for the already marginalised groups that disproportionately fall within the net of the criminal justice system are considered in Chapters 5 and 7. Yet it is important to recognise at this juncture that the focus on problematic drug users aligns with notions of protection through war – as it seeks to protect society by placing dependent drug users within the criminal justice system rather than diverting them into a health-centred environment. Some writers argue that this is a process which ultimately harms rather than helps drug users (Buchanan, 2004).

PROTECTION THROUGH HARM REDUCTION

Despite such punitive frameworks dominating contemporary developments in drug policy in England and Wales, the mantra to punish first should not be seen as a fait accompli. Indeed, prior to the turn towards a more punitive stance on drug users in the mid-1990s, British drug policy had centred on a public health approach (Stimson, 2000). This was built on a momentum developed in the mid-1980s for policy to recognise the needs of those who used drugs. At this time, it became apparent that the availability and types of illegal drugs were increasing, as were the numbers of people using them. Whilst a significant number of people were therefore choosing to use illegal drugs, there were few available services which they could turn to for support and guidance. Hence, we see the emergence of harm reduction services, which were 'based on containing, rather than eradicating the problems associated with certain drugs' (Monaghan, 2012:30).

An initial motivation to develop harm reduction services at this time was concern around the spread of HIV amongst injecting drug users. Whilst support for these schemes partially emerged through a desire to contain the spread of the disease from drug users to non-drug users (McKeganey, 2011), it began a process whereby the needs of drug users themselves were recognised. Hence, despite drugs being illegal, there was an appreciation that some people do take them and in order to address the harms that such use provokes (for the individual drug user in the first instance but also wider society) there was a need for services which could respond accordingly.

Clearly, however, harm reduction sits awkwardly with those who advocate that drug prohibition should emphasise a 'just say no approach' – in this sense, providing advice and assistance to those who use drugs represents an acknowledgement that prohibition is failing to deter everyone from using them. Simultaneously, it may be seen as weakening prohibition's deterrence affect by making drug use less risky and therefore more attractive. Resultantly, there are concerns that the development of harm reduction services represents a softening of drug policy or even that they may provide a back door to drug policy reform (Forston, 2006). Hence, harm reduction and drug prohibition can make for uneasy bedfellows. Despite this, harm reduction approaches have had a continued presence in drug policy since the 1980s and are embedded into contemporary society. Examples include pragmatic drugs education, which explains how to use illegal drugs in the safest fashion; needle exchanges, which allow those who inject drugs to access sterile works; drug-checking facilities, which test the chemical makeup of illegal substances to alert users to the existence of potentially harmful content; and drug treatment services, which provide replacement drug therapy, counselling and residential rehabilitation facilities.

It should be noted, however, that the UK government's austerity programme from 2010 onwards reduced public funding for such services, stagnating their availability, especially for recreational drug users to the point of almost elimination (Fisher and Measham, 2018). Simultaneously, drug policy since the 1990s has prioritised (treatment) services for those who are 'causing trouble (the criminal needy)' rather 'those wanting help (the healthy needy)' (Simson, 2000:261) meaning that resources have been disproportionately invested within a criminal justice rather than community context. Meanwhile, certain harm reduction strategies, for example, drug consumption rooms (whereby (injecting) drug users can access sanitary, private spaces to use drugs), remain in their infancy in the United Kingdom due to being politically or legally unpalatable. In this sense, an adherence to a more punitive mentality continues to limit opportunities to protect drug users.

PROLIFERATING DRUG-RELATED HARM

An inherent contradiction in harm reduction strategies employed under the guise of prohibitionist drug policies is that they attempt to mitigate the harm prompted not only by drug use itself but also by the wider environment of drug prohibition. For example, drug-checking services are only necessary because illegal drugs are unregulated and have unknown contents. Despite the existence of harm reduction services, the primary aim of policies of drug prohibition is to protect society by discouraging illegal drug use. Key to this strategy is that illegal drug taking should be framed as unattractive and indeed as risky as possible. By design, therefore, drug policy enhances the likelihood of harm for those who engage with drug markets in order to reinforce its deterrent message. Hence, if someone wishes to use illegal drugs, they have to navigate the illicit drug market, engage with criminal entrepreneurs and use substances of unknown quality and strength, increasing the apparent likelihood of health problems, overdose and death (Buchanan, 2015a).

Subsequently, illegal drugs tend to be generically presented as dangerous with the outcomes of such use framed as negative and unwanted, linked as they are to notions of criminality, addiction and an inability to socially function (Taylor, 2016). These constructions can lead to the stigmatisation of drug users, especially those dependent on drugs, who are labelled as addicts and junkies – with drug policy primarily focusing on the problems presented by this group (Ayres and Taylor, 2022). Resultantly, we centre attention (and indeed resources) on the issues presented by a minority of 300,000 (Hay et al., 2018) problematic drug users with comparatively scant recognition of the drug-using majority, nor of their needs (Taylor, 2011). For example, rates of last year drug use amongst young people increased between 2013 and 2020 (ONS, 2023a), yet levels of engagement with drug services declined during this period (Public Health England, 2018), which Webster (2018) contends was a direct result of a reduction in funding for such services.

This relative omission of the wider body of drug users within drug policy is odd given the consistent policy goal of preventing all drug use – as without recognising that approximately one in ten of the 16 to 59-year-old population in England and Wales report using an illegal drug within the last year (ONS, 2023a), we fail to acknowledge the drug-using majority. As a result, drug policy has historically overlooked what motivates most drug use, especially non-dependent drug use, despite this being crucial to realising its ambition of preventing this – as without understanding why the majority of drug users use drugs, drug policy will struggle to prevent it. Furthermore, a resilient belief in the gateway theory (Beckett Wilson et al., 2017) indicates that addressing 'lower level' drug use should be a priority if we are to prevent progression onto 'harder' substances. For critical drug scholars, however, this oversight serves a seeming purpose, as it evades a deeper questioning of the systematic use of illegal substances within society. It therefore avoids a recognition that for the majority, drug use represents a tangential element of their civilised, functional and law-abiding lives (Askew and Salinas, 2019); an appreciation that experimental or (in)frequent illegal drug use is a leisure pursuit engaged by a significant minority of the population; and an acknowledgement that many find solace, release and pleasure within their drug-using second lives (Presdee, 2000). It therefore avoids any acknowledgement of drugs as a positive experience (Holt and Treloar, 2008). Instead, drug policy frames drugs as bad, associates drug use with a certain population of problematic drug users and encourages society to 'just say no' despite this in effect, rendering a key policy ambition redundant.

An outcome of this relative omission of most drug users from drug policy is that it potentially enhances the harms associated with *all* illegal drug use. Through stereotypical representations of the problematic drug user, we develop the stigmatising processes outlined previously. Simultaneously, these dominant stereotypes (and systems) seemingly dissuade those users who may (or may not) be experiencing drug-related problems (especially those who do not associate themselves as 'junkies') from engaging with organisations offering support (Lloyd, 2010; UKDPC, 2010b) due to fear of (social or indeed legal) reprisal – a fear that seems well grounded given that a drug conviction can have life-long consequences relating to education, employment, housing, insurance, healthcare, finance, travel and relationships (Taylor et al., 2016). In this sense, drug prohibition ensures that those who use illegal drugs *purposefully* face greater risks of harm than if those same drugs were legally regulated and the needs and rights of users were recognised.

Furthermore, those who are arrested for infracting drug laws are again *purposefully* harmed as part of prohibition's deterrent/punitive methods. For those who break the law and amass within drug prohibition's net of criminalisation, this harm is perpetuated throughout their lives through an ongoing process of stigmatisation. The study of Lenton and colleagues (2000) on cannabis users provides a good illustration of this. The study compared a sample of 68 South Australians who received an informal response (an infringement notice) to a minor cannabis offence with a sample of 68 West Australians who received a criminal conviction for such an offence. They found that the group who had received a criminal conviction were more likely to report negative consequences in relation to employment (32% vs. 2%), further problems with the law (32% vs. 0%), relationships (20% vs. 5%) and accommodation (16% vs. 0%) because of this. As Lenton and colleagues (2000:257) observe 'while neither conviction nor infringement deterred subsequent cannabis use for the vast majority, the negative social impacts of conviction were far greater than those resulting from an infringement notice'.

These findings emphasise the potential harm prompted by a drug conviction and resultantly how drug users can be marginalised. This is particularly important when one considers the demographical profile of those who encounter the criminal justice system in relation to drug offences. For example, despite minority ethnic groups reporting lower levels of drug use than White populations in England and Wales, they experience disproportionate levels of stop and search by the police and a higher percentage of these are for drug offences compared to White groups (UKDPC, 2010a). These trends are further considered in Chapter 6.

The ability of drug policy to therefore protect society appears to be partial. Whilst it does seemingly attempt to protect those who do not use illegal drugs, by its very nature, it simultaneously attempts to enhance the harms faced by drug users themselves. Yet whilst those from minority and already marginalised groups appear more likely to experience the harms associated with the criminalisation of drug possession, the harms proliferated by prohibition are not restricted to those groups, nor to those who use illegal drugs, nor to those penalised for breaking drug laws. Taylor and colleagues (2018) contend that the pervasive nature of drug prohibition means that all members of communities can in fact be susceptible to such harms, arguing that regardless of whether prohibition is enforced with tenacity or apathy, its ability to enhance harm permeates much more widely than those directly involved in illegal drug markets. For example, the construction of drug users as dangerous prompts anxieties within communities where drug use is prevalent as non–drug-using residents are informed more by fear-inducing drug war rhetoric than factual information (Taylor et al., 2018), whilst attempts to eradicate illegal crops in Afghanistan and Colombia result in community instability and environmental damage (Dávalosa et al., 2009; Mansfield and Pain, 2007), whilst the war on drugs afforded President Duterte of the Philippines a veneer to commit genocide (Simangen, 2018).

Resultantly, contemporary drug policy, justified by its purported ability to mitigate drug-related harms, concurrently serves to enhance their scope and severity. Whilst these outcomes may be construed as an unfortunate but necessary by-product of a policy which is for the greater good, a growing body of scholars argue that such outcomes are not unfortunate but the result of a purposeful policy of condemnation and criminalisation that targets certain groups – a process which Taylor and colleagues. (2016) refer to as the *drug apartheid*. They argue that instead of viewing drug prohibition 'as a "war on drugs" there is a need to see it as a "war between drugs" a system of drug apartheid that has privileged the use of certain substances and outlawed the use of other substances, a corrupt system that has much to do with who uses the drugs and little to do with the risks posed by the drugs' (Taylor et al., 2016:459).

THE DRUG APARTHEID

Whilst the outlawing of certain substances is therefore justified by drug prohibition's apparent ability to protect society from drug-related harms, the validity of this justification can be questioned. This has led to accusations that drug prohibition's mantra of public protection represents a façade which provides legitimacy to a policy grounded in moral, political and economic reasoning (Ayres and Taylor, 2023). In this section, we therefore explore the arguments put forward by a series of critical criminologists who view drug prohibition as a tool of control by the state that affords the continuation of the capitalist status quo.

In this vein, Taylor and Colleagues (2016) contend that the key to unveiling the significance of drug policy is to view it as a system of apartheid that has created a hierarchy of institutionalised segregation, which privileges certain substances and their users whilst criminalising and punishing others. This drug apartheid represents a system of inclusion and exclusion, which provides cultural acceptance, competence and identity to some, whilst meting out stigmatisation, imprisonment and death to others. This framework allows those with the means of production to profit from legal regulation, whilst those located within the most marginalised economic groups are held responsible for a plethora of social ills and criminalised. Resultantly, whilst the drug apartheid proliferates drug-related harms most acutely on those populations who are already economically and politically marginalised, its remit is said to permeate the entire social strata.

Taylor and colleagues (2016) therefore argue that our response (in a social, legal and political sense) to substance use is governed more by the profile of who manufactures or uses a drug than the inherent toxicity or risks associated with it. So, whilst pharmaceutical companies, the alcohol and tobacco industry, purveyors of caffeine and food and drink manufacturers who laden their products with sugar are said to cause the greatest proportion of drug-related harms, they simultaneously enjoy a position of legal privilege (Ayres and Taylor, 2020, 2022, 2023). The powerful industry backing, corporate respectability and profitability of these industries, however, legitimise legal regulation. Illegal substances meanwhile lack such credentials, and perhaps more importantly, their consumers lack such respectability (Measham and Moore, 2008).

We therefore arrive at the juxtaposed status quo whereby certain substance use/users is/are constructed as problematic while other substance use/users is/are constructed as civilised (with such substances socially accommodated and their use indicative of a wider cultural competence). So, whilst brands like Krug or Cristal champagne are coveted, evoking notions of cool with their consumption eliciting envy, illegal heroin is seen as dirty with users perceived as addicts, criminals and failures, warranting arrest and imprisonment and eliciting contempt (Ayres and Taylor, 2020). Such hierarchies (and their subsequent privileges or exclusions) according to Taylor and Colleagues (2016) are founded upon the power differentials of wealth and status – rather than any scientific assessment of harm (as demonstrated by Nutt and colleagues (2010) ranking of alcohol as more harmful than heroin illustrated in Figure 4.1) – resulting in a hierarchy of substance use, which recognises and rewards those manufacturers, suppliers and users of licit substances, whilst allowing the arrest and punishment of those involved with illicit markets. It achieves this through framing the *drug problem* in two ways.

Firstly, through the drug apartheid and the subsequent cascading downwards of the war on drugs, we increasingly frame the *drug problem* as relating to a minority group of problematic drug users. Alexandrescu (2018) highlights how the construction of this group as dysfunctional addicts, drawn from the lower classes, who commit crime to fund their use, frames them as a redundant population. Hence, they are seen as serving a crucial purpose, acting as a generic metaphor of all illegal drug use, providing vivid visual and narrative evidence that 'drugs are bad' and that people should not take them (Taylor, 2016). Yet this use of stigmatisation to deter drug use is not the only purpose that this construction of the drug problem is said to serve. Simultaneously it also affords the impression that drug use or more pertinently the problem of drugs is restricted to a specific subpopulation based on notions of class and race – indicating that we can still win the war on drugs if we can just address the behaviours pertaining to these groups. It therefore frames these groups as a key social problem, justifying ever punitive and intrusive measures to control them with the practices of the drug apartheid disproportionality applied to the most marginalised in society who we continue to coercively treat, curtail the welfare benefits of and even sterilise.

Whilst drug policies rightly distinguish that socially marginalised populations are more likely to develop problematic patterns of (illegal) drug use, it is argued that they simultaneously place the responsibility for this on people's individual decision to use drugs – which in turn places the onus of becoming drug (and therefore crime) free on the individual level (Taylor, 2008). As Taylor and colleagues (2016:462) observe 'it may be politically expedient to present lives that have been damaged by deindustrialization, poverty, unemployment, exclusion, abuse and/or trauma as caused by "drugs", however, chronic problematic drug use is more often a symptom of wider underlying issues, not the causal factor'. Hence, whilst recent drug policy in England and Wales has led to a welcome extension of support and treatment provision for drug users, this is primarily provided within a criminal justice context. It therefore encompasses such support within a coercive framework (see Chapter 7), motivated by a desire to mitigate the problems such users pose as much as any sincere concern over their health and well-being. Consequentially, we offer problematic users the carrot of help but if they fail to take this, or are unsuccessful in their rehabilitative efforts, we respond with a punitive stick. This enables the criminal justice system to 'offer' support to these individuals whilst doing little to address the underlying issues of poverty, education, accommodation and employment, which characterise many problematic drug users' lives. Concurrently, punitive responses to the failure of such users to become drug free are seemingly justified due to the need to minimise the risks such users present to society. Conversely, this is a process which (via criminalisation and stigmatisation) can exacerbate extant underlying problems, with drug use becoming the key defining factor in users' lives, influencing future relationships, employment, education, accommodation, medical care, financial options, insurance cover and travel. Here, the drug apartheid intensifies the harms experienced. Resultantly, the already marginalised become even more so whilst the role of structural social inequalities are sidelined.

Secondly, the drug apartheid is said to frame which drugs (and drug producers and suppliers) represent the *drug problem* and in doing so, takes attention away from the damaging outcomes of legal drug use (Taylor et al., 2016). Ayres and Taylor (2022) argue that the most prominent harms prompted by the drug apartheid are those pertaining to the invisibility of non-drugs – with this serving to camouflage the most destructive drug-related harms within society, such as obesity, tooth decay, loss of sleep, liver disease, cancer and the prescription practices of the medical profession (Ayres and Taylor, 2023). Drug prohibition has played a crucial role in this process through its iteration of what substances constitute 'drugs' and therefore what harms are constructed as drug-related (Buchanan, 2015a). Through the MDA, we outlaw those substances considered dangerous drugs, whilst we permit the corporate promotion of sugary foods, alcohol, caffeine, tobacco, cosmetic procedures and pharmaceuticals. Here, the drug apartheid, despite an increasing recognition of the harms associated with legal substances, ensures their social, legal and political construction as non-drugs endures (Ayres and Taylor, 2023).

The arguments put forward by critical criminologists contend that the two pillars on which drug prohibition is built – that illegal drugs represent the most dangerous drugs and drug prohibition protects society – are both therefore illusory. Instead, they contend that drug prohibition plays a purposeful role in the drug apartheid as it allows for the control and criminalisation of the so-called problematic populations whilst legitimising the more destructive practices of legal drug markets. Taylor and colleagues (2016) conclude that until the drug apartheid is deconstructed and the arbitrary dichotomy between privileged and prohibited drugs is broken down, the harms associated with legal 'drugs' will continue to be prevalent and that until we develop a socio-legal understanding that *all* drugs are *drugs*, we will continue to deflect the harms of capitalism onto the drug using practices of a problematic minority and, in doing so, enhance the harms experienced by all of society, but especially those experienced by marginalised groups.

CONCLUSION

Drug prohibition and the subsequent drug policies devised under its guise pertain to be based on notions of evidence-based utilitarianism – using the best evidence they outlaw the most dangerous drugs to protect society from drug-related harm. In one sense, this claim appears to be a legitimate one, with most of society abstaining from illicit drug use, strategies of harm reduction utilised for those who do and the nefarious nature of drug markets and problematic outcomes prompted by drug use well illustrated. Yet as this chapter illustrates, whether drug policy *is* evidence based, whether strategies of harm reduction *are* well utilised, whether illegal drugs *are* the most dangerous drugs and whether drug policy *does* protect society can all be questioned. Furthermore, the concept of the drug apartheid highlights how drug prohibition can conversely play a pivotal role in extending the harms experienced by specific populations and wider society through its stigmatising processes and concealment of non-drugs. Whether we should therefore construe drug prohibition as a benevolent effort to safeguard citizens from the scourge of illegal drugs, or as a policy rooted in notions of control and economic bias, which ultimately serves to proliferate rather than mitigate drug-related harms, is a moot point. Despite this, drug prohibition retains its global drug policy dominance meaning that the criminalisation of those who infract drug laws continues unabated.

SUMMARY

- **Drug prohibition outlaws the most dangerous drugs in society but it is unclear why certain substances are classified as dangerous and others are not.**
- **Drug prohibition is legitimised by its ability to reduce drug-related harms but it may conversely increase the scope and severity of these.**
- **The 1971 MDA classifies substances into three typologies: Class A, B and C based on their harmfulness although some question the accuracy of this.**
- **The war on drugs has morphed into a war on drug users, particularly those who are disproportionately drawn from marginalised populations.**
- **The drug apartheid affords certain substances and their users a position of legal privilege whilst others are criminalised.**

Here are some points and questions for you to consider after reading this chapter:

1) How does drug prohibition attempt to protect society and mitigate drug-related harms?
2) Critically consider the 1971 MDA's classification of illegal substances – do you feel this is accurate and/or evidence based?
3) Identify the key issues raised by the drug apartheid concept and how these question the legitimacy of the current system of drug probation.

Here are some useful resources for those wanting to further explore the issues raised in this chapter:

- Ayres, T. and Taylor, S. (2020, December) The 12 dichotomies of drug policy. *British Society of Criminology Blog*. Available at: https://thebscblog.wordpress.com/tag/drug-apartheid/

  This blog maps out a series of dichotomies that are evident within prohibitionist drug policy. In doing so, it identifies a series of contradictions that appear to characterise societal, political and legal responses to substance use.
- Ayres, T. and Taylor, S. (2024, January) Are we in a drugs apartheid? *Talking Drugs*. Available at: https://www.talkingdrugs.org/are-we-in-a-drugs-apartheid/

  This short online article provides an overview of the drug apartheid including an analysis of how contemporary developments in drug policy are struggling to move beyond this and remain haunted by the ghosts of prohibition.

- Nutt, D. (2012) *Drugs without the Hot Air: Minimising the harms of legal and illegal drugs.* Cambridge: UIT.

  This seminal text considers drug-related harms in a pragmatic and scientific fashion. It identifies how we might measure drug-related harms and whether certain substances should be viewed as more harmful than others, incorporating a number of engaging case studies.

5
UNDERSTANDING THE DRUG–CRIME LINK

Overview

This chapter aims to provide you with:

- An overview of the relationship between drugs and crime.
- An understanding of the different links between drugs and crime.
- A critical analysis of the drug–crime relationship to illustrate its complexity and over-exaggeration.
- Examples of the link drugs have with different crimes using homicide/organised crime/terrorism as illustrative examples.

You will be introduced to the key terms:

- Drug offences
- Drug-related offences
- Spurious
- Causal

INTRODUCTION

The previous chapter contended that drug policy reform only has the potential to be progressive when drugs policy is no longer conceptualised through the lens of crime, criminalisation and criminal justice. Building on this further, this chapter will examine the relationship between drug use and crime in the contemporary political economic context of neoliberal consumer capitalism on both a local and global scale. Looking at the drug–crime relationship and the five most common explanations (drug use causes crime, crime causes drug use, both are caused by a third factor, the relationship is reciprocal and the relationship is spurious) before critiquing them, this chapter focuses on both behaviours being caused by a third factor, which is an under-researched area and a topic not given much space or time in other texts.

The previous chapter examines drug prohibition, highlighting how economic alongside socio-political factors have played influential roles in determining the criminalisation of the manufacture, supply, possession and use of some substances, but not others. Historically, Chapters 2 and 3 reveals how drug policy and legislation have been used to control marginalised populations and reinforce social hierarchies via the criminalisation of drugs (e.g. Chinese immigrants and opium), which has had lasting legacies that are reflected in laws and their enforcement and thus the drug–crime relationship. The criminalisation of drugs leads to an obvious association with crime and criminality attributable to their illegal status, which is largely the only connection some drugs like cannabis have with crime and criminality (Pedersen and Skardhamar, 2009), illustrating the role prohibition plays in the drug–crime connection.

The link between drugs and crime is well established and there is undoubtedly some connection between drug use and criminality. However, the exact nature of the drug–crime relationship is heavily contested and multifaceted. For decades, research has tried to disentangle the relationship to better understand the connections that exist between drug use and crime, which will be the focus of this chapter.

DRUGS AND CRIME

Historically, the relationship between drugs and crime is well documented. Early legislation implemented penalties for the use of drugs like laudanum and chloroform, which were used to 'stupefy things' in order to commit crime (e.g. 1851 Act for the Better Prevention of Offences) and there were occasional cases of murder by opium (see Berridge, 1999). One of the key reasons for the prohibition of opium was the number of overdoses, particularly the phenomenon of infant doping among the working classes – largely a response of women needing to work – which led to opium being seen as a public health problem (Berridge, 1999). There was also a well-documented link between alcohol and crime in Victorian Britain. Alcohol or the 'demon drink' as it was more commonly known was seen as a causal factor in evils like social disorder, crime, deviance, prostitution and poverty as alcohol was seen as a source of moral, social and financial ruin (see Berridge, 2013; Greenaway, 2003; Hands, 2018). As Chapters 2 and 3 illustrate, the control and criminalisation of certain substances and groups of people (e.g. poor, ethnic minorities) reflect the interests of powerful groups and the role of systemic inequalities in criminalisation, which is reflected in the drug–crime relationship today. In contemporary society, drugs and alcohol are still associated with crime, deviance and disorder, particularly among certain groups, a relationship that is the bastion of media reports, fiction, popular culture and scientific/academic investigation, which is reflected in the vast and ever burgeoning literature on drugs and crime.

The literature on drugs and crime is gargantuan. Even by the 1980s, the drug–crime literature was already being described as vast, complex and varied (Gandossy et al., 1980). Since the literature and research crosses countries and cultures, employs varied methodologies and definitions and tends to focus on treatment samples and/or offender populations (see Bennett and Holloway, 2007; Gossop et al., 2005) drawing comparisons, amalgamating findings and identifying gaps in the knowledge has proved problematic. Despite this, there are several texts on drugs and crime (e.g. Bean, 2014; Bennett and Holloway, 2005a; Hammersley, 2008; Stevens, 2011a; Tonry and Wilson, 1990) – including this one – and the literature on the drug–crime connections is considerable and ever expanding (for reviews, see Bennett and Holloway 2005a, 2005b, 2009; Caulkins and Kleiman, 2011; Chaiken and Chaiken, 1990; Gandossy et al., 1980). Thus, disentangling and deciphering the drug–crime relationship has proved problematic. What is clear is that a lot of people commit crime and take drugs, with research identifying that each is a high-risk indicator of the other. However, research also shows that the majority of drug users commit no crime other than those associated with prohibition (see Chapters 4 and 6), and not all criminals are drug users, illustrating the complexity, and to a certain extent controversy, surrounding the drug–crime relationship.

Despite the multifaceted nature of the relationship there is a 'taken-for-granted assumption' that drugs are linked to various forms of criminality in myriad of ways. Whether we are talking about the manufacture and supply of drugs linked to organised crime groups (OCG) (see page 135–136) and in some instances terrorism (narcoterrorism) (see the Box on page 136) or the disorder and violence attributed to drugs like cocaine and alcohol in the night-time economy (NTE), the link is well established and rarely questioned or critiqued. Instead, it is taken as fact, legitimised – in policy and legislation – despite the finer nuances surrounding this relationship.

DEFINITIONAL PROBLEMS AND ISSUES OF CAUSATION

What constitutes a drug and/or a crime is historically, socially and culturally specific (see Chapters 2 and 3), which also impacts the relationship that exists between these socially constructed phenomenon (see Hammersley, 2008 for an in-depth overview of this). What constitutes a crime or a drug is constantly changing and being redefined and reclassified. Also establishing causation is problematic, not just when looking at the drug–crime relationship (see Seddon, 2000) but also when trying to establish any causal connection between complex and multifaceted human behaviours, which cannot be distilled down to a singular micro, meso or macro factor (see the Box below). Instead, drugs and crime tend to result from a complex interplay of all three.

Micro – the individual: there is much research attributing drugs and crime to factors located in the individual like impulsivity, nervousness, neuroticism, trauma, coping strategies and personality disorders (see Chapter 1).

Meso – the group/organisation: research highlights the importance of family, school and peers traditionally locating drugs and crime in deviant subcultures and gangs (see Chapter 1).

Macro – the system (global/national): there is less research focusing on the wider socio-political-economic system when it comes to explaining drugs and crime, although some does exist (e.g. Ayres, 2023; Hall et al., 2008; Seddon, 2006; Stevens, 2011a).

When research starts to disentangle the relationship between drugs and crime, the finer nuances of the relationship start to emerge, which depend on the substance being looked at, race/ethnicity, class/socio-economic status, gender and severity of use (controlled/recreational versus uncontrolled/problematic). For example, some substances are more likely to be associated with certain crimes:

- Alcohol with violence (Lammers et al., 2014) including homicide (see the Box on page 32), domestic violence (IAS, 2014; WHO, 2006) and violence in public spaces that includes the ever burgeoning NTE (Finney, 2004; Hall and Winlow, 2006).
- Heroin/opiates and crack tend to be related to higher rates of offending, particularly acquisitive crime (crimes committed for financial gain) (Home Office, 2017; Pierce et al., 2017) and sex work (Surratt et al., 2005).
- Anabolic steroids have been linked to violence (Klötz et al., 2007) as has cocaine (Goldstein et al., 1991) and crack (Carvalho and Seibel, 2009).
- Date rape drugs (Rohypnol/Roofies, ketamine and gamma-hydroxybutyrate) have been linked to drink spiking, sexual assaults and rape, although alcohol is always a factor too (Albright et al., 2012; Lawyer et al., 2010).

Despite these well-established and taken-for-granted relationships, their prevalence is often over-exaggerated and not as common as we are led to believe. While there is no denying there are incidents when certain substances are linked to certain crimes, when you delve deeper into the research, most of these relationships are largely attributable to other factors, which are largely ignored and omitted from the official discourse. Instead, individual drugs are blamed – scapegoated – and the relationship over-simplified. For example, when you look at the relationship between crack and violence, 'the socio-demographic characteristics, mood and non-cocaine substance use disorders that make some individuals more likely to use crack cocaine than powder cocaine, are perhaps responsible for the increased prevalence of violence observed among crack users, rather than crack itself, compared to powdered cocaine users' (Vaughn et al., 2010:185). Also, as Weiss and Colyer (2010:350) argue, 'there has been little empirical evidence to suggest that drug-induced sexual assault, as embodied in the roofies narrative, is anything more than a rare but tragic occurrence'. When it comes to the link between drugs and crime, the atypical is made typical and multifaceted connections and pathways distilled into mono-causal explanations. Although the drug–crime link differs by substance, it also differs by age, gender, race/ethnicity, class and severity of use illustrating its complexity.

Age: the onset of drug use and offending are for a large percentage of adolescents a fundamental, even normal, part of growing up (Aldridge et al., 2011; Moffitt, 2003). Drug use and crime/delinquency are typically initiated in adolescence around the same age. The onset for drug use ranges from 7 to 15 years old (Farabee et al., 2001; Nurco et al., 1999), and the onset of offending is between the ages of 8 and 14 (age–crime curve) (Farrington, 1986, 2011). For most, both behaviours will be confined to adolescence and will be a normal part of growing up (adolescent-limited), while for a small minority, both behaviours will persist into adulthood and become an integral and permanent feature of their lives (life-course persistent) (see Moffit, 1993, 2003). The majority of drug users and offenders will progress up a hierarchy of severity after initiation for both drug use and crime. Legal drugs like alcohol and tobacco precede illicit drug use (Pudney, 2002), while minor low-level delinquency tends to precede more serious crimes (Farrington, 2011). For some, drug use will be initiated first, while for others, offending will be initiated first, although the research on which behaviour comes first is inconclusive, contradictory and complex (cf. Farabee et al., 2001; Kaye et al., 1998, for a review see Bennett and Holloway, 2007). The age of onset for both drugs and crime varies, based on gender and/or ethnicity/race (Theobald and Farrington, 2014; Vasilenko et al., 2017), but all research shows that an earlier age of onset is more closely associated with escalation to more serious and problematic drug use and/or crime (Farrington, 1986; Hser et al., 2007). Due to societal changes, particularly in the West/Global North, people's life courses have changed since a lot of the research was undertaken (e.g. as they stay in higher education, delay settling down and getting married or moving out of the parental home due to cost of housing/living) meaning that substance use and/or criminality are being carried on into early adulthood (Aldridge et al., 2011; Parker et al., 1998). Adults have always used drugs (Pearson, 2001) as have old-age pensioners (Badrakalimuthu et al., 2010), there is just less research on these groups, probably due to the illicit nature of both behaviours and people's reluctance to admit it.

Gender(s): the drug–crime relationship varies between gender(s). Men tend to be the most socially visible when it comes to drugs, while women and lesbian, gay, bisexual and trans (LGBTQ+) people have been largely excluded despite evidence to suggest LGBTQ+ people have high rates of drug use (NEPTUNE, 2016). While there is a dearth of research on the drug–crime relationship among LGBTQ+ people, there is more on women, who use and supply drugs as well as commit crime (Farrington, 2011; Fleetwood, 2015; Holloway and Bennett, 2007). There are, however, gender differences in the drug–crime relationship, particularly between men and women. Research has shown women use different drugs for different reasons than men, and their pathways into drug use and crime differ from males and drug use seems to play a greater role in women's involvement in crime than is the case for men (Boys et al., 2001; Makkai and Payne, 2003; Melrose, 2004), particularly among sex workers where it is also linked to violence (Johnson, 2004). There is also evidence to suggest female drug users differ in the amount and rate at which they consume certain drugs when compared to men as well as the risk factors underpinning drugs and crime (Farrington, 2011; Holloway and Bennett, 2007; Johnson, 2004). Gender differences in the drug–crime connection is an under-researched area, but overall female arrestees committed different crimes (more income-generating crime, shoplifting, sex work, vehicle theft and supply offences) and were more likely to use economic necessity and poor judgement to explain the link between their drug use and offending than their male counterparts (Holloway and Bennett, 2007). Research has also shown that it is often a combination of factors in a woman's life (not just drug use) that leads to crime, creating a complex web of social problems, and criminalising women just reinforces the abuse and oppression that already characterises their lives (Moe, 2006). It must be acknowledged however that the criminal justice system and its agents also treat women and LGBTQ+ people differently (Heidensohn, 2006; Mogul et al., 2011) and it is widely recognised that drug-related offences disproportionately impact upon and discriminate against women around the world (PRI, 2023), particularly when it comes to the death penalty for drug offences (see Fleetwood and Seal, 2017).

Race/Ethnicity: the statistics on drug use and crime between different ethnic groups is problematic due to the structurally embedded and institutional racism that pervades most countries and their criminal justice systems. The result is that drug-related offences disproportionately impact and discriminate against ethnic minority groups. Whether is it the over-representation of Black males in prison for drug offences in the United Kingdom and United States (Tonry, 2011; Wacquant, 2009), or Aboriginal people in Australia, particularly women (PRI, 2023), inherent inequalities influence/skew the perceived relationship between drugs and crime, particularly when it comes to race/ethnicity and official statistics. In the United States, largely due to drug and crime control initiatives, Black men 'have been five to seven times more likely than White men to be in prison, are much more likely to receive decades-long sentences or life without the possibility of parole, and are much likelier to be on death row' (Tonry, 2011). In the United Kingdom, 'Black people were stopped and searched for drugs at almost nine times the rate of Whites, while Asian people and those in the "mixed" group were stop-searched for drugs at almost three times the rate of Whites' (Shiner et al., 2018). In fact, drug prohibition has been described as akin to the Jim Crow Laws (Alexander, 2010). These racial inequalities and inherent racism around drugs and crime exist around the world and are more indicative of structural inequalities and racial bias than actual reality (see Koram, 2019; Tonry, 2011; Wacquant, 2009). Many of these inequalities actually reflect the historicity of drugs and their prohibition, but all seek to further complicate and distort the actual relationship that exists between drugs and crime. Historically, drugs and their markets have been racialised (e.g. crack epidemic in the United States and United Kingdom) despite most evidence suggesting that these racialised stereotypes/tropes are over-exaggerated and not supported by the evidence (Contreras, 2012; Coomber, 2006; Tonry, 2011 – also see Chapters 2 and 3), particularly since they often ignore social class/socio-economic status.

Social Class: no one talks about social class anymore, but a lot of the research on drugs and crime locates them both in certain neighbourhoods and countries where both play an important/integral role in the communities and lifestyles of people from the lower social classes. Although drug use and supply cut across social class (see Aldridge et al., 2011; Ayres and Ancrum, 2023), research has continually linked drugs and crime to social exclusion and disadvantage, particularly when it comes to looking at more problematic patterns of drug use (Buchanan, 2004; Melrose, 2004; Pearson, 1987, 2001; Seddon, 2006). As Buchanan (2004) argues, 'drug-related crime' cannot be adequately understood without also examining the underpinning issues of poverty and exclusion. In fact, drugs and crime tend to be concentrated in socio-economically deprived areas and neighbourhoods (Pearson, 1987). In this context, drugs and crime can be about surviving, obtaining status and respect, creating a strong street identity, providing structure to people's lives and/or providing economic security as well as the cultural markers of success contemporary consumer society tells us we need (e.g. Range Rover, designer clothes) (Ayres, 2023; Collison, 1996; Hall et al., 2008). As Hammersley (2008:77) says:

> Drugs and crime can bring cash in to social networks and neighbourhoods that have few other economic resources. . . pull the drug dealing from some areas and there would be almost no economy.

Inequality contributes to the unequal distribution of drugs and crime in certain areas among certain groups of people through complex pathways that are influenced by a plethora of factors. Drug prohibition, however, tends to disproportionately target these groups and has been described by Wacquant (2009:61) as criminalisation of the poor that amounts to 'a guerrilla campaign of penal harassment of low-level street dealers and poor consumers' particularly those that use drugs problematically and are socially excluded as a result.

Severity of Drug Use (Problematic/Uncontrolled versus Controlled/Recreational): much of the drug–crime literature and research, particularly that which supports the notion that drug use causes crime, stems from the 1980s heroin epidemic in the United Kingdom. This batch of research established and consolidated that problematic drug users (e.g. those that use heroin and crack) commit crime to fund their habit, convictions increase following the onset of heroin use (Jarvis and Parker, 1989) and the most prolific offenders are usually the most problematic drug users (Bennett and Holloway, 2005a) (see Chapters 3 and 6). This, however, is a minority of both the drug-using population, a minority of the offender population and a minority of the drug-using offender population (see Figure 5.1), illustrating that for the majority of drug users and/or offenders, there is no link between their drug use and criminality. This stands true even for recreational users of heroin (see Shewan and Dalgarno, 2005; Warburton et al., 2005). Even among the minority of people for whom drugs and crime are linked, the relationship is not static and changes over the course of their lives (Simpson, 2003). The majority of recreational drug users control their drug use and never commit crime bar that associated with prohibition, unless they are already criminals and even then, the pathways into drugs and crime is multifaceted and highly individualistic, even when looking at problematic drug use and crime (see Hayhurst et al., 2017).

Therefore, the drug–crime relationship is multifaceted and becomes even more complex when intersectionality is taken into account. For example, the most problematic drug users tend to live in the most deprived and socially excluded communities, be from a minority ethnic group and be poor. The inherent inequalities discussed here and in Chapters 2 and 3 influence and in some instances skew the perceived relationship between drugs and crime, particularly when these identities intersect to create unique modes of discrimination (and privilege) that influence people's experiences with drug use, criminalisation and the criminal justice system. As shown here (see also Chapters 2, 3 and 6), these disparities can also lead to unique vulnerabilities to certain drugs and crimes. As Mogul and colleagues (2011) highlight, 'poor White women, free women of colour, immigrant women, LGBTQ+ peoples, tend to be swept into criminal legal archipelagos for sexual promiscuity, prostitution and crime'. What is clear is that prohibition discriminates along the lines of gender, race/ethnicity and social class, disproportionately impacting on women, ethnic minorities and the poor, which skews the realities of the drug–crime relationship. This has resulted in the drug apartheid (see Taylor et al., 2016 and Chapter 4). Instead, official statistics tend to reflect inherent structural inequalities, the priorities of law enforcement and policy initiatives rather than the reality of drugs and their relationship to crime. Instead, certain drugs and certain populations (e.g. poor, ethnic minorities, women and LGBTQ+ people) have been historically scapegoated and blamed for crime, while alcohol and wider structural issues are largely ignored (Ayres et al., 2024; Taylor et al., 2016). The inequalities evident in drug prohibition and the War on Drugs replicate those evident in capitalism, which have been exacerbated by neoliberalism and consumer capitalism, as drug prohibition alongside treatment and testing all prioritise the exigencies of capitalism. In fact, evidence suggests that anti-drug policies sustain and prioritise the global expansion of capitalism and have been a tremendous source of profit for state–corporate entities and have facilitated global exploitation by the West/Global North of the East/Global South (Ayres, 2020b; Courtwright, 2001; Paley, 2014). Therefore, the focus of this chapter is to critically look at the drug–crime relationship.

The Drug–Crime Relationship

The most obvious, but overly simplistic relationship between drug use and crime is that most drug use is prohibited and their possession, production and supply criminalised. These types of crimes are commonly referred to in the literature as drug offences. In fact, it is important to distinguish between drug offences and drug-related offences, although the two terms are often used interchangeably in the literature.

Drug Offences: refers to the criminalisation of substances classified as having the potential for abuse/misuse and dependence. Drug offences include possession, supply, manufacture/production and allowing your premises to be used for drug use/supply (see Chapter 6).

Drug-Related Offences: the use of drugs is often associated with various crimes, particularly acquisitive crimes and violence (see Chapter 7).

For some substances like cannabis and ecstasy, the only crimes they are linked to are drug offences (e.g. possession and supply) (Hendrickson and Gerstein, 2005; Pedersen and Skardhamar, 2009). Although there is also research to the contrary (de Looze et al., 2015; Niveau and Dang, 2003; Vaughn et al., 2015), there are usually other factors that need to be considered (e.g. co-morbidity, socio-economic context). This should also include the balance of probabilities (e.g. cannabis is the mostly widely used drug, so a significant proportion of criminals use cannabis, however to assume cannabis is linked to their offending would be erroneous), illustrating the underlying causal mechanism(s) of the drug–crime relationship are likely to be more complex and the relationship is often subject to inductive fallacies.

The amount of crime attributable to drug use has been over-exaggerated since much of the research focuses on treatment samples and/or offender populations, which invariably skews the statistics. Scholars have also emphasised the importance of using longitudinal studies over cross-sectional research when examining the relationship between drugs and crime, so temporal ordering can be established (Hayhurst et al., 2017), particularly since for many drug-using offenders, crime precedes drug use, even if they eventually end up committing crime to fund their drug use. Research already differentiates between drug-using offenders who are primarily criminals who use drugs and those who are primarily drug users who commit crime (see Best et al., 2008; Nurco, 1998), a distinction that also influences the relationship between drugs and crime. What is well established is that one is a high-risk indicator of another. Drug use is a key risk factor (predictor) for criminality (Lammers et al., 2014), while delinquency and criminality are seen as risk factors for drug use (Doherty et al., 2008). Although the amount of crime attributable to drug use may have been over-exaggerated and distorted, it does not prevent it from being legitimised in drug policy and strategy.

DRUG POLICIES AND DRUG STRATEGIES

Drug use causing crime has been the mainstay of any UK drug strategy since its inception (Labour and Conservative) (see Chapter 3). As such, it puts problematic drug users at the centre of the strategy since this group are associated with a high proportion of drug-related offences (see Chapter 7). Crime is considered to be one of the harms arising from drugs, particularly from those who use drugs problematically. Drug policy in the United Kingdom has historically been premised on the notion that drug use causes crime, a view which is maintained in the current drug strategy drug strategy for England and Wales called 'From Harm to Hope: A 10-year drugs plan to cut crime and save lives' that is justified 'because drugs cause crime and crime ruins innocent lives', 'drive half of all homicides', 'destroy lives, they shatter families and they plague neighbourhoods around the country, fuelling violence and acquisitive crime' (Home Office, 2021:4–5). The aim of policy is 'in the next three years, we will reduce drug-related offences, death, harm and overall drug use' (Home Office, 2021:7). Although it targets specific drug-related offences (acquisitive, organised gangs (OCGs), firearms, money laundering, violence, human trafficking, slavery and exploitation), it also aims to focus on:

> The vulnerable victims of the vile county lines gangs, dragged into the world of organised crime from as young as seven.
>
> The innocent families whose homes are broken into by addicts seeking to feed their habits, and whose neighbourhoods are blighted by the criminals who supply them.
>
> The small business owner who endures repeated shoplifting and anti-social behaviour on their high street.
>
> The 300,000 heroin and crack addicts in England who, between them, are responsible for nearly half of all burglaries, robberies and other acquisitive crime.
>
> Because drugs cause crime and crime ruins innocent lives. (Home Office 2021:4)

Like the media, official discourse tends to be reductive, over-simplifying the drug–crime relationship into binary opposites that embody good and evil, innocent and guilty. These emotive, simplistic and over-exaggerated statements are taken as fact, and used to legitimise the prohibition of drugs and the draconian penalties/punishments implemented, despite their problematic evidence base. Whether it is long-term imprisonment, the death penalty or the confiscation of passports or driving licences for recreational drug users proposed by the new strategy, some of the harshest penalties/punishments/sanctions are reserved for drugs, their producers, suppliers and users. Drugs not only cause crime, but drug trafficking according to the National Security Strategy and Strategic Defence and Security Review (2015) is a threat to national security. Although these statements are supported by statistics – as statistics equal unequivocal evidence that drug use causes crime – a lot of the statistics come from the criminal justice system and its agents (e.g. the police who implement testing on arrest, which was initially called the NEW-ADAM programme (see the Box below) and was used to monitor patterns/trends around drug use and crime) or drug treatment, which tends to skew the evidence base. Official statistics also reflect recent policy or policing initiatives as much as they reflect drug use/supply and do not account for the inherent structural and systemic disparities and inequalities that pervade the criminal justice system and the application of drug laws (see Chapters 2 and 3).

The New English and Welsh Arrestee Drug Abuse Monitoring (NEW-ADAM)

A programme launched in 1999 ended in 2002 (3 yrs) – each year surveys were conducted in 16 police force areas – face-to-face interviews and testing urine samples. It aimed to assess the prevalence and patterns of drug use among arrestees and explore the links between drug use and criminal behavior. The findings were used to inform drug policy, particularly in targeting drug-related crimes.

In fact, trying to gauge the extent and nature of drugs, let alone their relationship to different crimes, 'is like trying to do a jigsaw with most of the pieces missing' (ISDD, 1995 as cited in Barton, 2011:23). Despite being used extensively in the official discourse, official statistics on both drugs and crime must be treated with caution, due to methodological issues and sampling deficits, but mostly due to their illicit nature, which means both are substantially under-reported, leaving the evidence base piecemeal and patchy.

Despite the problems of accurately gauging/measuring both drugs and crime, the reduction in crime is an outcome measure for success in most drug strategies. Although there is an acknowledgement of the impact wider social issues can have on the drug–crime relationship (unemployment, marginalisation), drug policy remains premised on there being a causal relationship between drugs and crime. The emphasis remains that a reduction in drug use will lead to a reduction in crime.

It is not just drug policy and treatment that perpetuates the relationship between drugs and crime, it is also perpetuated by the media and research, official statistics and popular culture. Drugs and crime have become so inextricably linked that it is taken as fact despite the evidence illustrating the opposite.

THE DRUG–CRIME LINK

The five dominant explanations for the drug–crime relationship are:

1) Drug use causes crime
2) Crime causes drug use
3) Reciprocal relationship

4) Common aetiology
5) Spurious relationship

1. **Drug Use Causes Crime:** is the most common relationship perpetuated by official discourse and indoctrinated as fact. Premised on Goldstein's (1985:5) tripartite framework that originally focused on violence in New York, the relationship can be broken down into three explanations:
   i **Psychopharmacological:** proposes that the effects of intoxication (including disinhibition, cognitive–perceptual distortions, attention deficits, bad judgement and neurochemical changes) cause criminal (especially violent) behaviour.
   ii **Economic Compulsive:** drug users engage in crime (e.g. robbery) to generate money to pay for their drugs and support their drug habit.
   iii **Systemic:** 'refers to the traditionally aggressive patterns of interaction within the system of drug distribution and use', which includes 'disputes over territory between rival drug dealers, robberies of drug dealers'.

Despite being used extensively to explain the relationship in drugs and crime, and being the crux of much government policy/strategy (and briefings), it has been heavily criticised. Stevens (2011b) critiques Goldstein's tripartite framework on the following grounds:

- Over-exaggerated
- Lack of empirical evidence underpinning it
- The focus is murders in New York
- Ignores other explanations (e.g. the role of alcohol was ignored)
- Dubious categorisation
- Uni-directional causal link

Other research that supports the notion that drugs cause crime shows that poly-drug users commit higher rates of crime over longer periods (Newcomb et al., 2001), those with problematic addiction commit higher rates of crime and treatment reduces both drug use and crime (Holloway et al., 2006). Even when we start to look at populations who have admitted that their drug use is linked to their crimes (e.g. drug-using offenders), the link is over-exaggerated. Drug strategy states that heroin and crack users – the most problematic drug users – commit a disproportionate number of drug-related acquisitive crimes (45%), showing that the most prolific offenders tend to also be the most problematic drug users. However, this group of offenders only comprise 13% of the offender population. In fact, contrary to the dominant ideology, the majority of arrestees, although drug users, are not problematic users and report little to no connection between their drug use and offending (Ministry of Justice 2013; UKDPC, 2008) (see Figure 5.1). According to UKDPC (2008), although about 3 in 5 offenders (59%) report drug use of some kind, fewer than a quarter (13%) of these report heroin and crack use. In fact, only 22% of drug-using arrestees reported heroin and crack use, which is even lower when we look at all arrestees (13%). The majority of drug-using offenders have less problematic patterns of drug use – 46% had used but not problematically and 41% had not used in last year, but of these, only 5% committed crime to get drugs and 8% offended while intoxicated (see Figure 5.1).

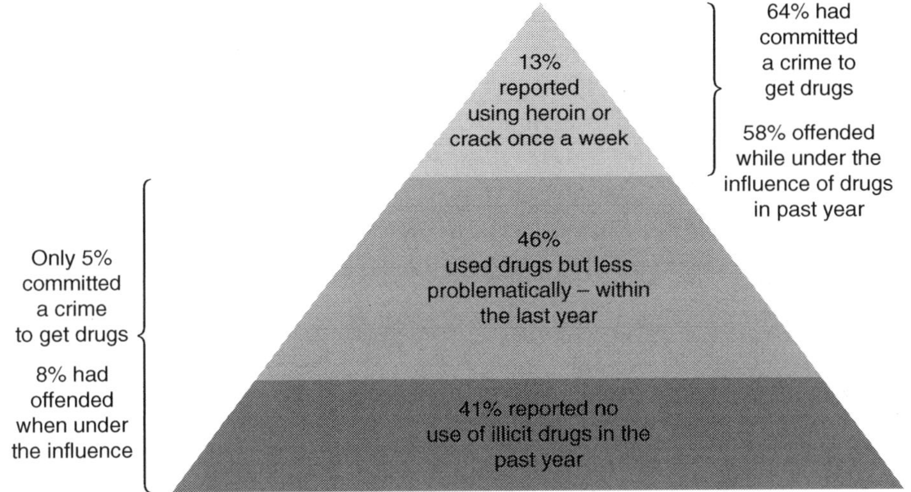

Figure 5.1 UK Drug Policy Commission (UKDCP, 2008)

Therefore, those that commit crime to pay for drugs constitute a minority (a third) of all drug-using offenders, illustrating how the relationship between drugs and crime has been over-exaggerated. Like the general population, a large percentage of offenders use drugs, but they do so unproblematically and there is very little connection between their drug use and offending. Instead, both drug use and crime may be underpinned by another third factor (have a common aetiology).

2. **Crime Causes Drug Use:** is probably one of the least explored areas in research, particularly longitudinal/sequential research that shows crime predates drugs, and overlaps heavily with the reciprocal and common aetiology explanations. Drugs might be used to facilitate a crime, celebrate a crime or provide a means of self-medication for dealing with the consequences of crime (live with what you have done) and/or for coping with prison that may be their punishment for committing crime (Ayres and Treadwell, 2012; Boys et al., 2002; Wright and Decker, 1997). Crime also provides the money to buy drugs (see Bennett and Holloway, 2005a). This explanation is premised on the notion that deviant individuals are more likely than non-deviant individuals to select or drift into social situations, (sub)cultures and lifestyles in which heavy drinking, drug use and crime are condoned, even encouraged particularly in today's consumerist society (Bourgois, 1995; Collison, 1996; Hall et al., 2008; Hobbs, 1995). Therefore, drug use can be seen as an extension of delinquency, criminality and its associated criminal lifestyle; however,

criminality could also as easily be an extension of a drug-using lifestyle, making even this relationship difficult to disentangle and simplify, since both may be a response to a third – common – factor (e.g. socio-economic deprivation, social exclusion and poverty).

3. **Common Aetiology:** both drugs and crime are attributable to a third factor and have a common aetiology often known in the literature as risk factors. It is a robust finding that the more the risk factors a person is exposed to during childhood, the more likely they are to become an offender and/or a drug user. For example, Kaplow and colleagues (2002) found children with two or more risk factors had more than a 50% chance of early-onset drug use compared to children with no risk factors, while Farrington, et al. (2009) found that over 80% of convicted offenders had four or more risk factors before the age of 10. Therefore, research has continually identified a plethora of risk factors (and protective factors) that underpin drug use and crime. The more risk factors a person has, the more likely they are to commit crime and use drugs (Farrington, 1995).

Risk factors often fall into the following categories and are often used in treatment and rehabilitation programmes:

Family: from as early as birth (e.g. Bowlby's 1951 attachment theory) through to parenting and socialisation, adverse experiences in the family can impact childhood development and increase the risk of drug use and criminality in adolescents and adulthood. Crime and drug use runs in families and it can be argued that it can be transmitted intergenerationally (from parent to child) and intragenerationally (from sibling to sibling), although the mechanisms of transmission are unclear (e.g. modelling, social learning or the transmission of other risk factors like harsh parenting) (Bandura, 1977; Farrington, 2011 also see Chapter 1). The risk factors associated with both drug use and crime include poor parental supervision, maltreatment/abuse, parental drug use and/or criminality/imprisonment, coming from a large family, parenting practices and socio-economic circumstances (Farrington, 2011; Nurco et al., 1996). Familial pathways and risk factors into drug use and crime, however, are unclear, particularly since research shows that other factors often mediate these relationships/pathways (e.g. school/education and peers).

Peers: peer group and schooling have been linked with the onset of both drug use and crime for some individuals (Becker, 1963; Farrington, 2011; Fergusson and Horwood, 1999). Antisocial activity and drug use are used by peer groups to demonstrate maturity and status via rebellion, particularly during adolescence (Moffitt, 1993). According to Moffit (1993), deviance, crime and drug use increase ten-fold in adolescence, when most people mature out of these behaviours (Moffitt called this group the adolescent-limited offenders). Moffit (1993) found for the adolescent-limited offenders, criminality was due to antisocial peers and a gap between their biological and social maturity, which meant they were trying to act more adult by being delinquent to establish their independence, whereas life-course persistent offenders were more likely to seek out delinquent peers. While antisocial peers are a risk factor for drug use and crime, prosocial peers act as a protective factor against the initiation of delinquency and drug use (Fallu et al., 2010; Farrington, 2011). Delinquent individuals are often more likely to be rejected by their prosocial peers, which increases the likelihood they will associate with other delinquent drug-using peers who they can relate to. For example, Friday and colleagues (2005) found delinquent children were five times more likely to associate with delinquent peers than non-offenders, while Nurco and colleagues (1994) found that even at age 11, problematic drug users had a strong disposition towards selecting deviant associates. The peer group provides environments where attitudes conducive to delinquency and drug use are shared, alongside techniques and information, as well as drugs themselves (via social supply), which all reinforce drug use and crime (Akers, 2009; Aldridge et al., 2011; Becker, 1963; Farrington, 2011). This mutual influence that occurs between peers is often referred to in the literature as 'peer contagion' or 'deviancy training' (Akers 2009; Dishion and Tipsord, 2011). Thus, drug use and crime are an important part of socialising with peers and conforming to group norms, to the extent that peer groups do not always see their behaviours as antisocial. It is difficult to distinguish between peer influence, group conformity, peer pressure and group offending since research rarely differentiates between them (McGloin and Stickle, 2011). However, the use of more explicit and coercive forms of peer pressure traditionally thought to encourage drug use and offending are largely unsupported, and instead they provide a reference point of acceptable and unacceptable behaviour, social norms, values, information and a safe environment in which to experiment with drugs, be delinquent and develop individual identities (Aldridge et al., 2011; McGloin and Stickle, 2011). Peer influence is thus important in adolescence but wanes in adulthood and can have both short- and long-term effects on an individual's behaviour (Dishion and Tipsord, 2011). Thus, the relationship between peers and their influence on the initiation of drug use and offending is multifaceted and unclear, particularly since it is also affected by a number of other factors (for a review, see Müller and Minger, 2011), which also depends on social context (e.g. neighbourhood, school).

School and Education: school can act as a protective factor against drug use and crime, and having strong bonds to school predicts lower levels of initiating deviant behaviour, including delinquency and drug use (Farrington, 2011; Hawkins et al., 1992; Payne, 2009). Misbehaviour and delinquent behaviour in school predict criminality and drug use (Weerman et al., 2007). School might be where drugs are purchased to use, problem behaviour in school before age 15 is related to problematic drug use (Hser et al., 2007), while attending a high delinquency school is a key risk factor for early onset of offending (before age 20) (Farrington et al., 2009), illustrating the role of school in the initiation of crime and drug use, which is also influenced by:

- Bullying is a predictor of delinquency and drug use, particularly early initiation, (Bender and Lösel, 2011; Bolognii et al., 2007).
- Truanting and exclusion increase the risk of antisocial behaviour and drug use, particularly problematic drug use (Berridge et al., 2001; Fothergill and Ensminger 2006).

- Early school dropout has been attributed to existing drug use and delinquent behaviour (e.g. criminal careers have usually started before being excluded from school) (Berridge et al., 2001).
- Low school achievement is one of the strongest predictors of onset of delinquency, offending and drug use, including problematic use (Farrington, 2011; Fothergill and Ensminger 2006), although the direction of the relationship is contested. Failure to do well at school, however, leads to failure to get a job, lower wages and higher levels of unemployment, which effect crime and drug use in adulthood.

Abuse and Trauma: neglect and mental, physical and sexual abuse are all linked to drug and alcohol abuse as well as mental ill health among women and men (see Chapter 1). Child abuse increases the odds of early onset of antisocial behaviour, serious juvenile delinquency, drug-related arrests in adulthood, being a persistent career criminal and drug use including problematic drug use (Conroy et al., 2009; Farrington, 2011); however, the exact nature of the relationship remains ambiguous and not fully understood, particularly for men (see Chapter 1). In fact, offenders experience higher levels of cumulative childhood trauma and drug use than the general population. In some cases, adults will use drugs and/or commit crime, to alleviate the negative affect and strain associated with the childhood trauma, but evidence also suggests that drugs are often used to cope with the negative emotions induced by the trauma experienced in childhood (Agnew, 2006; Ayres, 2020c; Hammersley, 2011; Ruiz and Strain, 2014). Thus, the relationship between trauma, drugs and crime exists for men and women, particularly for drug-using offenders (Matheson, 2012). It is not just abuse in childhood that increases the risk of drugs and crime in someone's life, abuse in adulthood has also shown to have an effect on both drug use and criminality (see Chapter 1). Trauma is also linked to developing a mental illness later on in life (Everett and Gallop, 2000).

Mental Illness: rates of mental illness are higher among drug-using offenders, especially women, which is linked to both their offending – especially violent offending and sex work – and substance use (Johnson, 2004; McClellan et al., 1997). In fact, mental illness and crime are more prevalent among those that use drugs, particularly among those who use drugs problematically, than in the general population. A recent review of the literature in this area showed that comorbid mental illness and substance use disorders were 20 times higher in prison populations than in the general population and were associated with adverse criminal, social and health outcomes. The review found that around half of those in the prison population with non-affective psychosis or major depression also had a comorbid substance use disorder, which included both alcohol and drug use disorders (Baranyi et al., 2022). Personality disorders are also higher among the prison population than in the general population. Personality disorders are highly prevalent co-morbid conditions among addicted individuals and criminals (Hammersley, 2008). While there is evidence to suggest certain personality disorders (e.g. anti-social personality disorder (ASPD)) predict criminal behaviour (Grella et al., 2003; Kranzler et al., 1997), others do not (Bovasso et al., 2002; Hernandez-Avila et al., 2000). Substance users with ASPD were also more criminally active than substance users without an ASPD diagnosis (Fridell et al., 2006), and although non-ASPD subjects were criminally active, ASPD subjects were more criminally active and more likely to commit multiple types of crimes and be registered for theft or other property crimes (Friddell et al., 2008) (see also Hammersley, 2008).

Individual Factors: there are many individual traits, which have been linked to crime and drug use (e.g. impulsivity, moral reasoning, self-control, mental illness) (see Chapter 1). Establishing causation, however, between individual traits is almost impossible since individuals cannot be isolated from other factors (e.g. environment, family, peer).

Environment and Socio-Economic Circumstances: The socio-economic/ disadvantaged, socially excluded, under-employed and particularly minority women are vulnerable to abuse (physical and sexual), drug use and criminal offending (Luck et al., 2004; Melrose, 2004). As already mentioned, the poorest neighbourhoods have tended to become more rundown, more prone to crime and more cut off from the labour market, particularly since deindustrialisation (think of the mining towns/ villages), and this is often where the drug dealers and more problematic drug users are also concentrated. Therefore, although drugs and crime are often a response to exclusion and disadvantage, once initiated, drugs and crime tend to entrench many of these disadvantages further (Melrose, 2004). This is exacerbated even further since people with fewer resources/support affect the dominance and maintenance of drugs and crime as part of the individual's identity and general lifestyle. For those living in these high-drug and high-crime areas, both drug use and dealing provide them with a lifestyle, focus/purpose and identity, and they become busy/purposeful, an important figure to those in the area (Preble and Casey, 1969). Crime is also often not just a result of drugs and their markets but can also be understood as a response to social and economic exclusion and marginalisation, just like drugs (Bourgois, 1995; Hammersley, 2008; Stevens, 2011a). Drugs and crime are an integral part of many people's lifestyles and necessary for their survival in society and/or just part of their consumerist lifestyle. Drug use and crime are initiated and used by some to cope with the stresses, strains and negative emotions encountered in everyday life (Agnew, 1991, 2001), to achieve status (Collison, 1996), gain respect (Bourgois, 1995) and fulfil/achieve the demands placed on them to succeed in life and for upward mobility (Hall et al., 2008). Although drugs and crime can be seen as a response to strains and negative life events, they are also about hedonism, fun, excitement and thrill seeking (Katz, 1988). They are also about consumerism. In fact, there is a growing body of work in this area linking consumerism to drugs (both recreational and more problematic use) and crime (Ayres, 2019, 2023; Hall et al., 2008; Hayward and Turner, 2019), illustrating that drugs and crime cannot be divorced from the wider socio-political and economic context.

The issue when looking at both drug use and crime being caused by a third factor that underpins both behaviours is also problematic. Although some of the factors discussed are stronger predictors of drugs and/or crime than others, their interconnectedness and mediating influence make it difficult to disentangle the risk factors or their contribution and establish causation (Farrington and Welsh, 2007), particularly when looking at the development of two entwined behaviours like drug use and criminality. Even when it comes to identifying a common aetiology underpinning both drug use and crime, it may still be indicative of a spurious relationship.

4. **Spurious Relationship:** here drugs just 'coexist with other conjunctive factors in the same situation' and have no causal or reciprocal relationship (Bennett and Holloway, 2005a: 91; Chaiken and Chaiken, 1990). Chaiken and Chaiken (1990) found high-rate offenders who commit crime are also like to use many different types of drugs. Therefore, drugs and crime just coexist in some people's lives within a complex set of events and backgrounds. Both behaviours are often just two behaviours in a cluster of other problems/issues in these individuals' lives.
5. **Reciprocal Relationship:** Research has shown that drug use predicts delinquency/crime (Green et al., 2010) and delinquency/crime predicts drug use (Doherty et al., 2008), and the severity of delinquency is linked to the severity of drug use (White et al., 1999), indicating a reciprocal relationship that is stable over time. Once both behaviours have been established in someone's life, they invariably influence each other. For example, as drug use escalates so does crime, although other factors also mediate the relationship between severity of substance use and crime (Lammers et al., 2014).

The five common explanations for the drug–crime relationship, however, can also all be present for one crime type depending on the individual as illustrated in the research examining sex work and drugs (see the Box below). This example shows there is evidence to support the different drug–crime relationships, highlighting the multi-faceted and individualistic nature of this connection and the problems surrounding its simplification into five reductionist discourses. This is also illustrated in the relationship between drugs, organised crime (see the Box on page 135) and terrorism (see the Box on page 136). The evidence supporting all five drug–crime relationships underscores the need for a multifaceted and holistic approach to drug policy rather than relying on overly simplistic reductionist discourses.

The (Complex) Relationship Between Sex Work and Drugs

- The relationship between sex work and drug use is complex and multifaceted. Both sex work and drug use are often interconnected due to various social, economic and psychological factors. For example, sex workers from minority ethnic groups who use drugs often face intensified discrimination and policing compared to their White counterparts, which leads to higher rates of arrest and incarceration.
- For some, sex work leads to drug use (crime leads to drugs), while for others, pre-existing drug use leads to sex work (drug use leads to crime) indicating a bi-directional and often mutually reinforcing relationship, which traps individuals in sex work and drug use cycles (Cusick and Hickman, 2005).

- According to Melrose (2009:84), however, it is important to distinguish between 'sex-working drug users' and 'drug-using sex workers': '"sex-working drug users" may be, for instance, sex workers who are also recreational drug users, "drug-using sex workers" may be those individuals for whom drug usage has become problematic and/or those who engage in sex work specifically to fund their drug use'.
- The majority of street sex workers report working to fund their problematic drug use/addiction (economic compulsive crime), particularly when addiction creates a pressing financial need. This is particularly true among street sex workers who are also problematic drug users. Drugs may also be used as a form of currency within the sex work economy (e.g. sex workers may be paid in drugs rather than money) (Cusick et al., 2003; Maher and Daly, 1996).
- Coping: many sex workers use drugs as a way to cope with the emotional and physical demands of their work, including dealing with trauma, stigma, abuse and violence as a form of self-medication, particularly since they also have a high prevalence of mental health issues. Research has also identified many of these factors as leading to both drug use and/or sex work independently (a third factor).
- The criminalisation of both sex work and drug use also impacts the relationship and can lead to stigma, shame, increased vulnerability to violence, exploitation and health risks, as individuals may avoid the police and health services to evade arrest. Female sex workers who use drugs often face compounded stigmas. Stigma can deter individuals from seeking medical help, further exacerbating health issues like substance use.

(Read Cusick and Hickman, 2005; Cusick et al., 2003; Maher and Daly, 1996; Melrose, 2009, for more information)

Drugs and Different Crimes

Drugs (use and supply) have been linked to an array of different crimes that vary in severity, from low-level disorder and acquisitive crimes to more serious organised crime and violence, including terrorism and homicide. The relationship is, however, complicated and often mediated by a variety of different factors as illustrated by the example below that focuses on homicide (see the Box below).

Drugs and Crime: Homicide

- The new drug strategy states that drugs 'drive half of all homicides' as statistics show that drug-related homicides have increased over the last decade, from 39% in 2010 to 48% in 2020; this increase reflects wider tends in all homicides (ONS, 2021). More recently, 'between April 2018 and March 2023, 838 of 3,148 cases in the Home Office Homicide Index met the criteria for a systemic, economic

(Continued)

(Continued)

compulsive, and/or psychopharmacological link to drugs. This represents 27% of all homicides' (ONS, 2024b:5). These are linked to being intoxicated at the time of the homicide (psychopharmacologically driven) and drug dealing (systemic violence), particularly in relation to county lines (see Chapter 8).

- According to the Homicide Index, almost a third (30%) of homicide victims and 43% of suspects were known to be drug users, and about a quarter (26%) of suspects and 15% of victims were known to be drug dealers. At the time of the homicide, a third (33%) of homicide victims were under the influence of alcohol (19%) and/or illicit drugs (7%) or both (7%), while a third (31%) of suspects were under the influence of alcohol (16%) and/or illicit drugs (4%) or both (10%). This proportion was higher among male victims and perpetrators than female victims and perpetrators (ONS, 2021). Statistics indicate once again that alcohol played more of a contributory role than drugs.
- The relationship between drugs and homicide, however, is often multifaceted as research suggests many of those involved already had a history of violence, mental health service contact and personality disorders, patterns replicated in the statistics in knife crime in England and Wales (e.g. 56% who carried out knife possession offences had special educational needs, 83% were persistently absent from school and 21% had been permanently excluded) (Ministry of Justice, 2018). The majority of homicide victims were White (69%), while 16% were Black and 8% were Asian. Although the majority of homicide victims were White, Black people had higher rates of victimisation, which were around six times higher for Black victims than White victims and almost four times higher than victims of other ethnicities (ONS, 2022d).
- There are also strong links between mental ill health and homicide, although official records are split over sources and different categories (Appleby et al., 2022; ONS, 2022). Across the United Kingdom, 11% of people convicted of homicide were mental health patients under mental health care (Appleby et al., 2022), further complicating the relationship between drugs and the crime of homicide.

Drugs have also been linked to organised crime, which is often used to provide a clear illustration of the drug–crime relationship by demonstrating how the illicit drug trade fosters a wide array of criminal activities (e.g. violence/homicide, human trafficking, arms trafficking, money laundering), particularly in official discourse. Rarely is the impact drug prohibition and criminalisation have on the relationship between OCG and drugs considered by those in power; instead, drugs and OCGs are blamed for fuelling crime, violence and an array of other problems plaguing the society. The omission of states, politicians and large organisations (e.g. banks like HSBC) that partake in very similar activities to OCGs are largely ignored, even when their misconduct is criminal and on par with the OCGs (e.g. see HSBC laundering drug money in Chapter 9). This is particularly problematic since it is estimated that some 70% of illicit OCG profits are likely to have been laundered through the legitimate financial system (UNODC, 2011), illustrating how the distinction between legitimate state actors and organisations and OCGs is blurred and often interconnected. In fact, government legislation – the

1914 Harrison Narcotics Tax Act – set the stage for the involvement of OCGs in drug trafficking primarily by criminalising certain substances and creating a black market for drugs, which is illustrated in the prohibition era in the United States that led to the rise of organised crime syndicates in the illegal alcohol trade (see Chapter 2). This set a precedent for organised crime involvement in illegal markets, including drugs, that was firmly established with the emergence of powerful drug cartels, which cemented the role of OCGs in the drug trade and eventually led to OCGs being linked to terrorists creating the term narcoterrorism (see the Box on page 136). This framing, however, according to Dawn Paley (2014) posits that the presence of organised crime and the threat of terrorism are used as pretexts to justify military interventions and state violence in the war on drugs, which coincide with neoliberal economic policies that benefit multinational corporations, while diverting attention away from the structural issues and economic policies that contribute to the drug trade, organised crime and terrorism to create the crime–terror continuum (see the Box below). This is part of what Paley (2014) refers to as 'Drug War Capitalism.'

Crime–Terror Continuum

The crime–terror continuum (Makarenko, 2004) is a conceptual framework that illustrates the fluid and often overlapping relationship between organised crime and terrorism. It highlights how these two entities can evolve, cooperate or transform into one another under certain conditions. Increasingly there has been a blurring between terrorism and organised crime. Terrorist groups often engage in drug trafficking to finance their operations (e.g. Taliban in Afghanistan) and OCGs might adopt terrorist tactics for political goals; they may also share resources, infrastructure and networks to enhance their operational capabilities. Both entities also participate in human trafficking, arms smuggling and the trade in counterfeit goods to raise funds.

Organised Crime Groups

- Transnational organised crime is estimated to generate $870 billion a year (UNODC, 2011), although it is difficult to know how many OCGs operate globally or even nationally as these are largely based on (gu)estimates (e.g. the National Crime Agency was aware of 4,600 OCGS operating in the United Kingdom in 2018) as very little is known about OCGs' role in drugs due to a dearth of research in this area (see Chapter 9).
- The link between OCGs and drugs is largely attributable to prohibition that has created an illegal market that moved underground. Most OCGs are now transnational, meaning that their criminality is of an international nature with more than one country involved.

(Continued)

(Continued)

- OCGs are involved in drugs to make money and seek maximum profit for minimum risk from trading in highly profitable commodities, including drug trafficking, smuggling of migrants, human trafficking, money laundering, trafficking in firearms, counterfeit goods, wildlife trafficking and cybercrime. Out of all of these, drug trafficking is the most lucrative with an estimated annual value of $320 billion (UNODC, 2011).
- It is contested how organised OCGs are, as it varies significantly as some are highly structured (e.g. cartels, Mafia-type organisations), while others are more fluid and disorganised (e.g. street gangs) (Hobbs, 1995). The activities of criminal networks also vary in their scale, sophistication and success.
- OCGs have recently been linked to county lines drug trafficking in the United Kingdom (see Chapter 9).

Narcoterrorism

- The term narcoterrorism gained prominence in the 1980s and 1990s, with increased recognition of the intersection between drug trafficking and terrorism (see Chapter 2).
- Prior to 9/11, which changed the face of terrorism, powerful drug cartels (e.g. Medellín and Cali Cartels), which were involved in violent conflict and terrorism, used their profits to fund violent operations against the state and rival groups. While some OCGs might be considered terrorist groups, this is not always consistently applied. The FARC and Shining Path guerrilla movements in South America both funded their activities through cocaine production and trafficking and are the forerunners of narcoterrorism.
- After 9/11, the United States and the United Kingdom began to more explicitly connect drug trafficking to terrorism, particularly the Taliban's involvement in the opium trade, which was used to finance their insurgency against the US and NATO forces.
- The connection between drugs and terrorism continues to evolve, but it is often difficult to differentiate OCGS from terrorist groups, particularly as both suffer from definitional issues, and a dearth of evidence, since research on terrorist organisations, let alone their connection to drugs, is minuscule.
- Narcoterrorism has been described as a political myth that has driven both American and international drug and counter-terrorism policies, leading to a focus on militarisation and law enforcement rather than addressing the root causes (e.g. poverty, lack of opportunity and political instability) (see Miller and Damask, 1996).

CONCLUSION

The relationship between drugs and crime is multifaceted and largely ignores the socio-economic and political – structural – conditions that foster both drug use and/or supply and crime. For example, people who commit crime to pay for drugs probably commit crime to pay for anything due to financial restrictions/shortages, an argument that applies equally to drug trafficking, organised crime and terrorism. Drugs are only a major driver of crime because official discourse frames it that way and ignores the wider structural issues that may lead to both, which is why this chapter focused on drugs and crime having a common aetiology. Therefore, to fully comprehend the drug–crime relationship, it needs to be understood in the broader context of criminalisation that examines the interplay between drug policies, social control mechanisms, economic conditions, political climate and cultural context. Instead connecting drugs to crime, especially transnational crimes like terrorism and organised crime, justifies prohibition via military interventions and state violence, while diverting attention away from the structural root causes (e.g. inequality, poverty). These structural factors have also played a part in which drugs are criminalised, shaping prohibition and determining how drug offences are policed and proceeded against via the criminal justice system, which is the focus of the next chapter.

SUMMARY

- **Drug use is higher among people who commit crime (drug-using offenders).**
- **The drug–crime relationship is over-exaggerated.**
- **For the majority of drug users and criminals, there is no link between their drug use and criminality bar that associated with prohibition.**
- **Research and official statistics skew the drug–crime relationship by focusing on vulnerable/problematic groups of people (e.g. offenders, homeless, treatment samples).**
- **Drug policy and drug strategy are historically premised on the notion that drug use causes crime, which is maintained in the current strategy/policy.**
- **Drugs and crime are influenced by a variety of different factors that further complicate people's pathways into drugs and crime.**
- **The drug–crime relationship is influenced by gender, race/ethnicity and class/socio-economic circumstances.**
- **Even among the minority of people for whom drugs and crime are linked, the relationship is not static and changes over the course of their lives.**
- **It is impossible to establish a causal connection between drug use and crime, despite it being legitimised in drug policy/strategy.**

Here are some points and questions for you to consider after reading this chapter:

1) Summarise the factors that contribute to the relationship between drug use and crime being over-exaggerated.

(Continued)

(Continued)

2) Why does drug policy/strategy perpetuate the notion that drug use causes crime?
3) Which theories in Chapter 1 can be applied to the relationships between drugs and crime discussed in this chapter?

Here are some useful resources for those wanting to further explore the issues raised in this chapter:

- Hammersley, R. (2008) *Drugs and Crime*. Cambridge: Polity.
  This book critically examines and unpicks the complex relationship between drug use and crime, challenging simplistic assumptions that drugs inevitably lead to criminal behaviour.
- Bennett, T. and Holloway, K. (2007) *Drug-Crime Connections*. Cambridge: CUP.
  Drawing on empirical research, this book discusses the connection between drug use and criminal activity, providing an in-depth analysis of how these two behaviours are interrelated.
- Stevens, A. (2011a) *Drugs, Crime and Public Health*. London: Routledge.
  This seminal book takes a critical public health approach to understanding the relationship between drugs and crime, arguing that both should be addressed through health-based interventions rather than solely through the criminal justice system.

6
DRUG OFFENCES

Overview

This chapter aims to provide you with:

- An overview of drug possession and supply offences.
- An insight into the policing of drug offences on the international and domestic level.
- An analysis of the use of stop and search in England and Wales.
- An analysis of the sentencing of drug offences in England and Wales.

You will be introduced to the key terms:

- Drug supply
- Drug possession
- Stop and search
- Sentencing

INTRODUCTION

In previous chapters, we have established that drug prohibition criminalises the possession and supply of illegal substances and explored the often-complex nature of the relationship between drugs and crime. In this chapter, we investigate the mechanisms of drug prohibition, exploring how drug laws are imposed/implemented and how drug supply and possession offences are policed and proceeded against via the criminal justice system. We discuss these issues with two key questions in mind: What are their outcomes? What are their wider ramifications?

DRUG OFFENCES

Here, we focus on what Chapter 5 refers to as 'drug offences'. On a domestic level, this translates as infractions of the United Kingdom's 1971 Misuse of Drugs Act (MDA), which stipulates that the importation/exportation, production/supply and possession of those controlled substances listed in the Act constitutes a criminal offence. Before we embark on our analysis of these offences, however, it is important to set a contextual scene.

Drug offences represent around 3% of police-recorded crime in England and Wales (ONS, 2023c). We know that these statistics are not an accurate reflection of overall drug offences, as the Crime Survey for England and Wales reports much higher rates of drug use than are reflected in the criminal justice system's data on drug offences. We also know that as a category, drug offences fluctuate in number, determined in large part by their (de)prioritisation by the police. Figure 6.1 illustrates how rates of police-recorded drug offences in England and Wales have witnessed considerable change over the past 20 years.

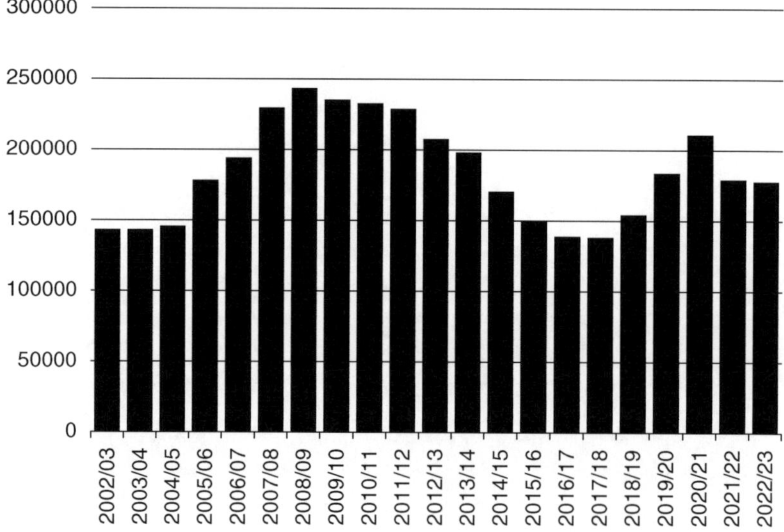

Figure 6.1 Number of Recorded Drug Offences in England and Wales From 2002/03 to 2022/23

Source: Adapted from ONS (2024).

The drug offence data in Figure 6.1 comprises two different categories: drug trafficking offences (which incorporates drug importation, production and supply) and drug possession offences. The bulk of these offences fall into the latter category and within this, the vast majority are for the possession of cannabis. In 2022/23, for example, there were a total of 179,539 drug offences, of which 24% were for trafficking and 76% for possession, with three quarters of these possession offences relating to cannabis (ONS, 2024a). Whilst these figures are perhaps unsurprising – as drug users outnumber drug suppliers and cannabis is the most widely used illegal drug – they illustrate how the criminal justice system, in volume at least, primarily criminalises those who possess cannabis rather than supply illegal drugs. Referring to the variations in overall drug offences highlighted in Figure 6.1, when these are broken down into the different offence types (see Table 6.1), including the separation of possession offences for cannabis and all other drugs, we see that cannabis possession offences largely determine the level of this fluctuation. That said, drug trafficking offences have recently begun to increase in both number and as an overall percent of all drug offences, a development linked to the increased attention and resources being employed to police county lines drug operations (see below). Yet most recorded drug offences continue to be for possession, with those relating to cannabis consistently making up the bulk of these.

As Table 6.1 illustrates, alongside offences of possession and supply, there exists a third category of 'other drug offences'. These includes offences related to permitting the use of premises for the supply or production of a drug. The rates of these offences, however, are comparatively rare compared to those of possession and supply, for example, there were only 756 of these recorded in 2022/23.

It should be noted that there are some additional drug offences that fall outside the remit of the MDA. Firstly, there are those which relate to the 2016 Psychoactive Substances Act (PSA). The PSA, a response to concern around the availability and outcomes of so-called Novel Psychoactive Substances (NPS), bans the production, distribution, sale and supply of psychoactive substances for human consumption with a maximum penalty of seven years' imprisonment. Possession of psychoactive substances is not an offence, unless this takes place in a custodial institution – a direct response to the apparent prevalence of NPS use (especially the synthetic cannabinoid referred to as 'spice') by prisoners (see Chapter 8). Again, however, recorded offences under the PSA are relatively rare. The initial period of the new laws being implemented, whereby 'head' shops which had legally sold NPS could no longer do so, saw a peak in convictions, yet these soon became relatively sparse – with approximately 110 individuals sentenced in 2018 (Home Office, 2018; Sentencing Council, 2019). Interestingly, 25% of recorded PSA offences in England, Wales and Northern Ireland are for possession in a custodial institution with mandatory drug testing data showing that NPS is more prevalent in prisons than all other drugs combined (Home Office, 2018) – an issue we return to and unpack in Chapters 8 and 11.

Table 6.1 Drug Offences by Offence Category – Bi-annual From 2002/03 to 2022/23

	2002/03	2004/05	2006/07	2008/09	2010/11	2012/13	2014/15	2016/17	2018/19	2020/21	2022/23
Total drug offences	143,320	145,837	194,233	243,536	232,922	208,003	170,689	139,184	154,415	211,097	179,539
Trafficking offence	22,435	24,190	26,550	29,885	32,336	29,746	27,368	25,933	30,478	42,901	43,868
Possession offence	119,896	121,647	167,683	213,651	200,586	178,257	143,321	113,251	123,937	168,196	135,671
Of which cannabis	X	88,263	130,395	167,950	160,733	142,627	110,297	84,729	91,910	134,513	101,761
Other drug offences	989	781	680	1,123	1,142	1,034	779	1,084	806	1,025	756

Source: Adapted from ONS (2024) – Note that offences recorded by Greater Manchester Police were omitted for the years 2018/19 to 2020/2.

Secondly, there is the offence of drug driving, which became law in 2015 under the guise of the 1998 Road Traffic Act. This makes it an offence 'to drive, attempt to drive, or be in charge of a motor vehicle with a concentration of a specified controlled drug in the body above the specified limit' – with limits for illegal drugs 'set in line with a zero-tolerance approach but ruling out accidental exposure' (Sentencing Council, 2023:1). It also makes it illegal to drive with over a specified limit of legal (prescription) drugs in your body. Police can investigate the presence of illegal drugs by a roadside drug test (for cannabis and cocaine) and if arrested, assert the limits of any of the 17 drugs included in this offence, by a blood test at the police station. A maximum penalty of an unlimited fine and six months custody, alongside a mandatory licence disqualification, is applicable to those caught driving or attempting to drive. Recorded drug driving offences are increasing year on year and therefore becoming more prevalent with 12,391 convictions in 2019 (Webster, 2021), indicating that this is an important trend to consider in relation to the future of drugs and crime scholarship, policy and practice.

Despite it being imperative to have an awareness and understanding of these additional drug offences, when we consider issues of drugs and crime, they remain, statistically speaking, much less widespread than those infractions of the MDA, which make up the bulk of drug offences. Here then, we turn our attention to these – looking firstly at drug supply before considering drug possession offences.

DRUG SUPPLY

Over the past half century, the UK economy has changed from one centred on production and manufacturing to one increasingly concentrated on service provision. Resultantly, our homes are littered with goods that have familiar stamps, such as 'Made in China'. The United Kingdom, as a set of islands, represents the final destination for these items, which are produced, transported and dispensed via an orchestrated web of organisations, logistical mediums and actors. In the same way, most illegal drugs consumed by UK citizens are, with the exemption of cannabis in recent years, imported. Here we see established traders and indeed trade routes import cocaine from South America, heroin from Asia and ecstasy from Europe to meet the demands of the UK drug consumer, all of which are coordinated through a multiplicity of countries and people. Simultaneously, attempts to identify, intercept and confiscate this contraband whilst apprehending those involved are undertaken by a similarly complex web of international and domestic organisations, working in partnership to stop the production, transit and distribution of these substances and the profits emanating from them. In Chapter 9, we work through the diversity of those involved in the supply of illegal drugs, but for the purposes of this chapter, we focus on how these substances are policed, in their widest sense, both before they arrive in the United Kingdom and domestically when such actions inevitably fail to stem their supply.

Here then, we provide a critical overview of efforts to police drug offences on firstly the international stage and secondly the domestic stage. Whilst these efforts are in essence a futile undertaking – as history shows that every type of illegal drug is available to those who wish to seek it out – this represents a pivotal, and indeed symbolic mechanism that sits on the front line of the war on drugs, incorporating political, economic and military action.

THE INTERNATIONAL STAGE

In 2015, Netflix aired the first season of the series 'Narcos', which focuses on the 1980s cocaine trade in Colombia and some of the infamous drug suppliers associated with this. In doing so, they showcase not only how the drug trade is synonymous with certain areas and people but also how the language of drug trafficking has entered mainstream discourse. Whilst legitimate business has Jeff Bezos, Elon Musk and Bill Gates, the drugs trade has Pablo Escobar, Frank Lucas and Joaquín Guzmán. Whilst Amazon, Tesla and Microsoft have Chief Executive Officers overseeing their operations, the illegal narcotics trade has drug lords, kingpins and barons coordinating their efforts (these examples frame drug trafficking as being dominated by men but see Fleetwood (2014) and Chapter 9 for a critique of this). Whilst largescale companies are known as global corporations, those organisations which facilitate the global cocaine trade are referred and revered as cartels or more recently 'super cartels'. And whilst those states in which legitimate businesses thrive are models of consumer capitalist society, those jurisdictions where the illicit drug trade is so apparent are construed as narco-states where narco-politics and indeed narco-terrorism prevail.

The language of the illicit drug trade indicates that whilst it has equivalence in the legitimate business world, it represents a separate entity, and indeed, the highest echelons of the trade referred to within such language, whereby illegal substances are produced and distributed on a wholesale level, were a key catalyst for the war on drugs. Various writers (Brownstein, 2013; Hari, 2015; Pryce, 2012) explain the reasoning for why the war on drugs emerged, when it did and what its motivations and purposes were. Here, however, our focus is clearly upon drugs and crime and how efforts to enforce drug prohibition were and are primarily centred upon eradicating the drug trade at source since on the most simplistic level, if a product is not available, then people cannot use it – a logic that applies to recent developments to stop the sale of flavoured cigarettes or the use of single-use plastics. This means that even though consumer demand for such products may be ongoing in destination countries, there is a global effort to enforce those regulations set out in the 1961 United Nation Single Convention on Narcotic Drugs (see Chapter 4). On the surface, this represents an easier strategy than persuading users not to use drugs – if for example we take fast food as a key cause of obesity, instead of attempting to prompt cultural change across multiple nations by encouraging people not to eat it, it would appear simpler to remove it from these societies, leaving people with no choice but to move on to apparently healthier alternatives. This, however, becomes much more difficult when that product is illegal – and even more so when it is largely imported from developing to developed countries, with the trade playing a crucial role in the former's economic stability, meaning that organised crime groups (OCGs) often have powerful political influence. Hence, those states seeking to eradicate the illegal drugs trade – which have been predominantly from the Global North, led by the United States – have utilised a variety of techniques to enforce prohibition and the criminalisation of those involved in drug markets by manipulating the domestic affairs of countries in the Global South where illegal drugs, particularly heroin and cocaine, disproportionately originate (Bourgois, 2018).

The US government has attempted to do this in several ways within the regions of South and Central America, where most illicit drugs transited into the United States originate. It has better-resourced governments in these countries – in the form of additional funding, the training of law enforcement professionals and the secondment of individuals to share knowledge and expertise – in a bid to eradicate the supply of, in particular, cocaine. Such policies have also seen the encouragement of proactive measures to wage war on the drugs trade, such as crop eradication, which targets illicit growing operations using airborne chemicals. Whilst such support has been welcomed by certain countries, others have been more resistant to such outside influence/pressure. This has led to financial sanctions being applied to certain states, leading to the prohibition of US citizens/businesses from engaging in transactions with organisations from such countries. Alongside these overt strategies, more clandestine operations have involved the US Central Intelligence Agency in 'many dubious drug related alliances in the name of national security' (Bewley-Taylor, 2001:167), which some have described as a process of 'narcocolonialism' (Villar, 2007).

Yet the emergence and indeed continued application of these various strategies have failed to stem the supply of illegal drugs. Whilst such measures may therefore negate the flow of drugs from within specific states, this vacuum is quickly filled by others – one only has to consider the cocaine trade in South America to see how a reduction in production in Colombia in the 2000s and 2010s was accompanied by increased productivity in Peru and the Plurinational State of Bolivia, ultimately leading to record levels of cocaine manufacturing (UNODC, 2022b). It also fails to address the vacuum prompted by interruption to what has become an essential – and often coerced – labour market within certain countries, meaning that when efforts are made to abolish crops, for example, this fails to take account of the limited alternatives to push people away from the trade as well as the pressures placed upon them to continue. Finally, this approach frames the drug problem as being confined to 'uncivilised' societies where illegal networks prevail – yet this again sees the drug trade occurring in a vacuum – as for every drug trafficker making money from illicit endeavours, there exists a legitimate enterprise that can launder and therefore legitimise their profits.

As Ayres (2023) highlights, in some countries, the illicit drug trade surpasses the size of the legitimate economy, while the infiltration of illicit drug profits into the legitimate economy is so widespread that it is difficult to tell where the boundaries lie, let alone unravel them. This is intensified by those legitimate people and businesses who are also involved in the illicit drug trade, such as lawyers, accountants and bankers.

A good example being HSBC Bank, which in 2012 was fined $881 million for laundering drug cartel money but never indicted. Instead, HSBC agreed to be observed by a court-appointed watchdog and instructed to pay a $1.92 billion settlement. Such cases demonstrate how those legal actors and businesses involved in the illicit drug trade avoid criminalisation and are instead – as is the case with most corporate criminality – regulated and fined.

Resultantly, outside of attempting to persuade or interfere with those states associated with the production of illegal drugs' domestic affairs, there has been an international effort to develop intelligence and the policing of those involved in the narcotic trade and indeed their profits, across the globe. This sees transnational policing organisations such as Interpol working alongside national military personal as well as those domestic organisations leading on these matters (e.g. the Serious Organised Crime Agency in the United Kingdom). Most of this work centres upon known OCGs operating across the globe – many of whom are involved in criminal activities that traverse illegal drugs, weapons and human trafficking – with the profits accrued by some said to fund terrorism (hence the phrase 'narcoterrorism' – see Björnehed, 2004). We consider the diversity of actors involved in OCGs, as well as how trade routes are becoming increasingly blurred due to online crypto markets in Chapter 9.

The efficacy of these combined strategies, however, is negligible. The United Nations Office on Drugs and Crime's World Drug Report 2022 identifies the number of people using drugs worldwide has increased by 26% over the last decade, indicating that demand for illegal substances is greater than ever and that this is being matched by record highs in drug manufacturing. For example, the production of cocaine is said to have more than doubled since 2014 (UNODC, 2022b). Whilst seizures of these drugs by various authorities may also be increasing, the fact remains that attempts to eradicate drug production and intercept those drugs which are in transit have and are failing to stem their availability in consumer countries.

The last line of external defence against the international drug trade for England and Wales is the UK Border Force. Despite investing considerable resources into disrupting global drug supply, illegal substances still reach the UK shores in considerable quantities. Notwithstanding their best efforts, however, the Border Force and their partners only manage to stop a small proportion of drugs from entering England and Wales – they are certainly unable to fulfil the UK government's wish of securing the border with 'a ring of steel to stop drugs entering the UK' (Home Office, 2021:7). This is illustrated by Pudney and colleagues (2006) who estimate that approximately 12% of the heroin and 9% of the cocaine which forms the UK drug market are seized by the authorities, meaning that most illegal substances bound for England and Wales successfully arrive at their destination.

THE DOMESTIC STAGE

The scale and scope of drug supply in the United Kingdom are both varied and complex. At one end, there are large-scale importers – often part of wider criminal networks – who traffic considerable quantities of illegal drugs into the United Kingdom (and indeed other international sites popular with British holidaymakers such as Ibiza) whose distribution is then cascaded down through various actors until they are sold to the end users themselves. This is a process which involves ever smaller quantities yet increased numbers of people as we move down the supply chain. The involvement of different people is also markedly different – some will simply drive a package from one location to another, some will only have possession of a drug for a short amount of time, some will supply the drug for profit, others for respect, some will sell the drug to fund their own use, others to sort out their friends. This makes summarising the domestic drug trade difficult and the policing of it even more so.

The number of drug seizures in England and Wales in 2021 was numerically dominated by the Police rather than the Border Force. Whereas 89% of seizures were made by the former (198,361), just 11% (24,745) were made by the later. The Border Force, however, are responsible for the seizure of much greater quantities of drugs due to the scale of their operations. For example, in terms of Class A drugs, the Border Force apprehended 85% of the total quantity of cocaine seized, 92% of heroin and 73% of ecstasy in 2021 (Home Office, 2022a). Yet the amount of illegal drugs seized is well below the level required to have an impact on consumption rates, as enforcement agencies are only removing a 'tiny fraction' (McKeganey, 2011:78) of those drugs available on the streets of the United Kingdom.

The main focus of domestic enforcement activities has centred upon those involved in the organised end of the drugs trade although targeted policing operations are often determined by the resources available and whether the policing of drugs is made a priority. So, for example, in recent years, domestic cannabis cultivation in the United Kingdom has attracted comparatively little attention from the authorities than those distribution networks referred to as county lines. A key reason being that the political climate surrounding county lines has meant that greater funding has been made available by central government due to how these networks sell drugs as well as how they are said to simultaneously exploit vulnerable (young) people (Home Office, 2021). For instance, this saw £3.6 million spent in 2018 on a new National County Lines Coordination Centre, which brought agencies together to develop national intelligence and provide oversight on resultant activities. This continues a historical trend whereby the focus of policing is drawn to apparently new or emerging drug market phenomena that are construed as a threat (Ayres and Taylor, 2023). As such county lines has been framed as a 'new' problem requiring greater attention and more proactive policing. It is, however, questionable whether this should be understood as an emerging episode (see Chapter 11) or more accurately as a predictable evolution of drug markets, which sees recognisable trends (such as exploitation, the expansion of drug networks, etc.) centre around different distribution methods (in this case mobile phones and the cuckooing of residential homes).

The framing of this phenomenon as exploitative also requires critical thought – whilst county lines undoubtedly involve individuals who are coerced into participating, for others, the drug market represents a rare opportunity to realise ambition within the confines of their socio-economic positioning (see Chapter 9). Spicer (2021) has highlighted how operations such as county lines may well exploit people – but also how some of those involved make an active choice to engage in such networks – as they represent (whether real or imaginary) a way of illegitimately attaining the cultural goals of money and status that may seem otherwise unobtainable through legitimate means (Merton, 1938). As such, there is a blurring between choice and coercion and subsequently of understanding these actors as victims or perpetrators. In one sense, this is unproblematic as all those concerned are committing drug offences and are therefore liable to arrest and punishment. Yet this becomes problematic when we see those involved as being exploited, through illusory promises, threats of violence or debt bondage. Most often than not it is the lower echelons of drug networks that are the most visible or liable to arouse suspicion and attention from the authorities, people who are simultaneously more likely to have been coerced into these illicit activities – for example, female drug mules who transit illegal substances (Fleetwood, 2014). Yet by arresting such people and criminalising them, we risk victimising them twice, which questions the utility of targeting these lower-end drug market actors.

These drug market blurred lines are further evident when it comes to those who supply drugs on a localised level. Among groups of friends, such as those who collectively visit clubs or festivals, it is common for one individual to order and collect the drugs they intend to take – the benefits being that buying in bulk can make the drugs cheaper, everyone within the group uses the same drugs and therefore hits the same high and it reduces the number and risks associated with criminal transactions. This process of 'social supply' or 'minimally commercial supply' (Coomber and Moyle, 2014) sees user–dealers (some of which may have a dependency on substances) as being distinct from those suppliers motivated by financial gain with many of those involved said to be motivated by a desire to help out friends whilst minimising the risks posed by engaging with the illegal drug market (Taylor et al., 2020). This category of drug supply is notably absent within the UK government's current drug strategy 'From Harm to Hope' (Home Office, 2021), unlike county lines, which is mentioned no fewer than 35 times in its 67 pages. Indeed, this prioritisation of disrupting county lines appears to have stimulated the increase in the overall number of recorded drug trafficking offences that is apparent in Figure 6.1. In turn, this has led to a growth in the number of offences prosecuted within the criminal justice system, with the majority of those convicted sentenced to imprisonment. In 2021, for example, the outcomes for those convicted of trafficking saw 57% result in an immediate custodial sentence, 28% receive a suspended custodial sentence, 10% a community sentence and 5% in other outcomes (Ministry of Justice, 2022b).

Resultantly, we have seen an increase in the overall numbers incarcerated for drug offences with minority ethnic groups more likely to receive an immediate custodial sentence for drug supply compared to White people (Sentencing Council, 2021). In 2022, approximately 14,500 individuals were in custody in England and Wales for drug offences. This comprises approximately 16% of the sentenced prison population, 24% of the untried prison population and 34% of the convicted unsentenced population (Ministry of Justice 2022c). Previous research has indicated that 88% of those sent to prison for drug offences were guilty of supply offences with 71% involving Class A drugs, 28% Class B and 1% Class C (Cuthbertson, 2017). It is also important to note that the average length of custodial sentences for those found guilty of drug trafficking is also increasing, moving from 32.5 months in 2012 to 43.6 months in 2020 (Allen and Tunnicliffe, 2021).

Clearly, therefore, the policing of drugs and indeed the processing of drug supply offences constitutes a significant element of domestic criminal justice activities. Whilst a body of people are prosecuted for such offences, however, policing efforts and resultant punishments fail to have a considerable impact on the availability and distribution of illegal drugs. McKeganey (2011:79) notes in relation to Scotland that when 'enforcement activities are unable to seize even 1% of the heroin available on the streets... it is hard not to wonder at the effectiveness and cost-effectiveness of drugs enforcement'. Illegal drugs then, notwithstanding efforts to stem their supply, continue to flow into the hands of those consumers whose propensity to use drugs instigates the drug market in the first instance.

DRUG POSSESSION

As discussed previously, drug policy within the United Kingdom has morphed from a focus primarily on drug suppliers to one on drug users themselves. This has taken two paths. Firstly, through the ad hoc enforcement of drug laws by the police, which includes the use of stop and search as a strategy to identify potential drug users (with the police appearing to often use the *suspicion* of drug possession as a rationale to stop and search individuals of wider interest, particularly young Black men). Secondly, through a focus on those drug users who commit other crimes. In this section, we focus on the former of these populations before moving our attention to the latter in the proceeding chapter on drug-related offences.

As outlined in Chapter 4, the likelihood of being reprimanded for the possession of drugs is very low, with only 135,671 possession offences recorded by police forces in England and Wales during 2022/23 (ONS, 2024a), whilst an estimated 3.1 million people used an illegal drug during this period (ONS, 2023c). The majority who use drugs can be referred to as law-abiding criminals (Askew and Salinas, 2019) as their drug use represents an unspectacular element of their otherwise legitimate lifestyles. Hence their use of drugs, even though it may take place in public, for example, bars, nightclubs or festivals, does not arouse the attention of authorities (although it may lead to conflict with other agents of policing in the form of private security staff). This is coupled with the proactive policing of drug possession taking a historically low priority – unless it serves a greater purpose than simply arresting someone for a drugs offence.

A good example of this is the reclassification and subsequent re-reclassification of cannabis in the 2000s. In 2004, cannabis was reclassified from Class B to Class C within the MDA, a move that was then reversed in 2009. One would assume that cannabis became a Class C drug because it was conceived as less harmful – and that this would consequently see its policing deprioritised even further. But what we saw during 2004–2009 was an increase in recorded drug possession offences, which then tailed off once cannabis returned to Class B. On the surface, this appears both contradictory and nonsensical. Yet, at a time when police forces were attempting to enhance their performance statistics, arresting drug users was as an easy and effective way of manipulating these (Shiner, 2015). Hence, there was a considerable rise in the number of cannabis possession offences from 88,263 in 2004/2005 to 167,950 in 2008/2009 (ONS, 2024a). Writers have identified how this was achieved by 'an intensification of police efforts targeting minor possession offences' and motivated by a wider need to bolster performance indicators via the targeting of specific groups of 'low-hanging fruit'' (Shiner, 2015:698). Here then, the likelihood of drug users being charged and convicted for a possession offence related directly to the purpose that these offences served the police. This is further demonstrated by the period following cannabis' return to Class B in 2009, which saw an equally pronounced decrease in recorded possession offences from 167,950 in 2008/2009 to 80,808 in 2016/2017 (ONS, 2024a). This trend has been explained by the deprioritisation of policing drugs alongside overall reductions in police stop and search procedures (Allen and Kirk-Wade, 2020), which coincided with a period of less intense political scrutiny of police performance indicators.

Interestingly, during the COVID-19 pandemic, with police time and resources freed from other duties, a rise was once again evident in drug possession offences (ONS, 2022a). This corresponded with increased political appetite for enforcing drug laws, with a key ambition of the 2021 drug strategy for England and Wales being a generational shift in demand for drugs. This includes making drug use less attractive by further enhancing its policing and associated punishments. The Government's White Paper which followed the publication of the drug strategy 'Swift, Certain, Tough: New Consequences for Drug Possession' (Home Office, 2022b) proposed a series of increasingly punitive measures for those found in possession of drugs, including mandatory drugs awareness courses, random drug testing, confiscation of passports and driving licences, wearable drug monitors and exclusion orders prohibiting attendance of particular venues (Holland et al., 2022). This has been accompanied by a narrative shift, whereby so-called middle-class drug users are being publicly shamed by leading politicians and senior police officers for the wider harms their drug use prompts (Ayres and Taylor, 2020). All of which would suggest that drug possession is going to be more aggressively policed moving forwards.

Yet how this will ultimately play out is a different factor altogether, especially in those locations where there exists a *liminality of drug prohibition* – meaning that in relation to a drug such as cannabis, notions of the licit and the illicit have become blurred to the point that its use is a normative aspect of community life and its possession and use effectively decriminalised (Taylor et al., 2018). This is compounded by the fact that where offences of cannabis possession are processed, these are most commonly dealt with via out-of-court disposals (see the Box below), which sits at seeming odds with the 'swift, certain, tough' mantra espoused by the UK government. This is underlined by the Home Office (2022c) report on Crime Outcomes in England and Wales 2021/22, which identifies the stark differences in how offences of cannabis possession are resolved in comparison to other drugs with cannabis possession having a much lower charge/summons rate (14.2%) than other drug offences (32.1%), reflecting that possessions of small amounts of cannabis for personal use will often be dealt with by way of an out-of-court disposal such as a Cannabis Warning or Community Resolution, which do not constitute a criminal record. To illustrate, nearly half of all cannabis possession offences were assigned such outcomes, compared with 12.9% of possession offences involving other drugs in 2020/21 (Home Office, 2022c). Consequently, the overall charge rate for possession of drug offences has been driven by the charge rate for possession of cannabis.

Out-of-Court Disposals for Cannabis

In the 2000s, a series of reports (May et al., 2002; Police Foundation, 2000; Warburton et al., 2005) highlighted that the policing of cannabis was resource consuming and that to avoid the time it took to process possession offences, police officers often employed informal discretionary techniques, for example, the confiscation and disposal of the drug without any official record, which fed into wider tensions in certain communities prompted by drug law enforcement. Within this context, a pilot project in the London Borough of Lambeth took place between July 2002 and 2003. The Lambeth Cannabis Warning Scheme (LCWS) saw those caught in possession of cannabis issued with a warning rather than arrested – a response that was then implemented nationally in 2004.

Whilst the LCWS brought about apparent savings in police time, allowing further focus on other crime, it also led to a 110% increase in the number of interventions concerning cannabis (Crowther Dowey, 2005). A trend that persisted locally well after the LCWS ended (Adda et al., 2014). Whilst the LCWS in one sense appeared to represent a softening of drug law enforcement, it had a net widening effect with the official processing of those who may have previously been informally dealt with. This is an important factor to consider as 47.8% of recorded cases of cannabis possession in 2021/22 resulted in out-of-court disposals (which include Cannabis Warnings, a Penalty Notice for Disorder or a Community Resolution) (Home Office, 2022c). It can also lead to escalated action if the same person is caught for the same offence, that is, for a second offence, they should receive either a fixed penalty notice, simple caution or conditional caution and a third offence will result in prosecution (Metropolitan Police, 2020).

(Continued)

(Continued)

For some, this timely processing of minor drug offences is used as an argument for the decriminalisation of cannabis possession (Taylor et al., 2016). For others, it is used as evidence that the supposed war on drugs is a misnomer as multiple infractions of the MDA are required before a prosecution even takes place (Hitchens, 2012).

Another key trend in rates of drug possession offences is geography – or more specifically, the rates of recorded offences in London. For example, of the 168,021 possession offences recorded across England and Wales in 2020/21, just over 30% of these occurred in London (Allen and Tunnicliffe, 2021). Given that population estimates (ONS, 2022b) indicate that the population of London represents 17.75% of the overall population of England and Wales, this shows that those living in London are disproportionately more likely to be apprehended for a drug possession offence. This is important as London is the most ethnically diverse region in England and Wales (ONS, 2022c), which feeds into wider trends in drug-related stop and searches.

The employment of drug possession as a key justification or 'reasonable grounds' to conduct stop and search under the guise of the 1984 Police and Criminal Evidence Act has become an issue of great public debate (see Chapter 4). Statistics for England and Wales show that whilst the use of stop and search has fallen dramatically over the last decade (although the COVID-19 period did see a resurgence in its use), the proportion of these where drugs are cited as the reason for the search has increased from 36% in 2008/09 to 65% in 2021/22, making suspicion of illegal drugs the most common reason for stopping someone (Home Office, 2022d). Whether suspicion of drug possession is a genuine motivation for such searches or merely provides a justification for engaging a person of interest whom the police may not have any other reasonable grounds to stop is a moot point. Clearly, however, stopping and searching someone for a possible drug offence allows the police an opportunity to legitimately intervene with someone they may suspect of involvement in other criminal activity even if no drugs are found. Furthermore, if drugs are found, it allows the police to arrest someone for a drugs offence, which they can potentially use as a gateway to monitor an individual of interest or as leverage to investigate other crimes (via the provision of information by the individual charged with a drug offence).

Given that 71% of stop and searches require 'no further action' and just 13% lead to an arrest (Home Office, 2022d), one must question the way that they are justified and utilised. As noted in Chapter 4, the disproportionate use of stop and search on minority ethnic groups is a serious cause of concern. Using data from 2019/20, Allen and Tunnicliffe (2021) identified that Black people represent 3.7% of the population of England and Wales in 2021 but represent 16.3% of those stopped and searched for drugs, whilst Asian people represent 7.6% of the population of England and Wales, but 12.6% of those stopped and searched for drugs. Comparatively, White people represent 84.4% of the population but just 50.4% of those stopped and searched for drugs. Overall, minority ethnic groups make up 33.8% of those stopped and searched for drugs when they represent just 15.6% of the population (Allen and Tunnicliffe, 2021) – see Figure 6.2 for an illustration of these rates. The Home Office (2022d) acknowledges that based on self-defined ethnicity, individuals from a Black or Black British background are searched at a rate 6.2 times higher than those from a White ethnic group, with those identifying as Asian or Asian British being searched at a rate 2.1 times of those from a White ethnic group.

	Searches for drugs		All searches		Population estimate
	Number	%	Number	%	
White	173,241	50.4%	282,123	49.8%	84.4%
Asian (or Asian British)	43,295	12.6%	60,287	10.6%	7.6%
Black (or Black British)	55,950	16.3%	97,308	17.2%	3.7%
Chinese or other	5,966	1.7%	10,239	1.8%	2.4%
Mixed	11,050	3.2%	18,474	3.3%	1.9%
Not Stated	54,449	15.8%	98,009	17.3%	-
Total	343,951	100.0%	566,440	100.0%	100.0%
Total ethnic minority	116,261	33.8%	186,308	32.9%	15.6%

Figure 6.2 Stop and Searches by Self-Defined Ethnicity Compared to General Population in England and Wales 2019/20

Source: Adapted from Allen and Tunnicliffe (2021:11). Contains Parliamentary information licensed under the Open Parliament Licence v3.0.

Aside from the crucial issue of whether such actions are indicative of institutionally racist practices being employed by police forces, the disproportionate stopping of minority ethnic groups begins a process which leads to them being disproportionately represented within the criminal justice system. For whilst we have identified that only a small percentage of those stopped and searched for drugs are ultimately arrested, we simultaneously have to recognise that the number of stop and searches undertaken are directly related to the number of police-recorded drug offences – hence during the COVID-19 lockdown period, increased use in stop and search was mirrored by an increase in drug offences, reflecting that whilst a small percentage of people who are stopped for reasons pertaining to drugs are arrested, these offences are often discovered through stop and search (Home Office, 2022d). The stop and search process, therefore, is the beginning of the disproportionate representation of minority ethnic groups within the criminal justice system and one which continues the trend of their differential treatment. Previous research has shown that Black people are arrested for a drugs offence at 6 times the rate of White people; are more likely to receive a harsher police response for possession of cannabis and cocaine than their White counterparts; are subject to court proceedings for drug possession offences at 4.5 times the rate of Whites; are found guilty of this offence at 4.5 times the rate; and are subject to immediate custody at a rate of 5.0 times that of White people (Eastwood et al., 2013). This illustrates how those from minority ethnic groups 'are more likely to be sentenced to prison than people from the White ethnic group and higher proportions of people in prison from BME [Black and Ethnic Minority] groups are there for drug offences' (UKDPC, 2010a:5).

Taylor and colleagues (2016) contend that drug laws, or more precisely how drug laws are implemented, represent inherently racist practices. This is a process evident across the globe and one which continues to be evident even in places where drug law reforms have taken place. For example, the disproportionate arrest of Black people for drug offences in US states which have moved towards a legalised cannabis market. Whilst there are other clear trends in the demographics of those arrested for drug offences – the vast majority being both young and male (Home Office, 2022d) – the over-representation of Black people in stop and search statistics and their inordinate treatment by the criminal justice system cannot be construed as anything other than prejudiced. In this sense, drug laws are used as a tool to subjugate and criminalise specific populations, a process which has been ongoing for a century (see Chapters 2 and 3) and further bolsters the argument that drug laws are not implemented to protect society but rather as a tool of oppression (see Chapter 4) with the sentencing and punishment of drug users being methods through which this is achieved.

In relation to this, Sentencing Council (2021) data for the year 2019/20 show that a total of 23,032 adults were sentenced for drug possession offences with 35% of these being for Class A drugs, 63% for Class B and 2% for Class C. Figure 6.3 provides a breakdown of these outcomes, illustrating how a fine is the most common response (making up 60% of sentences) with an absolute or conditional discharge (which sees the individual receive a criminal record, but no further action taken) being the outcome in 20% of these. An immediate custodial sentence is relatively rare, but a total of 893 individuals were sent to prison in this period, representing 4% of all those sentenced. The average custodial sentence length for possession offences in 2020 was 3.9 months (Allen and Tunnicliffe, 2021).

	Class A	Class B	Class C	Overall
Absolute and conditional discharge	13%	23%	37%	20%
Fine	63%	59%	35%	60%
Community sentence	10%	8%	11%	9%
Suspended sentence	4%	2%	4%	2%
Immediate custody	6%	3%	6%	4%
Otherwise dealt with	5%	6%	7%	5%

Figure 6.3 Proportional Outcomes of Adult Offenders Sentenced for Drug Possession Offences in 2019/2020 (Some Columns do Not Total 100% due to Rounding Up/Down)

Whilst a significant number of drug possession offences are therefore responded to by way of out-of-court disposals, a substantial quantity result in a court appearance and criminal record, the majority of which relate to cannabis. Given the fractional chances of a drug user being identified and processed by the police, these individuals may be framed as unlucky to have come to their attention, but this belies that the policing of drug possession offences is used as a purposeful strategy and one that is disproportionately employed by the Metropolitan Police against minority ethnic groups.

CONCLUSION

Despite considerable time and resources being invested into the global and domestic policing of illegal drugs, they remain in ample supply in the United Kingdom. Whilst the agencies and organisations involved may have an earnest belief that their efforts are productive in terms of disrupting the supply of drugs, seizing them and deterring/punishing their possession, these efforts have little but symbolic value (Coomber et al., 2019) as attempts to control drugs 'at source, in transit and at retail level has not produced significant reductions in the drug market and associated criminality' (Reuter and Stevens, 2008:475). Whilst nefarious drug suppliers are pursued to protect societies from their sinister products, the majority of drugs which make up domestic drug markets make it into the hands of those who wish to use them, and whilst the possession of these drugs is illegal, the vast majority of those who use them go unnoticed and, even when apprehended, are likely to receive an out-of-court disposal. One must therefore question whether the situation with drugs, in terms of the number of people who supply and or use them, would be vastly different if these efforts were to cease overnight. Indeed, whether drug prohibition is enforced with leniency or more punitive zeal seems to have little impact on the level at which people consume drugs (Stevens, 2019) or their availability.

Yet drug laws create drug offences and in doing so result in a body of individuals, whether they be involved in international trafficking, domestic supply or who simply possess drugs they intend to use, being brought into contact with criminal justice systems. Demographical data show these people to be disproportionally young, male and from a minority ethnic group – a trend that is most profound in relation to drug possession. Given that the UK government has promised new investment to 'deliver an expansion in the capacity of forces to deal with drug possession offenders, ensuring that more people face the consequences of their use', it would seem likely that England and Wales will see an increase in such recorded offences 'through a consistent, swift and certain approach to drug possession' (Home Office, 2021:48). Doing so, however, risks further cementing the prejudiced practices of the drug apartheid (see Chapter 4), which sees drug offences as a method of controlling and criminalising certain populations.

When this is considered in relation to a key message of this chapter, that the policing of drug offences is shaped as much by the priorities of the government/police and the wider purposes that enforcing drug laws serve, this emphasises the spurious nature of how drug offences are policed and therefore how drug prohibition is imposed. Whilst processing this body of individuals costs considerable time and resources, reformists argue that the decriminalisation of drug possession would see an end to inequalities in 'justice'. That said, as Aickenhead (2012: 1), summarising Peter Hitchens' argument in his book *The War We Never Fought*, observes:

> It is nonsense to say the war on drugs has failed, Hitchens contends, when in actual fact we have never even tried to wage it. Drug-taking was, in effect, decriminalised by the Misuse of Drugs Act 1971, ever since when the authorities have deployed the rhetoric of toughness to conceal the truth that we are free to take drugs with impunity, knowing our crime will probably be ignored... It suits the liberal elite to pretend the draconian rhetoric is true, because it justifies their claim that the law is unjustly repressive and should be abolished altogether. The solution to the alleged failure of the war is not to give up and give in, but to start fighting it.

Regardless of what one believes the shape of drug laws should look like, the current situation in relation to the policing of drug offences does not appear to satisfy anyone – as drugs continue to be available and people continue to use them, largely with impunity. For a body of people, however, a criminal record for drug supply and/or possession has substantial ramifications (see Chapter 4). Yet drug policy has entered a new phase, one which has moved its focus primarily from drug offences to one centred on drug-related offences, something which is premised as a response to the most pressing drug-related issue, that of the problematic drug user – an issue that we now turn to.

SUMMARY

- **Drug offences refer to infractions of the 1971 MDA as well as including offences relating to the 2016 PSA and the offence of drug driving under the 1988 Road Traffic Act.**
- **The policing of drugs on a global and domestic level involves a multiplicity of actors, yet these fail to stem the supply of drugs into England and Wales.**
- **The number of recorded drug offences in England and Wales fluctuates depending on their prioritisation by the government/police.**
- **The most common outcome of a drug possession offence is an out-of-court disposal.**
- **Minority ethnic groups, particularly young Black males, are disproportionately represented at every level of the criminal justice process for drug offences.**

Here are some points and questions for you to consider after reading this chapter:

1) Is the policing of drug supply and possession a worthwhile activity? What does it achieve?
2) What are the implications of processing almost half of all drug possession offences by way of out-of-court disposals?

3) What is the significance of approximately 16% of the sentenced prison population having committed drug offences?

Here are some useful resources for those wanting to further explore the issues raised in this chapter:

- Coomber, R., Moyle, L. and Knox Mahoney, M. (2019) Symbolic policing: Situating targeted police operations/'crackdowns' on street-level drug markets. *Policing and Society*, 29(1), 1–17.

  This article considers the meaning and outcomes of police crackdowns on drug suppliers. The authors argue that whilst these can lead to inadvertent and unwelcome consequences, they still allow the police to achieve symbolic objectives.
- Home Office. (2021). *From harm to hope: A 10-year drugs plan to cut crime and save lives.* London, Home Office.

  This is the current drugs strategy for England and Wales. An executive summary provides a succinct overview of the strategy's key aims and objectives before each of these is considered in further depth in specific chapters. These include insights into how drug offences are policed and responded to.
- Shiner, M. (2015) Drug policy reform and the reclassification of cannabis in England and Wales: A cautionary tale. *International Journal of Drug Policy*, 26(7), 696–704.

  This article offers a critical overview of the period during which cannabis was downgraded in the MDA to a Class C drug before being returned to Class B. It provides a fascinating analysis of the impetus for these reforms and their wider/unintended consequences (including how cannabis was consequently policed).

You can find the most up-to-date statistics relating to drug offences at the following sites:

- Crime in England and Wales. Available at:

  https://www.ons.gov.uk/peoplepopulationandcommunity/crimeandjustice/datasets/crimeinenglandandwalesappendixtables

  This site provides an annual statistical overview of recorded drug offences. It also provides historical data on these. These data are useful for looking at trends in drug offences.
- Crime outcomes in England and Wales. Available at:

  https://www.gov.uk/government/collections/crime-outcomes-in-england-and-wales-statistics

  This site provides statistics that map out the outcomes assigned to recorded crimes, including drug offences. These data are useful for considering how drug offences are responded to by the criminal justice system.
- Offender management statistics quarterly: Available at:

  https://www.gov.uk/government/collections/offender-management-statistics-quarterly

(Continued)

(Continued)

This site provides quarterly statistics on those in prison and on probation, including for drug offences. These data provide insight into trends within the criminal justice relating to those convicted of drug offences.

- Prisons data. Available at: https://data.justice.gov.uk/prisons

  This site provides statistics related to the prison population. This real-time data afford insight into the proportion of this population who have been convicted of drug offences.

7
DRUG-RELATED OFFENCES

Overview

This chapter aims to provide you with:

- An overview of drug-related offences and problematic drug users.
- An insight into the bespoke criminal justice process for drug users.
- A critical analysis of the use and effectiveness of court-sanctioned drug treatment.

You will be introduced to the key terms:

- Drug-related offences
- Problematic drug users
- Bifurcated criminal justice system
- Court-sanctioned drug treatment
- Drug Rehabilitation Requirement
- Recovery

INTRODUCTION

This chapter focuses on *drug-related offences*, which we define as being acquisitive crimes (e.g. burglary, robbery and theft) committed by adults who are dependent on drugs. In the 1990s, concern over the volume of drug-related offences linked to so-called problematic drug users (PDUs) saw the emergence of a bespoke criminal justice system, which differentially processed drug-related crimes and drug-using offenders. This system used drug testing as a medium through which to identify drug users who were arrested, embedded opportunities to engage with drug services into every stage of the criminal justice process and introduced a new sentence – the Drug Testing and Treatment Order, which sought to blend punishment with treatment. This, it was hoped, would enable PDUs to address their drug use and in doing so cease their criminal activities. The chapter provides an overview of drug-related offences and the system designed to engage PDUs, considering its development, structure and effectiveness. It then provides a critical examination of the wider symbolism and ramifications of this system before offering a re-imagining of how drugs, crime and the criminal justice system might be decoupled. Our focus here is on responses to drug-related offences in a community setting with a specific analysis of interventions delivered in custodial settings provided in Chapter 8.

PROBLEMATIC DRUG USERS (PDUS) AND DRUG-RELATED OFFENCES

The 1990s saw a paradigmatic change in the focus of domestic drug policy in England and Wales from one centred on health to that of crime control (see Chapter 4). The key reason being that increased numbers of heroin users were accompanied by increased rates of crime (Seddon, 2007b). Synonymous with this context is the emergence of a now longstanding folk devil who was framed as being responsible for a wide body of crime – the PDU – an individual dependent on heroin and/or crack cocaine who committed swathes of property crime to fund their drug use. This framed not only drug offences but also *drug-related offences* as a matter for the criminal justice system. Amid an epoch of risk management, this problematised and indeed criminalised addiction with fears centring on the addict–offender (Flacks, 2024). This led to the envisioning of a bifurcated justice process (meaning that the criminal justice system adopted a twin-track approach) whereby those who were dependent on certain substances and committed certain crimes were treated differently to non-drug users.

The rationale for the anxieties relating to PDUs were/are rooted in positivistic beliefs about addiction, crime and treatment. Whilst we discuss (and critique) the causal link between drug use/addiction and crime in Chapter 5, from the 1990s onwards, studies using samples of drug users in contact with the criminal justice system illustrated an apparently definitive relationship between the two and a seeming epidemic of drug-related crime. This research also highlighted a series of significant trends to support this contention. Notably that drug use is considerable amongst arrestees; that amongst those testing positive for heroin/cocaine, there are high rates of offending; that those offenders self-report that their drug use is related to their offending; and that illegal income amongst heroin/cocaine users is considerable (Bennett, 1998; Budd et al., 2005; Hearnden and Magill, 2004). Figure 7.1 highlights the scale of this, showing that most property crime is apparently motivated by drug use. Resultantly, offenders who use heroin, cocaine or crack cocaine are said to commit between a third and a half of all acquisitive crime – the cost of all crime totalling £58 billion with drug-motivated crime being responsible for £19 billion of this (Home Office, 2010).

The emergence of this data in the 1990s coincided with the New Labour government's rise to power in the United Kingdom (see Chapter 3). An element of their election success in 1997 was their positioning on law and order, which was encapsulated by their mantra 'tough on crime, tough on the causes of crime'. Then Prime Minister Tony Blair (cited in The Guardian, 2001:1) emphasised this when he stated:

> We will take further action to focus on the 100,000 most persistent offenders. They are responsible for half of all crime. They are the core of the crime problem in this country. Half are under 21, nearly two-thirds are hard drug users, three quarters are out of work and more than a third were in care as children.

'Hard drug users', or rather those seen as being addicted to drugs, were therefore construed as being one of the key causes of the 'crime problem' and whilst addressing other causes, for example, unemployment, would require fundamental changes to social policies which could take decades to bear fruit, resolving the drug dependency of PDUs offered a more realistic and immediate pathway forward. In this sense, the criminal justice system was viewed as ideally placed for targeted drug interventions due to the large number of (problematic) drug users who came into contact with it. Hence, the 'further action' that Blair refers to was, in the first instance, to differentiate crimes/criminals associated with drug use and the individual's committing these from other crimes/criminals. Hence an individual who shoplifts but does not take illegal drugs is an offender committing a crime, but an individual who shoplifts and takes heroin became a PDU committing a drug-related offence (see the Box below).

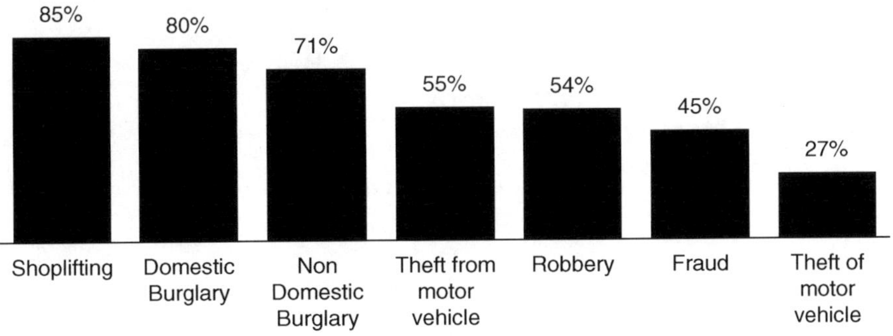

Figure 7.1 Percentage of Different Crimes Motivated by Drug Use
Source: Adapted from Prime Minister's Strategy Prime Ministers Strategy Unit (2003:25).

The second action was to develop a bespoke criminal justice process for those who committed drug-related offences which sought to blend punishment and treatment. In a bid to assist recovery from drugs and therefore remove the motivation for drug-related crimes, this meant identifying/arresting PDUs and engaging them in treatment via the criminal justice system. Treatment would stop them using drugs and, consequently, stop them offending. Importantly, engagement with treatment was made mandatory via court-ordered sentences, meaning that if someone failed to comply, they would face further punishment, including being potentially incarcerated. The result it was said would be a significant reduction in crime – a simple, attractive and ostensibly workable proposition.

Differentiating Drug-Related Offences

Several issues are raised by differentiating between drug-related and non–drug-related crime and the development of a twin-track criminal justice system. These include:

- Is it fair/ethical to process people who commit the same crimes differently just because one may use drugs?
- Why are only certain drugs, for example, heroin and crack/cocaine, construed as resulting in drug-related offences whilst others, for example, cannabis, are not?
- Framing drug use as the cause of criminal behaviour and responding to individuals in a differential fashion may encourage people to buy into the cause of their offending being drug use itself (as, on the surface at least, they are treated in a more 'lenient' manner). This behaviour is also then seemingly easier to justify, that is, 'it's not my fault, it's the drugs'.
- The twin-track system could provide an incentive to commit crime. For example, Stevens (2010:167) notes 'one of our interviewees commented that if he got away with theft, he got to buy heroin, but if he did not, at least he could get treatment'.
- The key indicator of whether a case is processed as a drug-related offence is a drug test undertaken on arrest at a police station. If this is positive for heroin/cocaine, the offence is labelled as drug related. Yet as Simpson (2003) notes, it could be that an individual is a 'persistent user' rather than a dependent user, and there is no way of establishing whether their drug use is linked to their offending, but a positive drug test seemingly confirms that the two variables are connected.
- Is it fair that individuals who commit crime to fund their drug use/dependency are given priority over those who do not commit crime in terms of access to treatment?

Criminal Justice Drug Interventions

New Labour detailed their vision for a twin-track criminal justice system in the 1998 drug strategy *Tackling Drugs to Build a Better Britain*. Whilst certain elements of this had been apparent previously (such as the ability of a court to mandate treatment for someone who used drugs – although this was rarely used), it was the strategy's desire to develop a seamless and more encompassing end-to-end system of drug interventions that was novel. This started with the introduction of drug testing on arrest/charge for certain trigger offences (burglary, theft, robbery) in police custody suites. This testing formed one element of arrest referral schemes, which afforded those who had committed certain crimes and who tested positive for either heroin or cocaine to be identified and given a priority referral to a drug service. This test result, as well as their subsequent engagement with the drug service, could/would then be documented in the pre-sentence report prepared by the Probation Service for their court appearance. If suitable, the individual could then be sentenced to a Drug Treatment and Testing Order (DTTO) – which was used as a direct alternative to custody – whereby an individual who was dependent on drugs and was thought would benefit from treatment, would be supervised in the community by the Probation Service but also engage with healthcare professionals and drug support services. For the duration of the DTTO (which could be between six months and three years), the individual would have to undertake regular drug testing (see the Box below), with a failed test in theory meaning a return to court and a punitive response. The individual also had to attend reviews of their progress in court. If an individual failed to comply with the requirements of the DTTO, they could be resentenced, potentially to custody.

The Pivotal Role of Drug Testing

A crucial influence on the formulation of the twin-track criminal justice process was the technological advancements that accompanied it. Mandatory drug testing in prisons began in 1996 and seemingly offered a magic bullet – for the first time, it could be proven whether an individual had used illegal drugs. This was initially used to police drug use, in the sense that prisoners were tested to see if they had used any illegal substances and, if this proved positive, receive punishment (in the form e.g. of additional time added to their sentence). It was then rolled out in the community with criminal justice interventions employing it in a more targeted way. Here it was used not only to identify drug users on entrance to the criminal justice system but also, and perhaps most importantly, as a method of monitoring their compliance with community sentences. It enabled 'help' to be offered but at the same time provided a surveillance tool, which monitored whether an individual was complying with their court-sanctioned treatment. Whether sentences such as the DTTO would have been rolled out without this tool is questionable. As Bean (2014:65) notes:

> From the mid-1990's onwards British governments have shown an increased willingness to fund and thereby increase the range of treatment facilities for substance abusers. There has been a corresponding willingness to increase drug testing. Governments have done so because they recognise that

(Continued)

(Continued)

> treatment provides one of the few options for containing the drug problem, coupled with a belief that it breaks the link with crime. Drug testing is included because it is thought that, without that backup, treatment will fail.

We do have to question, however, what drug testing ultimately achieves in the different arenas in which it is used whilst recognising how concerns around drug-related offences legitimised what can be seen as a deeply intrusive method of state surveillance. In the same vein that electronic or global positioning satellite monitoring has increased the scope of our ability to monitor an individual's movements, drug testing takes this a step further by affording the ability to observe what an individual puts into *their* body. Arrestees do not have the legal right to refuse a drug test as not giving a sample is an offence which is punishable by a prison sentence of three months and/or a fine of up to £2500. The 2021 drug strategy states that the government wish to extend the scope of who can be drug tested whilst also touting the possible use of drug tags, which would monitor an individual's blood for drug use in the same way already employed in relation to alcohol (otherwise known as a sobriety tag). This raises questions over the justification of employing this method of social control in relation to the civil liberties of people who may use drugs.

This system was developed and indeed evolved over time. Drug testing in custody suites was made mandatory and expanded to include a wider scope of offences with positive tests leading to compulsory appointments at a drug service. Referrals to drug services are ongoing and engagement with such services can be used as a condition (or restriction) of bail. Different drug-specific sentencing options have been implemented, some of which continue (such as accredited cognitive behavioural therapy programmes like Addressing Substance Related Offending), some of which are now defunct (such as the Drug Abstinence Order and Drug Abstinence Requirement, which aimed to engage non-dependent drug users whose crimes were still seen as drug-related offences with drug testing/support) whilst others have evolved (the original flagship sentence, the DTTO, was replaced by the Drug Rehabilitation Requirement (DRR), which lowered the tariff level of the sentence from a direct alternative to custody meaning that it could be applied to a greater spectrum of offences and indeed drug users and no longer had a minimum sentence length).

Notwithstanding these changes, the central tenants of the system introduced over a quarter of a century later remain. We have a criminal justice process with intervention points at every stage for those who are seen as being dependent on drugs and commit drug-related offences with treatment opportunities available from the point of arrest through to the end of a sentence, whether that be served in the community (Figure 7.2 illustrates how this process works in relation to the DRR) or in custody (see Chapter 8). The 2021 drug strategy indicates that this model will continue for the foreseeable future, emphasising as it does the government's commitment to breaking the drugs–crime link via criminal justice interventions, mapping out that they will increase the number of referrals from police, courts and probation into drug treatment and guarantee a treatment place for every offender with an addiction, which will contribute to some 740,000 crimes being prevented (Home Office, 2021).

Sitting alongside these court-sanctioned measures have been a series of police-led schemes focusing on persistent drug-using offenders. These gained traction with the 2004 Prolific and Priority Offenders programme, which encouraged the police and partner agencies to focus on those small number of offenders who were committing disproportionate levels of crime. This saw the roll out of schemes such as the Communities Against Drugs (CAD) project, which used intelligence (gathered from informants) to identify the 20 most prolific drug-using offenders in Liverpool. This epitomised New Labour's 'tough on crime, tough on the causes of crime' mantra. The CAD saw the police specifically target individual drug users, approach them before their release from prison or even on their doorsteps and offer them enhanced access to drug services (with the proviso that they would be drug tested to monitor their progress) but informed that if they refused this 'help' they would be placed under surveillance and arrested for any further offending behaviour. In essence, they were told in no uncertain terms that help to address their drug dependency was available, but if this was not taken up that they would be proactively put under surveillance, ensuring they were arrested for any further offences. Project ADDER (Addiction, Diversion, Disruption, Enforcement and Recovery), which began in 2021, is a more recent example of such practices. A key focus of ADDER is that it attempts to tackle 'drugs misuse through a coordinated action combining targeted and tougher policing with enhanced treatment and recovery services' (Home Office, 2021:8). As such, it highlights that the carrot (the offer of treatment) and stick (punitive responses to non-compliance) approach that depicts UK governmental efforts to address problematic drug use is set to continue.

Whilst Hollingworth (2008) has argued that we have seen a shift in the focus of drug policy – from punishment to treatment, the current approach represents a hybrid of the two. A characteristic of this has been multi-agency working with organisations and services previously based outside the criminal justice system being drawn more centrally into it. Drug services in particular have had to follow the funding and increased resources for criminal justice rather than community referrals has seen many organisations prioritise referrals from this group. This means that over the past three decades, a cultural change has taken place whereby health and drug services share information with the police and probation services pertaining to those individuals engaged with such treatment. Previously, this information might have been regarded as confidential, but it now provides a picture of whether an individual is complying with their coerced treatment or not. It has also meant that drug services represent the carrot in the coercive treatment paradigm but that the information they provide their criminal justice partners is used to weaponise the stick that can be enacted upon drug users. As such, they are essential to the processing and policing of PDUs and indeed to the court-sanctioned treatment associated with these.

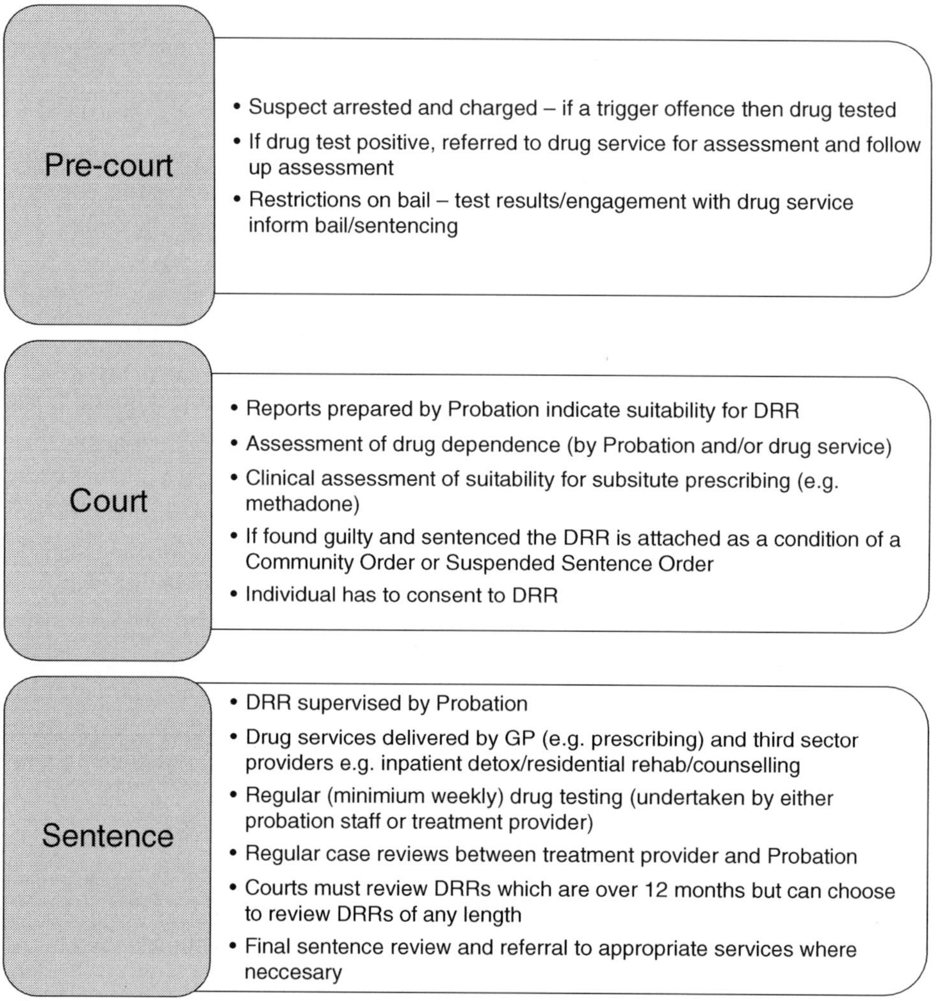

Pre-court

- Suspect arrested and charged – if a trigger offence then drug tested
- If drug test positive, referred to drug service for assessment and follow up assessment
- Restrictions on bail – test results/engagement with drug service inform bail/sentencing

Court

- Reports prepared by Probation indicate suitability for DRR
- Assessment of drug dependence (by Probation and/or drug service)
- Clinical assessment of suitability for subsitute prescribing (e.g. methadone)
- If found guilty and sentenced the DRR is attached as a condition of a Community Order or Suspended Sentence Order
- Individual has to consent to DRR

Sentence

- DRR supervised by Probation
- Drug services delivered by GP (e.g. prescribing) and third sector providers e.g. inpatient detox/residential rehab/counselling
- Regular (minimium weekly) drug testing (undertaken by either probation staff or treatment provider)
- Regular case reviews between treatment provider and Probation
- Courts must review DRRs which are over 12 months but can choose to review DRRs of any length
- Final sentence review and referral to appropriate services where neccesary

Figure 7.2 Process for Drug-Related Offences/Offenders in Relation to the Drug Rehabilitation Requirement
Source: Adapted from (NOMS, 2014).

COURT-SANCTIONED DRUG TREATMENT: THE DRR

The DRR in Numbers (Ministry of Justice, 2023a, 2023b)

- In 2022, a total of 5,930 DRRs were made, representing 3% of all Community Orders and 4% of all Suspended Sentence Orders made in this period. DRRs were most commonly combined with a Rehabilitation/Supervision Requirement (91%);

Unpaid Work Requirement (12%); Accredited Programme Requirement (7%); and/or Curfew Requirement (7%).

- Of those sentenced to a DRR in 2022:
  - 86% were male and 14% were female.
  - 21% were under 30 years of age, 42% were aged 30–39, 29% were aged 40–49 and 8% were aged 50 and over.
  - 87% were White, 4% Asian or British Asian, 4% Black or Black British, 4% Mixed and 1% Chinese or Other ethnic group.
- A total of 3,353 DRRs were terminated in 2022. Of these, 62% were successfully completed whilst 38% were revoked due to either a failure to comply with the requirements (9.5%), conviction of a further offence (18.5%) or for other reasons (10%).

It is important to note that despite previously painting a picture of a criminal justice system which seamlessly processes people for drug-related offences, and which then effectively supervises their court-sanctioned drug treatment, a series of recent reports indicate that this system is in turmoil. The Black Review (2021) and a joint inspection by HM Inspectorate of Probation (HMIP) and the Care Quality Commission (HMIP, 2021) together identified that in England (much less so in Wales), this process has taken a backwards turn. They note that whilst the number of offenders entering and sentenced to treatment via the criminal justice system increased throughout the 1990s–2000s, since then there has been reduced use of drug testing, less referrals into treatment and a fall in the number of DRRs ordered by courts.

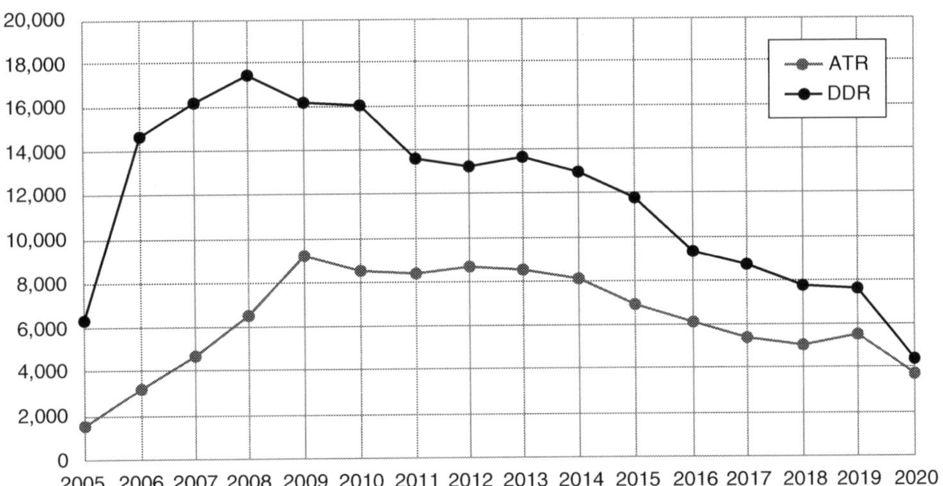

Figure 7.3 Trends in the Number of Drug Rehabilitation Requirements (and Alcohol Treatment Requirements) Commenced Under Community Orders and Suspended Sentence Orders in England and Wales, 2005–2020 (HMIP, 2021:46)

Source: Contains public sector information licensed under the Open Government Licence v3.0.

In 2022, a total of 5,930 DRRs were made (Ministry of Justice, 2023). This compares to 2008 when, at the height of its use, over 17,000 DRRs were ordered by the courts (see Figure 7.3) with the number being in steady decline, reaching the lowest rate during the COVID-19 period (see Table 7.1). One explanation for this decrease could be that drug use has simply become less prevalent amongst those arrested for drug-related offences – although there is no evidence to currently support this. Another is that a reduction in the number of DRRs does not necessarily mean that those who commit drug-related offences are not engaging with drug interventions. Whilst (problematic) drug users *can* be sentenced to a DRR, not all will be. Other community sentences can be employed for individuals who use drugs – for instance, the Supervision Requirement of a Community Order may implicitly include probation (or indeed drug services) undertaking specific work around substance use to address drug-related issues. There is also evidence to suggest that a recent decline in the use of the DRR has meant that many PDUs are being sentenced directly to custody (Black, 2021) where drug interventions can again take place.

Table 7.1 Number of Drug Rehabilitation Requirements Commenced Under Community Orders (CO) and Suspended Sentence Orders (SSO), 2012 to 2022, in England and Wales

	2012	2013	2014	2015	2016	2017	2018	2019	2020	2021	2022
CO	9,290	9,138	8,396	7,352	5,932	5,254	5,069	5,143	2,646	3,203	3,601
SSO	4,004	4,526	4,555	4,428	3,766	3,465	2,703	2,481	1,773	2,071	2,329
Total	13,294	13,664	12,951	11,780	9,698	8,719	7,772	7,624	4,419	5,274	5,930

Source: Adapted from Ministry of Justice (2023).

That said, the statistical drop off in the use of the DRR has been stark. The Community Sentence Treatment Requirement Programme launched in 2017 was a direct response to this decline, aiming to ensure greater use was made of treatment requirements as part of community sentences, including the DRR. Greater numbers, however, have failed to materialise, in fact the numbers of DRRs remain at one of their lowest levels. This sits within the wider context of a 38% decrease in the volume of people starting Community and Suspended Sentence Orders between 2009 and 2018 (Ministry of Justice, 2020) and a 26% drop in all community sentences between 2019 and 2020 (during the COVID-19 pandemic). Resultantly, in 2019/20, there were only 2,890 recorded referrals into drug treatment for those under probation, including DRRs and other community sentence supervision, a figure that has again been reducing since 2008 (HMIP, 2021, see Figure 7.4). This indicates that court-sanctioned drug treatment and drug interventions more generally are witnessing a dramatic downturn.

Accompanying this decrease in the use of DRRs has also been a deterioration in the quality of service and indeed management. It seems that 'programmes and structures previously put in place to identify and refer offenders with a drug problem to treatment

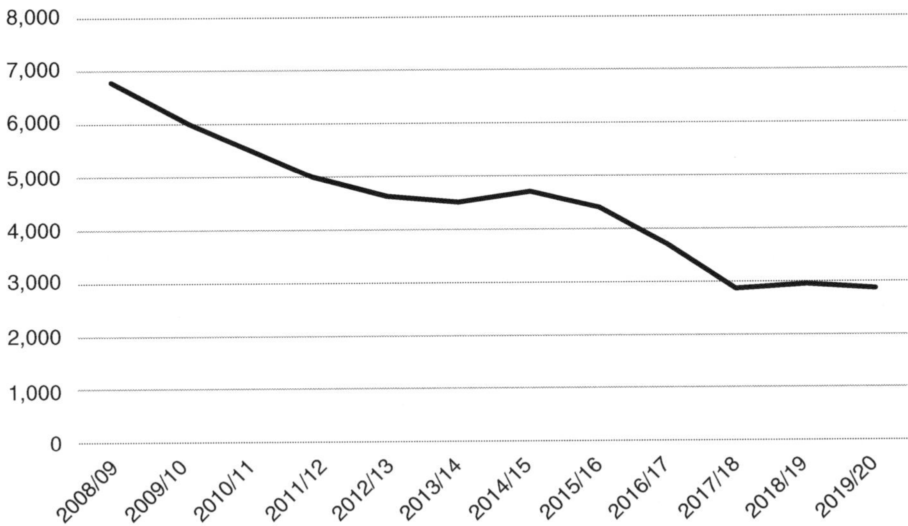

Figure 7.4 Probation Referrals Into Substance Misuse Treatment (New Presentations to Treatment) for England 2008/09 – 2019/20 (HMIP, 2021:27)

have withered on the vine' (HMIP, 2021:5). HMIP (2021:5) outlines the impact of this on a practical level, observing that:

> Of the 60 cases we inspected of people on probation with a serious drug problem, 50 were known to drugs services, but only five had treatment plans that had been shared between probation and a drugs agency and only 10 were being drug tested to see if they were staying off drugs. Probation managers were unable to tell us how many class A drug users they had on their caseloads or how many were in treatment – a major information gap. Even where people had been referred to treatment, our inspectors were unable to find out if appointments had been kept or drug tests carried out.

As noted above, of the 60 cases reviewed by HMIP, only 10 had received any recorded drug testing despite the sample containing 23 DRR cases. Whilst this report coincided with COVID-19 and the upheaval this prompted, the lack of testing, which represents a key facet of a DRR, is stark.

There are several reasons as to why this situation has arisen. In England at least, a change in how drugs service provision was co-ordinated and funded saw, at a time of austerity, disinvestment and a resultant erosion of all aspects of drug testing/service delivery. This saw an end to national schemes such as the Drug Interventions Programme (which provided oversight and funding for drug testing on arrest and referrals into treatment, including the Tough Choices initiative which made these mandatory), leading to services being 'commissioned in a fragmented way, without a guiding mind to organise and control progress' (HMIP, 2021:5). Funding for drug treatment was consequently passed from central to local authorities at a time when budgets were reduced, leading in turn to disinvestment in drug treatment, meaning that some local authorities have 'reduced treatment expenditure by 40%' (Black, 2020:6). The effects of this have been wide ranging. Certain police forces have scaled back drug testing on arrest to the point of stopping it entirely (Home Office, 2022b), a trend which removes the ability to identify PDUs and refer them to services and, therefore, to recognise those who may be suitable for DRRs. Drug services themselves have also reduced in size and capacity with some disappearing altogether. Simultaneously, these developments coincided with reduced policing budgets, the impact of COVID-19 and seismic changes to the Probation Service, which was part privatised in 2014 before being renationalised in 2021. An outcome of this has been a negative impact on the multi-agency partnership working arrangements that are so crucial to supporting drug users and indeed to assessing someone's suitability for a DRR and then effectively managing this.

A further outcome of this perfect storm is that PDUs are no longer being sentenced to community-based sanctions but are receiving custodial sentences instead. As Black (2021) notes:

> Same-day sentencing requirements in court and ineffective probation supervision have contributed to a fall in the number of these sentences because there is often neither the time nor the expertise available to help arrange such a disposal. In these circumstances, the judiciary inclines towards custodial sentences, particularly when the availability and quality of local treatment and recovery services are in question.

As such, the status quo with DRRs and drug treatment more widely is a precarious one. The current situation is also challenging to assess, as what meaningful work is being undertaken with drug users, even those sentenced to DRRs, is unclear. This malaise, however, provided a catalyst for action. The government, recognising the decline in all aspects of drug interventions, including court-sanctioned drug treatment, committed (via the 2021 drug strategy) to considerable re-investment. That said, the long-term implications of this erosion and whether this renewed promise will be enough to counteract the detrimental impacts of the last decade are unknown. One of the main conclusions of the Black Report, however, was that additional funding for drug treatment alone will not be sufficient. It contends that the co-ordination of drug services requires central government oversight with a recommissioning of specific services and a rebuilding of capacity, including recruiting many more professionally qualified staff and trained support workers – who, it is argued, are critical to the provision of effective treatment.

EFFECTIVENESS OF COURT-SANCTIONED TREATMENT

Having explained how the criminal justice system responds to drug-related offences and indeed PDUs, we now turn our attention towards the efficacy of criminal justice drug interventions, particularly court-sanctioned treatment. Again, this is not easy terrain to navigate as judging whether sentences such as the DTTO and DRR were/are effective depends on the outcomes one is seeking to assess.

The two most obvious measures of effectiveness for drug treatment delivered within a criminal justice context are its impact on drug use and/or crime. Even these, however, can be complicated variables to gauge in terms of whether court-sanctioned treatment has been successful. For example, a heroin user sentenced to a DRR may considerably *reduce* the level of their drug use and offending for the duration of their order (and/or beyond this) but not desist from either of these. For some, this may be construed as an effective outcome – the individual is clearly addressing their drug-using behaviour and less crime means less victimisation. For others, however, this might be interpreted as a failure, as for a DRR to be truly effective, it must prompt full abstinence from drugs (a measure that gained traction from 2010 onwards with greater governmental emphasise on the need for full recovery, see Home Office, 2010) and desistance from all offending behaviour. These 'hard' indicators, however, have formed the key performance measurements of most research studies into criminal justice drug interventions. Yet these indicators lack a nuanced appreciation of drug use, drug users and drug treatment. Sitting alongside these, therefore, are several 'soft' but nonetheless equally important indicators, which might be considered in relation to effectiveness. For example, has the sentence led to greater knowledge around how to minimise drug-related harms, or a reduction in health-related issues, or an improved lifestyle, or the (re)building of relationships with families and loved ones.

Adding to the complexity of evaluating what works is that evidence surrounding criminal justice drug interventions delivered in community settings is both limited and dated (Sirdifield et al., 2020). It is also at times contradictory, with research findings being ambiguous even around singular outcomes (McSweeney et al., 2007). If we take the use of drug testing as an example, there appears to be a lack of consensus surrounding the impact of this 'at different points in the criminal justice system on illicit drug use, offending behaviours and on engagement with treatment services' (McSweeney et al., 2008:24). In their evaluation of the Tough Choices element of the Drug Intervention Programme (DIP), which had oversight of the provision of mandatory criminal justice drug testing and treatment referrals in England and Wales for almost a decade before ending in 2013, McSweeney and colleagues (2018:62) conclude that there was 'no association between compliance and engagement with treatment services, rates of retention and successful discharge' nor was it associated with 'reductions in the rate and volume of reoffending'. Resultantly, they question its effectiveness and value for money. Meanwhile in their respective studies of the DIP, Best and colleagues (2010) found some evidence of this being linked to reductions in re-offending, whilst Collins, Cuddy and Martin (2017:12) concluded that the DIP 'successfully reduces economic costs of crime and also increases quality of life of individuals'. This apparent empirical ambiguity led Turnbull and Skinns (2010) to surmise that the DIP was neither a success nor a failure.

This uncertainty over effectiveness is also apparent in studies focusing on court-sanctioned treatment. Perhaps surprisingly, no research has been undertaken on the DRR – something which feasibly represents assumed knowledge that drug interventions are effective and that coerced treatment works. In a review of the impact of Community Orders and Suspended Sentence Orders on re-offending, Mews and colleagues (2015:14) note that they did not examine the DRR 'as it was felt that the complexity of this requirement made results difficult to interpret without further in-depth research focusing on the particular treatments available'. Fortunately, its predecessor, the DTTO, was considered by a body of studies with certain thematic findings emerging.

Studies indicated that the DTTO was associated with reductions in drug use, reductions in offending and improvements in health (Eley et al., 2002; McSweeney et al., 2007). That said, 'engagement and retention on the DTTO was particularly problematic' (Hollingworth, 2008:134). Turnbull and colleagues (2000) in their evaluation of the initial DTTO pilot scheme found that after commencing a DTTO, average spending on drugs went down from £400 to £25 per week, with drug-related offences also reducing significantly. The completion rate, however, was 47% with the remaining cases being revoked (due to either breaches of the order or further offending). In their two-year reconviction follow-up study, Hough and colleagues (2003) found that of those sentenced to DTTOs, just 30% completed their orders, with 67% having these revoked. The overall two-year reconviction rate was 80%, but for those who had their order revoked, the rate was 91% compared to a much lower 53% for those who had completed their orders.

These findings highlight two issues. Firstly, that of targeting and the importance of who was sentenced to a DTTO. What represents effective targeting, however, is another moot point. For example, one might view these findings in a negative light – as so many orders were revoked, this indicates failure as the DTTO was seemingly setting people up to fail and not being applied to those who were perhaps ready and/or able to commit to treatment. Alternatively, it could be argued that, as a direct alternative to custody reserved for high tariff offenders, these findings are unsurprising due to the nature of PDUs and that the DTTO was therefore being effectively targeted. Here, high non-completion rates can be understood as both success and failure. Interestingly, the box below illustrates that the rate of completion in 2022 for the DRR sat at 62% with 38% of these being revoked. Whilst these indicate that the DRR appears more likely to be successfully completed than the DTTO, it should be recognised that as this is not used as a direct alternative to custody, the individuals it engages may be at different stages in their drug use and offending pathways.

These are significant issues as studies showed that completing the DTTO was crucially important as the longer someone engaged with treatment, the more positive the outcomes, with those completing orders generally showing declines in drug use and crime (McSweeney et al., 2007). Given the high rates of failure among those sentenced to DTTOs, this raises the question of whether individuals coerced into drug treatment by the courts are ready to engage and likely to remain engaged for the duration of the sentence. Whenever we, as humans, try to change our behaviour, whether that be dieting, stopping smoking or lessening screen time, our mental and physical outlooks influence whether we are ready, prepared and motivated to enact such changes, so is coercing individuals into making such changes likely to work? Stevens (2010) makes three salient points in relation to this. Firstly, that whether an individual voluntarily refers to treatment or is ordered by the court, a level of coercion may still exist (such as pressure from friends and family). Secondly, that those sentenced to treatment are no more or less likely to be at a higher stage of readiness to change than those who refer voluntarily. Thirdly, that in terms of outcomes (around drug use, offending, physical and/or mental health), there are no significance differences between those who enter treatment voluntarily or via DTTOs/DRRs.

Lipton (1995) has identified that motivation to enter treatment is less important than retention in treatment as rates of retention appear relatively unrelated to whether someone refers voluntarily or via a court (McSweeney et al., 2007). This advances support for coerced treatment with retention leading to more positive outcomes regardless of original motivation. Nevertheless, this generic application of effectiveness overlooks that drug treatment is highly personal. Coomber (2013), whilst acknowledging that the longer an individual stays in treatment, the better the outcomes, also stresses the importance of the availability of treatment that matches an individual's needs, indicating that a one-size-fits-all approach does not work. This underlines the importance of services being commissioned to meet a range of needs (McSweeney et al., 2007), which in the current climate of treatment service regression might question the ability of drug services to provide effective individualised treatment, whether that be in relation to voluntary or coerced referrals. In terms of treatment fitting the individual, the majority of those sentenced to the DRR in 2022 (see the Box above) were White (87%), male (86%) and over 30 years old (79%). Given this, we must also be mindful of whether drug services are foremostly accustomed to working with these demographics and question how this might impact on treatment outcomes. Additionally, Coomber (2013) emphasises that a continuum of care is equally as significant, meaning in the case of court-sanctioned treatment, it is essential that access to appropriate services are ongoing both throughout the sentence and, where necessary, after its completion, to ensure that service users do not experience a cliff edge when their sentences end.

A final point in relation to studies evaluating criminal justice drug interventions is that measuring these is problematic. When we consider the 'hard measures' of impacts on levels of crime and drug use, there are issues around how long after sentencing these are monitored for and whether a control group which mirrors that of the research sample has been utilised. It is also near impossible to claim that specific drug interventions sanctioned by the criminal justice system have led to a reduction in crime or drug use. Drug treatment delivered within the criminal justice context often contains a series of differential elements, for example, methadone prescribing, drug testing, counselling, wider support from agencies relating to accommodation, employment, etc., so identifying which of these alone or together are most effective is difficult. It is also challenging to generalise in relation to sentences like the DRR in terms of treatment as different probation areas have different treatment providers and partner arrangements. In addition, the DRR is used alongside other elements of a Community Order or Suspended Sentence Order, most regularly with the Supervision/Rehabilitation Requirement (see Mews et al., 2015), which sees other work undertaken alongside the drug treatment element, which may equally influence any current or future desistance from drug use or crime. We must also realise, as noted previously, that treatment and recovery from drugs is a personal journey – aspects such as age, gender, ethnicity and history of drug use all being variables which can influence an individual's experiences of treatment and indeed whether this is ultimately effective or not.

CRITICAL ANALYSIS: TREATMENT BY COERCION

Despite levels of coercion, motivation and outcomes being more similar than different among those who either voluntarily refer or are coerced, we must recognise the negative impacts that court-sanctioned treatment may have, which should always be incorporated into considerations of its effectiveness. A lapse or relapse (Prochaska and DiClemente, 1983) when attempting recovery from drugs can be problematic but when such occurrences result in potentially punitive consequences, the implications may be worsened, leading some to criticise the criminal justice system's coercive approach to treatment. That said, being able to access drug treatment, regardless of whether one feels ready or not, is also essential and the investment in drug treatment services throughout the 1990s and 2000s saw the number of adults in treatment double with 'England having one the highest rates of heroin users in treatment in the world and average waiting days fell from 12 weeks to five days' (Black, 2020:18). Despite referrals into treatment more recently regressing, the very notion of increasing the numbers engaged in drug treatment is problematic for some as it reduces its effectiveness through a lack of specific targeting (see the Box below).

Stevens (2010) also interprets the targeting of DTTOs and indeed DRRs as a failure. He observes that despite the DTTO being used as a supposed direct alternative to prison, that the prison population continued to rise throughout the period it was used, stating that 'It seems – in line with Cohen's (1985) gloomy predictions of net-widening – that

DTTOs and DRRs have been used in addition to, rather than as a replacement for, imprisonment' (Stevens, 2010:166). In this sense, court-sanctioned drug treatment has failed to reduce the prison population but may also have targeted less serious offenders than premised, which has had the effect of up-tariffing the sentences received by drug users – and that even with this dilution of seriousness, revocation rates were/are still high, ultimately leading to further, arguably disproportionate punishment for those sentenced.

Whether or not drug treatment by coercion is construed as effective or not, its utility to some is still debatable on wider grounds. The very notion of forcing someone to undertake drug treatment and testing can sit uncomfortable on a human rights level. This is countered by the fact that the DTTO/DRR required/requires an individual's consent and a willingness to comply with the requirement. Whether this consent is coerced, however, especially when we look back at the DTTO which was a direct alternative to prison is a debateable point. Worryingly, HMIP (2021:40) observed in their study of 24 DRR cases that consent was obtained and recorded in only five of these, asking 'whether orders are being made too expeditiously at court, without a proper legal basis established'.

Yet court-sanctioned drug treatment, for a time at least, has afforded a more expedient route to access treatment for a body of drug users. Whilst there has been a prioritisation of criminal justice over other referrals, meaning that for some drug users' access to treatment continues to be a challenge, especially given the recent reduction in such services, the belief that treatment works – no matter where an individual is referred from – is a strong one. Yet we must accept that for some, treatment has not yet worked. We have an ageing cohort of heroin users in England and Wales (Black, 2021), many of whom have engaged with treatment on multiple occasions (via both the criminal justice system and otherwise). Substitute prescribing (usually of methadone) has formed one element of this engagement, and for some, this has been ongoing for extended periods of time with almost 30,000 individuals having received continuous prescriptions to address their opiate use for over five years (OHID, 2021). This 'parking' of people of methadone with little clear pathway to abstinence has received increasing criticism since drug policy turned towards the goal of full recovery in 2010, but is a trend that continues nevertheless.

The Need for a Drug Treatment Revolution

For some writers, the dominant approach to treatment, even before the degradation of service provision evident in recent years, is ineffective. Neil McKeganey (2011) argues that the notion underpinning this – that the greater the numbers engaged with drug treatment the better – is fundamentally flawed. Whilst we may therefore point to an

(Continued)

(Continued)

increase in both the professionalism of drug services and the number of people accessing these throughout the 1990s and 2000s, the investment which prompted this was potentially misplaced. It may not be the case, as is promised by the 2021 drug strategy that we need 'a treatment place for every offender with an addiction' (Home Office, 2021:9), as we instead need to revisit who we engage with treatment, what form this takes and what it ultimately aims to achieve.

In terms of effectiveness, McKeganey (2011:64) argues that in 'the UK the drug treatment service that is provided with the least frequency (residential) is the one that is most closely associated with addicts becoming drug free. By comparison, the treatment that has the lowest rate of success (methadone maintenance) in terms of addicts becoming drug free is the one that is provided with the greatest frequency'. Meanwhile he outlines that in the long run, methadone is not cheaper than residential treatment but allows many users to be simultaneously treated – therefore we increase the numbers of those entering treatment, yet the priority should be on people leaving treatment drug free. McKeganey (2011) therefore proposes a drug treatment revolution, which has five key ambitions:

1) Reduce the numbers engaged with drug treatment and refocus on recovery.
2) Differentiate between those who do not stand any prospect of becoming drug free and those who can and invest resources in the latter.
3) Clarify the purposes of drug treatment – is it to reduce harm or to become drug free? If it is the latter, then drug treatment should not be available to all, just those seeking full recovery.
4) Treatment users need to commit to change, with a time limit on the (free) services they engage with, for example, a, maximum two-year prescription of methadone.
5) Professional drug treatment should engage with abstinence-based self-help organisations, for example, Narcotics Anonymous.

According to national data on treatment outcomes (OHID, 2021), of those who left treatment for opiate use in England during 2020–21, 25% successfully completed this with an average time in treatment of two and half years. Whilst 23% of those starting opiate treatment in 2020–21 were referred via the criminal justice system, the majority were voluntary self-referrals (OHIB, 2021). These figures indicate that drug treatment for heroin use is demanding in terms of remaining engaged and doing so for an extensive period. It is also a reminder that for some, treatment may not work whether that be when court sanctioned or otherwise. We must also recognise that many of the drug interventions offered by the criminal justice system attempt to stimulate change on an individual level, and they therefore tend to 'have limited influence or success in addressing broader situational and structural problems linked to relationships, access to suitable accommodation, educational, training and employment opportunities and other forms of capital', which 'is important given the main causes and drivers of both dependency and criminality are disproportionately associated with poverty and structural disadvantage' (McSweeney et al., 2018:64).

Those PDUs whom frequent the criminal justice system then tend to have common demographical backgrounds. Indeed, as Stevens (2007:92) contends, both problematic drug use and crime are afflictions of inequality and focusing on the relationship between the two (and using the criminal justice system as a site to address this) rather than considering 'the links of both to inequality suits the interests of powerful groups within and around the British state'. What responding to the drug-related offences of PDUs has therefore achieved is a solidification of the ideology that drug addiction and drug treatment are criminal justice issues – and PDUs are the property of the criminal justice system. This has fed into PDUs being framed as outsiders, creating notions of 'them' being a threat to 'us' (Taylor, 2008). This has occurred during an epoch of penal populism framing the criminal justice's carrot-and-stick approach as something resembling benevolence rather than a series of intrusive measures enacted upon some of the most socially and politically marginalised. That those from the most deprived sections of society access treatment via the criminal justice system whilst those from more affluent sections pay to access private treatment facilities is less ironic that it is symbolic. Meanwhile, the roll out of drug testing and increased prescribing of methadone have meant that profits have flowed into the private sector.

CRITICAL ANALYSIS: DECOUPLING DRUGS, CRIME AND CRIMINAL JUSTICE

A commonly held belief amongst critical drug scholars from within the discipline of criminology is that if they had their way, they would be out of a job. That is because most criminologists working within the drug field would prefer to see drugs re-framed as a public health rather than criminal justice issue. Rather than seeing renewed governmental commitment to breaking the drugs–crime link via criminal justice-led interventions, they would prefer for dependent drug users to be diverted away from the criminal justice system with treatment for drug addiction responded to more directly as a health issue. That is not to say that this is an easy task – many PDUs commit large volumes of crimes, which have many victims and the criminal justice system needs to respond to this in some way – yet such a paradigm shift is not outside the realms of possibility.

In essence, to decouple drug dependency from the criminal justice system would mean that when someone is arrested, drug tested and/or sentenced, they are then diverted into drug treatment that sits outside the punitive reaches of criminal justice and is managed by the National Health Service or a third sector provider. This may include a suspension of criminal justice proceedings with the targeting of this and how compliance is monitored/managed requiring careful consideration. Perhaps more importantly, however, the provision of drug treatment would simultaneously need to be expanded in the community with an aim that this be available for all those who seek it out. Whilst this would provide drug services for all, an ambition would be for PDUs to access this before they become PDUs. This would mean that they engage with drug treatment prior to encountering the criminal justice system. Nevertheless, just because an individual engages with drug treatment does not necessarily mean they would not be offending so we may need to think more radically around how we might address this.

One potential avenue is through heroin-assisted treatment (HAT). HAT involves the prescription of diamorphine (laboratory-grade heroin) to those dependent on heroin. This usually requires individuals to attend a clinical facility where their use is supervised by trained professionals and where they have access to wider support services. Evidence indicates that HAT can reduce not only health-related harms but also drug-related offences (HMIP, 2021). There has, however, been a reluctance towards implementing HAT in England and Wales although a small number of pilot projects are ongoing. This is perhaps odd as if we are to believe the basis of the policy through which we currently respond to PDUs – that heroin leads to drug-related offences through a need to fund this use, surely, if we were to remove this financial motivation by prescribing free heroin, then this would have the same effect as someone stopping using heroin – they would stop committing crime. There is clearly an argument here that the state should not sponsor someone's drug use, nor should it accommodate a drug dependency as the goal should be recovery and becoming drug free. That said, given that most PDUs are already prescribed methadone with a body of those who receive such prescriptions having done so for a great many years (OHID, 2021), why not change this – or at least offer as an alternative, a drug that more closely mirrors the effect of heroin, and, if the belief that drugs cause crime is true, would mitigate this link. Admittedly, HAT is not a standalone panacea (Wakeman, 2015) and would need to be integrated with other drug treatment services which attempt to incorporate wider work around the structural social equalities PDUs experience in a bid to build towards recovery.

One way of doing this would be to extend the availability or divert PDUs into therapeutic communities (TCs). TCs employ a more holistic pathway directly towards abstinence, viewing drug dependency as a symptom of an individual's underlying and/or outstanding psychological, interpersonal and/or social difficulties – in essence, as a disorder of the whole person with full recovery only achievable if all these elements are addressed. Scott and Gosling (2016:53) have questioned whether TCs 'can be promoted for substance-using lawbreakers as part of a wider prison abolitionist strategy aiming to reduce social harms and challenge social and economic inequalities'. They argue that TCs represent a politically plausible and radical alternative to prison sentences – for our purposes, however, TCs could credibly be used as an alternative to any criminal justice sanction. Scott and Gosling (2106:63) argue that 'its logic of support is the antithesis of the punitive trajectory' and that TCs, 'when promoted as part of wider strategy to tackle social inequalities and social injustice, may be an intervention that can help ameliorate, rather than exacerbate, some of the worst harms, pains and injuries generated in advanced capitalist societies'.

CONCLUSION

This chapter has provided insight into how the criminal justice system responds to those drug-related offences committed by PDUs. It offers an explanation as to why a bespoke criminal justice system materialised which differentially processes drug and non-drug users. Whilst that system once provided end-to-end drug interventions, including court-sanctioned drug treatment to PDUs, the organisation and management of this and indeed the availability of drug services have been depleted over the last decade. The renewed investment promised by the 2021 drug strategy, however, indicates a continued belief in the relevance and efficacy of this approach. In one sense, this seems well founded given the apparent link between drugs and crime and the ability of court-sanctioned treatment to reduce rates of both, as well as bringing other benefits to an individuals' health. That said, research into the effectiveness of such approaches is patchy and dated – the absence of studies focusing on the DRR being indicative of this. Additionally, whilst drug treatment can reduce crime, it does not eradicate it (Seddon, 2000). There are also strong arguments made about the negative impacts of drug interventions being located within the criminal justice system and particularly around the intrusive nature of methods such as drug testing and the ethics of coerced drug treatment. Furthermore, that drug treatment has been brought into the fold of the criminal justice system has simultaneously framed PDUs as a societal threat who are compassionately offered help, which if they do not take opens them up to punishment. Regardless of which path is trodden, neither the carrot nor the stick of coercive sanctions addresses the underlying issues of social, political and economic marginalisation, which characterise PDUs' lives. Consequently, drug users are still disproportionately evident in both community and custodial criminal justice settings.

SUMMARY

- **Drug-related offences refer to acquisitive crimes committed to finance drug use.**
- **The volume of drug-related crimes committing by PDUs prompted a bifurcated criminal justice system which differentiates between drug-using and non–drug-using offenders.**
- **Drug testing is used to identify and monitor PDUs.**
- **The criminal justice system has drug interventions at every stage, enabling PDUs to access drug services.**
- **Drug interventions employ a carrot-and-stick approach whereby PDUs are offered help but if they fail to engage/comply face punitive responses.**

- **Court-sanctioned treatment can be made via a DRR as part of a Community Order or Suspended Sentence Order.**
- **The effectiveness of coerced drug treatment is questionable, but studies generally show that it can reduce levels of crime and drug use, with the length of time an individual is retained in treatment being key.**
- **Coerced drug interventions can be questioned in terms of their wider effects on dependent drug users and whether they are overly intrusive.**

Here are some points and questions for you to consider after reading this chapter:

1) Is court-sanctioned drug treatment delivered via the criminal justice system effective?
2) The idea of testing drug-using offenders is controversial. What are the advantages and disadvantages of this?
3) Drug treatment appears to reduce but not eliminate crime – what issues does this raise?

Here are some useful resources for those of you who want to further explore the issues raised in this chapter:

- Black, C. (2021) Review of drugs part two: prevention, treatment, and recovery. Available at: https://www.gov.uk/government/publications/review-of-drugs-phase-two-report/review-of-drugs-part-two-prevention-treatment-and-recovery

  This is the second part of Dame Carol Black's independent review prepared for the UK government, which focuses on drug treatment. It argues that the current system is unfit for purpose and provides a blueprint for how this needs to be overhauled.
- Hucklesby, A. and Wincup, E. (Eds.) (2010) *Drug Interventions in Criminal Justice.* Maidenhead: Open University Press.

  This text offers the best insight into the evidence base for today's bifurcated criminal justice system. It maps out the drug interventions evident at every stage of the criminal justice system, from the policing of PDUs to drug testing to treatment outcomes.
- McKeganay, N. (2011) *Controversies in Drugs Policy and Practice.* Basingstoke: Palgrave Macmillan.

  This seminal text offers some very different ways of thinking about drugs. For those interested in reading more about a potential drug treatment revolution, see the chapter titled 'Drug Treatment: So What's All the Fuss About?'.

8
DRUGS IN PRISON

Overview

This chapter aims to provide you with:

- An overview of drugs in prison and the prison drug strategy.
- An understanding of why people use drugs in prison.
- A critical overview of how prisons reduce the use of drugs as well as their supply using examples.
- A critical understanding of recovery in the prison context.

You will be introduced to the key terms:

- Demand and supply reduction
- Recovery
- Integrated drug treatment system
- Mandatory drug tests
- Recovery

INTRODUCTION

The prevalence of drugs in prison is well established globally. Not only are people sent to prison for drug offences (see Chapter 6) but prisoners also have higher rates of drug use than general population samples, which has led some to conclude that there is undoubtedly a connection between drug use and criminality (see Chapter 5). Understanding the role of drugs in prison and the challenges it poses to prison services around the world will be the focus of this chapter. Looking at drug use (both problematic/uncontrolled and non-problematic/controlled), the ensuing discussion will examine prison drug use and the supply of substances, including how HM Prison Service endeavours to stop drugs entering their establishments while also offering treatment. It will look at the extent and nature of drugs in prison and the challenges drugs pose in terms of security and violence. This chapter will cover traditional drugs, novel psychoactive substances (NPS), illicit use of prescribed and over-the-counter medications, as well as alcohol.

Drugs are readily available and used in prisons around the globe. Ironically, however, they also hold and punish people sentenced to prison for drug offences – possession and supply. Although criminal sanctions for drug possession have been removed in more than 30 countries and 50 jurisdictions, half a million people (470,000) worldwide are in prison for drug possession for personal use (Penal Reform, 2022). In fact, it is estimated that overall, 2.2 million people worldwide are in prison for drug offences with some of the longest prison sentences and severest punishments saved for drug trafficking/dealing (see Chapters 6 and 9). Several countries retain the death penalty/capital punishment for these offences. At least 285 people were executed for drug offences in 2022, a 118% increase compared to 2021 (Penal Reform, 2023).

Globally, prisons operate a zero-tolerance approach to illicit drugs – their use and supply – in prisons. The current Prison Drug Strategy (2019) in England and Wales adopts the same twin-track approach as seen in the national drug strategies – demand and supply reduction – and also replicates the 2010 and 2017 strategy's focus on building recovery (see Chapter 3). Developed by the Ministry of Justice and Her Majesty's Prison and Probation Service (HMPPS) it aims 'to tackle the problem of drug misuse in prisons' by preventing 'drugs being available in prisons (restrict supply)', to 'support prisoners to reduce and avoid drug misuse (reduce demand)', and to 'provide the help and treatment they need to maintain their recovery (building recovery)' (HMPPS, 2019:5) (see Figure 8.1). In prison, drugs – use and supply – have been linked to violence, bullying and crime – including organised crime – increased vulnerability, self-harm and suicide, all of which 'threatens safety and the ability of our hard-working prison staff to deliver effective regimes' (HMPPS, 2019:3).

Adopting a whole-system approach, it focuses on five areas:

1) People – that prisons have the right staff, with appropriate skills and support.
2) Procedural – that prison processes are clear, fair and effective.
3) Physical – that prison conditions are safe, clean and decent and promote well-being and recovery

To reduce drug misuse in prisons, we will		
Restrict supply	**Reduce demand**	**Build recovery**
• Minimise the supply of drugs into prisons through guidance, processes and technology. • Find drugs that do enter prisons using searching, intelligence and drug testing. • Disrupt the trade of drugs within prisons, working with law enforcement, sharing information and tackling corruption.	• Ensure there are the right incentives in prisons to encourage and support prisoners to make good decisions. • Provide productive opportunities and constructive relationships with staff to steer prisoners away from drugs. • Engage with families, friends and peers to help prisoners develop networks that will support them to avoid substance misuse.	• Collaborate with health partners to ensure successful commissioning and delivery of substance misuse services. • Share successful initiatives from the Drug Recovery Prison pilot to build a whole prison, recovery focus. • Work with community partners to ensure that prisoners receive continuity of care when released from prison.

Figure 8.1 Prison Service Drug Strategy (HMPPS, 2019)

4) Population – that prisoners have positive relationships and engage in constructive activities.
5) Partnership – that all the organisations contributing to achieving our aims work together effectively.

A whole-system approach involves multi-agency cooperation and partnership working that includes National Health Service England/Public Health England, local authorities and providers of substance use services both within and outside prison, which vary depending on those operating in the local area. As illustrated in Chapters 2 and 3, the history of drug policy and the changing dominance of the Home Office and the Department of Health over its direction is also reflected in prisons. The responsibility for the funding and commissioning of drug treatment in prisons has also alternated between the National Offender Management Service and the Ministry of Justice and the Department of Health/Public Health England.

The whole-system approach adopted by the prison service uses integrated offender management (IOM) as a framework to facilitate multi-agency cooperation aimed at recovery and abstinence. IOM ensures a coordinated approach of expertise and local teams of professionals who follow them through prison to release. Aimed at the most prolific and persistent offenders, IOM aims to reduce crime and reoffending, and increase public safety, and varies across localities to reflect local priorities (Home Office, 2015). Prolific offenders are those who commit over 5% of all reoffences, despite constituting less than 1% of all prisoners, and have a reoffending rate of 75% (MoJ, 2013a:21). Evidence underpinning the efficacy of IOM is mixed however (see Hadfield et al., 2021; Senior et al., 2011) but nonetheless operates across the prison estate.

CONTEXT AND THE PRISON CRISIS: ARE DRUGS TO BLAME?

While drugs and their use have been blamed for contributing to violence and self-harm while also having a negative impact on prisoner well-being (HMIP, 2023), the reality is that the prison estate has been in crisis for over 50 years. While over recent years there has been a rapid deterioration in safety across the prison estate as rates of violence, self-harm and suicide/death have reached record highs with one-third of prisoners fearing for their safety (HMIP, 2019; PRT, 2024), these issues are not solely down to drugs and their use. A lack of purposeful activity, a reduction in funding, a decline in standards and reduced staffing – particularly experienced staff – have all resulted in regime restrictions, with some prisoners spending the majority of the day in their cells (HMIP, 2023; PRT, 2024). Despite restricted regimes, drugs are still easily available in prison (HMIP, 2023). In fact, according to Carol Black's review (2020, 2021), drug use in prisons is closely linked to the amount of purposeful activity available to prisoners.

A reduction in purposeful activities is a consequence of a reduction in staff across the prison estate, meaning prisoners are locked in their cells for up to 23 hours a day, which results in increased drug use, mental ill health, resentment, boredom and poor staff–prisoner relationships. Alongside other security issues (e.g. increased violence, lockdown being used to manage dangerous/risky situations), understaffing also weakens the prison's ability to detect and disrupt the supply of drugs (Blakey, 2008; HMIP, 2019). In fact, there is a growing acknowledgement that prisons are more 'inhuman and degrading (in England and Wales, in conditions of high security) than they once were' (Liebling, 2011:532), which is evidenced by the HM Chief Inspector of Prisons, who said prisoners were living in 'some of the most disturbing prison conditions we have ever seen – conditions which have no place in an advanced nation in the 21st century' (HMIP, 2018:7). Substances and the use of drugs in prison are not only a result of these conditions but they also contribute to them and have been continually linked with violence, bullying and debts while also undermining the rehabilitation, healthcare and treatment provided in prison, all of which are already significantly lacking (HMIP, 2018, 2019).

To try and tackle the most persistent and urgent problems facing some of the more difficult prisons, the government launched the 10 Prisons Pilot Project, which aimed to enhance security, improve standards and strengthen leadership. The £10-million project focused on tackling violence, improving safety and decency (e.g. by improving residential areas inside the prisons), boosting leadership capabilities through new training and tackling drugs and mobile phones via improved security (e.g. x-ray body scanners, metal-detecting equipment, drug trace detection machines and toilet traps to collect flushed contraband). Overall, the pilot was deemed to be a success as there was a reduction in assaults and a reduction in positive drug tests across the prisons (see MoJ, 2019). As a result, many of these initiatives have now been rolled out across the prison estate. Despite this increased security, drugs are still readily available in prison, with some prisoners stating they are easier to obtain in prison than they are outside of prison (O'Hagan and Hardwick, 2017; PRT, 2024), which may explain why substance use is so high among prisoners.

EXTENT AND NATURE OF DRUG USE IN PRISONS

The rate of substance use among prisoners is higher than the general population and about 1 in 3 people in prison are problematic/addicted drug users (Black, 2021; PRT, 2023). In fact, the majority of prisoners report having used drugs prior to prison, although this varies across studies (60–82%) (Boys et al., 2002; MoJ, 2013b; PRT, 2024; UKDPC, 2008). The prevalence of drug use among prisoners also varies by gender with women being more likely to report entering prison with a drug problem/addiction (37%) than men (25%), although 1 in 10 women and 1 in 8 men report developing a drug problem since their arrival in prison (this includes illegal drugs and prescribed medications) (Boys et al., 2002; PRT, 2023). Just under a quarter of prisoners (22%) admitted drinking every day before coming to prison, with women being significantly more likely (23%) than men (15%) to have a problem with alcohol upon arrival (PRT, 2023). Globally, the increase of drug users in the prison population is evident (EMCDDA, 2001; Hiller et al., 1999). Although the majority of prisoners have used drugs and some initiate drug use in prison, some drug users also use prison as a means of desisting from drugs and using the time and support available to help them take a break from the chaos and to cease using drugs and, in some instances, achieve abstinence. Some prisoners will even get themselves sent to prison because they have a better chance of receiving drug treatment in there than in the community as waiting lists can sometimes be long and criminal justice referrals take priority.

The substances used in prison tend to reflect those used on the outside and include traditional illicit drugs (e.g. cannabis, cocaine and heroin), NPS (e.g. synthetic cannabinoids), prescribed medications (e.g. painkillers and opiate substitutes), illicit alcohol and vaping, since prisons are now smoke free. Although traditional drugs like cannabis and opiates still dominate drug use in prisons, there has been an increase in the use of NPS – mostly synthetic cannabinoids – and diverted medications, although this varies by establishment, with drugs being worse in local category C male prisons (Black, 2020, 2021). While cannabis remains the drug of choice among prisoners, the introduction of mandatory drug tests (MDTs) displaced some cannabis users onto heroin in the 1990s (see the Box on page 187). According to MDTs – that are supposed to show drug use patterns in prison – in 2020, 42% of positive MDTs were for cannabis, 30% for NPS and 15% for opiates, although positive tests for cocaine have increased by 398% since 2015 (HMPPS Annual Digest, 2019/2020). It was not just illicit drugs, but prisoners also said that it was easy to get alcohol in prison (PRT, 2023) (see the Box below). It must be noted however, that patterns of drug use amongst prisoners' change over time (see HMIP, 2015). The drugs being used in prison also depend on the category of prison and its security, types of prisoner, sentence lengths, country and geographical region within countries (Wakeling and Lynch, 2020), all of which differ greatly across the prison estate.

Alcohol in Prison: Hooch and Moonshine

The presence and impact of alcohol in prisons is a global phenomenon, with inmates obtaining it through smuggling, illicit brewing (referred to as hooch, moonshine or prison wine) using yeast and/or fruit/vegetables and/or corrupt staff. Alcohol use in these environments poses challenges related to security, health and rehabilitation. Efforts to control alcohol in prisons include searches, intelligence-led operations and staff training to detect and prevent smuggling. Treatment programmes for alcohol dependence are also implemented (e.g. Alcoholics Anonymous) (OHID, 2022).

Although the majority of prisoners use drugs (60–82%), they do so unproblematically (recreationally/controlled) (87%), and fewer than a quarter (13%) of these report more problematic patterns of use (e.g. heroin and crack use). Just under a quarter of drug-using arrestees reported heroin and crack use, which is even lower when we look at all arrestees (13%) (UKDPC, 2008 and see Chapter 5). A small percentage of prisoners (4%), however, report intravenous drug use while in prison, with a quarter (25%) of these initiating this practice while in prison (Boys et al., 2002). Allwright and colleagues (2000) also found about a fifth (21%) of intravenous drug users reported first injecting in prison, but more worryingly, 71% of this group reported sharing needles in prison, thus increasing the likelihood of transmitting bloodborne viruses (e.g. hepatitis C, hepatitis B, HIV/AIDS). Although intravenous use of drugs decreases among prisoners who normally inject, when prisoners do use drugs intravenously in prison, they are more likely to do so in an unsafe manner as there are no needle exchanges in UK prisons and few resources to clean needles smuggled in (e.g. availability of bleach tablets, but these are not consistently supplied and are ineffective at sterilising needles).

Evidence also suggests that drug use, particularly problematic drug use, is linked to higher rates of self-harm and suicide, mental illness including personality disorders, as well as bullying, violence, debts, medical emergencies and costly treatment, while drug-using prisoners also have higher recidivism and mortality rates than non-drug users (Boys et al., 2002; PRT, 2023). It is estimated that there are about 300,783 problematic drug users in England with 70,000 of these passing through the prison system yearly and 39,000 being present at any one time (HOL/HOC, 2005), meaning that prison provides an opportunity to engage this hard-to-reach vulnerable population in treatment. Prisoners constitute a vulnerable population and have not only higher levels of substance use but also poorer rates of physical health, higher rates of mental ill health, social problems and more adverse childhood experiences than the general population, meaning their needs are some of the most complex and thus difficult to treat.

Mandatory Drug Tests

MDTs were introduced in 1996 and are implemented in five ways: a random computer-generated list of names of both remand and sentenced prisoners is created monthly; suspicion testing (suspect a prisoner has used drugs); part of frequent testing for those with a history of drug use; all new arrivals to prison are tested on reception; and as part of a risk assessment (e.g. if the prisoner is applying for a privileged position or a job). The aim of MDTs is three-fold:

1) To deter prisoners from using drugs.
2) To provide information on patterns of drug use.
3) To identify individuals in need of treatment.

Between 5 and 10% of prisoners are tested each month. Prisoners are required to provide a sample via law – the Criminal Justice and Public Order Act 1994 – and a positive MDT will be charged under prison rules where a stipendiary magistrate can give up to 42 additional days as a punishment. Prisoners may also lose privileges and be put in segregation or on closed visits, and it may also affect their parole chances and prisoner category as a punishment. A failure to provide a sample is as serious as giving a positive test, and if prisoners try to evade MDTs by saying they cannot give a sample, they can be kept in segregation and given water until they do. Positive MDTs are highest in local prisons (HMIP, 2015) and cost £4.4 million in 2018/2019, 'twice the cost of running a credible drugs reduction and rehabilitation programme, and around half the total healthcare expenditure for a prison' (Gore and Bird, 1996:1124).

When MDTs were first introduced, there was evidence to suggest some prisoners switched from using cannabis to using heroin in prison as it could be eliminated from their system quicker (3 days) than cannabis (over 14 days), thus allowing them to avoid a positive test (Farrell et al., 2000; MacDonald, 1997; O'Hagan and Hardwick, 2017) although evidence on the extent of this is mixed (Edgar and O'Donnell, 1998). This was also seen more recently when prisoners switched from using cannabis to using synthetic cannabinoids – 'spice' – in prison. The main reason provided by prisoners for switching to synthetic cannabinoids was to avoid positive MDTs since they were undetectable in drug tests. This happened not only in the United Kingdom but also in countries around the world (EMCDDA, 2018, 2019; Hvozdovich et al., 2020; Rodrigues et al., 2022). Therefore, research illustrates the adverse impact drug policy can have on prisoners and their substance use, with users switching to potentially more harmful substances, or in relation to synthetic cannabinoids, of unknown harm. NPS have been linked to 117 deaths in prison (2013–2018) (PRT, 2023). Initially, the addition of synthetic cannabinoids to the drug tests led to an increase in positive tests in 2018 (11,093) – 48% were NPS – which led to the highest number of positive MDT tests since 1999 (11,313) (HMPPS Annual Digest, 2019/2020).

(Continued)

(Continued)

MDTs, however, have been heavily criticised as 'no longer an accurate measure of drug use in British Prisons' as many of the diverted medications used by prisoners cannot be detected in MDTs, thus underestimating the level of drug use reported (HMIP, 2015:4). There is also evidence that the MDT system is not being implemented effectively in 46% of prisons (HMIP, 2015).

WHY USE DRUGS IN PRISON?

Drugs are used in prison for a variety of reasons that vary across drugs, users and instances. Some may use drugs recreationally at weekends, while other prisoners will use them on a daily basis. According to Wheatley (2007 in Jewkes, 2007), there are five explanatory reasons on why people use drugs in prison:

1) **Self-medication model:** can operate on several levels and include both recreational/controlled and problematic/uncontrolled use of substances as a way to self-medicate. Self-medication occurs on a continuum of severity. From minor mood enhancements or mood alleviation to using drugs to forget about life's problems and to escape from reality. At the more serious end of the spectrum, some individuals use drugs (to varying degrees) as a form of self-medication, to block out traumatic and negative life events, to deal with stress, to cope with particular lifestyles (e.g. homelessness, sex working), to alleviate mental illness and as a palliative for failing to achieve societal goals and/or because they are unhappy with their life. This is true outside and inside prison, but there are specific reasons why people initiate drug use in prison as a form of self-medication, including not being able to obtain prescription medications (Cope, 2003). Prisoners do not passively undergo imprisonment, and it has been extensively shown that prison can cause lasting damage to many prisoners; something that is also acknowledged in the current prison drug strategy (HMPPS, 2019:19) – 'being in prison can often exacerbate poor mental health and wellbeing and prisoners can turn to drugs'.
   Prisoners will often self-medicate with drugs in prison due to:
   - **Past Trauma** – The prevalence of childhood trauma and drug use is much higher among offenders than in general population samples. Prisoners experience higher levels of cumulative childhood trauma and drug use, with problematic drug users being over-represented in the prison population (Messina et al., 2007). The relationship between trauma and substance use exists, particularly among offenders (Ayres, 2020c; Boys et al., 2002; Grella et al., 2005; Reavis et al., 2013) but is somewhat complex and mediated by a range of factors that includes coping style (Ayres, 2020c; Min et al., 2007), ethnicity and gender (Grella et al., 2005; Lansford et al., 2010; Min et al., 2007; Widom et al., 2006). While research shows a consistently strong relationship between childhood

trauma and adult substance use among women, it is less clear for men (see Chapters 1 and 8).

- **Pains of Imprisonment** – Sykes (1958) identified 5 pains of imprisonment – deprivation of liberty, goods and services, heterosexual relationships, autonomy and security – that prisoners endure. As a response to these pains and tied to the self-medication model above, some prisoners may turn to drugs to help them to cope with these pains (Ayres et al., 2024; Crewe, 2005). Whether drugs are a way to regain control, reduce anxiety, alleviate boredom or help them to sleep, prisoners give an array of reasons of why they turn to drugs whilst in prison (Ayres et al., 2024; Boys et al., 2002; Bullock, 2003; Crewe, 2005). Drug use helps to alleviate the pains of imprisonment and avoid/escape the psychological impact prison has on the individual's psyche.
- **Mental Ill Health:** Prisoners have higher rates of mental illness than the general population, particularly higher rates of comorbidity (HMPPS, 2019; Singleton et al., 1999). The majority of women (76%) and half of men (51%) report having a mental health problem (PRT, 2023) and those with mental health issues are also significantly more likely to report problematic drug use (HMIP, 2015). In fact, most problematic drug users have complex social, physical, dependence and mental health issues (HMIP, 2015). The more complex and higher number of psychiatric diagnoses statistically predicted heroin and cocaine use (Boys et al., 2002). Boys and colleagues (2002:1557) also found that prisoners with 'an adult diagnosis of antisocial personality disorder were approximately three times as likely to have used cocaine and/or heroin'. The relationship between mental ill health and substance use is complex and an array of factors have been associated with psychiatric issues among prisoners that include truancy, expulsion from school, abuse, trauma, unemployment, socioeconomic status, ethnicity and age (Singleton et al., 1998). The use of PS in prison has also led to an increase in mental health issues (e.g. paranoia, anxiety, psychosis, psychiatric complications), rates of self-harm and suicide and even death (HMIP, 2015; Home Office, 2014; PRT, 2023). Prison can lead to poor mental health and/or exacerbate existing mental health issues leading prisoners to use drugs (HMPPS, 2019).

2) **Time Management Model** – Drug use helps prisoners to pass the time in prison, particularly when they are locked in their cells for most of the day. Whether it is a way of regaining control or about coping with the situation, prisoners use drugs to 'manipulate how they experience time' (Wheatley, 2007:404). Cohen and Taylor (1972 as cited in Wheatley, 2007) refer to this as mindscaping, where drugs are used to escape the confines of prison and their physical surroundings as they escape reality. Prisoners talk about killing time, relaxing and making the walls disappear. Drugs can offer 'sanctuary, diversion and relief' (Crewe, 2005:463). Also, sleeping is often not about resting but instead it is used to control and suppress time in prison (Cope, 2003).

3) **Social Network Model** – As on the outside, drugs are used to socialise in prison and provide prisoners with a sense of camaraderie and belonging (Ayres et al., 2024; Crewe, 2005). Although these social networks are often premised on associates rather than friendships, their instability and fragility are unimportant since they provide users with a common interest and shared experiences, although some also spoke of forming friendships over drugs (Crewe, 2005). Overall, drug use is seen as an integral part of social life in prison, although it must also be noted that drugs can also undermine prisoner relations and what Crewe (2005:466) refers to as 'inmate solidarity, trust and goodwill'.
4) **Status Model** – Drug use and drug dealing can infer power and status on prisoners (Crewe, 2005). It is widely acknowledged that supplying drugs facilitates status and respect (Collison, 1996; Hall et al., 2008; Preble and Casey, 1969) and this is also true in the context of prison (Crewe, 2005), where its hyper-masculine environment values anti-authoritarian, macho behaviour and risk-taking as the norm. As Crewe (2005:469) highlights, drug dealing 'carries considerable kudos as an organized, entrepreneurial, high-risk and potentially very lucrative endeavour. Inside prison, there is no question that, through the cost and desirability of their product, drug dealers can become extremely influential and comfortable figures'.
5) **Economic Model** – Most drug dealers supply drugs to make money (see Ayres and Ancrum, 2023) and this is also true in prison. Drug trafficking gives prisoners financial power (Crewe, 2005), both inside prison and on the outside since many will continue to deal drugs despite being in prison as a way to make money and even support their family.

The reasons given for using drugs in prison and the types of drugs used also depend on the population (e.g. adult or young offenders), geographical area/country, security category of the prison and changing trends in drugs that can often present the prison service with new challenges both in terms of supply and demand reduction. A clear example of this is the recent use and supply of synthetic cannabinoids (see the Box below), which has led to new procedural and security measures to prevent their supply into prison, as well as created new challenges for the staff (e.g. violence/aggression, convulsions, inconsistent effects, unknown toxicity, lack of pharmacological treatments, psychosis, hospitalisation and even death), which was exacerbated by the inability of drug testing to pick these substances up (HMIP, 2015; Ralphs et al., 2017; User Voice, 2016), making its identification and treatment in prison difficult.

Synthetic Cannabinoids in Prison

- Synthetic cannabinoids (spice, Black Mamba) became popular in UK prisons around 2010 with a marked increase in usage by 2013–2014 when it was said to be having a devastating and destabilising effect, causing a national panic that something needed to be urgently done.

- Recent reports suggest that while the prevalence of synthetic cannabis may have declined from its peak, it still poses significant challenges. In 2010, spice was seized 15 times in prison, compared to 737 times in 2014, and remained the most common substance seized in 2023 (32% of all seizures compared to 19% cannabis and 12% cocaine) (PRT, 2023). It was also an issue in American prisons (Hvozdovich et al., 2020).
- It became popular in prisons due to its legal status, potent effects, affordability, purity, ease of access, the difficulty in detecting it through standard drug testing methods (MDT), to relieve boredom, self-medication and coping with pains of imprisonment and it was not only relatively easy to smuggle into prisons, often disguised as legal substances or even sprayed onto paper and mailed to inmates, but replaced existing drug use, particularly cannabis use, as unlike natural cannabis it had no smell (Ralphs et al., 2017; User Voice, 2016; see also Chapter 11).
- Due to the varying potency and its inconsistent effects, prisoners are being used as 'spice pigs' or 'mamba muppets' to test new strands of synthetic cannabis, which were then often videoed suffering from the adverse effects of intoxication and posted on YouTube or TikTok (McMann et al., 2022).
- The adverse effects include seizures, psychosis, loss of motor control, mental ill health, self-harm, addiction, an irregular heartbeat and death. According to the ONS (2023) between 2017 and 2019, death certificates of 37 prisoners mentioned synthetic cannabinoids, making it the most commonly implicated drug in deaths in custody. The use of spice was also linked to debt, violence, bullying and intimidation (HMIP, 2016; Ralphs et al., 2017; User Voice, 2016), all of which created significant challenges for prison management and healthcare services, particularly as there was no treatment for synthetic cannabinoids.
- In response to the rising issue, the UK government and prison authorities implemented several measures that improved detection (e.g. MDTs that do detect synthetic cannabinoids) and prevention (e.g. photocopying the mail stopped letters soaked in synthetic cannabinoids from reaching prisoners) and education. Prisons introduced several measures to the Psychoactive Substances Act 2016, making it illegal to possess NPS, including synthetic cannabis in a custodial institution (see Chapter 3).

DEMAND REDUCTION

Demand reduction in prison focuses on a range of psychosocial and clinical interventions that operate in differing combinations across the prison estate (see Figure 8.2). These include:

- Integrated drug treatment system (IDTS)
- Drug services/workers
- Maintenance prescribing and detoxification

Figure 8.2 Demand Reduction in Prison (HMPPS, 2019)
Source: Contains public sector information licensed under the Open Government Licence v3.0.

- Compact-based drug testing
- Drug-free wings and orisons (see the Box on page 199)
- Rehabilitation programmes (see the Box on page 200)

Integrated Drug Treatment System

IDTS is an evidence-based approach that provides improved clinical management that is delivered by multi disciplinary teams to provide psychosocial and pharmacological treatment to those identified as problematic drug users during their first 28 days in prison (see Marteau et al., 2010 for a history of IDTS). Evidence shows that the first 28 days in prison increases the risk of self-harm and is when half of all self-inflicted deaths occur, with the majority (62%) of these being among problematic drug users

(Drug Strategy Unit, 2006). It ensures those engaged with IDTS are assessed upon arrival and a care plan created relating to their substance use, which relies on the drug services/workers (previously referred to as Counselling, Assessment, Referral, Advice and Throughcare (CARATS) workers) and includes maintenance prescribing and detoxification programmes. IDTS aims to increase the quality and volume of drug treatment available to prisoners and improve continuity of care from the community to prison.

Key Term

The CARAT (Counselling, Assessment, Referral, Advice and Throughcare) service was an initiative within the UK prison system aimed at addressing drug use among inmates. Upon arrival in prison, inmates were assessed by CARAT workers to determine their level of drug use and the necessary interventions to create a personalised treatment plan tailored to the specific needs of each inmate. They also offer advice (e.g. life skills), deliver counselling (individual and group) and refer them to appropriate drug treatment programmes, both within the prison and in the community (e.g. detoxification programmes, therapeutic communities) upon their release to ensure continuity of throughcare, starting from their time in prison through to their release and reintegration into the community.

MAINTENANCE PRESCRIBING/OPIATE SUBSTITUTION THERAPY AND DETOXIFICATION

The IDTS means all new arrivals to prison are assessed for substance use and withdrawal from alcohol and drugs, usually through urine testing. Problematic/dependent substance users are an at-risk group, particularly in the first 24 hours to five days arriving in prison when they are more likely to start withdrawing from drugs (HMIP, 2015; Jacobson et al., 2007). While this was not always the case, the importance of clinically assessing prisoners upon arrival to prison for substance use acknowledges the high rates of self-harm and suicide among problematic drug users, particularly in the first 28 days in prison (Drug Strategy Unit, 2006). There are only two drug withdrawals that are life threatening, and that is withdrawing from alcohol or benzodiazepines (e.g. as Xanax, Klonopin, Ativan, Valium), illustrating the importance of assessing all new arrivals in prison. Those who are physically dependent on a substance should be offered low-dose substitution therapy – this is where they prescribe a pharmacologically similar substance to stave off withdrawal symptoms. Those prisoners who arrive already prescribed substitute therapy in the community will usually have it maintained in prison to ensure continuity of care and stabilisation. Maintenance prescribing operates sporadically around the world's prisons (EMCDDA, 2022) and has led to court cases in a number of countries (see the Box on page 195).

Key Terms

Maintenance/Substitute Prescribing/OST – where a drug user is prescribed a pharmacologically similar substance to the main drug that they use as a substitute to illicit street drugs. For opiates, prescribing a stable dose of methadone or buprenorphine over a sustained period of time.

Detoxification – also known as assisted withdrawal, supports the user to reduce their reliance on substances via a planned regime that reduces the dose being taken daily – either of the drug or the substitute drug – until they are drug free (abstinent).

Retoxification – prisoners who reduce their drug use and/or achieve abstinence in prison may be vulnerable to relapse and overdose on release, particularly in the first few weeks. Released prisoners are 40–50 times more likely to die than the general population (over 90%) as a result of drugs, meaning that 1 in 8 prisoners overdose on heroin within 2 weeks of release and male prisoners are 29 times more likely to die and women were 69 times more likely to die the week following release (Farrell and Marsden, 2008). This also happens in Europe (EMCDDA, 2001). Thus, some prisons retoxify prisoners with a pharmacologically similar substance before release to avoid death by overdose.

An increase in maintenance prescribing is partly the reason for a decrease in heroin use, and while opiate substitution therapy (OST) is an effective intervention for heroin use and dependence (PHE, 2014), it is one of the medications commonly diverted in prison (HMIP, 2015). The most commonly diverted medications in prison are those that have a depressant effect and include opiate substitution medicines (e.g. buprenorphine, benzodiazepines, antidepressants and painkillers) largely because of their low cost, availability, perceived undetectability and guaranteed effect (Bullock, 2003; HMIP, 2015). While some prisoners sell their medication – to make money – others have it taken from them against their will (e.g. through theft or bullying), which leads to violence/disorder, debts, unexpected drug interactions and occasionally death (HMIP, 2015; Tompkins, 2016).

Public Health England has stressed that while opiate substitution treatment (OST) is an effective intervention for heroin use and dependence, the medication itself and accompanying psychosocial/recovery interventions need to be optimised to give the user the best chance of recovery and sustained abstinence (PHE, 2014). There is, however, much controversy over maintaining drug users in prison versus abstinence. Even Her Majesty's Inspectorate of Prisons said they 'welcomed a shift in emphasis from long-term methadone maintenance prescribing towards a recovery-orientated drug treatment approach' (HMIP, 2011:12), although why remains unclear. It must be acknowledged, however, that abstinence is not achievable or appropriate for everyone. In fact, as a treatment objective, abstinence-focused recovery has been heavily criticised (Best et al., 2010) and has left the aims of drug treatment tense and confused (see the recent debate about harm reduction and abstinence, cf. McKeganey, 2011; Neale et al., 2013). Therefore, there is much debate about the focus on recovery.

Study Question: Is Opiate Substitution Therapy/Methadone Maintenance a Human Right?

- Prisoners are sent to prison for punishment and not for further punishment, and as such, they are entitled to the same standards of healthcare that are available in the community (UNODC, 2015), so prisoners entering prison were forced to withdraw from heroin with no medical help or support, meaning they involuntarily had to endure the physical and psychological symptoms of withdrawal without their consent.
- As a result, 197 prisoners in the United Kingdom sued the Home Office for compensation as they claimed it breached their human rights against torture (mental or physical) and inhuman or degrading treatment or punishment (Article 3), the right not to be discriminated against (Article 14), the right to health and to life (Article 2) and the right to live your life privately without government interference (Article 8).
- It also raised serious ethical issues for prison healthcare providers as it potentially violated the basic principle of beneficence and nonmaleficence (e.g. to help and do no harm, which includes not inflicting pain and suffering) (Bruce and Schleifer, 2008).
- Similar law suits have also occurred in other countries including the United States and Australia.
- Methadone is recommended by the National Institute for Clinical Excellence (2007) and has a substantial evidence base underpinning its efficacy.

BUILDING RECOVERY: DRUG TREATMENT

The focus of more recent drug strategies has shifted towards recovery (and some would argue, abstinence), which has become the aim of drug treatment (HMPPS, 2019) (see Figure 8.3). The evidence however shows that prison drug treatment mostly constitutes stabilising prisoners with no aim of achieving long-term recovery (Black, 2020).

The concept of recovery is not a new phenomenon and has been revived, largely due to the backlash against methadone maintenance and requests from the abstentionist movement, that abstinence-based treatment is not only more effective but also what users want (see McKeganey, 2011). Some commentators believe users are being denied the opportunity to become drug free (Gyngell, 2011; McKeganey, 2011) as drug treatment in prison is ill-equipped to facilitate and support long-term recovery, and community treatment struggles to cope with the numbers being coerced into the system (Black, 2021). While drug treatment is available in prison, short sentences mean that two-thirds are in it for less than six months, with many in it for less than a month, meaning there is not enough time for treatment to effect change (Black, 2021). This is exacerbated further by the lack of continuity of care for most prisoners

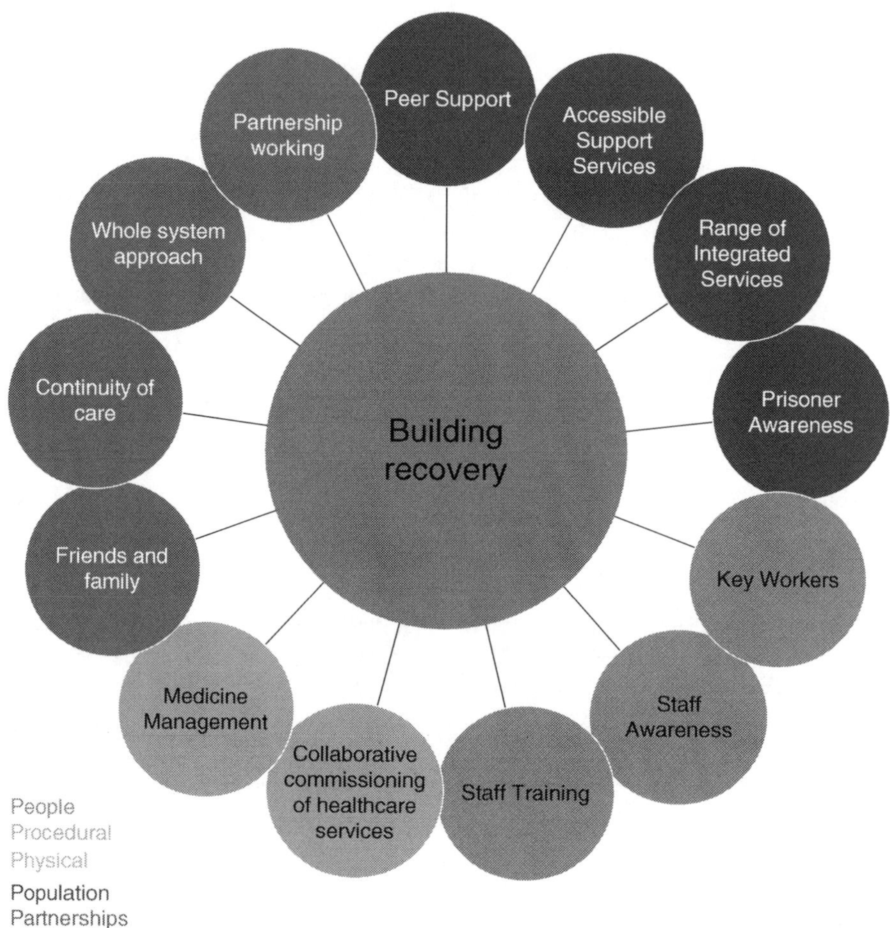

Figure 8.3 Recovery in Prison (HMPPS, 2019)
Source: Contains public sector information licensed under the Open Government Licence v3.0.

on release as only a third of people referred for community treatment after release go on to receive it within three weeks, which for non-opiate users is even lower (1 in 10) (Black, 2021), which has led to an increase/refocus on Through the Gate services (see Millings et al., 2019; Taylor et al., 2017). There is also a need for better multi-agency co-operation when people are transitioning from prison to the community, particularly for substance users, who have a higher mortality rate on release than non-substance users.

Although there has been an emphasis on strengthening Through the Gate services across the prison estate, less than a quarter of men in prison reported they were receiving help with getting into employment upon release, and even fewer (20%) with setting up education/training and housing or being offered drug treatment (only a fifth said they had received it) (PRT, 2023). In 2023, over a third said they did not know where they would be living when released and two in five people in prison said they would accept help for their drug problem if they were offered it (PRT, 2023), illustrating that continuity of care is still inadequate/problematic. This has implications for rehabilitation and achieving long-term recovery despite evidence showing that being released with unsuitable accommodation and support undermines any drug recovery/rehabilitation work undertaken in prison (Lloyd et al., 2014).

DRUG TREATMENT IN PRISON

Drug treatment in prison is estimated to cost £106 million a year with approximately 20,815 individuals in prison-based treatment for drugs (Black, 2021), which is about 20% of all prison healthcare spending (PRT, 2019). Although 'prison-based drug treatment services have improved dramatically in England over the past 10 years' (HMIP, 2015), prisoner engagement is often too short to make a significant difference or achieve any long-term changes in their drug-using behaviour, since many drug users, particularly the most problematic opiate and crack users, only receive treatment for two weeks or less (Black, 2020). In fact, three-quarters of adults receiving drug treatment in prison do so for less than six months, with less than 5% receiving treatment for two years or more (Black, 2021). About 75% of men who had a drug problem on entry to prison received help (Black, 2021), although the quality and quantity of this help varied across the prison estate and are easily undermined by staff shortages, lock downs, restricted regimes and the presence of illicit substances. Also, the substances being used by those presenting to treatment are increasing, problematic and complex to treat. More opiate users presenting to prison treatment are also using crack cocaine, possibly reflecting the higher harms related to this polydrug use. There is also a slightly higher percentage of people presenting with crack only use (not with opiates) in prison alongside 1 in 8 presenting with problematic synthetic cannabinoid use (Black, 2021; PRT, 2019). These new synthetic cannabinoids are more potent than cannabis and have unknown pharmacological risk profiles that have led to seizures, behavioural disturbances, violence, convulsions, bullying and paranoia; they have even been attributed to some deaths (PRT, 2019). While effective treatment has been shown to improve quality of life, reduce drug use and lower recidivism rates thus saving money in the long run (Lloyd et al., 2014), the evidence base underpinning effective drug treatment in prison is mixed and inconclusive.

Key Term

Compact-Based Drug Testing, which includes Voluntary Drug Testing, Incentive-Based Drug Testing and Voluntary Testing Units, also referred to as drug-free wings (see PSI 31/2009), is where prisoners provide the prison with urine samples to be drug tested often to prove they are clean/abstinent from drugs. They cost the prison service £70,000 in 2018/2019 in terms of drug testing kits and analytical services.

Drug use by prisoners is also associated with adverse outcomes post-imprisonment, including lower rates of employment, more housing difficulties, worse physical health and an increased risk of death compared to prisoners who do not use drugs (Bukten et al., 2020). It is not only the efficacy of the support and treatment provided in prison that has been questioned; the failure to provide continuity of care both in prison and on release not only undermines the recovery and rehabilitation work that does go on in prison but it has also been attributed to a 274% increase in post-release deaths during supervision in the community, suggesting that better Through the Gate services and joined-up healthcare provision on release are needed alongside housing (Lloyd et al., 2014). Unless accommodation and support are available to prisoners upon release, drug recovery work in prisons is futile (Lloyd et al., 2014), emphasising the important of Through the Gate services and a joined-up prison approach that supports prisoners into the community. Through the Gate services aid with resettlement – drug treatment, housing and employment – and integrated local services take a holistic approach to promoting recovery and rehabilitation, in accordance with the Transforming Rehabilitation Agenda. Through the Gate services depend on each area and are often a postcode lottery.

Key Term

The Transforming Rehabilitation Agenda (2013–2016) was a reform programme aimed at reducing reoffending while protecting the public by changing the way offenders are managed in the community. It aimed to 'open up the market to a diverse range of rehabilitation providers and incentivise innovation by paying providers by results'; 'extend statutory rehabilitation to 45,000 short sentenced offenders released from prison every year, who have the highest reoffending rates and yet currently receive no supervision after release'; and 'resettle offenders "through the gate", with continuous support from custody to community' via a network of resettlement prisons (MoJ, 2015:1).

Those without suitable accommodation on release are at an increased risk of not only using substances but also reoffending (HMIP, 2019; Lloyd et al., 2014). It also illustrates that recovery is more than just about drug treatment and the support services provided in prison. Successful recovery is also grounded in the community and upon release (Best and Laudet, 2010). Meaning housing, employment and social care on release are equally as important and can undermine any rehabilitative and recovery work undertaken in prison (Black, 2020, 2021), emphasising the importance of a holistic joined-up approach, which adopts a whole-prison, whole-person approach.

The whole-prison approach emphasises the importance of looking at the entire offender journey, from induction through to working with reducing reoffending partnerships and resettlement teams upon release. The whole-prison approach is essential for creating a rehabilitative culture that everyone is responsible for and can impact, and which the whole regime has the potential to support or undermine (Mann et al., 2018; Møller et al., 2007). The whole-prison approach was used in the Drug Recovery Prison, which was a pilot project to test and develop new ways of addressing the supply and demand of illicit substances across the prison estate, improving health as a result of reduced drug use, supporting recovery and reducing reoffending on release into the community (see Ayres et al., 2023).

Drug Free/Rehabilitation Wings

- Prisons were given licence to develop their own Drug Rehabilitation Wing (DRW) models to reflect local needs.
- The resulting pilots were very varied: capacity ranged from 20 to 140 beds – therapeutic content varied from structured, full-time programmes to little more than the basic support offered elsewhere in the prison. Some were abstinence based but some only involved harm reduction. Some were run by uniformed prison officers and others by third sector drug treatment professionals. Some were segregated from the rest of the prison, while others shared the wider regime.
- These often rely on voluntary/compact-based drug testing to ensure the wings are drug free.
- Abstinence-focused DRWs experienced difficulties attracting prisoners on OST and evidence showed that in reality none of them were drug free. In all but one DRW cannabis, NPS (spice) and diverted medications (Subutex) were reportedly readily available, which is unsurprising since evidence shows that drug dealers will often target DRWs as the prisoners on them are vulnerable and can easily be tempted (Tompkins, 2015). Maintaining a therapeutic regime was problematic as therapeutic input could not fill the whole day, particularly if the DRW was trying to maintain a degree of segregation from the rest of the prison. For the most part, prisoners' physical and mental health declined over the course of their time on the DRWs and there was little evidence of improving attitudes or hopes for the future. Prisoners were disappointed by the level of preparation for release, the worst being housing and being released to a hostel or funded bed and breakfast.
- Outcomes: Those that were followed up six months after release showed considerable reductions in drug/alcohol use and self-reported offending. However, reoffending was still quite common (See Lloyd et al., 2014).

The nature and structure of drug treatment regimes in prison vary across the estate, from drug recovery wings (see the Box above) to drug treatment programmes (see the Box below). Drug treatment in UK prisons is tailored to meet the individual needs of inmates, thereby aiming to reduce drug dependency, improve health outcomes and reduce reoffending rates, which poses a similar question to that in Chapter 3 about drug policy being more about crime reduction than drugs: ***are drug treatment programmes delivered in prison about reducing crime and reoffending or drug use (see the Box below)?*** What is clear is that according to the Nelson Mandela Rules

(UNODC, 2015), Rule 24, 'the provision of health care for prisoners is a State responsibility. Prisoners should enjoy the same standards of health care that are available in the community, and should have access to necessary health-care services free of charge without discrimination on the grounds of their legal status.' If this is the case, then ***why are there no needle exchanges in UK prisons, despite international evidence suggesting they work effectively (see Lines et al., 2006)?***

Drug Treatment Programmes in Prison

Short Duration Programme (SDP) – is a four-week intervention, based on CBT and harm minimisation for prisoners on remand or with less than six months left to serve.

Prison Partnership Twelve Step Programme (PPTSP) – based on the 12-step programme, it is aimed at medium– to high–risk-dependent drug users whose offending and drug use appear to be linked. Abstinence is the overall aim.

Rehabilitation of Addicted Prisoners Trust (RAPt) – offers three prison-based programmes – Alcohol Dependency Programme (ADP), Bridge Programme and the Substance Dependence Treatment Programme (SDTP) – based on the 12-step model, these programmes vary in duration from six to 22 weeks and are underpinned by cognitive strategies of behaviour modification and motivational enhancement. Abstinence is the overall aim.

Alcohol-Related Violence (ARV) – is a cognitive behavioural programme aimed at reducing reoffending for problematic drinkers with alcohol-related crimes of violence.

Building Skills for Recovery (BSR) – is a group-based psychosocial programme aimed at reducing problematic substance use and reoffending. The aim is to achieve the goal of recovery by formulating a person-centred recovery toolkit.

Control of Violence for Angry Impulsive Drinkers (COVAID) – aimed at aggressive and violent drinkers to reduce violence, this is a CBT programme aimed at binge drinkers and those who get into trouble on social drinking occasions.

Therapeutic Communities – HMP Grendon is a therapeutic community and a lot of other prisons have wings that operate as a therapeutic community. It is the most intense form of drug treatment since it operates 24 hours a day and uses CBT alongside social learning. It aims to reduce drug use and reoffending among medium– to high–risk-drug dependent offenders by giving them new skills and values to live drug- and crime-free lives.

Prison Addressing Substance Related Offending (P-ASRO) – is a CBT programme designed to assist prisoners to address illicit drug use and related offending, which aims to enhance motivation to change, strengthen self-control, develop strategies to avoid relapse to problem substance use and encourage lifestyle change to reduce the risk of a return to substance use and offending. It is intended for prisoners with a low to medium severity of dependence on substance use. This programme is no longer delivered.

FOCUS – is a CBT programme designed to assist prisoners with moderate to severe substance use problems address factors relating to substance (drug and alcohol) use, which are linked to their offending. This programme is no longer delivered.

(see page, 2017 for a review).

Supply Reduction

The rationale underpinning supply reduction is that a reduction in the availability of drugs leads to a reduction in drug use (Bullock, 2003; Grace et al., 2019). As the supply of drugs are reduced, however, it also increases the price, often reduces the quality and occasionally displaces use onto other substances that are more readily available (e.g. prescribed medications). Preventing the supply of drugs into prison has led to many procedural changes, which are constantly having to be reassessed as supply routes change and evolve in response to new security measures (Norman, 2022). These new security measures can also have unintended consequences (e.g. resource intensive) and infringe policies protecting personal privacy (e.g. photocopying the mail) (EMCDDA, 2022) (see Figure 8.4).

Supply reduction in prison tends to be achieved by increasing security; however, security alone is also not enough to stop the supply of drugs (e.g. it needs to be supported by effective staff training, capacity and deployment). In prison, there are three main types of security. Physical security (e.g. window restrictors, bars, new search areas), which includes new technologies (e.g. a millimetre wave scanner, a magnetic resonance scanner and a full-body X-ray scanner), procedural security (is the system and processes deployed to create safety and security like staff and room searching, patrols and intelligence gathering) and interpersonal security (is how information is acquired through conversations, interviews, covert intelligence, information gathering, relationships and procedural justice principles). These were all piloted in the Drug Recovery Prison (see Ayres et al., 2023).

The prison drug strategy (HMPPS, 2019:8) states that 'the availability of drugs in our prisons is a threat to safety and security, obstructing recovery for prisoners with drug misuse issues and leading others to develop issues while in prison'. Drugs enter prison in a variety of ways, including coming through the front gate via staff and deliveries, thrown over the wall/perimeter, through visits and the mail, inside prisoners/people entering or returning to prison and via new technologies like drones (Blakey, 2008; EMCDDA, 2022; HMPPS, 2019).

To reduce the supply of drugs, each prison has a local security strategy that implements a range of security measures aimed at enhancing physical, procedural and interpersonal security, which include:

- **Drug Dogs:** both passive and active drug dogs are used in all prisons to check the mail, search goods and vehicles, detect drugs on visitors and staff and to search the prison and all vehicles.

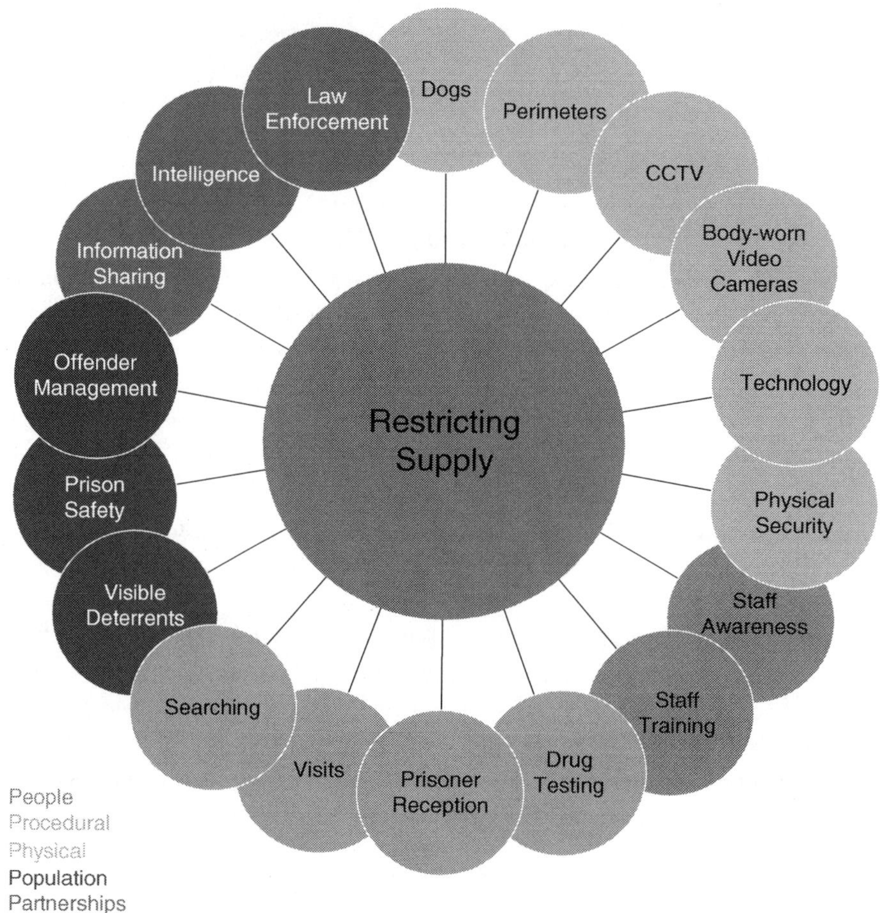

Figure 8.4 Supply Reduction in Prison (HMPPS, 2019)

Source: Contains public sector information licensed under the Open Government Licence v3.0.

- **Technology:** CCTV surveillance is used throughout the prison including on visits, while technology to detect mobile phones and drugs now includes body scanners, metal-detecting equipment, analysis of recovered handsets and SIM cards, drug trace detection machines, X-ray scanners for bags, number plate recognition and toilet traps.
- **Intelligence:** intelligence is gathered on prisoners and visitors to identify those supplying drugs in prison. Drug testing also provides intelligence (e.g. who is using drugs and what types of drugs). Working closely with the police – each prison usually has a prison liaison officer – those supplying drugs are targeted both inside and outside prison. 'HMPPS National Intelligence Unit is working with prisons, probation and law enforcement partners to pro-actively develop intelligence on offenders who present the greatest threat to prison security and public protection, including those involved in the supply of drugs' (HMPPS, 2019:11), which includes

staff. Intelligence on staff is gathered by prisons and law enforcement to identify staff who use their position for illicit gain.

- **Visits and Visitors:** CCTV and low furniture in visits make it more difficult to pass drugs, and visitors suspected of bringing drugs in may be searched, scanned/x-rayed and only allowed closed visits (e.g. through a screen), while in some instances, visits might be banned completely.
- **Prosecution and Punishment:** all visitors found bringing drugs into prison will be arrested and prosecuted as will all staff and prisoners, who will often invoke internal sanctions (e.g. losing privileges or put in solitary confinement) and be sentenced to extra days by a stipendiary magistrate.
- **Staff:** to increase staff resilience against corruption, training is provided and there is a new Counter Corruption Policy Framework (see the Box on page 204 on staff corruption).
- **Prescribed Medications:** working with healthcare providers to ensure prescribed medications are not diverted and used by other prisoners (e.g. implementing safe handling, transportation and storage, supervised consumption).

Prison Rules for Searching

- Prison Rule 41 – allows for every prisoner to be searched when taken into custody on reception, after visits and subsequently whenever deemed necessary. Prison officers have no legal authority to conduct an intimate search but can undertake strip searches.
- Prison Rule 71 – all persons seeking to enter or leave the prison, including visitors and their children, staff and prisoners' babies may be searched.
- All areas of the prison are Crown property and prison management has the power to have them searched at any time.

Increased security is the traditional approach to reducing the supply of drugs in prison, even though evidence shows that as soon as one supply route is disrupted, pressure is increased on the other routes, which is known as the balloon effect (Blakey, 2008). For example, if there is increased security for visits and the mail, drugs will start coming into the prison via staff or over the wall. Evidence also shows enhanced security needs to be supported by effective staff (training, capacity and deployment) and staffing issues (understaffing, poor retention and inadequate training and experience) continually undermine security and safety in prisons (Beard, 2019; HMIP, 2019). Security and safety alongside good intelligence and information sharing are also crucial to promoting recovery and creating a more reformative and rehabilitative culture in prison (Mann et al., 2018). Rather than stop the supply of drugs, however, the implementation of many security measures has often had a detrimental impact on the prison, prisoners and the staff (e.g. markets switch to supply more harmful drugs; prices increase and debts rise; new routes are found; disorder increases and debts escalate, which negatively impacts on relationships, violence, intimidation bullying and conflict in the prison)

(Blakey, 2008; Edgar and O'Donnell, 1998). Also, despite the increased technology, it is not always used consistently and the staff are not always adequately trained to use it (HMIP, 2022).

Supply of Drugs: Corrupt Staff

- Blakey (2008) estimates that there are 1,000 corrupt staff overall or seven corrupt staff per establishment.
- According to the Ministry of Justice, the number of staff found taking contraband into prisons in England and Wales has risen by 57% from 2012 to 2017, with 341 staff either dismissed, excluded, convicted or cautioned by police.
- In 2017, there were 71 cases of staff smuggling compared with 45 in 2012, and between 2020 and 2022, 80 officers were involved and 22 were convicted of bringing drugs into jails, while a further 58 were dismissed from the service or excluded from their workplace despite anti-corruption training and measures.
- Staff corruption has been attributed to staff cuts and a larger proportion of inexperienced officers, which has meant that those in post are more vulnerable to corruption.
- The new scanners implemented across the prison estate mean that since July 2020, 28,626 suspicious items have been identified (MoJ, 2023).

Despite security, drugs are still trafficked into prison. The drug trade in prison is lucrative (see the Box below) and many prisoners continue to run their drug-dealing businesses from prison via the use of illicit mobile phones, which are used to arrange deliveries (e.g. via visits, mail or packages thrown over the wall) and facilitate a continuous supply of drugs (Tompkins, 2015). The profit that can be generated by drug sales in prison is up to four times greater than that in the community (Crewe, 2005), while the profit to be made on NPS (synthetic cannabinoids) is 30 times higher in prison than on the outside where it can be bought for £3 per gram and resold in prison for £100 per gram (Ralphs et al., 2017). This is largely because prohibited commodities like drugs fetch higher prices in prison due to the risks taken to smuggle them in and their scarcity in prison compared to out in the community. The high profit margins make drug dealing an attractive and easy way to make money, which is why organised crime groups are often involved in prison drug markets (EMCDDA, 2022). Drugs in prison also tend to be of poor quality to maximise profits. A few countries have also reported cases in which people are believed to have deliberately breached their (parole) licence in order to take advantage of the high profits afforded by supplying drugs in prison (EMCDDA, 2022).

The Prison Drug Trade

- 3 ounces (tablespoons) of heroin will sustain the illegal drug trade for one month (Ministry of Justice, 2009).

- The drugs trade in UK prisons is estimated to be worth £100 million (Chambers, 2010), making it highly profitable.
- It is guesstimated that 22,000 kilos of drugs are smuggled in to British prisons every year.
- The illicit drug trade undermines security, drug treatment and rehabilitation schemes and is linked to violence, bullying and debts (Blakey, 2008; Djemil, 2008; HMIP, 2015).
- There are also huge profit margins with spice as outlined by Ralphs and colleagues (2017:61) 'wholesale prices (purchases of 100 g or more), an ounce (28 g) could be widely obtained for as little as £84 (£3 per gram) outside the prison via online sellers or high street headshops and resold inside the prison, typically compressed in the lid of a soft drink for an astounding £100 per gram.'

Globally, research has identified three drug market levels and main suppliers of drugs in prison (EMCDDA, 2022; Norman, 2022):

1) **Established Enterprises:** involves a network of multiple distributors that sell to prisoners and distributors are paid in drugs. Distributors deliver the drugs, collect payments and use violence to collect debts. These are similar to drug markets in the community and operate like a sophisticated business. Corrupt prison staff are often involved in these enterprises.
2) **Separate Suppliers:** is where individual prisoners opportunistically sell drugs to make a profit for themselves. They will often obtain a privileged position – enhanced prisoner status – that allows them more time out of their cell and thus more movement around the prison. Separate suppliers act autonomously sourcing, distributing and selling their own drugs and often only sell to prisoners they know and trust to reduce the chances of getting caught.
3) **Social Supply/Sharing and Trading:** in a form of altruistic/reciprocal supply, prisoners with drugs will share them with other prisoners, with the expectation that when they have drugs, they will share them with them. Trade between friends is common in prison where drugs are shared or exchanged for other items.

Those involved in drug supply can thus vary from large-scale suppliers and organised crime groups to opportunistic sellers taking advantage of their circumstances (EMCDDA, 2022); the actors vary (see Figure 8.5). Various methods are also used to distribute drugs in prison (e.g. via Listeners and other enhanced prisoner positions), which vary not only from prison to prison but also around the world. In France, walks and 'yoyos' (i.e. exchange through windows between people housed on different floors) are used to exchange drugs (EMCDDA, 2022), while in Guyana, certain positions in the prison are a key part of the supply chain as well as using trained animals (e.g. rats, cats and dogs) to move drugs (Ayres et al., 2024).

Roles and actors in the supply and distribution of drugs in prison

Prison supplier: an outsider who systematically supplies drugs to prison. These can be established individual drug suppliers based in the community, or organised crime groups.

Importer: a person who takes drugs into prison. Importers can be prison visitors, staff, friends and family of the people in prison, or people new to prison or re-entering prison.

Seller: an insider who sells or trades drugs. Sellers can be prison dealers with larger supplies and a range of importation sources or user-sellers with limited supplies and fewer sources.

Runner: an insider who moves drugs and goods around the prison, enabling transactions, most often a person in prison.

User-sharer: a person in prison with limited individual supplies entering into reciprocal sharing of drugs with other people in prison.

Figure 8.5 Roles and Actors in Prison Supply Chains (EMCDDA, 2022)
Source: Creative Commons 4.0.

Regardless of the supplier, drug markets in prison rely on prisoner relationships; they all use the same supply routes and are characterised by high prices, poor quality and the threat of violence if debts are incurred (Crewe, 2005). Despite the expenditure on supply reduction measures and enhanced security, research illustrates their inefficacy at stopping or even disrupting the supply of drugs into prison (Blakey, 2008; Crewe, 2005). Instead, it merely displaces supply routes and the drugs being used (Blakey, 2008), showing the ineffectiveness of supply reduction measures to stop drugs entering prisons.

CONCLUSION

Drugs in prison present an array of challenges to the prison service, as prisons operate a zero-tolerance approach to drugs with the overall aim being drug-free prisons (we have smoke-free prisons). This would seem to be both unrealistic as most prisons around the world have problems with drugs. It is also undesirable for many, which includes staff and prisoners alike, as some drugs keep the prison quiet: a stoned jail is a quiet jail. Replicating the twin-track approach inherent in the wider drug strategy (see Chapter 3), prison aims to reduce demand and restrict supply. Since prisons remain a wash with drugs, however, it would appear that like the wider drug strategy, the prison's drug strategy is also failing to meet its objectives as drugs continue to be used and supplied in prison. The next chapter focuses on drug supply more widely.

SUMMARY

- **The prison drug strategy replicates the national drug strategy and maintains the traditional twin-track approach to supply and demand reduction, alongside a focus on recovery.**
- **The prison drug strategy is failing as drugs and their use have not been eliminated from prisons, while many of the initiatives implemented to reduce supply and demand have also shown to have adverse effects that may be harmful (e.g. MDTs).**
- **The rate of substance use among prisoners is higher than the general population, and problematic drug users are over-represented in the prison population. Some people will initiate drug use in prison.**
- **People use drugs in prison for a range of reasons (e.g. recreation, socialising, coping, self-medication, status and respect) in both controlled/recreational and more problematic/uncontrolled ways. Prison itself and the pains of imprisonment are one of the reasons prisoners give for using drugs in prison.**
- **Drug treatment is inconsistent across the prison estate despite the IDTS as are Through the Gate services and continuity of care. Although the focus has shifted to recovery, the resources are not there to help prisoners achieve and sustain long-term recovery.**
- **Increased security is the traditional prison approach to reducing the supply of drugs, even though evidence shows that as soon as one supply route is disrupted, pressure is increased on the other routes. Supply cannot be stopped while there is a demand for drugs in prison.**
- **Drug strategy is failing as prisons remain awash with drugs, with some initiating drug use in prison and coming out addicted/dependent on drugs.**

Here are some points and questions for you to consider after reading this chapter:

1) Why do people use drugs in prison? And if we did have drug-free prisons, would we see an increase in self-harm, suicide and mental ill health?
2) Why might positive MDT tests be higher in local prisons that serve the courts?
3) Is methadone maintenance a human right for drug-using prisoners?

Here are some useful resources for those wanting to further explore the issues raised in this chapter:

- Malloch, M. (2008) *Women, Drugs and Custody: The Experiences of Women Drug Users in Prison.* Waterside Press.

  This book explores the experiences of women drug users in the UK prison system, focusing on how drug use intersects with gender, incarceration and social

(Continued)

(Continued)

marginalisation, which shows that many women in prison for drug-related offences are also grappling with issues such as poverty, trauma, mental ill health and domestic violence that are exacerbated by imprisonment.

- Shewan, D. (2013) *Drug Use in Prisons*. London: Routledge.

  This book provides an in-depth examination of drug use within prison environments, discussing the factors that contribute to the high prevalence of drug use among incarcerated individuals (e.g. availability, culture, behaviour) and the difficulties of controlling drugs in prison.
- Wheatley, M. (2007) Drugs in Prison in Y. Jewkes (ed.) *Handbook on Prisons* (pp. 399–422). Collumpton: Willan.

  This chapter offers a comprehensive overview of drugs within the prison system, exploring how and why drugs are so commonly found and used in prison, including the methods used to smuggle drugs into prisons, the reasons prisoners use drugs, the impact of drugs on the prison environment and the challenges it poses to security and rehabilitation.

9
DRUG SUPPLY

Overview

This chapter aims to provide you with:

- An overview of drug production and supply.
- An understanding of drug supply: markets and dealers, including systemic violence.
- A look at how drug markets have changed/evolved.
- A critical overview of drug dealing, including whether it constitutes a form of work.
- Illustrative examples of drug supply using cannabis farms, county lines and cryptomarkets.

You will be introduced to the key terms:

- Drug dealer/trafficker
- Drug markets
- Differentiated
- Cryptomarkets

INTRODUCTION

This chapter will look at drug supply on a local (e.g. cannabis grown for personal use, user–dealers), national (e.g. county lines and cannabis farms) and international scale (e.g. drug mules, see Box on page 221–222, and organised crime groups (OCGs) – OCGs and narcoterrorism are covered in more detail in Chapter 5), including how the war on drugs has failed to stop or even lessen the supply of drugs. Instead, drugs have become global commodities. The main focus of this chapter will be on the drug dealer. It will focus on the people and organisations that participate in the production and supply of drugs and the methods used (e.g. cannabis farms, county lines, cryptomarkets) to deal drugs. Looking at how drug supply has evolved and changed alongside technology, this chapter will examine online markets in the supply of drugs, including the use of cryptocurrency and the problems this causes for law enforcement.

Drug production is participation in the process of producing an illegal drug.

Drug supply is the act of passing a controlled substance to another person whether it is for financial gain/profit or not.

Drug dealers/traffickers are those people and/or organisations that are involved in the manufacture/production and supply of illicit drugs.

DRUGS: GLOBAL PRODUCTION AND SUPPLY

The production and supply of illicit drugs is a global billion-pound industry that is estimated to be worth around $360–400 billion a year, although this is a guestimate, since calculating the worlds drug trade accurately is impossible due to its clandestine nature. The drug trade, however, is one of the few businesses where:

> The average drug trafficking organisation, meaning from Medellin to the streets of New York, could afford to lose 90 percent of its profit and still be profitable. Now think of the analogy. GM builds a million Chevrolets a year. Doesn't sell 900,000 of them and still comes out profitable. That is a hell of a business, man. That is the dope business. (Robert Stutman, a former DEA agent)

Consequently, the drug trade is an attractive business for many different actors and organisations (see Ayres and Ancrum, 2023; Coomber, 2006). From college students, businesspeople, your next-door neighbour to terrorists, OCGs, states and legitimate businesses, the actors involved in the supply of drugs are diverse and varied. Drug markets are varied and heterogeneous or, as Coomber (2010) describes it, highly differentiated.

Reiterating Coomber's (2010) calls to reconceptualise how drug markets and drug dealers are understood alongside the structures and activities that characterise drug supply, as all are often over-exaggerated and erroneous, this chapter focus on drug supply. In fact, very little is known about drug dealing, particularly successful drug dealers and those that occupy the higher echelons of the drug trade. Academics have continuously tried to categorise drug markets and drug dealers. From Preble and Casey's (1969) work in the 1960s to Pearson and Hobb's (2001) attempts to map out the 'middle levels' of the United Kingdom's drug markets, very little is actually known about drug supply chains and those that operate within them. Annually, the United Nations Office of Drugs and Crime produces statistics guesstimating the global drug trade providing statistics on the production, supply and use of drugs around the world. While it remains a guestimate due to methodological limitations (e.g. irregular reporting, absence of data), which affect the reliability, quality and comparability of the information published, it does provide an overview of illicit drug production (e.g. crop cultivation or precursor chemicals) and global trends in the production and supply of individual drugs and their supply chains (see Chapters 2 and 3).

The stereotypical notion of drug supply chains being run by all powerful hierarchical monolithic entities (e.g. Mafia) whose tentacles reach around the globe is not supported by evidence (Hobbs, 1995, 2013; Pearson and Hobbs, 2001). Although there is little research on the higher stages/levels of drug dealing, the reality tends to suggest small organisations (autonomous of each other) involved in fragmented and disorganised crime that is characterised by networks and partnerships, which are often based on race/ethnicity (Hobbs, 1995, 2013; Paoli and Reuter, 2008; Pearson and Hobbs, 2001).

Pearson and Hobbs's (2001) research offers a four-tier classification of drug markets that suggests that after importation, there are three levels of distribution in a country (e.g. United Kingdom). There is the wholesale level that is mainly run by OCGs and businesspeople, which are often based on specific nationalities. This is followed by the middle-level drug brokers, who link the upper levels to the lower retail level, as the middle level dealer is someone who buys multi-kilo amounts and sells in smaller amounts (e.g. part-kilo amounts or ounces) at the lower retail level. The lower retail level focuses on those that deal drugs on the streets, which Pearson and Hobbs split into three types. The heavy-end single commodity dealer (e.g. heroin dealers who sometimes sell crack – some to support own habit), the single commodity dealers (e.g. those that mainly sell cannabis) and multi-commodity retail dealers who sell a variety of recreational drugs to multiple retail-level customers (see Figure 9.1).

While such categorisations may help us to understand the different levels of the UK supply chain and its 'distinctive market roles and functions', this does not mean that there are always four stages in the supply chain or that the categories proposed are rigid (Pearson and Hobbs, 2001:vi). The reality is that drug markets are largely decentralised, diverse and highly fragmented – a constantly mutating network where roles can be interchangeable, individuals can occupy dual roles and which can have numerous stages and intermediaries operating in the chain (Pearson and Hobbs, 2001). Drug supply chains also depend on the country being looked at as drug markets are dynamic and differ depending on the cultural context as well as the socio-political and economic

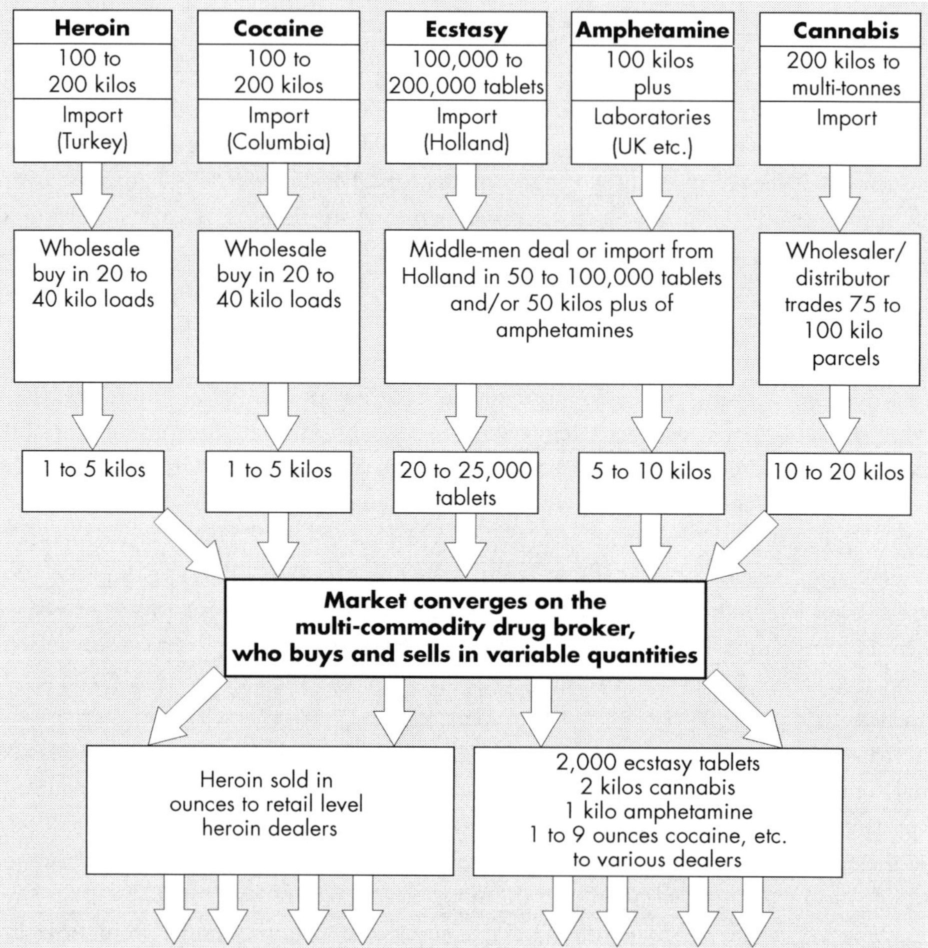

Figure 9.1 Mediating Role of Middle Market Multi-Commodity Drug Broker (Pearson and Hobbs, 2001)

circumstances of the states, organisations and people involved, factors that also influence the level of risk, violence and complexity of buyer/seller interactions. The risks involved at each stage of the supply chain tend to be reflected in the increase in price (see Reuter and Kleiman, 1986), with the mark up for drugs like cocaine increasing 550% from farm gate to the first dealer (see Wilson and Stevens, 2008). The categorisations provided by Pearson and Hobbs (2001) are also illustrative of their era, as the categorisations provided also ignore the role of the internet in drug supply and the concept of social supply.

Social supply is the sharing and/or reciprocal supply of drugs with friends and acquaintances for no profit (Coomber et al., 2016; Coomber and Moyle, 2014) that has also been described as sorting friends out (Parker et al., 1998:155). Sorting friends out –

social supply – is rarely seen as a criminal offence, which has seen the reconceptualisation of drug supply as being normal/normalised (see Aldridge et al., 2011; Coomber et al., 2016; Parker et al., 1998) (see the Box below). These developments/changes mean drug markets and drug dealing need to be reconceptualised to accommodate their transitional and constantly changing nature that extends the currently narrow focus, which concentrates on the usual suspects and illicit substances, excluding legitimate markets and organisations, like Big Pharma (see the Box on page 227).

The finer nuances/complexities inherent in international drug markets with its array of roles are rarely reflected in drug legislation or in sentencing (see Coomber, 2006; Fleetwood, 2015). Instead, the dominant definition of a drug dealer is narrow and often stereotypical focusing on amoral and inherently violent individuals – usually men – who are the personification of evil and who stand outside school gates preying on the young and the vulnerable, forcing drugs onto innocent bystanders in order to get them hooked. They are stereotypically seen as death dealers. The reality, however, is very different. Drugs are merely commodities people demand (Ruggiero and South, 1995). Drugs are pulled not pushed and are subject to market forces like any other commodity consumers' want and desire. Drug supply, like all other commodities, is driven and shaped by market forces. Also, despite drug users being routinely portrayed as the victims of drug dealers, drug supply is a largely victimless crime or at least a crime where the victim consents to any harm that occurs as a result of the drugs being sold and used, as mostly these are not forced down people's throats. This is problematised further since the evidence base underpinning prohibition, the criminalisation of drugs and their supply is largely missing, or at least not premised on scientific evidence (see Chapter 4), and yet, those that supply illicit drugs face some of the harshest punishments. Despite this, the stereotypical portrayal has distorted society's perception of the contemporary drug dealer, which has been indoctrinated as fact in drug policy and legislation, despite many of these actualities being shown to be 'urban legends' (Coomber, 2006). In fact, it is the mediated stereotypical representation of the drug dealer that dominates, as the hyper-reality surrounding drug supply and trafficking has become more real than reality itself as drug dealers have been historically demonised and othered, and myths created that are presented as fact, which alter alongside the ever-changing drug markets and those that operate within them.

Social Supply

- Social supply is where illicit drugs are supplied for no profit and/or for low amounts of money and/or drugs, which usually occurs among friendship groups (sorting friends out) and is rarely seen as a criminal offence by those involved (Aldridge et al., 2011; Coomber and Moyle, 2014; Coomber et al., 2016; Parker et al., 1998). It is also referred to in the literature as 'mutual societies', 'trading charities' and

(Continued)

(Continued)

'minimally commercial supply' (Dorn et al., 1992:10–13; Coomber and Moyle, 2014:157).

- 'Brokering' or acting as a 'go-between for friends' is also an aspect of social supply (Moyle and Coomber, 2015).
- Social supply also incorporates user–dealers and applies to all substances from cannabis to heroin (Moyle and Coomber, 2015). User–dealers also have very different motivations from commercial suppliers. Often the purpose is to produce their own supply of drugs, as they often see it as a less harmful and more convenient way of funding their drug use/addiction (e.g. than committing acquisitive crime or sex work) (Moyle and Coomber, 2015; Preble and Casey, 1969).
- Most social suppliers drift – slip – into the supply of drugs (Matza, 1964) and do not see themselves as deviant/criminal; to them, drug supply is normal (Coomber et al., 2016; Murphy et al., 1990; Parker et al., 1998), although they implement techniques of (soft) neutralisation (see Coomber et al., 2016 and Chapter 1). As such, social suppliers are increasingly seen as not being drug dealers proper, yet for the most part, they are traditionally treated by the law and criminal justice system the same as commercially motivated suppliers.
- Although the sentencing guidelines (2012) introduced provisions to differentiate social supply from drug dealing proper – seeing it as a lesser offence than supply for commercial gain – by introducing provision for more lenient punishments so they avoid imprisonment, there remains scope for disproportionate outcomes and for social suppliers/user–dealers who participate in supply to still end up being prosecuted as a commercial drug dealer (see Coomber and Moyle, 2014).

The Evolution of Drug Markets

Drug markets and their structure are not static and are constantly evolving and changing alongside technology. Whether it was pagers and mobile phones or more recently the darknet and cryptocurrency, technological advancements have changed the face of drug markets around the world.

Open to Closed Markets

There has been a shift from open to closed drug markets, largely due to technological advancements but also to reduce risk.

Open Markets: are often street-based where dealers are open to any buyer with few barriers to access and with no requirement for prior introduction to the seller.

Closed Markets: are often in spaces that are not openly accessible to just anyone as buyers need to be known to the seller and/or given access/introduced to the seller via a contact already known to them.

Open drug markets were prevalent up until the mid-1990s and were probably where most illicit drugs were sold (May and Hough, 2009). The invention and proliferation of pagers and mobile phones altered the way drug markets operate, and in the United Kingdom, it led to a substantial decline in open drug markets and the establishment of closed markets, which is now where most drugs are sold (Dorn et al., 1992; May and Hough, 2009).

Policing of drug markets has also impacted on the move towards closed drug markets and has transformed many open markets into closed markets, which potentially offer more protection to the seller as they are no longer openly visible on the street where they can be watched by the police. The proliferation of closed drug markets has seen dealing 'indoors' and 'off the street' that makes the seller less visible and thus less accessible to law enforcement (Coomber, 2006). May and Hough (2009) also refer to semi-open drug markets that take place in pubs and club-based retail markets, which are largely associated with recreational drug use. These changes, however, do not mean that open drug markets do not continue to operate in other countries, just as closed markets also operate across the globe and take on different forms (see Ayres and Ancrum, 2023; Coomber, 2006; May and Hough, 2009; Ruggiero and South, 1995), with both having their advantages and disadvantages.

Although different, open and closed drug markets share an array of similarities, which includes advantages and disadvantages for both the buyers and sellers. As May and Hough (2009:550) highlight, 'the main advantage of an illicit open street market – ease of locating buyers and sellers – is also its major drawback for the participants: it renders them vulnerable to policing'. As such, open markets may be seen as riskier as they provide the dealer with less security and make them more vulnerable to the police. Even in open markets, however, drug dealers will be cautious of and 'vet' prospective buyers and have regular customers who are known to them to minimise the risk by refusing to sell to strangers (Broadhurst et al. 2005; Coomber, 2006; May and Hough, 2009; VanNostrand and Tewksbury, 1999). In fact, some dealers reckoned they could detect police through verbal and non-verbal indicators and implemented methods of avoiding the police and protecting themselves if they did get arrested (e.g. no records of transactions) (VanNostrand and Tewksbury, 1999). Despite being less vulnerable to law enforcement/police, closed markets limit the choices offered to the buyer by the sellers they can access, while dealers are unable to 'pick up' any passing trade and therefore maximise their profits as sellers in open markets do (May and Hough, 2009). Both types of markets, however, offer counter-balancing advantages and disadvantages for both the sellers and the buyers.

Although mobile phones initially helped to transform drug markets from closed to open as they reduced the risks associated with illicit transactions (May and Hough, 2009) and are integral to the county lines model of drug dealing (Coomber and Moyle, 2018; Spicer, 2018; see the Box on page 220), this transformation has not continued with the evolution of mobile phones. In fact, smart phones are avidly avoided by dealers who prefer the old-style burner phones that do not collect and store data like smartphones do.

This is to minimise the chance/opportunities for police surveillance, phone tapping, the downloading/mining of data and thus prosecution. As in May and Hough's (2009) research, respondents also replaced their phones frequently to help with this. Digital technology (e.g. phones and pagers) includes the growth of the internet, which has allowed drug markets and supply to develop in new ways that have fundamentally changed drug interactions and the structure of drug markets (see Aldridge and Askew, 2017; Aldridge et al., 2017; Martin, 2014). The use of social media to deal drugs has also been a recent development in drug dealing (see the Box below).

Drug Supply on Snapchat and WhatsApp

- The use of social media apps (e.g. WhatsApp, Telegram and Snapchat) to deal drugs has become a growing concern as dealers leverage the anonymity, encryption, private messaging, temporary content (e.g. messages disappear), integrated digital payment systems and reach of these platforms to facilitate easy and quick transactions.
- A study by Leah Moyle and colleagues (2019) explored how drug dealers in the United Kingdom use Snapchat and Instagram to advertise and sell drugs using the ephemeral nature of these platforms' content, slang and emojis as key strategies to avoid detection.
- The advantages they provide drug dealers is a global reach while allowing them to maintain local operations, which enhances the scalability of their drug-dealing operations without the need for a physical presence in different regions, thereby expanding their customer base, reducing costs and minimising detection as it also reduces the need for intermediaries in drug transactions.
- OCGs have adapted to the digital age by integrating social media and cryptomarket technologies into their operations (e.g. to advertise products, arrange deals, and coordinate deliveries), which includes using these platforms to manage supply chains, advertise products, arrange deals, recruit buyers/members, communicate securely and coordinate deliveries with minimal risk of interception and detection, thus providing a low-risk, high-reward structure to expand their operations and increase profitability (Demant et al., 2018).
- These platforms provide dealers with the means to conduct business discreetly and rapidly, illustrating how dealers adjust their methods in response to law enforcement efforts, which has implications for policy and practice.
- Law enforcement agencies need to develop advanced surveillance techniques to monitor social media activities effectively, but may need the collaboration of social media companies that often pride themselves on their privacy to identify and prevent drug-related activities on their platforms. Using social media apps also poses unique challenges to the current laws and legal framework covering drug dealing and the use of cryptocurrencies for illicit purposes (Demant et al., 2018).

Drug markets are constantly changing and evolving to meet demand and/or avoid detection from law enforcement. Increased law enforcement efforts to intercept imported cannabis, particularly from countries like Morocco, led to a reduction in the availability of imported cannabis, which changed the cannabis market in the United Kingdom, which shifted from importing cannabis to domestic cultivation. In 2000, cannabis farms started to become more prominent as domestic cultivation allowed growers to control the quality and potency of the cannabis, as growing high-potency strains – skunk – was more profitable, due to high demand, relatively low production and a reduced risk of detection (e.g. less people involved and lower handling and transportation costs) (see the Box below). While illicit homegrown cannabis is criminalised and its producers punished, the United Kingdom is one of the main producers of medical cannabis and the main source/exporter of cannabis-based medicines (UNODC, 2022b), illustrating the hypocritical nature of drug policy in the United Kingdom (see the Box on page 271–272 of Chapter 11). UK policy has not only been described as hypocritical but those in government have been accused of hypocrisy and nepotism as the drugs minister at the time – Victoria Atkins – was married to the managing director of British Sugar, who was licensed to grow non-psychoactive cannabis and had an exclusive deal with the large pharmaceutical company GW (BBC, 2018) (see Chapters 2 and 3 where substances of the colony are discussed and compared to this example).

Cannabis Farms

- Domestic cannabis production grew steadily so by the mid-to-late 2000s, the number of cannabis factories – often located in residential properties, warehouses and industrial units – had increased substantially. In 2007/2008, 3,032 commercial cannabis farms were identified, 6,866 in 2009/10, 7,660 in 2010/2011, 7,865 in 2011/2012 and 276,676 in 2013/14, which had an estimated street value of £62 million (NPCC, 2012).
- Operations varied in scale from small setups with a few plants to large, sophisticated operations with hundreds or thousands of plants, as organised crime gangs (OCG) started to become involved. As the National Police Chiefs' Council (NPCC) (2012:3) highlighted 'with the UK street price of illegal drugs among the highest in Europe, a significant proportion of OCGs within the UK are now engaged in commercial cultivation.' Due to the scale of cultivation, the United Kingdom actually began exporting cannabis (Hagan & Parker 2016 as cited in NPCC, 2012).
- Initially, South East Asian and Vietnamese gangs were involved linking cannabis cultivation with illegal migrants, modern-day slavery and trafficking of children. Vietnamese children became the largest group of potential child trafficking victims in the United Kingdom, with many forced into illegal cannabis cultivation. Between 2009– and 2016, out of 198 Vietnamese immigrants, 115 (58%) were forced into cannabis cultivation (e.g. via debt bondage), the majority (67%) of whom were male minors at the time of exploitation. Despite the existence of legislation and guidelines protecting victims, many Vietnamese individuals, including children who have been recognised as victims of forced labour, were criminalised (ISAC, 2017).

(Continued)

(Continued)

- Although Vietnamese people initially constituted up to two-thirds of those being arrested for cannabis production, this changed. In the NPCC (2012) report, the majority of identified offenders were White British men aged between 25 and 34 years of age with a new trend of cultivation sites being controlled by White British OCGs that employed Vietnamese nationals (also see Daly, 2007).
- The involvement of Vietnamese OCGs led to claims of extreme violence by the police and media, and although there has been the odd violent incident associated with cannabis farms (e.g. BBC, 2008), the evidence shows that in reality, this is quite rare. The involvement of Vietnamese OCGs also appears to have been overinflated as 'Vietnamese criminal cannabis networks are relatively small; they are mono-ethnic (although recent evidence suggests that partnership working may be developing), rarely deploy violence, especially lethal violence, do not readily co-operate with authorities' and 'are not on the whole organised criminals by trade. . .but instead come from. . .those who migrated here over time' (ISAC, 2017:44).
- The increase in cannabis farms provoked a law enforcement reaction that involved raising awareness via scratch and sniff cards posted to homes countrywide in 2014, as most farms are detected by community intelligence-led operations (e.g. smell emanating from premises) and/or police responding to a fire, a consequence of bypassing the electricity metre. The police also raised awareness among landlords about renting to Vietnamese, which potentially breached the Race Relations Act and led to them struggling to rent houses (Daly, 2007; ISAC, 2017; NPCC, 2012).
- There has been a decline in cannabis farms in recent years or just less being detected as cannabis cultivators have become more sophisticated in avoiding detection (e.g. using heat-blocking materials, moth balls to hide the smell), ***but as domestic cultivation of cannabis is clamped down on, will the United Kingdom see a return to importing its cannabis?***

The (Dark)Net: Cryptomarkets

The internet has changed the way drugs are supplied (Bancroft, 2023 in Ayres and Ancrum, 2023; Martin, 2014). Sellers can set up virtual shops on the clearnet and darknet or exchange forums (e.g. silk road) to sell their products or use existing social media and communication platforms (e.g. Facebook, WeChat, WhatsApp) and payment can be made using credit/debit cards, bank transfers or cryptocurrency (Aldridge and Askew, 2017; Barratt and Aldridge, 2016; Martin, 2014; Moyle et al., 2019). They also show criminal innovation/entrepreneurship in drug supply as a response to law enforcement efforts (Barratt and Aldridge, 2016; Martin, 2014). This is largely because online trading offers drug sellers powerful protection and anonymity via complex encryption technologies and virtual currencies and the drugs are delivered by couriers, the postal services and dead drops. Online, sellers' market their products and buyers leave their feedback (on the seller and the product) like any other legitimate online business, with some even promoting their products as 'fair trade' (Martin, 2014). Cryptomarket users also communicate with one another to share information enabling drug market participants to make more accurate assessments of the drugs being used (e.g. drug purity and appropriate dosages), the sellers (e.g. reliability, quality of drugs), harm reduction strategies and the risk of apprehension, which have led to them developing their own counter-interdiction strategies (e.g. beginner guides to drug smuggling) and online intelligence to evade law enforcement initiatives (Aldridge and Askew, 2017; Martin, 2014). According to Aldridge and Askew (2017), the use of encrypted communication is often advocated as 'good practice', although it is not always employed even though it minimises detection. Cryptomarkets and their currency present a new and costly challenge for law enforcement officials (Martin, 2014).

It is debatable whether cryptomarkets present a more or less harmful alternative to the conventional illicit drugs trade as it has its benefits (e.g. reliable supply and income, predictable quality and safety, and reduction in systemic violence associated with drug supply) as well as its harms (e.g. buying unknown substances that are often different from the ones advertised – fentanyl instead of heroin) (Bancroft, 2023 in Ayres and Ancrum, 2023; Barratt et al., 2016; Martin, 2014). They cannot, however, be divorced from more traditional forms of drug supply, as the online and offline markets intertwine (Barratt and Aldridge, 2016; Martin, 2014). Bancroft (2023 in Ayres and Ancrum, 2023) highlights how online supply can reconfigure other drug markets in three ways. They:

1) Produce hybrid distribution strategies that combine online and offline, as cryptomarkets are not isolated from broader drug markets (see also Barratt and Aldridge, 2016);
2) Saturate some markets pushing previous dominant dealer networks to exploit previously marginal opportunities;
3) Open new exploitation vectors.

Depending on the drugs being sought and their availability, drug users often combine online and offline purchase methods, and despite its popularity, it has not overtaken more traditional forms of supply. In fact, Barratt and colleagues (2016) show that although many users test out darknet cryptomarkets, they desist from using them, preferring the more traditional face-to-face drug markets. It has, however, altered the middle-level drug market, and the types of dealers and customers that operate in online markets; they are different from those found in traditional middle drug markets. Dealers need different skills (e.g. technological) rather than a reputation for physical toughness, and they do not need the social networks necessary in the face-to-face market (Bancroft, 2023 in Ayres and Ancrum, 2023, 2023; Barratt et al., 2016). Although drug markets have moved online, the majority of drugs are still bought and sold offline. In fact, county lines drug dealing has said to have changed the face of heroin and crack markets as a new phenomenon, while other academics argue that county lines are nothing new and is largely how drug markets have always operated. County lines has been linked to gangs, violence and exploitation in drug distribution, but what is county lines drug dealing (see the Box on page 220)?

County lines operations are characterised by high levels of violence – often gang-related violence – including assaults, stabbings and shootings, which are used to establish and maintain control over territories and enforce debts. In fact, violence is considered to be a prominent feature of drug markets. In illicit markets, there is systemic violence (see Chapter 5), and in legal markets, there is the invisible violence inherent to our socio-economic order and its various hierarchies, that is, consumer capitalism (Ayres, 2020b, 2023; Hall et al., 2008). The difference is that the structural violence inherent in our daily lives is denied and omitted from the official discourse, which instead focuses on other forms of (subjective) violence that is often associated with specific types of behaviour (e.g. crime and drug use), excessive consumption and intoxication of substances (see Chapters 2 and 3) and drug markets, although there are many more. Whilst the stereotypical perception of drug markets, perpetuated by those in power, official discourse (see UK drug strategies or the war on drugs rhetoric) and the media, is inherently violent, this is not always supported by research in this area (see the Box on page 222), further illustrating the myths that swirl around drugs and those that supply them (see the Box on page 225–226).

County Lines

- County lines is used to describe gangs and organised criminal networks involved in exporting illegal drugs into one or more areas in the United Kingdom, using mobile phone lines or other forms of 'deal line' that exploits children and vulnerable adults to move and store drugs and money. It 'involves"outreach" selling from major supply hubs, direct to heroin/crack users in provincial satellite area' (Coomber and Moyle, 2018:1323).
- County lines often use coercion, intimidation, violence (including sexual violence) and weapons to manage their business using 'distinctive supply practices' that Coomber and Moyle (2018) call:
  Commuting, which describes the way in which dealers travel to satellite dealing locales (villages/towns) and sell throughout the course of the day, with the seller returning to their urban hub at close of business.
  Holidaying is a minor extension of commuting where county lines dealers stay overnight or for a few nights (e.g. in bed and breakfasts or other short-term lodgings) and then return to their home/hub location when done.
  Cuckooing describes the situation where a county lines dealer 'takes over' accommodation located in the provincial drugs market, using it as a local dealing base – not just here in the UK, but also in Canada and other places too. It is about optimising profits and keeping costs down.
- The benefits of county lines include a reduced risk of arrest (e.g. smaller municipalities have fewer police); rural communities often have more secluded houses, meaning dealers are less likely to be seen and thus caught, and higher profits, illustrating the financial benefit of county lines.

The violence used in drug markets can often be tied to constructions of identity and masculinity. For many, engaging in drug-related violence is a way to assert dominance, gain respect, build a reputation within their communities and maintain a sense of control and power in an otherwise oppressive environment (Collison, 1996; Contreras, 2012). Therefore, in relation to the manufacture and supply of drugs, it has been gendered, racialised and linked to socio-economic class, despite the actual knowledge of dealer demographics being limited. What is known is largely influenced and skewed by research (see Coomber, 2006), which shows:

Gender(s): The drug-dealing research and literature largely focuses on men. Traditionally, women were omitted from the official picture like much of criminology as there is a lack of research on women in the drug trade. A growing body of research has shown, however, that women also successfully deal drugs around the world (see Denton, 2001; Dunlap and Johnson, 1996; Fleetwood, 2014, 2015; Maher, 1997; UNODC, 2022a). Not only has this resulted from a change in drug markets (see Maher and Hudson, 2007), but as Fleetwood (2023 in Ayres and Ancrum, 2023) shows 'women's "emancipation" has resulted in women becoming more involved, and more seriously involved in the drug business' and 'women's labour is fundamental to all aspects of the global drug trade'. Although stereotypically perceived to occupy the lower echelons of drug supply (e.g. as drug mules), this is not the case, as both men and women operate at this level, including as mules (see the Box below).

Despite these changes, the drug trade continues to be stratified by gender (see Maher and Hudson, 2007) with the drug economy replicating the more formal economy (Maher, 1997). While there is evidence to suggest women remain marginalised in the drug trade, there is also research showing that women involved in drug supply are not always passive victims but resourceful, competent business operators who run complex drug-dealing businesses. Although they were often introduced to the drug trade by men and some relied on men (e.g. for protection), women also carved out their own reputations for violence and survived independently of men (e.g. some relied on the reputation of their family and/or support of their family), rather than being their employees and/or buyers (Denton, 2001; Fleetwood, 2014, 2015; Maher and Hudson, 2007; UNODC, 2022a). Evidence also suggests that drug markets and women's roles within them remain highly sexualised (Maher 1997), although some women used this alongside their feminine attributes to their advantage (see Maher and Hudson, 2007). As Maher and Hudson (2007:820) illustrate, however, 'little is known about how gender and ethnicity interact to shape opportunities for both men and women within particular drug markets and the broader drug economy.'

Drug Mules

A drug mule is someone who is paid, coerced or deceived into trafficking drugs across borders. Although Fleetwood and colleagues (2015:428) highlight that for many the

(Continued)

(Continued)

term 'drug mule' is derogatory, it 'usefully distinguishes between categories of carriers: those working for others (mules), self-employed couriers (working independently) and organisers (who invest capital and employ others, including mules)'. Although drug mules are predominately men, the majority of those arrested are women (see Fleetwood, 2014). Women are also more likely to receive the death penalty for drug-trafficking offences than men (see Fleetwood and Seal, 2017 and Chapter 5) and in the United Kingdom, about a quarter of foreign nationals are in prison for drug offences (PRT, 2022). While they occupy one of the lowest level roles in the supply chain, they often receive some of the longest and harshest sentences. While the Sentencing Guidelines (2012) have tried to reduce the sentences for drug mules to recognise their lesser role, which seem to be successful, the use of weight to determine the role of drug mules is problematic, particularly since evidence suggests drug mules often do not know the weight (or type) of the drugs they are carrying, meaning mules carrying large quantities are still likely to receive harsh sentences despite their lesser role (see Fleetwood et al., 2015). In fact, as Fleetwood and colleagues (2015:16) highlight, determining whether a person was involved due to coercion or financial gain remains problematic as 'the two are not mutually exclusive'.

For most men involved in drug supply, it is about making money, but for some men, drug supply has also been linked to masculinity, crime and violence. Drug supply is about creating a strong street identity that is about status, power, respect and consumerism, which often involves violence (Collison, 1996; Hall et al., 2008), particularly among Black men dealing drugs, which can affirm their masculinity and is often about survival when more legitimate channels appear unattainable (Contreras, 2012; Hook, 2004). In the drug-dealing literature, violence is depicted as a rational response and survival strategy within the high-risk environment of the drug market (Collison, 1996; Contreras, 2012; Hall et al., 2008).

Systemic Violence in Drug Markets

- The drug trade, both in the United Kingdom and globally, is frequently associated with significant levels of violence that is referred to as systemic (Goldstein, 1985; Reuter, 2009 – also see Chapter 4), which occurs at various stages of the drug supply chain, from production and trafficking to distribution and retail. Levels of violence however vary and need to be considered in the socio-economic and political context in which they occur as well as the structure of the drug market and law enforcement practices, although the role of law enforcement and prohibition in drug market violence is largely overlooked.
- Violence can occur between rival OGCs over territory and expansion of businesses or between criminal organisations and law enforcement (police or military) whether this is on a national or international level, although this violence is often intertwined

with broader economic and political interests and neoliberal policies that exacerbate the conditions that lead to and exacerbate violence in drug markets (e.g. economic instability, militarisation of the war on drugs) but serve the interests of states and corporate actors (Paley, 2014).

- Due to their illicit nature (prohibition), drug markets are characterised by violence as a form of regulation, and whether that is enforcing payment of debts or to expand their criminal enterprises, violence generally frames all illicit marketplaces (Hobbs 1995, 2013). Even then, 'most illegal drug markets are generally peaceable' (Reuter 2009:275).
- The extent of violence that is directly related to drug markets, particularly those in the United Kingdom and Europe, is often greatly overstated as 'much of what passes for drug market violence is in fact often the "culture of violence" that many of those involved in the drug trade live by anyway'. So violent individuals who have cultivated reputations for violence are often attracted to the drug trade (Ayres and Treadwell 2012; Hobbs, 2013).
- Research shows that most drug dealers are reluctant to become involved in violence and will implement other strategies characteristic of legitimate businesses (e.g. if there was competition, they would start a price war, give out free samples and discount on bulk buys) rather than hold a gun to their rivals head or use violence, although this did depend on the role they had within the drug business (e.g. those that taxed and robbed other dealers tended to be violent, Treadwell et al., 2018).
- Violence tends to be high in producer and transit countries (e.g. Colombia, Mexico, Brazil and the Golden Triangle) where cartels – OCGs – run the drug business and are extremely violent. These countries, however, are also politically unstable with high levels of corruption, meaning OCGs/cartels often act with impunity, deploying threats of extreme violence to aid corruption.
- Violence also increases when the state intervene – law enforcement and the military – cracking down on the drug trade both internationally and domestically. This is also true for law enforcement aimed at disrupting the drug trade, which can also involve significant levels of violence.

(see Broadhurst et al., 2005; Coomber, 2006; Paley, 2014; Reuter, 2009)

Race/Ethnicity: Drug production and supply has always been racialised. Whether referring to the Chinese opium dens of the nineteenth century (see Berridge, 1999) or the more recent Yardie gun wielding crack dealers (see Coomber, 2006), drug supply has always been associated with outsiders, others and foreigners. This is true across the globe (e.g. the United States, Australia). Drug supply has stereotypically been associated with minority ethnic gangs in poor dispossessed urbanised neighbourhoods (ghettos) (Contreras, 2012; Pitts, 2020; Wacquant, 2009), and while evidence suggests that certain ethnicities are associated with drug trafficking, this racialisation has also led to the over policing and criminalisation of minority ethnic groups when it comes to the manufacture and supply of drugs as they are over-represented in the criminal justice statistics (Eastwood et al., 2013;

Wacquant, 2009). Statistics show that in the United Kingdom, Black people were prosecuted at more than eight times the rate of White people and were sentenced to immediate custody for drug offences at 9.1 times the rate of White people (Eastwood et al., 2013). These racial inequalities are a result of drug prohibition, which has been described as akin to the Jim Crow Laws (Alexander, 2010) and reflects the wider structural inequalities and racial bias that pervades much of society (see Chapters 2, 3 and 5). The result is that drug laws and their enforcement, particularly when it comes to the manufacture and supply of drugs, become yet another attack on certain marginalised ethnic and socio-economically disadvantaged groups (Wacquant, 2009).

Social Class: Drug supply pervades all social classes from the underclasses to wealthy businesspeople and celebrities, and research shows that people from an array of socio-economic circumstances participate in drug markets (Ayres and Treadwell, 2012; Bourgois, 1995; Collison, 1996; Contreras, 2012; Hall et al., 2008; Hobbs, 1995, 2013; Mohamed and Fritsvold, 2010; Preble and Casey, 1969; Ruggiero and South, 1995; Salinas, 2018). Those from the more privileged socio-economic backgrounds tend to avoid serious encounters with the criminal justice system even when they are involved in drug supply (see Mohamed and Fritsvold, 2010; Murphy et al., 1990). In fact, the drug dealing of the well-off is largely overlooked, particularly by law enforcement agencies, illustrating how the stereotype surrounding drug dealers influences policing and thus prosecution decisions that nearly always exclude the 'boys and girls next-door' who are largely shielded from criminal justice scrutiny by race- and class-based privileges' (Mohamed and Fritsvold, 2023 in Ayres and Ancrum, 2023). As highlighted in Chapter 5, drug prohibition and the law enforcement initiatives that accompany it tend to disproportionately target low-level street dealers and those who live in poverty (Wacquant, 2009). Yet the myth of the drug dealer as a ruthless, atypical, amoral, even evil, individual who corrupts young children and deals in death prevails mostly due to the historical demonology and otherness that surrounds this group (see Chapters 2 and 3).

Historical Demonology of the Drug Dealer

Drug dealers have been historically demonised and scapegoated (Szasz, 2003). Blamed for many of society's problems, drug dealers have been portrayed as the personification of evil, responsible for the destruction of society and its citizens, and their otherness – particularly foreignness – is emphasised, which warrants their condemnation, vilification, exclusion and punishment (Ayres and Ancrum, 2023; Berridge, 1999, 2013; Coomber, 2006; Szasz, 2003). This is because illicit drug dealers are largely seen as something we are not – folk devils – and the implementation of the death penalty illustrates the belief that drug 'pushers are murders who should be executed' (Szasz, 2003:15), when the reality is, they are not very different from the rest of us or the legitimate manufacturers and suppliers of drugs; as such market distinctions are increasingly becoming blurred (Hobbs, 1995, 2013). In fact, the demonisation of drug dealers and mythology surrounding them dominate (see the Box below for an example).

Figure 9.2 'Too Much Bling? Give Us a Ring!' Posters

The stereotypical images constructed through popular culture (e.g. either young, White, working-class males on an estate or a young Black man, driving a BMW, dripping in gold and carrying a gun) dominate. They even pervade drug policy campaigns (e.g. Too much bling? Give us a ring! – see Figure 9.2). As Boyd (2002:398) illustrates 'the media's most hateful depictions are reserved for drug dealer/trafficker…as deranged or depraved…evil, sadistic, immoral, greedy, corrupt outsiders, who lure innocent youth, and draw moral women into drug addiction and crime'. The media, alongside political discourse, has constructed the drug dealer/trafficker within various guises of otherness, premised on race/ethnicity, gender, criminality and evilness, themes that have been replicated throughout history and have led to 'knee jerk' reactions and punitive responses that often lack a legitimate evidence base (e.g. Ayres and Jewkes, 2012). In fact, like much drug policy and legislation, the evidence base is either questionable or missing altogether.

Myth Versus Reality

- Drug dealers cut their drugs with dangerous substances – rat poison, arsenic, anthrax, glass and brick dust – and lace drugs like cannabis with other more addictive drugs (e.g. heroin) to get users addicted so they use and buy more of the product. They also lace sweets with drugs to entice children (e.g. blue star tattoo; strawberry quick).
- While drug dealers do cut their drugs with other substances, it is usually with substances that will not harm the user but enhance the product (e.g. glucose, benzodiazepines, lignocaine/benzocaine), which in some instances may be more dangerous than the actual drug (e.g. PMA/PMMA in MDMA).

(Continued)

(Continued)

- In response to this myth drug dealers said, it 'wouldn't be ethical ... seems ridiculous', 'because you would have to be crazy', 'because it is dangerous', 'I don't want to kill anybody'. They might sell '16 year olds aspirin and they believed it was "E". It didn't hurt me or them. I'd never use worming tablets – that's evil' (see Coomber, 2006:101).

This portrayal and its accompanying images can be seen throughout history, creating the stereotypical drug dealer, which has become a staple of popular culture and the media. Mythology has created urban legends (see Coomber, 2006) that have been indoctrinated into reality. A good example of this is the perception that drug dealers stand outside the school gates forcing drugs onto young children, a stereotype and myth that is indoctrinated in legislation and policy. The Drugs Act 2005 and the Sentencing Guidelines for Drug Offences require a court to take it into account as an aggravating factor (e.g. dealing near a school and/or supplying drugs to someone under 18 years old when sentencing). The reality is very different, with many drug dealers implementing a moral code never to deal to children and actually inflicting violence/punishments to anyone who did (Broadhurst et al., 2005). Mythology influences and has been indoctrinated into reality.

Drug policy and legislation have indoctrinated many of the myths spiralling around drug dealers and presented them as fact. While there is a need to calibrate the extent of these harms and differentiate myth from reality, particularly in this multi-mediated landscape, the mediated stereotypical representation dominates the view of the drug dealer/trafficker, which has distorted society's perception and thus the research and knowledge base in this area, while the impact of prohibition – and its subsequent legislation – is ignored. It is easy to blame drugs and the 'criminals that supply them' for 'blighting neighbourhoods' and delivering 'misery to so many neighbourhoods' (Home Office, 2021:4–5). When the reality is very different, as outlined in Chapter 5 where Hammersley (2008:77) outlines:

> Drugs and crime can bring cash in to social networks and neighbourhoods that have few other economic resources. . . pull the drug dealing from some areas and there would be almost no economy.

In fact, rather than destroying neighbourhoods or even countries (e.g. Afghanistan), illicit drugs and their supply are a key part of their economy and thus their economic survival. In some countries, the illicit drug trade far exceeds the size of their legitimate economy, while the penetration of illicit drug profits into the legitimate economy is so extensive that it is impossible to tell where the boundaries lie. Instead, most drug dealers are no different from any other law-abiding citizen, except that they sell drugs (see Ayres and Ancrum, 2023). While some drug dealers may fit the stereotypes, these are a minority/atypical. Most are responding to their need to make money (economic survival), often taking advantage of their networks – based on familial or friendship groups – and opportunities to do so (Coomber et al., 2016; Hobbs, 2013; Murphy et al., 1990; Pearson and Hobbs, 2001). For many, drug supply is often considered a form of work and about (economic) survival (Ayres and Treadwell, 2012; Bourgois, 1995; Collison, 1996; Contreras, 2012; Preble and Casey, 1969; Ruggiero and South, 1995; Treadwell et al., 2018). These myths and stereotypes serve a dual purpose by not only constructing the drug dealer proper so they might be identified and punished but is also determining who the drug dealers are not (e.g. states, governments, Big Pharma – see the Box below).

Big Pharma as Dealers of Drugs

The pharmaceutical industry sells drugs using many strategies similar to those found in the illegal drug trade, often selling more harmful substances than those available on the illicit market. While Big Pharma can legitimately manufacture and supply drugs legally, they inflict social harms, by engaging in unethical and illegal business practices in the pursuit of huge profits. Pharmaceutical companies often engage in aggressive marketing practices, sometimes misrepresenting the benefits and downplaying the risks of their products to increase sales, often without regard for the harm caused, as pharmaceutical companies prioritise profit over public health. The recent opioid crisis in the United States can be partially attributed to pharmaceutical companies prioritising sales over the well-being of patients, leading to widespread addiction and overdose deaths (see Chapters 2 and 10). Pharmaceutical companies have also been accused of exploiting vulnerable populations, including those from poor developing countries, for profit, particularly when it comes to testing drugs and clinical trials, sometimes engaging in practices that are not only unethical and harmful but also skirt the regulations, leading to legal penalties. For example, Johnson & Johnson, Purdue Pharma and others have faced substantial fines and legal action for their roles in the opioid epidemic or the Tuskegee Syphilis experiment that used poor African Americans, although no one was prosecuted for the deaths and injuries caused in this trial but the federal government did settle a class action lawsuit filed in 1973 for $10 million in 1974 (Pasquali et al., 2010; Schipper, 2008). This could be described as a form of medical colonialism.

Why do we not see pharmaceutical companies (and/or states and their agents) as drug dealers?

DRUG DEALING: A FORM OF WORK?

The manufacture and supply of drugs is a global criminal offence that varies from country to country. Drug dealers often receive some of the harshest punishments and longest prison sentences available, not only in the United Kingdom but also around the world, including the death penalty. The death penalty still applies in 35 countries for drug supply/trafficking (e.g. China, Singapore, Saudi Arabia, Iran and Vietnam) (HRI, 2023). In the United Kingdom, drug supply offences are prosecuted under the Misuse of Drugs Act, 1971, and the Psychoactive Substances Act, 2016, alongside supplementary legislation (e.g. Drugs Act, 2005) and sentencing guidelines to ensure consistency, which covers culpability, harm, personal circumstances and aggravating/mitigating factors (Sentencing Council, 2012). Despite being a criminal offence, the supply of drugs for many is seen as the only viable form of employment (Ayres and Ancrum, 2023; Coomber, 2006; Preble and Casey, 1969; VanNostrand and Tewksbury, 1999), which is often seen as a 'lesser offence' to other forms of criminality (e.g. burglary or mugging) as there are no victims or better than the low-level dead end jobs available to them (Broadhurst et al., 2005). Whether it is supplementing their legitimate income or their sole means of earning money, those involved in drug supply are eclectic and varied as drug supply has been democratised.

Drug supply is an equal opportunity employer that attracts people from all walks of life. Whether a football hooligan, criminal entrepreneur, self-employed business person, parent, former law enforcement personnel, gang member, student, professional person (e.g. professor, lawyer), taxi driver or serviceperson, those who supply drugs are diverse (Ayres and Treadwell, 2012; Bourgois, 1995; Collison, 1996; Contreras, 2012; Hall et al., 2008; Hobbs, 1995, 2013; Mohamed and Fritsvold, 2010; Preble and Casey, 1969; Ruggiero and South, 1995; Salinas, 2018). The motivations for drug dealing also tend to be interrelated and tend to evolve and shift over time (e.g. from financial need, to greed), which included being addicted to the lifestyle and liking the fast and easy money (VanNostrand and Tewksbury, 1999).

As Hobbs (2013:158) points out, there is an 'entrepreneurial symbiosis associated with a wide range of skills, acumen and logistics common to both criminal and legitimate enterprise', including drug dealing. In fact, the contemporary drug market and its transactions stress flexibility, autonomy and independence, reflecting similar trends in the legitimate market and its global gig economy as people increasingly occupy precarious employment with zero-hour contracts and/or cannot find employment at all, particularly employment that provides enough to live on and pay the bills. Therefore, drug dealers – on both a local and a global level – exploit the opportunities they have for illicit gains, using skill sets that are often no longer valued in the legitimate economy. Therefore, drugs – their production and supply – must be understood in the political economy of neoliberal consumer capitalism, which promotes the entrepreneurial values of competitiveness, self-interest, individual empowerment and decentralisation, creating self-interested actors who embody the neoliberal idea of market-orientated entrepreneurship.

Illegal entrepreneurship is defined as a process whereby entrepreneurs supply willing customers with illegal services/products or legal products/services using an illegal process/enterprise.

Criminal entrepreneurs choose to organise a criminal business enterprise in order to exploit illegal (and sometimes legal) market opportunities – where there is a profit to be made – locally as well as globally, which for many, focuses on the manufacture and supply of drugs (Hall et al., 2008; Hobbs, 2013; Ruggiero and South, 1995). What we know about drug supply, however, is limited and often shaped by the research on drug supply and trafficking, which is also limited and as Coomber (2023 in Ayres and Ancrum, 2023) argues, focuses on the most visible (e.g. what is assumed or 'known' from prior research) and 'sexy' topics, further skewing the knowledge base in this area as it continues 'to over simplify and over homogenise what, and who, a drug dealer *is* and what a drug market looks like'. Those that partake in social supply may be very different from drug dealers proper who sell drugs for commercial gain (see the Box on page 213–214 on social supply). As Coomber (2010:10) highlights, 'social suppliers, however, do not conform to the stereotype of the drug dealer in terms of activity, and they are also often not conceived of as drug dealers by those who know them or, indeed, by themselves', further complicating the diverse and differentiated nature of drug supply.

CONCLUSION

Drug supply is a billion-pound global industry that largely operates as part of the illicit economy due to prohibition, although disentangling it from the legitimate economy and big corporations (e.g. banks, pharmaceutical companies, governments/states and their agents) is increasingly problematic. The illicit drug market is not only dominated by criminal drug trafficking organisations but also involves legitimate businesses (e.g. banks, solicitors firms, delivery companies and even Royal Mail), although their role is usually overlooked and if it is noticed punished by way of a monetary fine, while the drug dealer proper is subject to some of the harshest criminal punishments (e.g. life imprisonment and death) despite the drug market being demand driven. Regardless of the stereotype, drug dealers do not need to push drugs, they are pulled, but mythology dominates and the stereotype of the drug dealer dominates, despite the vast array of actors involved in the drug trade (see Ayres and Ancrum, 2023). Drug markets vary in the level of risk, the amount of violence and the complexion of seller–buyer liaisons. These vary depending on the level (e.g. local, national or global) and context (e.g. country and culture). There has also been a diversification of drugs and their markets that reflects technological developments (e.g. pagers, mobile phones and the internet) and law evasion by drug traffickers as they attempt to avoid detection. Like most business, drug supply is about minimising risk and maximising profit by selling commodities that people want, but are prohibited, which is why reform is needed, which is the focus of the next chapter.

SUMMARY

- **All drug dealers implement the same survival strategies regardless of the level they operate at. They want to make a profit, collect debts, sell drugs and avoid the police/law enforcement and prison.**

- **Violence is characteristic of drug dealing (systemic violence – Goldstein 1985 – see Chapter 5). However, the evidence suggests most dealers are reluctant to become involved in violence. Instead, like most legitimate businesses, the majority of drug dealers would rather implement marketing strategies to attract customers and beat the competition.**
- **Drugs are not pushed by dealers, they are pulled by the users. The drug trade is demand driven. Drugs are merely commodities people demand and dealers' supply.**
- **The reality of drug supply is very different from the popularised representation. Many of the myths surrounding drug dealers and drug markets are not evidenced in reality, but continue to be indoctrinated in drug policy, practice and legislation as the hyper-reality is more real than the actual reality.**
- **Drug markets are differentiated and diverse, attracting people from all walks of life, genders, race/ethnicities and social stratas, with a plethora of motivations that can be explained by the theories in Chapter 1 (see also Box below). There are those who have always been drug dealers, those who drifted/fell into it (snowballed from a few friend to a business) and criminal diversifiers who started out in more mainstream forms of criminality and discovered profits to be made from selling drugs so switched.**
- **Women also deal drugs, although they are largely omitted from the official picture and there is less research on them than their male counterparts.**
- **The mechanics of drug dealing are similar to operating any legitimate business (e.g. there must be a supply, a supplier, regular good-quality stock, promotion/marketing efforts and a network of customers to sell to).**
- **Drug dealers implement marketing strategies (e.g. promotions like BOGOF, competitive pricing and freebies) to entice and keep customers.**
- **Drug market transactions stress flexibility, autonomy and independence, reflecting trends in legitimate markets. It also shows how many dealers exploit an opportunity they have and drift into drug supply.**

Theory: Drug Supply

- For some, drug dealing is a **rational choice**: the benefits outweigh the negatives/ punishment (e.g. prison is seen as an occupational hazard) and although these choices might be constrained by structure, they are not determined by structure.

- **Mertonian Strain**: Drug dealing is an innovative response to strain. Innovators are those that accept the cultural goals of society but reject the conventional methods of attaining those goals (e.g. via crimes like drug dealing).
- **Status Frustration**: Many youths who cannot gain status legitimately become frustrated and therefore try to gain status through illegitimate means via gang membership and drug dealing.
- **Pleasure from Transgression**: Drug supply is about excitement, with some dealers being addicted to the lifestyle (e.g. power and respect) and its easy money.
- **Labelling**: Being convicted and labelled as a drug dealer is a legal form of stigmatisation that can follow an individual for life, limiting their opportunities, freedoms and choices.

- **There has been a decline in street dealing (open markets) and an increase in closed markets.**
- **The internet, cryptomarkets and cryptocurrency have altered drug supply (e.g. methods, dealers and buyers), although most drugs are still bought and sold in conventional face-to-face markets.**

Here are some points and questions for you to consider after reading this chapter:

1) Should social supply of drugs be comparable to the commercial supply of drugs for financial gain/profit or conceived as separate in terms of motivation, intent and culpability, and thus punishment?
2) Do cryptomarkets and/or social media platforms present a more or less harmful alternative to selling drugs than the conventional way?
3) Which theories in Chapter 1 best explain drug markets and supply (see Box below to help you)?

Here are some useful resources for those wanting to further explore the issues raised in this chapter:

- Ayres, T.C. and Ancrum, C. (2023) *Understanding Drug Dealing and Illicit Drug Markets*. London: Routledge.

  This edited collection provides a comprehensive exploration of the structure and dynamics of illicit drug markets and drug dealing in contemporary society, including the array – diversification – of drugs and those now involved in their production and supply to show how drug markets operate in both physical and online spaces.
- Coomber, R. (2006) *Pusher Myths and Motives*. London: Free Association Books.

  This seminal text critiques the common stereotypes and myths surrounding drug dealers, particularly the image of the ruthless and violent drug pusher. It covers the diverse profiles of drug dealers and their varied motives to show the differentiated nature of drug markets.

(Continued)

(Continued)

- Martin, J. (2014) *Drugs on the Darknet*. Basingstoke: Palgrave Macmillan.
  This book provides an in-depth look at the online drug trade, focusing on darknet markets where drugs are bought and sold anonymously, and how these online platforms have transformed the drug market by offering access to a wider range of substances and enabling dealers and buyers to avoid traditional law enforcement detection.

10

DRUG POLICY REFORM AND THE DRUG–CRIME RELATIONSHIP

Overview

This chapter aims to provide you with:

- An overview and explanation of drug policy reform.
- An insight into drug policy reform within the existing framework of drug prohibition.
- An analysis of drug decriminalisation and legalisation.
- A critical reflection on the current drug policy reform movement.
- A consideration of a fully regulated system encompassing all drugs.

You will be introduced to the key terms:

- Drug policy reform
- Decriminalisation
- Legalisation
- Regulation
- The ghosts of prohibition
- Human rights

INTRODUCTION

Throughout this book, we have exposed a variety of problems associated with drug policy and the dominant model of drug prohibition. Each chapter has offered critical analysis of issues pertaining to drugs and crime and identified alternative ways of thinking about and responding to these. This chapter takes this further by considering how fundamental changes to drug policy might impact on the drug–crime relationship and overcome some of the obstacles currently apparent. It does this in two stages. Firstly, given the UK government's ongoing commitment to prohibition, it considers how drug policy reform might take place on a domestic level within this framework, offering a pragmatic way of moving beyond the status quo. Secondly, it discusses more radical reforms in the form of decriminalisation and legalisation, which could see a sweeping movement away from the prohibitionist model.

WHAT IS DRUG POLICY REFORM?

In simple terms, drug policy reform means that the current approach to illegal drugs is changed in order to improve it. This can equate to relatively mundane reform, which stimulates small-scale changes to existing drug policy, through to large-scale reform, which seeks a complete overhaul of this. It is worth noting that drug policy is in a constant state of reform – as it continually evolves to respond to the political narratives of the day (e.g. from a public health to criminal justice-orientated drug policy, or from maintenance to abstinence-focused responses to addiction) and/or emerging issues presented by drugs and their use (e.g. Novel Psychoactive Substances). When we talk about drug policy reform, however, this often relates to the growing desire to explore drug policies which are fundamentally different from those of the current day. In some cases, this can mean reform that leads to more punitive drug policy in a bid to strengthen prohibition, such as enhancing the policing and punishment of drug offences. Most of the time, however, in keeping with an increased momentum for change built by academic drug scholars and prominent pressure groups, this refers to so-called liberal reforms, which urge for more evidence-based, inclusive and less harmful drug policies (such as drug decriminalisation or legalisation).

The notion that drug policy reform can lead to less harmful drug policies is a particularly important one. This is well illustrated in Figure 10.1, which shows a spectrum of drug policy models in relation to the (social and health-related) harms associated with them. It highlights that severe (or 'ultra') prohibition lies at one end of the spectrum with a legalised, free market (or 'commercial promotion') model at the other. Crucially, both extremities are associated with the highest levels of drug-related harms. Sitting in between these models are a variety of drug policies, which seemingly have differential impacts on such harms although none of the models listed remove all harms. In this chapter, we identify and explore these alternatives to the current dominant model of prohibition. It should be noted that the legalisation of cannabis for medical purposes is not discussed here but is considered in Chapter 11.

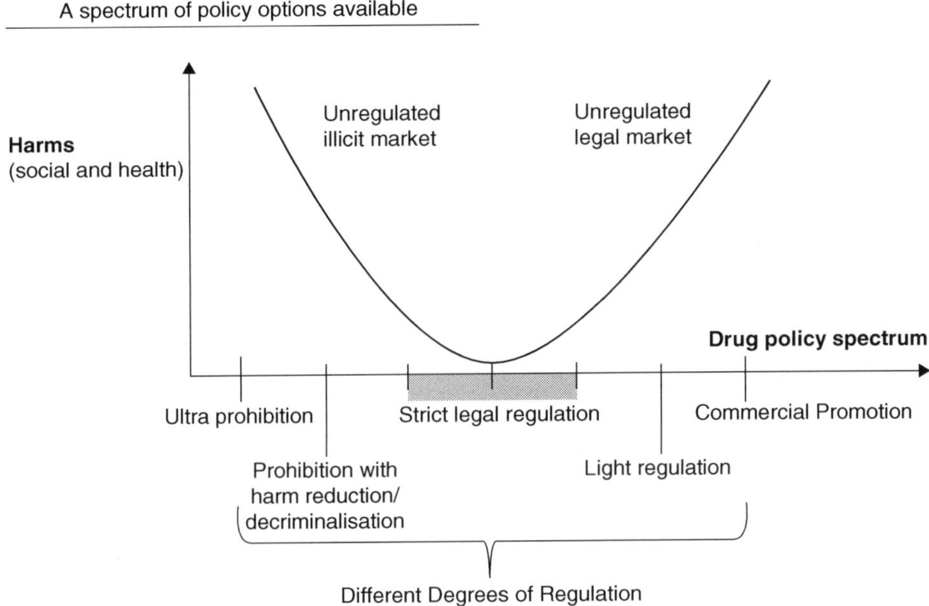

Figure 10.1 Different Models of Drug Policy and Their Associated Levels of (Social and Health) Harms (Scottish Government, 2023a:6)

Source: Contains public sector information licensed under the Open Government Licence v3.0.

THE CASE FOR DRUG POLICY REFORM

For some, drug policy in England and Wales is seen as effective. Most people abstain from taking illegal drugs whilst the last two decades have seen a relative stabilisation in rates of use among the minority that do. There has been a reduction in the numbers of those referred to as problematic drug users with, until recently, increased numbers accessing more professional treatment in quicker time. Accompanying this has been a significant reduction in acquisitive crime, a seemingly crucial proxy measure of success for a drug policy focused on addressing the drug–crime link. Meanwhile, an enhanced health focus has seen the formalisation and dissemination of drugs education (such as the FRANK website) and the piloting of harm reduction techniques (such as drug checking and heroin-assisted treatment).

Despite these apparent positives, several prominent problems remain, which critics argue are grounds for reform. These include the continuation of supply and demand for/of illegal drugs; the continuation of problematic drug use; the normalisation of so-called recreational drug use, particularly among young people; and record numbers of drug-related deaths. In addition, drug policy itself is increasingly viewed as a cause of harm (e.g. the disproportionate stop and search and discriminatory processing of Black people within the criminal justice system; the impacts of criminalisation; the unethical nature of coerced treatment and drug testing; the redaction of drug services). These concerns couple with two other important drivers of reform.

Firstly, a belief that prohibitionist drug policy should be repealed on moral grounds. As noted in Chapter 1, Szasz (Friedman and Szasz, 1992:122) contends that '... in a free society it is none of the government's business what ideas a man puts into his mind; likewise, it should be none of its business what drugs he puts into his body'. Philosophical arguments like this have been used as an argument for drug policy reform throughout the last century. They are often tied to the interlinking issues of legitimacy (i.e. whether the law prohibiting people from taking certain substances is legitimate) and human rights (i.e. whether an individual should be free to use drugs). In essence, the contention here is that current drug laws are *illegitimate* and drug users *should* have rights, including the right to use drugs. Whilst these standpoints once predominated the reformist agenda, their prominence has waned over the last few decades. A key reason being that drug policy reformers have reacted to the governmental mantra of 'evidence-based policy' (even though, as mapped out in Chapter 4, whether drug policy *is* evidence based remains a moot point) by replacing such 'soft' philosophical arguments with hard facts. In one sense, this has seen a simplification of the drug policy reform debate as attention has moved from theoretical discussions about the moral and political positioning of drug policy towards more scientific, quantitative analysis.

Secondly, and as a direct result of the move towards this 'drug science', is the belief that evidence now exists, which suggests that drug policy reform can mitigate a variety of issues that prohibition presents. This argument is based on an emerging body of research from across the globe, which has found that harm reduction measures (such as heroin-assisted treatment and drug consumption rooms) as well as more fundamental policy overhauls (such as decriminalisation and legalisation) have positive effects and outcomes. This evidence base builds momentum for drug policy reform but simultaneously struggles to enact change due to inherent beliefs that drug prohibition is effective and warranted.

DRUG POLICY REFORM WITHIN THE PROHIBITION PARADIGM

Whilst public attitudes surrounding drug laws have softened over the past decades, meaning that people are increasingly open to the idea of more liberal drug policies, there remains generally widescale support for the ongoing prohibition of some, if not all currently illegal drugs. Despite the best efforts of organisations and pressure groups and the emergence of an evidence base indicating that alternative drug policies can be effective, the UK government's appetite for drug prohibition has not diminished. In 2014, the Home Office published the policy paper 'Drugs: international comparators', which reviewed evidence around what works in drug policies enacted in other countries. This noted that 'Looking across different countries, there is no apparent correlation between the "toughness" of a country's approach and the prevalence of adult drug use' (Home Office, 2014:51), yet the paper concluded that the UK's balanced approach to drugs enables reactive and flexible policy to emerge. It was telling that then Prime

Minister David Cameron (cited in Wintour, 2014:1) reacted to this publication by stating:

> I don't think anyone can read that report and say it definitely justifies this approach or that approach, but the evidence is what we're doing is working… I don't believe in decriminalising drugs that are illegal today. I'm a parent with three children; I don't want to send out a message that somehow taking these drugs is OK or safe.

Here, Cameron follows the normative cycle of governmental ministers responding to evidence/reports that offer support for drug policy reform by emphasising that prohibition and domestic drug strategies are effective and by reinforcing this with reference to the perils of illegal drug use (Taylor, 2016). He also dismisses this 'new' evidence and instead refers to the apparent evidence base that supports the status quo. In short, Cameron reaffirms governmental commitment to drug prohibition. Whilst there has, therefore, been a global weakening in the prohibitionist model over the past two decades and indeed a quiet revolution of drug policy reform (see below), the UK government remains steadfast in their belief that drug prohibition should continue.

That said, on one level, UK drug policy has proven itself to be both reactive and flexible. The previous chapters of this book are evidence of this, highlighting as they do a variety of pilot projects that have been implemented, from the Lambeth Cannabis Warning Scheme to trials of heroin-assisted treatment. Another recent example was the enhanced availability of naloxone (a drug which when taken reverses the effects of an opioid overdose) announced in 2024, enabling criminal justice and health practitioners to supply take-home supplies of this to certain drug users in a bid to reduce numbers of opioid-related deaths. These policy developments indicate that even within a structure of drug prohibition, policy can be innovative. Such advances, however, rarely address the more structural problems associated with drug policy – a key reason being that a misnomer seemingly exists, that even if prohibition continues, drug policy cannot be more dramatically changed.

Whilst the UN Control Treaties (1961, 1971, 1988) mandate that action be taken with regard to drug-related acts, punitive responses are by no means the only recourse available (Beckett Wilson et al., 2017). Indeed, the Police Foundation's Independent Inquiry into the Misuse of Drugs Act 1971 in 2000 observed that these 'in fact allow more room for manoeuvre than is generally understood' and that in the area of drug use, possession and related acts, 'there is express provision for imposing measures such as treatment, education, rehabilitation or social reintegration…either in addition or, more importantly, as an alternative to conviction or punishment' (Runciman, 2000:3).

When it comes to responding to drug-related issues – particularly those relating to crime and criminalisation – there is, therefore, greater freedom for drug policy reform within the framework of prohibition than has been envisaged or indeed implemented. A key reason for this is a rigid adherence to the drug war narrative and a seeming need for politicians not to be seen as soft on drugs. There is, however, scope for change, should this become politically palatable, and whilst a movement towards the decriminalisation or legalisation of drugs may be politically daunting (meaning this is unlikely to happen in the UK anytime soon, see the Box below), implementing reforms within the existing paradigm of prohibition may be more politically viable. Such reforms might also appeal to and appease critics of the status quo, especially if these address those enduring issues that have been so prominent under the guise of prohibition in the United Kingdom. Examples of potential reforms include:

- return oversight of drug policy to the health service, detaching it somewhat from the criminal justice system.
- rework the Misuse of Drugs Act 1971 (MDA) and change the sentencing guidelines for drug possession offences. This would not necessarily mean a move towards decriminalisation of drug possession but see a different approach to sentencing. This could take many forms; for example, it could see the sentencing threshold for possession offences lowered so that custody is removed as an option, or it could divert possession offences away from the criminal justice system, like the approach employed for speeding offences in the United Kingdom, with those caught in possession directed to attend drugs awareness courses.
- recalculate the MDA's current ABC classification system to ensure that drugs are in the appropriate category, consummate to the harms they are associated with (addressing the contradictions mapped out in Chapter 4).
- expand harm reduction services so that drug users are better supported. For example, the (wider) roll out of heroin-assisted treatment and the introduction of supervised drug consumption facilities.

Scotland and Drug Decriminalisation

In 2023, the Scottish government (2023a) published *A Caring, Compassionate and Human Rights Informed Drug Policy for Scotland*, which set out a definitive approach to drug policy reform. This was set against the backdrop of Scotland having the highest rate of drug-related deaths in Europe. The proposals put forward had public health and the reduction of harm as their underlying principles. These included (Scottish Government, 2023b):

- Decriminalisation of all drugs for personal supply progressed as part of a wider review of drug laws.
- Immediate legislative changes to allow full and proper implementation of harm reduction measures, for example, supervised drug consumption facilities.
- further exploration of drug law reform, focused on evidence and the reduction of harm, including an update of the drug classification system to be based on harms caused.

Summarising these proposals, the Scottish Minister for Drugs Policy, Elena Whitham, noted that 'We want to create a society where problematic drug use is treated as a health, not a criminal matter, reducing stigma and discrimination and enabling the person to recover and contribute positively to society' (cited in Scottish government, 2023b:1). The response from the United Kingdom's Conservative government (and the opposition Labour party), however, was unequivocal, with these being immediately dismissed. A spokesperson for then Prime Minister, Rishi Sunak, stated that he had no plans to alter his 'tough stance on drugs' (Christie, 2023:1584). Whilst enacting such changes would have required the devolution of specific powers to the Scottish government as drug policy is controlled by the UK government in Westminster, the way this was dismissed by the two dominant UK political parties indicated that any 'radical' movement away from prohibition is unlikely in the near future.

These options for pragmatic reform within a continued framework of prohibition would see all current drug offences remain illegal but differential approaches afforded to minimise drug-related harms. Whilst one intention of such reforms may be a genuine desire to improve drug user well-being (through less punitive responses to possession offences, enhanced access to support services, etc.), another ambition could be that these strategies would impact on the drugs and crime status quo. If we consider each of the above in turn, these might achieve the following:

- *oversight of drug policy to the health service*: this could see a repositioning of drug policy to allow issues of drugs and their use to be seen first and foremost as a health and social rather than criminal justice issue. Greater services could be provided for drug users, for example, enhanced drug education, harm reduction advice and access to drug services with those seen to be dependent on drugs supported within a health context rather than processed within the criminal justice system. This might include integrating drug treatment with sheltered housing, and medical and mental health care.
- *change the sentencing guidelines for drug possession offences*: this might change the way that drug possession offences are processed, meaning they cannot result in custodial sentences, or they are informally rather than formally processed, avoiding someone receiving a criminal record.
- *recalculate the MDAs current ABC classification system*: this might mean that drugs move categories within the MDA, for example, ecstasy might move from Class A to Class C to reflect its comparative level of harm (see Chapter 4). This would then mean that offences for ecstasy would fall into a lower sentencing threshold. Sentencing thresholds themselves might also be reduced, that is, the maximum sentence for a Class C possession offence is lowered from two years imprisonment to a community sentence.
- *expand harm reduction services*: this might see enhanced efforts to recognise the current harms associated with drugs and implement strategies and services to mitigate these. In essence, this would recognise that whilst drugs are illegal, people

still use them and there is a need to either encourage safer drug use or support drug users. This could enhance understandings of drug use and better inform drug-taking practices. For example, if drug checking services identify and communicate the exact contents of ecstasy tablets, this may influence whether someone uses the drug or how much they use at once – simultaneously engagement with such a service may allow users to learn about safer drug-taking practices, such as the recommended amount of water to drink.

Figure 10.1 indicates reforms involving harm reduction measures can seemingly lessen drug-related harms compared to a stricter model of drug prohibition. That said, it also illustrates that there are other models which might do this even more effectively.

DRUG POLICY REFORM: DECRIMINALISATION

The reforms set out above might have considerable impacts on how drugs and drug users are positioned and responded to within society. We also know, from those places that have implemented such policies, that evidence indicates these can reduce drug-related harms and have a positive impact on issues of crime and criminalisation (Taylor et al., 2016). That said, the breadth and scope of change these reforms enact might be perceived as relatively modest. Certain countries, however, have engaged in more radical shifts in policy. The most common methods being to either decriminalise the possession of cannabis or indeed all drugs or move to a legalised, regulated cannabis market.

Whilst policies of decriminalisation are usually introduced within an existing structure of prohibition – and therefore fit with those reforms outlined in the above section – for the purposes of this chapter, we present these separately as they entail a more fundamental shift away from a central tenant of prohibition, the criminalisation of drug users. This is because policies of decriminalisation, whilst varying widely in design and implementation, generally make possession of small quantities of drugs for personal use a non-criminal offence. In 2016, Release published *A quiet revolution: drug decriminalisation across the globe*. In this, they note that whilst policies of decriminalisation should not be considered new, as these have been evident around the globe since the 1970s, since the turn of the Century a 'new wave of countries have moved towards the decriminalisation model' leading to over 30 countries having such policies in place (Release, 2016:6). These include Portugal (see Box on page 242-243), the Netherlands (see Box on page 244-245) and Spain (see Box on page 245).

The motivation for those places that have moved towards decriminalisation varies – for some, it is due to a realisation of the harms caused by criminalisation, for others, it is part of a wider shift towards a more public health-orientated drug policy, whilst for others still it is to reduce the costs amounted by prosecuting such drug offences, or indeed a combination of these. The reasons underpinning such reforms, however, are incredibly important as they demonstrate what is driving these, which can include a recognition of the failures or faults of prohibition; an acknowledgement that illegal drug use is part and parcel of society and it makes little sense to criminalise people; or a realisation that whilst drug use is still illegal and therefore wrong, it is a minor offence that criminal justice systems do not have the resources to effectively respond to nor are they best placed to address.

MODELS OF DECRIMINALISATION

These different motivations influence the structure of decriminalisation policies – and these vary greatly. This is important as different decriminalisation policies have different advantages and disadvantages, the most common of which are mapped out in Table 10.1. This also illustrates some of the tensions that are inherent with the decriminalisation model and how it represents a seeming halfway house – or indeed a liminal space – between stricter prohibition and more liberal legalisation models.

Table 10.1 Common Advantages and Disadvantages Associated With Models of Drug Decriminalisation

Advantages of Decriminalisation	Disadvantages of Decriminalisation
Move away from strict prohibition	Prohibition remains whilst the black market continues to operate
Avoids criminalising drug users (although caveats may allow people to still be arrested e.g. using in proximity to a school)	Criminalisation remains for any non-decriminalised drugs
Allows users to possess drugs with impunity	Only possession of drugs up to a specified threshold limit is decriminalised
Allows police to focus on drug supply	How do the police distinguish between possession and supply?
	Supply remains illegal and criminalised
Removes discretionary policing	Discretionary/discriminatory policing may continue
Reduces criminal justice costs	Administrative costs are incurred through implementation whilst convictions can still occur
Encourages more health centred strategies to develop	Health centred strategies might not be implemented
Reduce stigma	Stigma remains as drugs remain illegal and certain users may still be criminalised
Greater pleasure from drug use	Potential increase in drug use
	Need to protect people from drugs via prohibition

If we consider two of the issues highlighted in Table 10.1, those of criminalising drug users and discretionary policing, what we see is that implementing decriminalisation is not straightforward. In terms of criminalising drug users, decriminalisation clearly seeks to avoid this; however, some may point out that current policy already does this to an extent, whilst others may contend that even within a framework of decriminalisation, people may still be arrested and charged for possession as stipulations continue to exist, such as the amount of drugs they have in their possession or whether the person is using the drug in public. This then feeds into the second point around discriminatory policing – on the surface, decriminalisation would remove this as possession of drugs would no longer be a criminal offence but the police are still likely to be able to stop and search someone for reasons pertaining to a drug offence – it is also probable that different police forces would approach possession in different ways, meaning the situation could be similar to the present.

Clearly, the scope of issues presented by moving towards a policy of decriminalisation depend on the model that is employed. It should be noted that in some countries, decriminalisation has always been evident as they have never criminalised drug possession (although such policies can perversely lead to harsher sentences for those caught with certain amounts of drugs, see Release, 2016). For those who have more recently implemented reform, however, two dominant models have emerged – the decriminalisation of the possession of cannabis and the decriminalisation of the possession of all drugs for personal use.

In terms of the decriminalisation of cannabis, these policies in general mean that the possession of cannabis is either legal or 'de facto legal' (meaning that whilst this is not written into law, it is in essence legal). In practice, this can mean that the police do not look to intervene with those suspected of possessing cannabis nor arrest them. Yet this is not necessarily the case as the police may still engage with such individuals, be permitted to confiscate the drug and begin a process whereby the individual is referred into an administrative or diversionary process (which may have outcomes such as a referral to a drug service or punitive sanctions such as a fine). This is because most countries with decriminalisation policies maintain the right to arrest people for possession depending on factors such as the amount of cannabis found and how many times the individual has previously been found in possession of the drug.

One of the fears regarding decriminalisation is that rates of drug use will increase when these policies are implemented – after all, that is one of the premises on which drug prohibition is built. The evidence suggests, however, that rates of drug use generally remain relatively stable (Release, 2016). Nevertheless, decriminalisation can simultaneously have a contradictory impact on those who do use drugs. For example, Hughes and colleagues (2016:6) identified that despite the introduction of various policies of decriminalisation in different Australian states, overall rates of drug use/possession detections continued to rise, meaning 'more people who use drugs risk getting charged, convicted and imprisoned for minor quantities…'. This net widening effect (Cohen, 1985) has also been seen in Portugal (see the Box below).

Decriminalisation of All Drugs in Portugal

In 2001, Portugal decriminalised the possession of all drugs for personal use, repositioning this as an administrative rather than criminal offence. Possession of drugs is permitted in line with threshold amounts that reflect what an average person may consume over a 10-day period (25g cannabis, 1g MDMA, 2g cocaine, 1g heroin).

Anyone found with amounts above these limits can face a criminal charge. Accompanying this legal reform was a change towards a health-focused drug policy with a greater ambition to support drug users and refer people to treatment services.
When an individual is found to be in possession of drugs (by the police), they are not simply released, instead their drugs are confiscated, and they are mandatorily referred to a 'Commission for the Dissuasion of Drug Addiction' (a panel of three experts which includes legal, social work and healthcare professionals). Whilst this panel can apply punitive sanctions (e.g. regular reporting to the panel, community service, suspension of a driving licence or a fine), they may also make (non-mandatory) referrals to treatment services for those with a drug dependency. For non-dependent, first-time 'offenders', proceedings are usually suspended with no sanctions imposed. Transform (2021:2) describes the panels as 'non-judgemental in nature, and a primary focus is safeguarding the right to health of those referred, their main aim is to encourage an individual to address their drug use'. Overall, these reforms are framed as a success. Transform (2021:1) indicates that:

- Drug-related deaths fell after the reform of Portugal's drug policy and have remained below the EU average since 2001.
- The proportion of the prison population sentenced for drug offences has fallen from over 40% to 15%.
- Rates of drug use have remained consistently below the EU average.
- Portugal has gone from accounting for over 50% of yearly HIV diagnoses linked to injecting drug use in the EU to 1.7%.

Despite these apparently positive trends, it is difficult to assert whether they are a direct result of decriminalisation. Meanwhile, Rego and colleagues (2021) dispute the overall progressive nature of these reforms. They contend that the last decade has seen an increase in criminal sanctions targeted at drug users, noting that 'prohibitionism has not been discarded' (Rego et al., 2021:2). Similarly, they identify that the majority of those referred to the Commission for the Dissuasion of Drug Addiction in 2019 were cannabis users, with just 10% of referrals classed as dependent drug users, indicating a potential net widening effect, whereby cannabis users are being drawn into more formal processes than previously. The outcomes of these panels are in the main suspensions (where no action is taken), but in 19% of cases, the decisions were classed as punitive. Finally, they argue that the harm reduction measures imagined at the beginning of the reform process, for example, drug consumption rooms, have failed to materialise. They conclude that policy reform has been enacted under conservative lines and that consequently, it has struggled to 'emancipate drug use from the stigma that associates it with either crime or pathology, where it is kept captive' (Rego et al., 2021:2).

The threshold quantities of drugs defined as decriminalised for the purposes of possession is another important point. Different countries have very different interpretations. Some ambiguously denote that 'small amounts' are permitted, leaving this very much open to discretion, whilst others provide specific but varying calculations.

For example, Portugal's thresholds are said to reflect what an average person may consume over a 10-day period, namely, 25g cannabis, 1g MDMA, 2g cocaine and 1g heroin. Yet Spain's thresholds, which reflect what an average person may consume over a 5-day period, calculate this as 25g cannabis resin, 2.4g MDMA, 7.5g cocaine and 3g heroin. Whilst Portugal therefore maintains a policy of decriminalisation of all drugs, to what extent this is true, based on the set threshold amounts, is questionable. Whilst 25g of cannabis over a 10-day period may be seen as a roughly proportionate amount for a regular user, 2g of cocaine might easily be used in a single event of drug taking. When we talk about the decriminalisation of all drugs based on thresholds, it is debatable whether in effect it is actually just cannabis that is decriminalised as the thresholds for other drugs are often very low.

The evidence from many places where decriminalisation has been implemented is still in its infancy. That said, it is growing in both scope and longitudinal nature. Whilst the varied nature of policies of decriminalisation makes generalisations of its outcomes difficult, some key themes and trends are identifiable. These are well summarised by Release (2016:7):

> decriminalisation when implemented effectively does appear to direct more people who use drugs problematically into treatment, reduce criminal justice costs, improve public health outcomes, and shield many drug users from the devastating impact of a criminal conviction. Decriminalisation when coupled with investment in harm reduction, and health and social services, can have an extremely positive effect on both individuals who use drugs and society as a whole.

Clearly, this evidence should be treated with caution, especially where it is based on short-term research as it could be potentially misleading due to the impacts of such transformative changes perhaps taking generations to be fully realised. For example, even if possession of heroin is decriminalised, a high degree of stigma will still be associated with the drug and its use, which may or may not change over time, but the outcome of which will have ramifications for its policing, the processing of those found in possession and the willingness of heroin users to proactively seek support should they require it.

Decriminalisation of Cannabis in the Netherlands

The Netherlands first enacted decriminalisation of cannabis possession in 1971, amending this in 1976 to separate cannabis from the wider drugs market so that young people were not exposed to 'harder' substances. Whilst cannabis is still technically illegal, it is 'de facto' decriminalised due to being regarded as the lowest priority of law enforcement (Release, 2016:25). The Netherlands is most well-known for its coffee shop model, which sees licenced and regulated venues (which have limits to the number of sales they can make, a minimum age of 18 and stipulations not to sell alcohol or cause public nuisance) permitted to retail cannabis. The policy does not extend to suppliers, however, meaning the sale of cannabis to these shops still relies on the unregulated black market, although a pilot scheme began in 2023 which permits the legal production (and therefore sale) of cannabis in certain cities.

The Ministry of Health has primary responsibility for drug policy and cannabis decriminalisation is one element of a much wider harm minimisation strategy aiming to support those with drug dependencies through the provision of harm reduction services and integrated support. Arrests and criminal records for use or minor possession are extremely rare in the Netherlands compared to other European states whilst there are low rates of problematic drug use (Scottish government, 2021). Cannabis use has remained stable and at similar levels to other European countries (Grund and Breeksema, 2017). The coffee shop model, however, has prompted some concerns related to public nuisance, leading to a 2012 scheme which aimed to restrict sales to registered residents to, in essence, make them into private clubs. This, however, was not universally embraced nor widely implemented.

Decriminalisation of All Drugs/Cannabis in Spain

Possession of drugs for personal use has never been a criminal offence in Spain. Although there are no set threshold limits defining possession, if someone is caught with above what is perceived as 5-day supply for personal use (100g of cannabis, 25g cannabis resin, 2.4g MDMA, 7.5g cocaine, 3g heroin), they may face prosecution.

It is in relation to cannabis, however, that the most interesting developments have emerged. In accordance with a Supreme Court ruling, personal exemption from criminal prosecution for possession was extended to collective exemption. This led to the emergence of 'cannabis social clubs', described as 'democratically-structured and not-for-profit private-member associations of adult cannabis consumers, the social club premises of which provide a space for the acquisition and consumption of cannabis sourced by the association board members for the use of members' (Release, 2016:32).

The legal positioning of these clubs, however, has been questioned, especially as membership of some has extended to thousands. Simultaneously, more people are subjected to administrative penalties for drug possession in Spain than in any other country in Europe (Release, 2016).

DRUG POLICY REFORM: LEGALISATION

Whilst decriminalisation may represent radical drug policy reform to some, for others it still operates in an overall structure of prohibition, meaning that it allows many associated drug-related harms to continue and does not challenge the fundamental problems of existing policy. The next model we turn to, drug legalisation, overcomes many of these criticisms as it replaces the prohibition of illegal drugs with a regulatory framework, meaning that illegal substances become like other commodified drugs, such as alcohol and tobacco. The only policies of legalisation that have currently been enacted across the globe, however, relate to a single drug – cannabis. In this sense, no single state has detached itself from the model of drug prohibition, nor has any country attempted to legalise any other drug. This prompts a question, which oddly, very few people seem to ask – why is it that cannabis is the first/only illegal drug that is legalised?

One reason may be that cannabis is thought of as a less harmful drug, although if we were to refer back to Nutt and colleagues (2010) rankings of drug-related harm (see Chapter 4), we see that cannabis lies in the middle of this scale – meaning that if such reforms were motivated by the apparent risks associated with a drug, other substances such as magic mushrooms, LSD or ecstasy might be more logically placed to be legalised. Cannabis, however, is the most popular illegal drug. It may therefore be argued that the scale of harm that can potentially be reduced by legalising cannabis (in terms of health- and social-related issues, including those pertaining to possession offences given they represent the bulk of drug offences in England and Wales – see Chapter 6) justifies this. Cannabis' popularity, however, also means that a move towards a legalised, regulated market is potentially very profitable.

These discussions again lead us to consider what exactly is motivating these reforms, with financial reasoning being an important influencing factor. A legalised cannabis market, open to private sector investment, has obvious business allure. That is not to say that every place that has legalised cannabis has created a commercialised private market (see the Box on page 250-251 which outlines the alternative state-governed model implemented in Uruguay) although this is the most common model. The tax revenue that can potentially be accrued is also very attractive to government – it is difficult to think of many other currently illegal activities (aside from perhaps sex work) that might be legalised meaning that instead of *costing* the government money (in terms of enforcing the law and prosecuting individuals), it provides an *income*.

Alongside this, cannabis is a drug that can now be produced domestically in most countries, meaning that unlike some other illicit substances, moving to a regulated market is relatively straightforward as the production, transportation and retailing of the drug can all be managed internally – if one were to legalise a drug which is produced in another country, this would bring the added complexity of additional regulations in the country of origin as well as along the transportation route. This issue was highlighted during Uruguay's move to legalisation, whereby US banks could not be involved in the financial operations of cannabis-related business as the drug is (on a federal level) illegal in the United States. That said, there is precedent here in terms of drugs such as opiates which are legally grown in various states around the world before being shipped to other countries for medicinal purposes.

Whether there are other non-financial ambitions at play in relation to the legalisation of cannabis is unclear. The Home Office (2014:6, emphasis added) report cited previously interprets the legalisation of cannabis in certain countries in an interesting manner, noting that:

> Uruguay and... American states... are adopting experimental policies which legalise and regulate the production, supply and recreational use of cannabis. *These policies have common aims – disrupting organised crime and exercising greater control over the use of cannabis...*

It continues saying that 'Black market production and supply may continue, undercutting the legitimate market and the ability of state authorities *to use taxes as a means of deterring consumption'* (Home Office, 2014:39 emphasis added). Indeed, it was telling that in the same year as this report was published, the then Deputy Prime Minister of the United Kingdom, Nick Clegg, stated 'If you are anti-drugs you should be pro-reform'. Drug reform in the form of legalisation then, whilst often heralded as liberal – or indeed being soft on drugs – may equally be motivated by a desire to further control drugs and drug users, and to align an illicit market with the dominant model of consumer capitalism through regulation, private profit and taxation. These mixed motivations are unfolding in a thought-provoking fashion in the United Kingdom, where centre-right groups such as the Centre for Evidence based Drug Policy (formerly the Conservative Drug Policy Reform Group), who receive funding from private sector cannabis business, are championing legalisation alongside established 'liberal' reform groups.

Yet one cannot ignore the fact that the legalisation of cannabis in those places where it has been introduced would not have happened without a relative groundswell of public support (although in the case of Uruguay, most of the public were opposed to legalisation when the policy was announced, see Laqueur et al., 2020). It has also been celebrated by both those who have long campaigned for legal reform – seemingly representing a first step towards an acceptance of illegal substance use – and by cannabis users themselves, who no longer face criminal prosecution. In relation to this last point, an interesting question is whether those previously prosecuted for offences relating to cannabis possession should be exonerated if the drug is legalised, an issue which US President Joe Biden addressed by pardoning those previously convicted of possessing small amounts of cannabis at a national level in 2022.

MODELS OF LEGALISATION

The number of places where cannabis is legalised is growing and currently includes Canada, Georgia, Luxembourg, Malta, Mexico, South Africa, Thailand (although this policy is currently under review), Uruguay, 24 US states and the Australian Capital Territory in Australia. That said, whilst all these places permit cannabis to be legally possessed and/or cultivated, only a few (Uruguay, Canada, Thailand and certain US states) have a distribution system for retail sales.

Advantages of legalisation	Disadvantages of legalisation
Drug offences removed	Offences remains for not following legal regulations
Removes criminalisation	Criminalisation remains for non-legalised drugs
Removes stigma of illegality	Stigma remains and may be enhanced for non-legalised drugs
Replace black-market with regulated system	Black-market will remain and people will use this to avoid regulatory restrictions
Ensures products of known quality and strength	Regulatory market may offer less variety than current black-market
Tax revenue	Costs associated with implementation
Reduce criminal justice costs	Increased administrative costs
Commercial model offers consumer choice and freedom	Commercial profit-driven model potentially problematic
Reduce social and health harms	Potential increase in use due to novelty/ greater availability
Allows greater focus on harm reduction	Harm reduction strategies might not be implemented
Greater pleasure from drug use	Need to protect people from drugs via prohibition

Figure 10.2 Advantages and Disadvantages of Drug Legalisation

Whilst different models of cannabis legalisation are evident in these countries, these differences are perhaps less pronounced that those pertaining to decriminalisation. For example, the US and Canadian (see the Box on page 250) frameworks are perhaps best characterised as 'commercial models', which involve a degree of regulatory restrictions coupled with a degree of free market liberty, whilst the Uruguayan system (see the Box on page 250-251) can be seen as a 'non-commercial' model, which sees a state operated framework with greater regulatory stipulations. Again, the underpinning reasons why countries move towards legalising cannabis is crucially important, as this effects both the overall framework in which cannabis is regulated and the practicalities of how this operates.

Moving towards a regulated cannabis market involves a variety of potential advantages and disadvantages, some of which are mapped out in Figure 10.2. Yet these beneficial and negative consequences are themselves guided by the overall motivation for such reform and the way that this policy is implemented. Regardless of such motivations, the advantages and disadvantages of this model, like those discussed previously in relation to decriminalisation, indicate some of the conflicts involved in legalisation.

If we take one of the points from Figure 10.2, that of replacing a criminal market with a regulated system, we can highlight some of these difficulties. Whilst a regulated system can ensure that drugs contain specific ingredients of known strength, moving away from the current unknowns of the black market, it might also lead to drugs costing more and being strictly controlled in terms of who, when and where they can be sold, issues which in themselves may prompt the continuation of a black market. Several of the contentious issues raised by the legalisation model relate to how it is implemented with numerous decisions about the practicalities of regulation facing anyone tasked with visioning how this will operate – the Box below provides examples of the many practical questions that must be answered if a model of legalised cannabis is pursued.

Practical Questions Facing Those Implementing a Model of Cannabis Legalisation

- Who will be permitted to produce cannabis?
- Will cannabis be solely produced by approved manufacturers or will individuals be allowed to cultivate it for personal use?
- Where will cannabis be sold? Will a licence be required? Can those with a criminal record hold a licence?
- Where will/can cannabis be used?
- How much tax will be implemented on cannabis production/sales?
- Will there be set pricing, or will this be at the discretion of retailers?
- What forms of cannabis will be available, for example, will edible cannabis products be permitted?
- Will there be any restrictions to the strength of cannabis available?
- How will cannabis be packaged? Will advertising be permitted?
- Will there be an age restriction applied to cannabis sales?
- Will there be a maximum purchase/possession limit for people buying/carrying cannabis?
- Will cannabis only be purchasable by residents of that country or open to visitors?

All those jurisdictions that have moved to a legalised cannabis market have had to respond to these questions – and have done so in different ways. The Box below explains how this has been approached in Canada, whilst the Box after that provides insight into the very different system operating in Uruguay. Whilst the evidence relating to drug decriminalisation may be viewed as in its infancy, evidence relating to policies of legalisation is even less developed as the policies in these countries continue to evolve. The outcomes of legalisation are therefore relatively unknown although early indications are that it can considerably reduce the number of people arrested for drug offences, result in significant criminal justice savings, has a minimal impact on rates of adolescent cannabis use and leads to substantial tax revenue (Drug Policy Alliance, 2018; Government of Canada, 2022).

Legalisation of Cannabis in Canada

Canada legalised cannabis in 2018. In doing so, the Canadian Government identified three key aims: protecting young people, protecting public health and reducing criminality associated with the black market. The federal government regulates the production of cannabis whilst local jurisdictions (provinces and territories) have the discretion to shape how legalisation works in practice, although certain stipulations generally apply:

- Adults over 18 are allowed to possess (and share with other adults) up to 30g of cannabis. This includes non-Canadians. In certain provinces, the minimum age is set at 19. In some provinces public use is permitted, in others not.
- Cannabis (initially herbal and oils but now edibles and concentrates) is available from regulated retail outlets and online sales. These retailers are either government operated or privately owned.
- Adults can cultivate up to four cannabis plants for personal use in most (but not all) provinces.
- Cannabis must be sold in plain packaging with clear health warnings and content information – minimal brand logo and details are allowed.
- Strict controls are in place on advertising and promotions, including bans on sponsorship, celebrity endorsements, and any information that targets youth.
- Access to cannabis for medical purposes is regulated under separate legislation/regulations.

As this model is implemented regionally, different issues have arisen in different places. Overall, however, drug use is said to have increased but at a relatively stable rate in keeping with the trends evident prior to legalisation (Government of Canada, 2022); there has been a significant decrease in people accessing cannabis directly from the illegal market although approximately one third of users still use the black market (Statistics Canada, 2023); the price of legal cannabis, whilst initially almost double that available via the black market, has reduced with the gap between the two narrowing (Government of Canada, 2022).

In 2022, there were 836 federal commercial licence holders permitted to produce cannabis and 3,200 retail stores. The market is dominated by 10 producers who, between 2019 and 2021, were responsible for 43.2% of dried cannabis production with 66% of all revenues attributed to them (Government of Canada, 2022). Yet commercial producers are seemingly facing financial problems, which are being partly attributed to the stringent regulatory system (Yousef, 2023).

Legalisation of Cannabis in Uruguay

Uruguay legalised cannabis in 2013 having previously decriminalised personal possession in 1974. In doing so, it became the first country to operationalise a legal system of cannabis distribution. Laqueur and colleagues (2020:2) outline that the motivation behind this 'was to eliminate the illicit drug trade and its associated violence and public health related harms'. According to Transform (2018), the main risk identified in relation to legalisation in Uruguay was commercial promotion – hence the strict, non-commercial model that has been pursued. This sees both production and supply controlled by government.

Cannabis is sold via licenced pharmacies with a variety of restrictions in place including buyers having to be registered, over 18 years old and only able to buy a maximum of 10g a week. Only two types of relatively low potency cannabis were initially available for purchase, sold in unbranded packaging. All advertising and sponsorship are banned. Pricing is set just below the illicit market rate. Home cultivation (of up to six plants) and 'user associations' (similar to cannabis social clubs in Spain, see the Box on page 245) of between 15 and 45 members are permitted with each again requiring registration.

Emerging research from Uruguay indicates that legalisation has not had an impact on rates of (adolescent) cannabis use (Laquer et al., 2020) although overall prevalence of those who have used the drug is said to have increased (Lissardy, 2019). As the pharmacy system did not begin until 2017, it is very early for any definitive research findings to emerge. One issue to arise is that the black market is still utilised by many to buy their cannabis for numerous reasons, including ease of access; because people want to avoid officially registering as cannabis users; due to it offering more variety than the restricted legal options; and because people cannot access user associations due to the restricted membership numbers creating long waiting lists.

DRUG POLICY REFORM: A PROGRESSIVE MOVEMENT?

When one considers the multiple problems presented by drug prohibition alongside the emerging evidence base that suggests that these can be ameliorated by drug policy reform, it seems that moving drug policy towards frameworks of decriminalisation or legalisation represents a progressive shift in our ability to produce a more rational and less harmful approach to illegal substances. Some writers, however, have provided some pertinent analysis which questions this direction of travel.

Firstly, Walmsley (2019) suggests that drug policy reforms continue to be haunted by the *ghosts of prohibition*. This is due to reform being motivated by the same factors that have driven prohibition – fear of drugs and a need to further control drug users. Resultantly, evaluations of drug policy reform – as can be seen in the example case studies presented in this chapter – measure effectiveness through a continued lens of prohibition, focusing on their impact on levels of drug use, crime rates and addiction, the scope of health-related harms, overdoses, deaths and treatment referrals. This means that the emerging evidence base around drug policy reform aligns with dominant prohibitionist understandings of drugs – that they are inherently harmful, cause crime, cause addiction, lead to health problems and require treatment. Consequently, we continue to view drugs and their use through a narrow, conventional lens, ignoring the wider inferences of this policy, for example, how reforms may enhance rights, enjoyment and benefits of drug users.

Further bolstering this argument is that one of the key proxy measures of drug policy reform is rates of drug use. Whilst we do not have the time to consider just how difficult it is to accurately gauge these, the key point here is that we see ghosts once again haunting reform. Why, we might ask, should rates of drug use be an issue here? The answer is that drug prohibition has instilled a belief that any rise in drug use is bad, as people should not be taking drugs, and therefore any policy that leads to an increase in use is a failure. This is a telling indication of what motivates drug policy reforms, demonstrating that these are not being introduced as part of a wider ambition to live with rather than without drugs but because these align with the fundamental tenant of prohibition – to control.

Secondly, the ghosts of prohibition are also evident in terms of the ongoing processes and trends relating to drugs and crime. Whilst reform can be liberal in nature, in places where policies of decriminalisation and legalisation have been introduced, people can still be arrested, charged and imprisoned for drug possession offences and even where administrative penalties are applied, these can still be punitive. Sitting alongside these are the continuation of discriminatory practices, which see the disproportionate representation of minority ethnic groups, particularly Black and Indigenous people, charged for such offences (Drug Policy Alliance, 2015; Government of Canada, 2022). Meanwhile, reforms can also enhance the scope of individuals drawn into formal processes – whether these be administrative or criminal – for those found in possession, indicating that drug policy continues to widen its scope and breadth. For example, in the case of Canada, the rates of young people receiving a criminal charge for cannabis possession have increased (from 32.5% in 2015 to 45.5% in 2019) since the drug was legalised (Government of Canada, 2022). Similarly, as Rego and colleagues contend (2021), despite Portugal's decriminalisation reforms being humanistic and pragmatic on the ground, these ultimately work in compliance with the war on drugs. Therefore, the criminalisation and discrimination that have been a hallmark of drug prohibition continue to haunt drug policy reform, indicating how drug policy is often a sypher for wider social issues, ambitions and prejudices.

Thirdly, Taylor and colleagues (2016) contend that drug policy reform might actually serve to bolster prohibition. Stand-alone policies of decriminalisation or cannabis legalisation may represent stepping stones to more liberal approaches to drugs and the dismantling of prohibition. Yet when enacted in a vacuum, without being integrated within a wider strategy that encompasses all legal and illegal drugs, these continue the drug apartheid's (see Chapter 4) arbitrarily focus on individual substances rather than the full spectrum of drugs and their use. They also, in relation to cannabis, may pose a risk to the momentum of the drug policy reform movement. As Buchanan (2015b: 1) argues:

> The global and united drug reform movement could be undermined by an unintended consequence of privileging cannabis to join the elite drugs and subsequently 'divide and rule' to maintain the bifurcation process. No doubt, and understandably, after the decades of oppression suffered by cannabis users, legalisation of their drug of choice will be met with a celebration of the new found freedoms and privileges, but possibly also by a lack of interest to fight to

> end the prohibition of all drugs. Indeed, further, it could give rise to a new momentum against 'drugs' or 'hard drugs' – as recently liberated cannabis users redefining themselves as herbalists or sensible recreational users of 'soft' drugs.

As Wakeman (2014:236) notes, whilst amendments which improve things on the ground in the now should be pursued, 'ultimately they will not suffice alone'. It is, therefore, questionable whether we should see incremental reforms as progressive if these are simultaneously complicit with the existing prohibitionist structure. An alternative is to seek a more radical contestation of existing structures in the pursuit of more sustainable long-term solutions. As Seddon (2016) notes, the notion of drug policy reform is an oxymoron as without a reconceptualisation of the term 'drugs', there can never be any genuine reform, ensuing that the ghosts of prohibition are emboldened. Hence, some have called for drug policy reform to have grander ambitions.

TOWARDS A REGULATED SYSTEM OF ALL DRUGS

Despite the apparent turbulence in global drug policy indicating a weakening of the historically dominant model of prohibition, the criminalisation of drugs continues. No single country has moved towards a fully legalised market for all illegal substances whilst those found in possession of drugs continue to be prosecuted, even in places where reform has taken place. Whilst we are therefore seeing a nibbling at the edges of drug prohibition, it still endures and in some places is actively being strengthened (see, for example, the UK government's addition of nitrous oxide to its list of banned substances in 2023).

Meanwhile, there seems to be growing support for prohibition of a different type, one pertaining to legal substances. An example being New Zealand's attempt in 2023 to introduce tobacco laws which aimed to create a smoke-free generation of young people by gradually increasing the legal age at which tobacco can be purchased. Such measures may seem justifiable from a public health perspective, but the many problems associated with prohibiting illegal drugs question whether banning legal drugs is the correct path to take.

Contrastingly, Julian Buchanan, a prominent critique of drug prohibition, maintains that the ideal drug policy reform would be that of a fully regulated system of legalisation, which encompasses all currently legal and illegal substances. This would see the regulation of all illicit drugs, allowing them to be legally produced, sold and consumed. It would also, however, see a strengthening of regulations pertaining to legal drugs like alcohol, tobacco and prescription medications. Whilst this model raises various dilemmas and difficult questions, it would ultimately see an end to prohibition. Yet again, however, the motivations behind such policy reform would be crucial. Buchanan (2015c) notes that if the ambition was to replace strict prohibition with strict (yet commercialised) regulation, this would result in 'Prohibition 2.0'. He therefore suggests that it is crucial to follow a 'human rights approach' which would allow a more nuanced, holistic and less harmful drug policy to emerge. Figure 10.3 illustrates how these two models differ in terms of their aims, methods and outcomes.

A Human Rights Approach to Drugs and Drug Reform

A human rights approach to drugs and drug policy focuses on ensuring that the development and implementation of drug-related policies and practices respect, protect and fulfil the human rights of all individuals. This approach emphasises the dignity, health and well-being of individuals and communities focusing on health, social support and justice rather than punishment. By aligning drug policies with human rights principles, societies can create more effective, humane and sustainable responses to drug-related challenges (see Bone, 2019; Buchanan, 2006; Lines, 2017; Szasz, 1992; Walsh, 2016).

In line with Mill's harm principle (see Chapter 1), individuals should have the freedom to make choices about their own bodies, including the use of drugs, as long as it does not harm others. This links to the ideas presented by Szasz (Friedman and Szasz, 1992) above around the human right to choose whatever one wishes to place in one's body.

Walsh (2016) uses the concept of cognitive liberty, which emphasises the importance of personal autonomy and the individual's right to self-determination as individuals should have the freedom to explore their own minds and consciousness through the use of psychoactive substances promoting the idea that people should have the legal right to explore different states of consciousness.

Human rights approaches tend to support drug policy reform advocating for decriminalisation/legalisation, harm reduction and the provision of comprehensive health services for drug users.

Whilst providing a clear set of principles, Figure 10.3 does not engage with the multiplicity of practical issues that moving towards a regulated market pose. Whether such a policy could be enacted by a single nation state is questionable due to potential issues with the manufacture and production of currently illegal drugs. It might also, due to the associated harms and stigmas attached to certain drugs, make many people feel deeply uncomfortable – whilst publics may feel relatively at ease at the thought of a cannabis café in their town, the thought of heroin or cocaine being available to buy over the counter might prove unnerving.

Nonetheless, a regulatory model, especially one based on the human rights approach (see the Box above) touted by Buchanan, would aim first and foremost to remove the link between drugs and crime by removing all criminal penalties. It would also seek to place the needs and well-being of drug users front and centre, developing a system that maintains their safety but also respects their right to use any substance of their choosing. It would attempt to encourage society to see all substances, whether currently legal or illegal, as drugs. It would seek to address drug-related issues as a whole – with a drug policy that considers the regulation, retail, benefits and harms of legal and illegal substances together. Whilst this may lead to MDMA being available via specialist pharmacies, it might equally see alcohol sales restricted to a small number of government-owned retailers, like the Swedish 'systembolaget', which sees alcohol sales not driven by profit but by a more restrictive policy that aims to limit the harmful effects of the drug.

Importantly, the human rights approach would look to include drug users rather than marginalise them. This is particularly novel, as seemingly absent from those drug reforms evident around the globe have been the voices of drug users themselves (Askew et al., 2022). Nowhere has reform seemingly been motivated by an ambition of recognising and respecting the right to use drugs nor the needs of drug users, which again questions the overriding motivations underpinning these policies.

12 Steps to Prohibition 2.0 via Legal Regulation	12 Steps to End Prohibition via a Human Rights Approach
1. Gangsters shouldn't be in charge of drug distribution – we must end prohibition.	1. Gangsters can't be in charge of drug distribution we must end prohibition.
2. Drugs are potentially dangerous, they all need to be legally regulated.	2. Commercially sold drugs should be regulated.
3. Only state approved and regulated companies should produce and distribute drugs.	3. Only approved companies should produce them for commercial distribution.
4. Only state approved regulated outlets should be allowed to sell drugs.	4. Only approved outlets should sell them.
5. Only approved legally regulated drugs should be sold.	5. Only approved regulated drugs should be commercially sold.
6. To support and protect the Legal Regulated market, possession of unregulated or non-approved drugs must be an offence.	6. Strict regulatory controls are placed on all business practices (advertising, packaging, distribution, sale etc).
7. To protect people from the dangers of drugs, only approved regulated drugs should be consumed.	7. Individuals can manufacture and/or cultivate ANY substance – for personal use only.
8. Strict enforcement and penalties should apply to all possession and supply of unregulated unapproved drug.	8. Individuals can possess and consume ANY substance – for personal use.
9. Because drugs can be dangerous, and we have a regulated market, individuals must not be allowed to manufacture or cultivate drugs.	9. Registered societies and clubs can meet exchange information, knowledge and equipment.
10. Law enforcement should be able to enter without a warrant if unregulated drug production/cultivation is suspected in a building.	10. The fundamental human right for a person to consume in their body, what they choose, without threat, controls or punishment from the state remain paramount and must always be protected.
11. Strict Regulation has successfully produced a Legal Regulation model which has state approved legal regulated drugs and outlawed underground unregulated drugs.	11. All drug prohibition has been abolished.
12. That may sound unnervingly familiar. A full circle, welcome back to Prohibition 2.0.	12. Welcome, we have a human rights approach to legal regulation.

Figure 10.3 12 Steps of Drug Policy Reform (Buchanan, 2015c)

CONCLUSION

This chapter has considered the inferences for drugs and crime in relation to drug policy reform, discussing the significance of this in relation to various micro-, meso- and macro-level issues identified throughout this book. We have seen how drug policy reform can be enacted, either within the existing paradigm of drug prohibition or through a more radical overhaul of policy via decriminalisation and legalisation – both of which, emerging evidence suggests, can have positive impacts on drug user well-being and health and lessen the harms of the criminalisation imposed by drug prohibition. That said, it is difficult to generalise about such reforms as across the world these have and are being enacted in different contexts, for different reasons and in different ways. Additionally, each of these models presents contentious issues, not least the continuation of some of the problematic trends and notions associated with drug prohibition. Perhaps, therefore, the answer is for a more ambitious fully regulated system for all drugs, yet this is a solution that in itself comes fraught with practical, political, social and health-related dilemmas. It should also be noted that whatever form drug policy takes, certain drug related harms will persist and other harms will emerge even where reform takes place.

Each model of drug policy reform, however, shares a key ambition – to address the relationship between drugs and criminalisation. Fundamentally, this is through restructuring how the criminal law reacts to offences of drug possession. Many reforms, however, also aim to destigmatise drug use and users, enact more public health-orientated drug policies and offer enhanced support and harm reduction services to drug users, all of which can impact on issues of crime more widely. Perhaps, however, the key message emanating from this chapter is that until we move away from the ghosts of prohibition, genuine drug policy reform cannot take place. As such, it is only when we stop conceptualising drug policy through the lens of crime, criminalisation and criminal justice that truly progressive drug policies might emerge.

SUMMARY

- **For some, drug prohibition is seen as effective and able to innovatively respond to emerging issues.**
- **Within the existing structure of drug prohibition, drug policy reform is possible but often pursues small-scale rather than root and branch changes.**
- **Decriminalisation refers to the possession of (certain) illegal drugs for personal use being made a non-criminal offence.**
- **Evidence suggests policies of decriminalisation can increase engagement with treatment services, reduce criminal justice costs, improve public health outcomes and lessen criminal convictions.**
- **Legalisation refers to (certain) illegal drugs being legally regulated. So far, the only drug to have been legalised anywhere in the world is cannabis.**

- **Evidence suggests legalisation can reduce the number of people arrested for drug offences, can result in significant criminal justice savings, has a minimal impact on rates of adolescent cannabis use and leads to substantial tax revenue.**
- **The evidence base relating to both decriminalisation and legalisation is still in its infancy.**
- **Policies of decriminalisation and legalisation vary widely and pose a series of practical questions as well as a spectrum of potential advantages/disadvantages.**
- **Whether drug policy reform is progressive can be questioned especially when viewed as being haunted by the ghosts of prohibition.**
- **The motivations underpinning drug policy reforms are crucial.**

Here are some points and questions for you to consider after reading this chapter:

1) Is radical drug policy reform necessary? Map out the arguments for the continuation of drug prohibition and what can be achieved by this.
2) Imagine that the United Kingdom has decided to legalise cannabis – what are the potential advantages/disadvantages of a regulated cannabis market? What would a regulated cannabis market look like? What practical issues should we consider when designing this?
3) Do you feel that drug policy reforms such as decriminalisation and legalisation are progressive? Why? Using a case study, identify what they achieve.

Here are some useful resources for those wanting to further explore the issues raised in this chapter:

- Hall, W. (2018) *The future of the international drug control system and national drug prohibitions. Addiction,* 113: 1210–1223.

  This article provides a pragmatic overview of not only drug prohibition but also drug policy reforms with the author ultimately identifying the best approaches that might be adopted for minimising harms from the use of different drugs.
- Transform (2022) *How to regulate Cannabis: A practical guide 3rd edition.* London, Transform Drug Policy Foundation. Available at: https://transformdrugs.org/publications/how-to-regulate-cannabis-3rd-ed.

  This guide provides an insight into how legal regulation of cannabis works in practice, drawing on best practice from those jurisdictions that have implemented regulated cannabis markets. In doing so it outlines a regulatory framework that aims to promote social justice and protect public health.
- Transform (2009) *After the War on Drugs: blueprint for regulation.* London, Transform Drug Policy Foundation. Available at: https://transformdrugs.org/publications/after-the-war-on-drugs-blueprint-for-regulation

(Continued)

(Continued)

This was the one of the first publications that attempted to provide a comprehensive guide to moving beyond drug prohibition. It offers five models for regulating drug supply, detailing the practical inferences of implementing each of these.

Here are some useful sites, which provide further insights into some of the issues raised in this chapter:

- Drug Decriminalisation Across the World. Available at: https://www.talkingdrugs.org/drug-decriminalisation/

  This site provides an interactive real-time map of drug decriminalisation across the world, allowing you to not only learn more about policies in specific countries but also search for different polices based on factors such as the legal model used, thresholds and types of substances.
- Julian Buchanan: Drugs, Human Rights & Harm Reduction. Available at: https://julianbuchanan.wordpress.com/

  The work of Julian Buchanan is discussed at length in this chapter, and this is his personal website. It contains a series of blogs and links to publications that provide an invaluable insight into different aspects of drug policy and drug policy reform.

11

DRUGS AND CRIME: MOVING FORWARD

Overview

This chapter aims to provide you with:

- An overview of key emerging and/or contemporary issues within the drugs and crime field.
- An understanding of the challenges presented by emerging types and patterns of drugs/use, developing drug markets and the evolution of responses to these.
- A critical insight into how we might expand our thinking about drugs and crime moving forward.

You will be introduced to the key terms:

- Simmering panic
- Recycled concerns
- Synthetic drugs
- Licit and illicit drug markets
- US opioid crisis

INTRODUCTION

This book provides a comprehensive overview of the drugs and crime field, considering its theoretical and historical foundations, exploring its relationships and critically analysing the ramifications of relevant policy and practice. The previous chapter offered insight into drug policy reform, identifying different pathways for moving drug policy forward whilst considering how these can/might impact on issues of drugs and crime. It is essential, however, to recognise that the form of drug policy in any jurisdiction, including whether drug policy reforms are implemented, and what shape they may take, is moulded by those contemporary drug market and broader socio-political issues, facing that place, at that time. In this chapter, we investigate such contextual factors, offering insight into a variety of emerging issues within the area of drugs and crime in not only the United Kingdom but also more widely, which may influence the future of drug policy and are therefore crucial to moving drugs and crime forward.

NEW ISSUES?

It has been argued that societies are in a continual state of 'simmering panic' in relation to drugs (Taylor, 2008:373). This is because they represent an omnipresent yet ever-evolving threat with a reductionist discourse, evident across the fields of media, public, politics, policy, research and academia, framing drugs as a persistent social problem, definitively associated with an array of damaging outcomes – dysfunctionality, ill health, addiction and of course, crime (Taylor et al., 2016). Resultantly, public understanding, dialogue and debate about drugs perpetually focus on the harms they present and the need to respond to these (Taylor, 2016). Yet these concerns are never fully allayed due to the cyclical nature of the simmering panic, as illustrated in Figure 11.1. This means that despite devising policies that respond to the issues of the day,

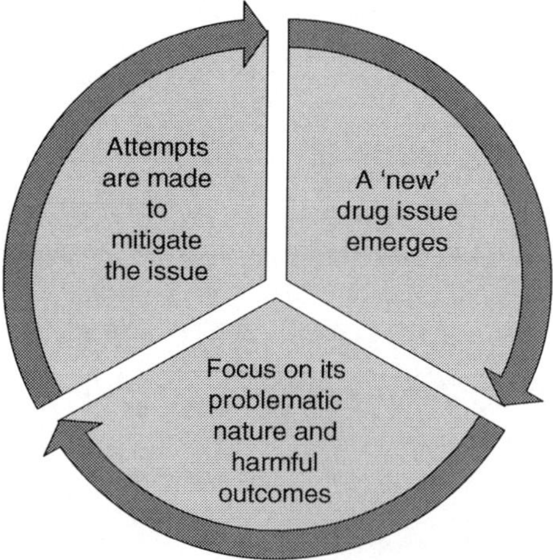

Figure 11.1 The Cycle of Simmering Panic Relating to Drugs

the next drug-related issue is never seemingly far away, giving the impression that new drug issues are continually presenting themselves to society.

Ayres and Taylor (2023), however, question whether any contemporary drug market developments should be construed as 'new'. They argue that whilst different types of drugs emerge (e.g. nitrous oxide, Novel Psychoactive Substances), as do different modes of manufacturing drugs (e.g., methamphetamine labs, hydroponic systems) and methods of drug supply (e.g., mobile phones, apps, the darknet, drones), these do not actually represent anything 'new'. Instead, they represent the evolution and modernisation of established trends within the drugs and crime sphere, most of which have been evident for over a century but are given a fresh twist meaning they are framed as novel. In doing so, these 'new' developments present drugs and their apparently dangerous consequences as a consistent threat, which we should be concerned about.

Potter and Chatwin (2018) support this contention, critiquing how Novel Psychoactive Substances have been framed as a separate and new typology of drugs, and in doing so, question the enhanced focus on such emergent issues. At the same time, however, they acknowledge that these issues need to be understood by those tasked with responding to them. This chapter then aims to identify those contemporary issues that appear important to developments within the field of drugs and crime moving forward. Yet it simultaneously recognises that these fit within the established parameters of the simmering panic and reductionist discourse relating to drugs, meaning that rather than representing new problems per se, they more accurately represent recycled concerns relating to four key issues: types of drugs, patterns of drug use, the nature of drug markets and the effectiveness of responses to these issues.

TYPES OF DRUGS

When we consider drugs and crime, arguably the most pressing issue is the emergence of new substances and indeed their criminalisation. History teaches us that drug use has always been evident in societies (see Chapter 2). It also indicates that new types of drugs/drug use perpetually appear, for example, LSD in the 1960s, ecstasy in the 1980s and ketamine in the 2000s. As they do, they reignite the touch paper of the simmering panic as the appearance of a 'new' drug captivates media attention with the ensuing reports detailing deadly effects and consequences. Whilst much of this reporting is both sensational and inaccurate (see the Box below), it emphasises the need that something must be done in response to such substances, meaning that legal and policy changes often follow. Yet recent decades have seen two phenomena emerge, which have accelerated and expanded developments and concerns within the drugs and crime sphere – an increase in the production of synthetic drugs and a heightened demand for illicit prescription/enhancement drugs. We shall discuss each of these in turn.

Synthetic drugs can be used to describe a multitude of substances, including some 'traditional' illegal substances (e.g. MDMA or methamphetamine). The term, however, has become synonymous with a swathe of substances, which, whilst mimicking the effects of traditional illicit drugs, comprise different chemical compounds. The issue of synthetic drugs gained momentum in the 2000s in the United Kingdom linked to concerns over the availability of 'legal highs' in certain head shops (see Chapter 3). These substances, for example, synthetic stimulants such as mephedrone and synthetic cannabinoids such as spice, were overtly labelled as 'not for human consumption' and/or as 'plant fertilizers' but were being covertly sold as recreational drugs. This ultimately resulted in a ban on the sale of such substances via the United Kingdom's Psychoactive Substances Act 2016.

The production and availability of synthetic drugs, however, continue to present issues. Despite the rates of these 'new' types of drugs being comparatively low compared to more established illegal drugs (ONS, 2023a), they continue to be framed as a threat. Media reports often position users of such substances as problematic, even positing them as inhuman cannibals or zombies (see Alexandrescu and Spicer, 2023; Atkinson and Sumnall, 2020), whilst focusing on their use by specific elements of society, such as homeless and incarcerated populations.

Ralphs and colleagues (2017) study of synthetic cannabinoids (or spice) among prisoners in an adult male English prison offers an interesting insight into this. They firstly found that most prisoners who they interviewed first used spice whilst incarcerated, the key reason being that it could not be detected by mandatory drug testing (see Chapter 8). Whilst drug testing for substances such as spice is now possible, the chemical compounds of illegally produced synthetic substances are continually changing, meaning they continue to prove difficult for drug testing to identify. This, combined with their cheaper pricing compared to more traditional illegal drugs (McCormack et al., 2023), means that their appeal to some remains.

The Case of Mephedrone

Mephedrone, or meow meow as the media colloquially referred to it, was one of the first 'legal highs' in the United Kingdom to attract public and political attention – a key catalyst being the deaths of two men in April 2010. The *Daily Mail* headline reporting the incident stated 'Action pledged on "Meow Meow" drug after two teen friends die within hours of taking "legal high"' (Brooke, 2010:1). The ensuing article outlined that the police had confirmed the drug appeared to have contributed to the deaths of two men who were characterised as normal, caring and hardworking with promising futures ahead. This prompted various follow-up articles across the popular press. For example, *The Mirror* informed us that the 'killer drug Meow Meow' was 'being flown into Britain every day by ruthless Chinese dealers' (Butler, 2010:1).

Whilst most of the United Kingdom had never previously heard of mephedrone, the media reported on children as young as eight using the drug and numerous suspected deaths. *The Sun* even launching a campaign to ban mephedrone (Fleming, 2010). Despite reservations by various organisations and some of its members, the Advisory Council for the Misuse of Drugs recommended banning mephedrone a month after the two deaths with it subsequently being classified a Class B substance under the Misuse of Drugs Act 1971. In June 2010, however, the coroner's report of the two men's deaths revealed that according to toxicology reports, neither of them had taken mephedrone.

This story indicates the difficulties faced by society in relation to the simmering panic surrounding drugs and how new types of drugs are responded to. Whilst mephedrone may have ultimately been banned regardless of this case, its prohibition was grounded in a myth. Ensuing research also found that after the drug was criminalised, its use became more popular (Wood et al., 2012) and played a role in an increase in overall legal high deaths (ONS, 2013).

Another key reason that synthetic drugs continue to present issues is that the process of manufacturing such substances offers flexibility to criminal entrepreneurs. This is because producing a synthetic rather than a plant-based substance (such as heroin or cocaine) means that producers are not necessarily tied to a geographical location. Instead, it is access to the relevant chemicals that is imperative and because these chemicals are often readily accessible and legal to precure, this again offers flexibility, meaning that alongside their potential profitability, synthetic drugs present an attractive proposition to black market operators.

The quasi-legal nature of this manufacturing process highlights an interesting capitalist quandary as the chemicals and equipment used to make these substances mostly originate from legitimate enterprises who are profiting from their products being used for illicit activities. This blurring between the licit and the illicit represents a crucial facet for the drugs and crime field moving forward as it highlights the contradictory nature of free market capitalism and the complex relationship between the licit and illicit economies involved in the production and consumption of illegal drugs. This interlinks with the regulatory model outlined in the previous chapter, as critiques of both drug prohibition and polices of drug reform contend that it is not until all drugs are legalised and regulated into a singular system that such tensions might be more comprehensively addressed.

Yet this grey area between drug-related licit and illicit economies is more complex than the issue of synthetic substances. Taylor and colleagues (2020) draw attention to those legally purchased products that are used by illegal drug users to mitigate the harms and enhance the pleasures of their substance use. They highlight the legitimate and flourishing marketplace of drug-related technologies such as drug-checking kits, vaporisers, stash devices, eye drops and snorting tubes (Taylor et al., 2020), all of which are marketed at illegal drug users and used for illicit purposes. This interlinks with other legitimate marketplaces, such as those pertaining to hydroponic systems used to grow cannabis, bongs and pipes to use a variety of different drugs and drug packaging which is widely available via a simple online search. Moving forward, therefore, it will be interesting to see how these different relationships between licit and illicit economies unfold and indeed are responded to.

A further example of this economic grey area brings us onto the second key issue within this focus on emerging types of drugs, that of heightened demand for prescription/enhancement drugs, leading to these being either illicitly produced or procured through illicit networks (see Hall and Antonopoulos, 2019). This process can take many forms but is broadly associated with a belief that these can offer improvements in health and well-being. For example, the use of Viagra for improved sexual performance (Loe, 2001), dietary supplements (EMCDDA, 2015) or image-enhancing drugs (Begley et al., 2017) for improved bodies or pharmaceuticals for improved pain management (Ayres, 2020a).

This latter category is a particularly important one. Rhodes (2018) identifies that in England, there are approximately 2 million users of non-prescribed painkillers. This brings attention to people self-medicating to address health-related issues via illicit marketplaces. Whilst such painkillers may be sourced from acquaintances who have been legitimately prescribed them, the demand for pain relief solutions is such that illegal drug suppliers have recognised the lucrative nature of this market, leading to the increased manufacturing of counterfeit versions of these drugs. In 2022, counterfeit pharmaceuticals/medicines were the seventh most seized product in the European Union (Europol, 2022) although their use is said to be particularly prevalent in the Global South (Ziavrou et al., 2022).

Here, we see yet more interactions between the licit and illicit drug economies, the complexity and ramifications of which are well illustrated by the US opioid crisis, which continues to see unprecedented numbers of drug-related deaths with over 80,000 fatal opioid-involved overdoses reported in 2021 (NIDA, 2023). The origins of the opioid crisis can be traced back to the practices of 'Big Pharma' with the increased prescribing of opioid painkillers during the 1990s in the United States creating greater consumer demand (see the Box below). This demand was initially met by legitimate prescriptions, then in turn by illegal heroin markets, and most recently by counterfeit versions of the synthetic opioid fentanyl, produced by criminal entrepreneurs. The prevalence of counterfeit painkillers in the United States is increasing (DEA, 2023) with their production associated with Mexican drug cartels (Bonello, 2023).

The US Opioid Crisis

The roots of the US opioid crisis were sewn in the mid-1990s and are closely associated with the production and promotion of the painkiller OxyContin by Purdue Pharma. OxyContin, as later admitted by Purdue when pleading guilty to criminal charges, was fraudulently marketed as less addictive than other opioids, meaning it could be used for a wider array of health-related issues and at higher doses (Raden-Keefe, 2021). This resulted in a 'profit-driven quadrupling of opioid prescribing' (Humphreys et al., 2022:555), which has seen more than 600,000 deaths in North America from opioid overdoses with a further 1.2 million people predicted to die by 2030 without substantial policy reform (The Lancet, 2022:495).

The Stanford-Lancet Commission formed in response to the crisis has stated that the approval of OxyContin by the US Food and Drug Administration as well as 'overly intimate relationships between opioid manufacturers and universities, professional societies, patient advocacy groups, and lawmakers, and aggressive product promotion to prescribers and (to a lesser extent) the general public' (Humphreys et al., 2022: 556), were the catalyst for the current situation. Whilst measures have been introduced in North America to restrict the prescription of opioid painkillers, the Commission simultaneously warns 'that pharmaceutical companies based in the USA are actively expanding opioid prescribing worldwide, and are using fraudulent and corrupting tactics that have now been banned domestically. This highlights risks of a repeat of the tobacco experience, in which an addiction-promoting industry adapted to tighter regulation in wealthy countries by expanding its business in lower-income nations' (Humphreys et al., 2022:557).

Here then, a key catalyst of the contemporary landscape were the practices of legitimate companies and the promotion and prescribing practices of licit drug markets. A key effect of this being that demand has increased and production has transcended into criminal markets, which continue to evolve. For example, Friedman and colleagues (2023) study of what they term tourist-orientated pharmacies in North Mexico highlights how controlled substances are now widely available without a prescription with counterfeit medications often being sold. They highlight that this has been prompted by the unaffordability of healthcare in the United States, a reduced prescribing of opioids and the emergence of counterfeit opioids.

Addressing these blurred lines will be of crucial importance to the future of drug policy. New drugs and indeed new patterns of drug use will continue to emerge, meaning that legal, regulatory and wider policy decisions will have to be made in relation to each episode. Yet whilst 'new' types of drugs may emerge, the issues they present are perhaps no different from those of other substances that have emerged previously. It is a perpetual cycle that will be ever evident whilst the demand for drugs (including demand prompted by legitimate enterprises such as pharmaceutical companies) continues and we have different legal classifications for different substances. Resultantly, decisions will need to be perpetually made even if the 'new' threat is only in essence recycling that of previous ones.

PATTERNS OF DRUG USE

Another key factor influencing how we move forward in relation to drugs and crime are the issues presented by trends in drug use itself. As we explored in Chapter 4, however, it is often the substance use of specific groups within society that is focused on, deemed problematic and therefore presented as a pressing issue. We return to this shortly, but when we look at patterns of drug use, there is one clear demographic whose rates of use appear to be both higher than other groups and whose use of illegal substances is employed as a barometer to measure the state of the nation – young people.

According to data collected by the Crime Survey for England and Wales, rates of drug use are highest among the 16- to 24-year-old age bracket, with approximately 18% (around one million young people) reporting drug use in the previous year (ONS, 2023a). Whilst rates of use among this group have shown some fluctuations since their lowest level in 2013, these currently appear relatively stable, and well below the highest levels reported during the 1990s/2000s when almost a third of young people reported using illegal drugs in the past 12 months (ONS, 2023a). Meanwhile, patterns of drug use among young people have also seen a significant change in the sense that the gap between male and female drug use has closed with the use of drugs among boys and girls aged 11–16 now being roughly equal (NHS, 2022).

These patterns will be particularly interesting to monitor moving forward given the recent context of COVID-19. The impact of COVID-19 on illegal drug use remains unclear, although some research has indicated that this period has seemingly influenced wider patterns of drug use. For example, the long-term decline in rates of smoking in England has seemingly stalled in the post-pandemic landscape, particularly among young people (ONS, 2023d). Meanwhile, alcohol use has also been declining among young people in England for some time, a trend evident in many high-income countries (Whitaker et al., 2023), with 23% of 18- to 24-year-olds in England reporting that they never drink alcohol (SIBA, 2023). These trends are mentioned as when we consider young people's use of illegal drugs, it is important not to do so in a vacuum.

Whilst we might therefore be seeing an overall decline – perhaps even a period of denormalisation – of both legal and illegal drug use among young people, we must also recognise the evolution of their wider consumption practices. For example, at a time when health and well-being is aggressively marketed, with consumers encouraged to use products that are promoted as being better for them, we have seen the decrease in young people smoking accompanied by an increase in the number of young people vaping. Consequently, illegal drug markets are also emerging around these principles with the BBC (2024) identifying the prevalence of tetrahydrocannabinol (this being the psychoactive compound in cannabis) vapes among young people. These vapes negate the need to smoke tobacco when using cannabis, which on the surface may offer a healthier alternative. Yet this trend has been accompanied by reports of vapes that contain synthetic cannabinoids, namely spice (Barton, 2023). Patterns of legal and illegal drug use therefore interact with each other, with changing patterns of consumption influencing the drugs and crime status quo.

Whilst young people represent an important group to consider, as they allow us to tentatively predict what issues society may face in the future, patterns of drug use among other sub-populations are equally important to the field of drugs and crime. As discussed in Chapter 4, ever since the 1990s, drug policy in England and Wales has centred on a minority of so-called problematic drug users who predominantly use heroin. Despite efforts to support these people towards abstaining from drug use, many continue to use heroin (often alongside other substances) and have been doing so for a considerable number of years. There is now, therefore, an ageing population of opioid users, who are presenting an ever-evolving array of personal issues (ACMD, 2019). Indeed, the wider health-related problems facing this group are potentially one of the reasons we have recently seen the highest recorded rates of drug-related deaths in England and Wales (ONS, 2023e).

This highlights that the ability to respond to issues presented by drug users is something that must be foreseen and planned for. In relation to the ageing cohort of opioid users, contemporary service provision has been described as 'insufficiently prepared to manage' their complex needs (ACMD, 2019:22). This might also apply equally to the emerging needs that health services are currently facing associated with other drug use, such as ketamine and bladder problems or nitrous oxide use and neurological issues. Furthermore, if the patterns of drug use described previously continue to develop, health services will need to be prepared to respond to issues presented by licit/legal drugs, such as prescription painkillers. It is therefore crucial that service provision evolves in advance of/in line with the emerging needs of drug users.

The ageing cohort of opioid users also poses direct questions about drug-related crime. Given that this group's patterns of drug use were a catalyst for drug policy moving into the realm of criminal justice in the 1990s, a key issue moving forward is whether the argument to maintain this policy will remain viable if contemporary patterns of drug use and crime evolve. Will we continue to see drug use and property crime as intrinsically linked in the landscape of tomorrow? Indications are that we shall as we are seeing a continued linking of patterns of (problematic) drug use and crime, associated with specific sub-populations, such as sex workers, the homeless and military veterans (Home Office, 2017). Additionally, geographical patterns of drug use amongst opiate and crack users were used in the UK government's 2021 drug strategy to identify the areas where their use was most prevalent to prioritise resources on these locations with a key rationale being their links to drug-related criminality. This focus on specific groups, specific patterns of use and specific places has been a hallmark of recent drug policy, so moving forward, it will be interesting to see if policy remains focused on these groupings or new priority groups (see the Box below), patterns of use and areas of use emerge.

Chemsex

Chemsex is a term used to describe the use of drugs before/during sexual activity, predominantly in relation to men who have sex with other men (Ralphs et al., 2023). It is an activity associated with specific types of drugs, such as mephedrone, GHB/GBL and crystal methamphetamine (McCall et al., 2015). The issue of chemsex gained traction during the 2010s and was identified as a priority issue in the UK government's 2017 drug strategy with this 'new' pattern of drug use touted as a concern as it was

(Continued)

(Continued)

said to carry 'serious physical and mental health risks including the spread of blood-borne infections and viruses' (Home Office, 2017:15).

Whilst there is a clear need for people to be provided with harm reduction advice around both drug use and sexual activity, the emergence of chemsex as a new phenomenon was interesting. People have, continue to, and always will combine drug use with sexual practices. Indeed, a motivation for using drugs is that they enhance sexual pleasure and vice versa, forming part of a wider process of pharmacosex (Moyle et al., 2021).

In that sense, chemsex was certainly not a revolutionary development. What prompted this pattern of drug use to gain social attention at that time was more to do with the types of drugs being used, the sexual practices involved and the subpopulation of people associated with these – similar to concerns in the 1960s over the Summer of Love and its association with the hippy counterculture of the time – highlighting how it is the 'new' patterns of drug use amongst certain subpopulations, who often have shared demographics along the lines of age, race, class, gender and/or sexuality that are highlighted as social issues/problems.

When new patterns and indeed practices of drug use emerge, there is undoubtedly a need for services to be able to respond with the appropriate educational and practical advice. It is imperative that health, harm reduction and, in the current climate, criminal justice services are alive to the issues faced by the drug users of today and prepared for the issues that will face the drug users of tomorrow. Yet whether these emerging issues should be regarded as 'new' is a moot point. Whilst patterns of drug use may change, the overriding issue remains the same – people continue to use drugs and whilst most users do so with few detrimental effects, a minority require often substantial support. Moving forward, this trend will endure meaning that a key question is whether we shall continue to frame new patterns of use as being construed as a new threat, when drug use and related harms appear to be an ever-present characteristic of society. Furthermore, whether we continue to associate such patterns of use with subpopulations of drug users, framing these patterns as novel, understanding them first and foremost as a concern when they are in fact characteristics of everyday life (South, 1999) in a global society of drug users, is an interesting conundrum.

DRUG MARKETS

The evolving demand for illegal drugs means that drug markets, whether these be licit or illicit, also continue to evolve. When demand changes, suppliers of illegal drugs, as illustrated by the production of counterfeit painkillers, can change their business models in line with what their consumers want. Yet suppliers of illegal drugs also evolve their business practices, alike legitimate organisations, in line with new innovations that offer greater opportunities. In terms of illegal drug markets, such methods offer the chance of not only doing better business but also further advancing the clandestine nature of their criminal operations.

The dance between drug suppliers and the authorities attempting to police them has been evident throughout drug prohibition and is certainly ongoing, with both sides utilising emerging technologies to better their efforts. When customs and other authorities attempted to enhance the patrolling of major drug-trafficking routes, the use of 'narco-submarines' developed. When the police began using thermal imagining cameras to identify cannabis factories, operations were moved from larger facilities to smaller-scale sites (a process often involving the use of coercion and debt bondage). When police operations targeted open drug dealing, closed markets materialised utilising pagers, then mobile phones, then encrypted social media services and darknet platforms. When enhanced security measures, such as x-ray scanners, were introduced by prisons, suppliers used drones to fly contraband over prison walls. This dance will never stop as despite new developments, the issue at hand remains the same – drug suppliers continue to supply drugs, the authorities continue to police them and the former do all they can to avoid the attention of the latter.

One of the key contemporary developments within this dance has been the emergence of online drug markets (see Chapter 9). These markets are indicative of the grey area previously discussed between licit and illicit drug markets, offering as they often do access to both illegal and illicit legal drugs. Whilst engagement with such markets has increased, a relatively small proportion of people currently report acquiring their drugs through such mediums across Europe (UNODC, 2023). This is because most people continue to obtain their drugs in person albeit in ever-evolving ways, with suppliers now using apps and proactively advertising their products through social media (see Figure 11.2) in ways that would have been unthinkable two decades ago (see Coomber et al., 2023). Moving forward, it will therefore be interesting to see how emerging types of drugs and patterns of drug use interact with these evolving drug markets and what the collective outcomes of these will be. In the meantime, those who police drugs will continue to develop their ability to monitor, disrupt and close down these markets as the everlasting dance between them and drug suppliers endures.

That said, moving forward, we must also be aware that the structure of drug markets will change. The involvement of organised crime groups in both the distribution of legitimately manufactured legal drugs or producing counterfeit versions of these is a critical contemporary issue. The profits resulting from such operations are immense and where this money ultimately ends up – and how and for what purposes it is used – is another important future issue within the drugs and crime field especially in the context of concerns around narcoterrorism (see Chapters 6 and 9). This evolution may not, however, be straightforward. A good example of this is the current situation in Afghanistan, where the Taliban have proactively prohibited the growth of opium, leading to a seemingly massive decline in its production – reported to be as much as a 95% reduction in a single year between 2022 and 2023 (UNODC, 2023). At a time when synthetic opioid use is prompting much concern in the United States, and indeed

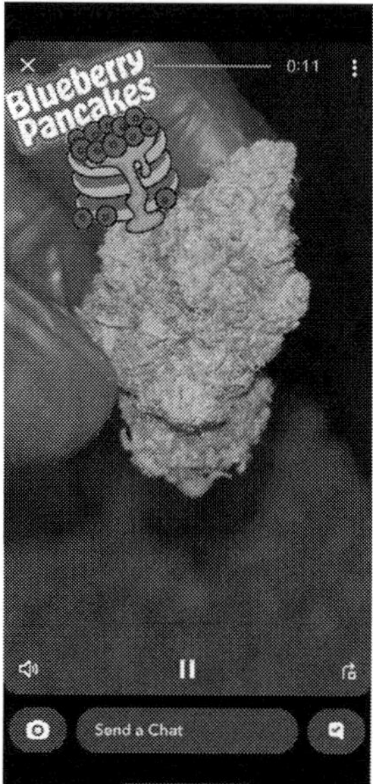

Figure 11.2 Examples of Social Media Promotions of Illegal Drugs From the United Kingdom

globally, it will be interesting to monitor whether another jurisdiction – as we have historically seen with cocaine production in South America (see Chapter 6) – increases opium production to fill this void or whether another type of (synthetic) drug, for example, fentanyl, is utilised as a replacement by drug suppliers. This is a reminder that the future of domestic drug markets can be moulded by geo-political events and that when considering issues of drugs and crime, it is imperative to expand our gaze to consider how contemporary events around the world impact the overall form, shape and nature of drug markets.

Yet it is not just clandestine drug markets that are vital to consider moving forward. It is equally as important to monitor the outcomes of drug market reforms across the world, especially in relation to cannabis. Cannabis is currently legalised for medical purposes in over 50 countries and either fully or partially legalised for recreational purposes in around 10 countries. As Chapter 10 demonstrates, legalisation, however, does not necessarily remove all aspects of crime and criminalisation associated with any given substance, nor does it simply evolve drug markets in a straightforward fashion.

In relation to those drug markets where cannabis has been legalised for recreational purposes, it will also be important to monitor the implications of this on a domestic as well as global stage. How the cannabis legally produced and sold in one jurisdiction impacts on established drug-trafficking practices and whether such products remain in their place of origin or are illegitimately transferred elsewhere are pertinent issues. Likewise, the legalisation of cannabis for medicinal purposes (see the Box below) prompts questions about the validity of reasons why this is being prescribed and whether prescribed medical cannabis is redistributed illegitimately. Furthermore, just because someone is prescribed medical cannabis does not necessarily mean they stop accessing the black market (Reed et al., 2019). Momentum, however, is very much building in relation to the potential medicinal and therapeutic benefits of other currently illegal substances aside from cannabis. This represents another fascinating area of future development in terms of whether substances like MDMA, ketamine or magic mushrooms might be legalised for medicinal purposes moving forward.

Again, whilst drug markets continue to evolve, and those with a vested interest in the drugs and crime field should keep abreast of such developments, it is questionable how 'new' the emerging issues mapped out here are. Whilst we continue to have legal and illegal drug markets, we shall continue to have grey areas between the two. Whilst legal drug markets may solve many issues prompted by drug criminalisation, they do not solve all of these and as we have seen previously with bootleg alcohol and counterfeit cigarettes, if demand is there, criminal entrepreneurs will ensure a black market remains. And whilst certain substances remain illegal, the dance between the authorities and those flouting the law will be ongoing. These are well-established trends evident over the past century, which show no sign of diminishing.

Medicinal Cannabis in the United Kingdom

In 2018, it became legal to prescribe cannabis for medicinal purposes in the United Kingdom. As we saw in Chapter 4, and previously in this chapter in relation to mephedrone, drug policy often develops based on the prominent issues of the day rather than wider reflections of available evidence – with a key catalyst for this change being the parent-led campaigns of two high-profile cases of children with epilepsy (Alfie Dingley and Billy Caldwell) who, after exhausting all other options, argued that medicinal cannabis was the only effective treatment available.

Despite its legalisation, in 2023, less than five people in the United Kingdom had received a National Health Service (NHS) prescription for cannabis although those with the resources have accessed it via private healthcare settings – leading to some amassing substantial debt and even re-mortgaging their homes (Beckett Wilson and Metcalf McGrath, 2023a). The reason for this lack of NHS prescribing is that the change in the law occurred in a vacuum due to the UK government's lacklustre implementation sitting alongside practical barriers (Metcalf McGrath and Beckett Wilson, 2023). For example, difficulties in supply and production meant that pharmacies were unable to supply such prescriptions nor have there been any state campaigns to educate and teach medical professionals about prescribing the drug (Beckett Wilson and Metcalf McGrath, 2023a). This has led to those seeking prescribed medical cannabis as occupying a liminal space – or living in limbo (Beckett Wilson and Metcalf McGrath, 2023b).

Furthermore, the wider context of cannabis criminalisation continues to haunt those who have been prescribed the drug for medicinal purposes. People report stigmatising

(Continued)

(Continued)

effects with some concealing their prescription due to anxieties over revealing this to family, friends and employers. Likewise, those prescribed the drug report incidents of police officers confiscating legitimate medication, reporting the use of the drug to social services and being refused entry to public events with their medication (Metcalf McGrath and Beckett Wilson, 2023).

Such experiences illustrate how, when legal changes to drug laws are made, they do not necessarily play out in a straightforward fashion and require careful planning and strategic direction. As Beckett Wilson and Metcalf McGrath (2023b: 8) contend, the UK government's ongoing 'commitment to prohibition of cannabis at all costs makes them reluctant to acknowledge the benefits of the drug', leading to a juxtaposed and contradictory status quo. How this develops moving forward will be interesting to see.

RESPONSES

This fourth and final element considers responses to drugs, encapsulating both drug policy directions and practical service-level provision. As mapped out in the previous chapter, perhaps the most paradigmatic shift within the drugs and crime field most recently has been that of drug policy reform and the movement away from criminalisation in various jurisdictions around the globe. Certainly, this should be an area of scrutiny for anyone interested in this field moving forward. Considerations of how polices of reform evolve in different places is a fascinating issue. For example, Thailand, after decriminalising cannabis in 2022, is currently considering new laws to re-introduce prohibition of the drug for recreational purposes. Likewise, in relation to legal drugs, in 2022 New Zealand passed legislation to introduce new tobacco laws, banning young people from purchasing cigarettes, yet this was rescinded in 2023. What this tells us is that moving forward, drug policy will be in a constant state of flux.

Yet equally as important as monitoring drug policy reform is the need to continue identifying the impacts of drug prohibition, which remains resolutely enforced across the globe. For example, in Sri Lanka, more than 29,000 individuals were arrested over a monthlong drive against drug traffickers in 2023 with almost 1,600 of those detained sent to compulsory military-run rehabilitation centres (Rahaman, 2024). Meanwhile, the former president of the Philippines, Rodrigo Duterte, is being investigated by the International Criminal Court for alleged crimes against humanity for what has been termed genocidal acts (Simangan, 2018) enacted under the mantel of the war on drugs. Amnesty International (2020) claim that in one six-month period between 2016 and 2017, more than 7,000 people were killed in the Philippines, whilst it is estimated that a total of between 12,000 and 30,000 were killed overall as part of Duterte's anti-drug campaigns (Iglesias, 2023).

On a domestic level in the United Kingdom, it is dubious whether wider drug policy reform will take place any time soon. That is not to say, however, that how drug policy evolves in the different nation states that comprise the United Kingdom is not of interest moving forward. Scotland, for example, has shown a greater appetite for drug policy reform, which has brought them into conflict with the UK government. Indeed, the United Kingdom's first drug consumption room was approved by the Scottish government to begin operating in 2024. This represents part of a wider drive in Scotland to address drug-related harms, including drug-related deaths. It will again be interesting to see how the different countries within the United Kingdom move forward and whether they take individualised approaches to drug policy or are restricted by the overarching United Kingdom-wide legal frameworks.

In terms of England and Wales, the most recent 2021 drug strategy has been criticised as being conceptually identical to previous strategies (Transform, 2022). Its promotion of 'unevidenced and harmful measures to deter drug use by means of punishment' is predicted to have 'deleterious impacts on people who use drugs' (Holland et al., 2022:215). Whether it will therefore have a positive impact on issues of drugs and/or crime moving forward is questionable. One key characteristic of the strategy is its promise to deliver a world-class treatment and recovery system by reinvesting in drug services and this perhaps reflects the area of most interest moving forward given the belief that engaging problematic drug users in treatment to address both their drug use and criminal behaviour has been a key driver of drug policy in England and Wales for over three decades. As mapped out in Chapter 7, however, drug services have more recently reduced in size and scope and so whether the promised reinvestment in these can achieve any outcomes that we have not previously seen will be noteworthy.

Perhaps, however, on a UK and global level, the most crucial factors moving forward should not be regarded as contemporary or indeed emerging issues – the ongoing disproportionate use of drug laws on minority ethnic groups and the inherently racist practices associated with the policing of these being a prominent example. It is crucial that when we focus on the future of drugs and crime that we consider intersectionality and how the disparate treatment of certain people based on demographics of gender, race, and sexuality continues regardless of these practices being so starkly visible. In 2023, Baroness Casey's independent review into the standards of behaviour and internal culture of the Metropolitan Police Service in London was published. The findings were damning, indicating that the Service was institutionally racist, misogynistic and homophobic. In relation to drugs, evidence was presented of a gay police officer being subject to malicious rumours that they used party drugs due to their sexuality, whilst another officer reported overt racism when a White woman was found buying drugs from a Black person. Such cultures feed into the policing of drugs and the ongoing disproportionately high rates of stop and search conducted on young Black males, which the Met themselves acknowledge (Casey, 2023). Yet as mapped out in Chapters 6 and 7, discriminatory practices are not only evident in the policing of drugs, they are also evident at every stage of the criminal justice system, from arrest through to sentencing. Whether such practices will be challenged and changed moving forward is a critical issue – although as mapped out in Chapter 4, if we understand drug laws as a tool of oppression rather than a tool aimed at the pragmatic management of drug-related harm, this infers that the ongoing discrimination is not an undesirable side effect but a purposeful aim of drug policy – and so whether these trends will ever dissipate is questionable.

The area of responses to drugs perhaps most profoundly questions the notion of whether developments in the drugs and crime field should be regarded as new. Yes, drug policy and drug strategies change, yet the tone, activities and impacts associated with these remain consistent. Perhaps, however, the outcomes of drug policy reforms represent the most novel aspect of drugs and crime moving forward, representing as they do a break from the historically dominant model of prohibition. As noted in the previous chapter, however, whether we continue to evaluate these through the lens of prohibition or develop fresh ways of considering their impacts is key to identifying new and exciting developments in the field. Hence, moving forward, as much as there is a need to monitor developments within the drugs and crime sphere, there is a need to develop the ways through which we look to understand these.

EXPANDING THE DISCUSSION

Whilst noticing, observing and responding to emerging issues are therefore valuable, recognising what issues are absent from contemporary discussions about drugs and crime is an equally important task, as moving forward, it is not only about what is currently present but also about what is currently overlooked. A good starting point here are the contents of this book, which, whilst providing a comprehensive analysis of pertinent issues within the drugs and crime field, tend to focus on a specific interpretation of drugs, drug users and drug-related crime – as such they could be criticised for feeding into the reductionist drugs discourse. The topics covered represent normative aspects of the drug and crime sphere, meaning that issues that sit outside these remain on the periphery.

A good example of this is that the potential pleasures and benefits that might be associated with drugs and crime remain largely disregarded. Indeed, the notion that drug use and crime lead to positive developments may represent an alien concept to many (Taylor, 2016). Yet this belies the contention that many individuals who use illegal substances and/or are involved in their supply take enjoyment and/or are advantaged by doing so. This can play out in numerous ways. For instance, for those who use or supply drugs, the fact that drug possession/supply *is* a crime provides a degree of edgework excitement (Lyng, 1990). In this sense, one of the attractions of being involved with illegal drugs is the deviance associated with it (Katz, 1988). As Presdee (2000:5) observes:

> The feeling of 'getting away with it' that comes as part of wrong doing, the buzz and excitement of the act of doing wrong itself, of living on the 'edge' of law and order, are all emotions that many seek out in the daily performance of their lives.

So, whilst we normatively associate illegal drug markets with negative outcomes, they also provide some with the opportunity to achieve things, both materially and personally, that they may not otherwise achieve through legitimate means. Whilst certain drug takers and suppliers actively avoid negative labelling from their activities (Askew and Salinas, 2018), for others, the status that emanates from using (Taylor et al., 2020) or selling drugs (Bourgois, 1996) can be either welcome or indeed sought after, especially among those who face social, political and economic marginalisation (Sandberg and Pedersen, 2011). For some, therefore, engagement with illegal drug markets can provide positive outcomes – whether that be in relation to feelings of identity and belonging, pain relief, hedonism, status or financial gain. This means that when one considers attempts to eradicate such drug markets, we might better understand why people continue to readily be involved in these, despite the associated inherent risks as well as why, moving forward, these markets will continue to be socially prevalent. Exposing and exploring such factors, however, has long been restricted by our focus on the simmering panic of drug-related issues and the normative gaze on drugs and crime as problematic, which have both been encouraged by the limited theoretical lens' employed to understand such issues. Future scholarship could, therefore, take greater advantage of those theoretical positions mapped out in Chapter 1 (such as critical/cultural criminology, ultra-realism and the deviant leisure perspective) to make further sense of these factors.

By doing so, a more nuanced, encompassing comprehension of the drugs and crime status quo may emerge. Drug policy reform, such as the legalisation of cannabis, is a good case study to illustrate this. Using a normative drug and crime lens we may consider, as mapped out in Chapter 10, what the outcomes of these reforms are and whether they should therefore be deemed effective. Yet if we extend this lens to consider wider sociological, political and economic factors in an era of consumer capitalism, a different set of issues are presented. For example, the legal cannabis market in the United States is dominated by those with the means to establish businesses within the new frameworks of legalisation. It is estimated that only 1% of cannabis dispensary owners in the United States are Black. White males are said to be mostly profiting from the legal market, in a process that some regard as a gentrification of the industry (BER, 2020) – a development compounded by the fact that in certain states, you cannot work within the cannabis industry if you have a criminal record, which may preclude those who were previously involved in the illicit cannabis trade who may wish to legitimise their business. Meanwhile, whilst the black market for cannabis continues to be evident even where cannabis has been legalised, few question what happens to those criminal entrepreneurs who may lose business as a result of any reduction in the illegal marketplace prompted by such reforms. Here, the movement away from drugs being a crime has consequences for those who previously relied on the illegal marketplace for employment, income, pride and status.

Expanding our gaze therefore leads us towards a wider consideration of issues when moving forward. Similarly, however, when we seek to interpret issues of drugs and crime, it is essential that we also look backwards. As noted in Chapter 2, recent theoretical developments within criminology have brought attention to the issue of colonialism and indeed the need to decolonialise how we understand issues such as drugs and crime. As Taylor and Ayres (2024) argue, the development of the modern-day drug apartheid (see Chapter 4) can be traced back to the emergence and establishment of capitalism and processes of colonialism, empire, slavery and exploitation. This is a view that is developing momentum. For example, in 2023, Bolivia began a review of the outlawing of the coca leaf within the 1961 UN Single Convention of Narcotic Drugs. According to Fordham (2024: 1), this scheduling was 'based on grotesquely racist and colonial prejudices regarding traditional Indigenous practices of the Andean-Amazonian region. Thousands of coca farmers, traders and consumers have suffered violence, scapegoating and criminalisation as a result while coca's many benefits have been ignored and maligned'. This, contends Fordham (2024:1), 'exposes the colonial and racist prejudices that lie at the heart of the international drug control system, which must urgently be addressed'.

Expanding the discussion of drugs and crime is therefore paramount to developing a more encapsulating account of the status quo, and indeed, the future. Recent considerations around the environmental implications of drug markets as well as their sustainability (UNODC, 2023) provide further evidence that developing the gaze of our analysis of drugs and crime can offer crucial insights. At a time of great social change in terms of how we view dominant frameworks of drug control across the world, moving issues of drugs and crime forward to explore different aspects, which have historically sat outside our normative gaze, represents a fascinating opportunity to reframe how we understand this field.

CONCLUSION

This concluding chapter highlights a variety of issues that might be regarded as pertinent to the future of the drugs and crime sphere. In doing so, it tentatively identifies how emerging trends relating to the types of drugs that are being used, patterns of drug use, the nature of drug markets and the shape and outcomes of responses to these represent crucial factors to consider. It therefore illustrates those existing and emerging trends that scholars of drugs and crime may wish to monitor due to the potential ramifications they will have in relation to crime, criminalisation and criminal justice – as well as drug policy and practice.

The consideration of these issues, however, is accompanied by a critical question: should these issues be regarded as 'new'? Whilst the use of drugs, the structure and shape of drugs markets and the response to drug use and supply continually evolve, how novel the emerging issues they present are is a moot point. Whether, therefore, we should regard developments within the drugs and crime sphere as new or instead see them as recycled concerns, often associated with a simmering societal panic about drugs and crime, is something to consider moving forward.

Finally, the chapter offers insight into how we might expand our understanding of drugs and crime towards more genuinely novel thinking and analysis. Widening the gaze through which we explore drugs and crime via the use of a wider array of theoretical lens might allow the field to move beyond dominant conceptualisations of drugs and crime, towards a more encompassing and insightful social, political and economic comprehension of these in the future.

SUMMARY

- **Drugs and crime remain crucial social issues due to the simmering panic that exists around drug use/supply.**
- **Whilst new drug issues continually emerge, we might question whether these present novel or recycled concerns.**
- **An increase in the production of synthetic drugs and a heightened demand for illicit prescription/enhancement drugs draws attention to the grey area between licit and illicit drug markets.**
- **Patterns of drug use among specific subpopulations will continue to draw attention with services needing to be alive to the needs of these groups.**
- **The dance between illegal drug market actors and the authorities charged with policing them is ongoing with technological advancements continually changing the shape of this.**
- **It is important to monitor the motivation, focus and outcomes of drug policies and the impacts of drug policy reforms moving forward.**
- **There is potential to develop our understanding of drugs and crime by expanding our exploration of the field to incorporate a broader array of factors.**

Here are some points and questions for you to consider after reading this chapter:

1. Do you think that we should regard contemporary and emerging issues within the drugs and crime field as new or as the recycling of established patterns?
2. What three issues do you think are of most importance when considering issues of drugs and crime moving forward?
3. Can you make a prediction of what the key developments in the drugs and crime field will be in the next 10 years?

Here are some useful resources for those wanting to further explore the issues raised in this chapter:

- Ayres, T. and Ancrum, C. (Eds.) (2023). *Understanding drug dealing and illicit drug markets.* Abingdon: Routledge.

(Continued)

(Continued)

This edited collection provides a comprehensive overview of traditional drug markets as well as new drugs, new technologies and new prospectives. It identifies established issues within the drugs and crime sphere and highlights some emerging trends and novel ways of thinking about these.

- European Union Drugs Agency (EUDA). Available at: https://www.euda.europa.eu/publications_en

  This site lists the most recent EUDA publications. These focus on emerging issues relating to drugs, crime and drug-related harm within the European Union, including the annual European Drug Report.

- United Nations Office for Drugs and Crime (UNODC). Available at: https://www.unodc.org/unodc/index.html

  This site contains links to the UNODC annual World Drug Report, which identifies drug market patterns and trends, highlighting contemporary developments within the drugs and crime field. It is a crucial source for accessing the most up-to-date developments in global drug markets as well as policy developments.

Here are some useful sites which provide further insights into some of the issues raised in this chapter:

- Crime Survey for England and Wales. Available at: https://www.crimesurvey.co.uk/en/index.html

  This site provides links to the most recent Crime Survey for England and Wales findings. These include estimations of illegal drug use amongst 16–59 year olds and trends within this.

- Talking Drugs. Available at: https://www.talkingdrugs.org/

  This site regularly publishes articles which focus on established and emerging issues within the global drugs field with a particular focus on drug policy analysis and harm reduction.

- Drug Science. Available at: https://www.drugscience.org.uk/

  This site provides access to independent evidence which aims to create the foundation for pragmatic and effective drug laws. It considers emerging drug market and drug policy issues but has a particular focus on research relating to the therapeutic use of currently illegal substances.

GLOSSARY

Abstinence: refers to the practice of voluntarily refraining from engaging in substance use and in the context of addiction and recovery is the complete cessation of substance use, with the goal of maintaining a substance-free lifestyle.

Acid house: a subgenre of house music that emerged in the mid-1980s.

Addiction: a term used to describe a pattern of behaviour whereby someone becomes dependent on drugs. Addiction is a contested term, with different writers explaining this in different ways. For some, addiction is seen as a choice, whereas for others, it is a biological or psychological process whereby a person becomes physically or mentally dependent on a substance. How addiction is defined, who is seen as being addicted and what reasons underpin addiction all vary widely.

Addict: a term that is used as a catch-all phrase to describe those who are seen as having an addiction.

Advisory Council on the Misuse of Drugs (ACMD): an independent body of experts that makes recommendations to the UK government on drug-related issues, including the control of dangerous/harmful drugs and the classification of these with the Misuse of Drugs Act, 1971. The body comprises academics and practitioners from within the field of substance use. The work of the ACMD involves collating evidence-based reports on specific drugs as well as wider drug-related issues which are used to advise the government.

Anti-social personality disorder (ASPD): is a mental health condition characterised by a long-term pattern of disregard for, or violation of, the rights of others. Individuals with ASPD often exhibit behaviours that are deceitful, manipulative and lack remorse. They may engage in criminal activities, act impulsively and fail to conform to social norms.

Apothecary: a historical term for a pharmacist and/or medical professional who formulates and dispenses medications to physicians, surgeons and patients. Apothecaries were among the predecessors of modern pharmacists.

Cannabis warning: is a formal but non-statutory police warning given to individuals caught in possession of a small amount of cannabis for personal use. It is given for the first offence and is part of a graduated response to low-level drug offences that aim to address minor drug possession without resorting to prosecution. Although a cannabis warning does not result in a criminal record, the information can still be used if further offences are committed.

Chemsex: refers to the practice of using drugs to enhance sexual experiences (e.g. to prolong sexual sessions, increase sexual arousal and reduce inhibitions).

Cognitive behavioural therapy (CBT): is a widely practiced form of psychotherapy that focuses on identifying and changing negative patterns of thought and behaviour, including substance use.

Colonialism: is a historical and political process where a nation establishes and maintains control over a foreign territory or people, which often involves the imposition of political, economic and cultural dominance by the colonising power and typically results in the subjugation of the indigenous population and the exploitation of resources.

Community Order: is a non-custodial sentence used in the criminal justice system of England and Wales, introduced by the Criminal Justice Act 2003 to address offenders' behaviour through various forms of supervision and rehabilitation without sending them to prison. Community orders provide an alternative to custodial sentences for less serious offences or for offenders who have been convicted of crimes but are deemed suitable for community-based rehabilitation/punishment.

Comorbid/comorbidity: in the context of mental health, as used in this text, it often describes the occurrence of a mental health disorder alongside another mental health issue or physical illness. For example, a person with ASPD might also have substance abuse disorders, depression and/or anxiety disorders.

County lines: is a term used primarily in the United Kingdom to describe a specific type of drug-trafficking operation that involves gangs extending their criminal activities from urban areas into rural or suburban regions, and using dedicated mobile phone lines to manage and coordinate drug sales across these different geographic locations.

Crime Survey for England and Wales (CSEW): is a national victim survey conducted annually in England and Wales that measures the prevalence and nature of crime, including drug use.

Criminalisation: refers to the process by which the use, possession, distribution and production of certain substances are defined and penalised as criminal offences rather than as a public health or medical issue.

Cryptomarkets: also known as darknet markets, are online platforms where illegal drugs and other illicit goods and services are bought and sold using cryptocurrencies like Bitcoin. These markets operate on the darknet, a part of the internet not indexed by traditional search engines and accessible only via specific software like Tor.

Darknet/web: refers to a part of the internet that is not indexed by traditional search engines and requires specific software (e.g. Tor), configurations or authorisation to access.

Decriminalisation: refers to the removal of criminal penalties for drug offences. Whilst varying widely in form and shape, it generally makes the possession of small quantities of drugs for personal use a non-criminal offence. Most jurisdictions that have implemented such policies have decriminalised the possession of cannabis, but in 2001, Portugal decriminalised the possession of all drugs for personal use.

Dependent drug use/drug dependency: are terms used instead of or alongside **addiction** to describe an individual's or group's reliance on substance use. Some scholars who question the concept of addiction use this term to indicate that a person may be dependent on substance use without necessarily being 'addicted' to it.

Deterrence/deter: are terms that describe the perspective that people can be persuaded not to act in certain ways if they belief the outcome of this behaviour will be unfavourable. Using drug laws as an example, it is believed that making the possession and supply of drugs illegal will deter people from engaging in such behaviours for fear of the ensuing consequences.

Detoxification (detox): is the medical or physiological process of removing drugs and alcohol from the body. Detoxification is typically the first step in a comprehensive addiction treatment programme and aims to manage acute intoxication and withdrawal symptoms, helping the individual achieve a substance-free state (abstinence).

Drug Abstinence Order/Requirement: court-ordered sentences, which were aimed at adults whose drug use was linked to their offending behaviour. This included non-dependent drug users and/or less serious offences than those associated with Drug Treatment and Testing Orders. They involved being supervised by the Probation Service whilst submitting to drug testing. They were used by courts in England and Wales between 2000 and 2005.

Drug apartheid: a concept that refers to the systemic and institutionalised inequalities in drug policy and enforcement, which disproportionately impact marginalised and minority ethnic groups. This term is used to highlight the ways in which drug laws and their enforcement create and perpetuate social and racial disparities.

Drug checking: refers to the process of analysing substances to determine their composition and purity, often conducted at events, festivals or harm reduction centres. The primary goal is to provide users with information about the contents of their drugs to reduce the risk of harm associated with consuming adulterated or misrepresented substances.

Drug driving: refers to operating a vehicle while impaired by/under the influence of drugs, whether they are illegal substances, prescription medications or over-the-counter drugs.

Drug Intervention Programme (DIP): was a UK initiative introduced in 2003 aimed at improving outcomes for individuals with drug problems who come into contact with the criminal justice system. It focused on providing access to treatment and support services while addressing underlying issues related to drug use, by diverting drug-using offenders out of crime and into treatment.

Drug offences/crimes: are specifically defined violations of drug laws, involving illegal activities directly related to controlled substances.

Drug prohibition: refers to the legal policy and practice of banning the manufacture, distribution, sale and possession of certain controlled substances that are enforced through laws and regulations that criminalise the production and distribution of specific drugs, which are subject to penalties ranging from fines to imprisonment. The aim is to reduce illegal drug use and its associated social, health and economic consequences. This approach is part of the broader 'War on Drugs' strategy and is intended to deter drug use and diminish the power and influence of drug-trafficking organisations.

Drug policy: refers to the set of laws, regulations and guidelines formulated and implemented by governments or organisations to manage and address drug use and its related issues. Drug policy encompasses a broad range of activities including the regulation of drug production, distribution, use and the response to drug-related crime and health issues.

Drug Rehabilitation Requirement (DRR): is a legal provision in the United Kingdom that allows courts to mandate drug treatment as part of a criminal sentence. Such requirements are made as part of a **Community Order** or **Suspended Sentence Order**.

Drug-related death: refers to a fatality that is directly attributable to the use of drugs via overdoses, poisoning or deaths resulting from complications related to drug use.

Drug-related harm: is the negative consequences and adverse effects associated with the use of drug, both directly and indirectly, that can affect individuals, communities and public health systems, and it encompasses a broad range of physical, mental, social and economic impacts.

Drug-related offences/crime: refers to criminal activities that are connected to drug use or supply/trafficking but are not limited to direct drug law violations. This can include a range of criminal behaviours influenced or exacerbated by drug use (e.g. shoplifting, burglary).

Drug strategy: refers to a comprehensive plan or framework developed by governments or organisations to address the complex issues related to drug use, including prevention, treatment, enforcement and harm reduction. A drug strategy outlines the goals, priorities and actions to manage and mitigate the impact of drug-related problems on individuals and society.

Drug supply: refers to the act of providing or distributing controlled substances and includes activities such as possession with intent to supply and other forms of drug distribution. Drug supply and drug trafficking, however, are often used interchangeably.

Drug trafficking: involves the illegal trade and transportation of drugs on a larger, often global scale, often involving multiple stages of the supply chain and organised criminal activity. Drug supply and drug trafficking, however, are often used interchangeably.

Drug treatment: refers to a range of interventions and therapies designed to help individuals reduce or stop their use of drugs (e.g. detoxification, CBT, substitute prescribing), address the issues related to drug dependency/addiction, improve overall health and well-being and support recovery and rehabilitation.

Drug Treatment and Testing Order (DTTO): was a type of community sentence in the criminal justice system of England and Wales, designed for individuals who have committed offences linked to drug dependence/addiction. The DTTO aimed to address drug addiction while holding offenders accountable for their actions. It combined treatment and regular drug testing to support recovery and reduce reoffending.

Folk devil: is an academic term used to describe a person or group that is portrayed as a threat to societal values, norms or safety – it is what we should not be. Often used in discussions about moral panics, where certain individuals or groups are depicted as the cause of widespread societal problems or fears.

Gateway theory: suggests that the use of certain substances, often perceived as less harmful (e.g. cannabis) or legal (e.g. alcohol), can lead to the use of more dangerous or illicit drugs (e.g. heroin, cocaine).

Global North: refers to the economically developed, industrialised countries primarily located in the Western Hemisphere and parts of East Asia, characterised by high standards of living, advanced technological infrastructure and significant global political and economic influence.

Global South: refers to the economically developing or less-developed countries primarily located in the Southern Hemisphere, as well as parts of South and Southeast Asia, characterised by lower standards of living, developing technological infrastructure and limited global political and economic influence. This term often includes regions in Africa, Latin America, South Asia, Southeast Asia and parts of the Middle East.

Harm reduction: is a public health approach designed to minimise the negative health, social and economic consequences – harm – associated with drug use and other risky behaviours, rather than solely focusing on the elimination of the behaviour itself. The primary goal is to improve the overall quality of life for individuals and communities by addressing the risks and harms associated with substance use and promoting safer practices.

Head shop: is a retail store that specialises in selling products related to drugs, their use and culture (e.g. cannabis smoking paraphernalia). Head shops used to sell legal highs/novel psychoactive substances.

Human rights: are fundamental rights and freedoms to which every person is entitled, regardless of nationality, ethnicity, gender, religion or any other status. These rights are inherent to all human beings and are universally recognised as essential for maintaining human dignity, equality and justice.

Heroin-assisted treatment (HAT): is a form of medical treatment for individuals with a heroin addiction, which involves the supervised administration of pharmaceutical-grade heroin (diacetylmorphine) to help stabilise and support people who have not responded to other treatment methods (e.g. methadone or buprenorphine therapy).

Industrial revolution: is a period of significant economic, technological and social transformation that began in the late eighteenth century and continued into the nineteenth century. It marked a major shift from agrarian economies based on manual labour and handicrafts to industrialised and mechanised production processes.

Intersectionality: explores how various forms of social stratification (e.g. race, class, gender, sexuality and other identity categories) intersect and interact to shape individual experiences and systemic inequalities that contribute to complex patterns of oppression and privilege.

Legalisation: refers to the process of making something that was previously illegal or prohibited by law legal under specific regulations or conditions.

Maximum Sentence: represents the most severe penalty allowed by law for a given offence, which is the upper limit set by the legislation and applicable in the most extreme and aggravated cases (e.g. for Class B offences under MDA, this is 14 years' imprisonment and/or an unlimited fine, or both).

Medicalisation: refers to the process by which the use, treatment or classification of drugs is framed within the context of medical discourse and practice, which involves reinterpreting behaviours or conditions previously understood in non-medical terms as medical issue/disorder requiring diagnosis and treatment (e.g. substance use disorders within diagnostic frameworks like the DSM-5 (Diagnostic and Statistical Manual of Mental Disorders) or ICD (International Classification of Diseases).

Medical model: in healthcare is a framework that views diseases and disorders as conditions that can be diagnosed, treated and potentially cured through medical intervention. It emphasises biological and physiological factors as primary causes, diagnosis and classification based on symptoms and signs and standardised treatment protocols (e.g. medication, therapy and rehabilitation).

Micro, meso and macro: are terms used to describe different levels of analysis or perspectives within various fields, including social sciences, organisational studies and policy analysis. Each level provides a distinct view of phenomena, from individual behaviour (micro) to large-scale social systems (macro).

Minority ethnic groups: are populations within a larger society that have different racial, national, cultural and/or linguistic characteristics from the dominant group. These groups are often distinguished by their unique heritage, traditions and experiences, and they may face varying degrees of marginalisation or discrimination.

Misuse of Drugs Act 1971: remains the key piece of legislation in the United Kingdom that regulates the use and distribution of controlled substances. The Act classifies drugs into three categories (Class A, B and C) based on their perceived harm and potential for abuse, setting out penalties for offences related to possession, trafficking and production, and staggering the punishments according to the offence and perceived harm of the substance.

Narco-colonialism: is the exploitation and control of a country's political and economic systems through the illegal drug trade. It implies a form of colonial domination where drug cartels and external powers manipulate and profit from the drug economies of less powerful nations.

Narco-state: is a nation where the government and various institutions are heavily influenced or controlled by drug cartels. In such states, the drug trade becomes a significant part of the economy and political landscape (e.g. Columbia, Mexico, Afghanistan).

Narco-politics: involves the interplay between drug cartels and political systems, where drug traffickers influence, control or collaborate with political actors and institutions.

Narco-terrorism: is the use of drug-trafficking profits to fund terrorist activities, or the convergence of drug trafficking and terrorism, where terrorist groups engage in the drug trade to finance their operations.

Narcotic: is a term with historical and contemporary connotations that varies based on the context in which it is used. Historically, the term referred to substances that produced a numbing effect or altered consciousness, typically through sedation or pain relief, which included both natural and synthetic drugs. In modern medicine, narcotics are often referred to as opioids.

Needle exchange: refers to a public health programme designed to reduce the transmission of bloodborne diseases among individuals who inject drugs. The programme involves providing clean needles and syringes to drug users in exchange for used ones, thus promoting safer practices and minimising health risks associated with needle sharing (e.g. HIV/AIDS, hepatitis B).

Neoliberalism: is a political and economic philosophy associated with Thatcher in the United Kingdom advocating for free markets, deregulation, privatisation, entrepreneurship and minimal government intervention in the economy.

Net-widening: is a phenomenon where new policies or programmes intended to divert individuals from the criminal justice system actually result in an increase in the number of people being brought into the system (e.g. as seen with cannabis and khat warnings). This can happen when alternatives to prison (e.g. drug courts or diversion programmes) capture individuals who might otherwise have avoided formal legal intervention.

Normalisation: is a concept that describes recreational drug use being more widely accepted and integrated into everyday life, including mainstream leisure pursuits and cultures.

Offence Range: the offence range often differs from the **Maximum Sentence** as it refers to the range of penalties that courts typically impose for these offences, depending on the severity of the case, the offender's culpability, and any mitigating or aggravating factors (e.g. for Class B offences under MDA, this can range from a fine (for the least serious cases) to 10 years in custody).

Official discourse: refers to the formal and authoritative communication and/or narrative propagated by government bodies, institutions or other established authorities, which reflects their perspectives, policies and ideologies on various issues.

Patent medicine: originating in eighteenth and nineteenth century, patent medicines are commercial products advertised and sold over-the-counter as a medical remedy without being subject to the regulatory standards that are typically required for medicinal drugs, often making them dangerous, although they were often accompanied by extravagant claims of effectiveness.

Pre-sentence report (PSR): is a document prepared by a probation officer or other designated official to assist the court in determining the most appropriate sentence for a convicted individual. It provides detailed information about the offender's background, behaviour and circumstances.

Problematic drug user: is an individual whose drug use leads to significant negative consequences in various areas of their life, such as health, social relationships, employment or legal status.

Project ADDER (Addiction, Diversion, Disruption, Enforcement and Recovery): is a UK government initiative aimed at tackling drug misuse by combining targeted enforcement with expanded diversion, treatment and recovery services.

Psychoactive Substances Act 2016: is a UK law that prohibits the production, distribution, sale and supply of psychoactive substances intended for human consumption, but excludes those already regulated under the Misuse of Drugs Act 1971.

Psychotropic substances: refers to substances or medications that affect the mind (e.g. mental processes), emotions, mood or behaviour that can have therapeutic uses in treating mental health conditions (e.g. antidepressants, antipsychotics) but they can also be associated with recreational or non-medical use.

Public health approach to drugs: focuses on addressing substance use and its related harms through evidence-based, health-centred strategies rather than through punitive measures, which prioritises the health and well-being of individuals and communities, aiming to reduce the negative health, social and economic impacts of drug use.

Rave: a large, often spontaneous or clandestine dance party featuring electronic dance music, where people gather to dance, socialise and experience a vibrant atmosphere of lights, sound and sometimes performance art.

Recovery: means different things to different people, but generally refers to the process of overcoming drug or alcohol dependence/addiction. Recovery is a holistic process involving medical, psychological and social components.

Regulation: refers to the legal and administrative framework established by governments and regulatory agencies to control the development, production, distribution and use of pharmaceutical drugs. This framework ensures that medications are safe, effective and of high quality, protecting public health and preventing addiction.

Rehabilitation: rehabilitation in the context of substance use and addiction refers to a comprehensive process aimed at helping individuals recover from drug or alcohol dependency and reintegrate into society as productive, healthy and responsible members. Rehabilitation encompasses a wide range of services and interventions designed to address the physical, psychological, social and behavioural aspects of addiction. In the context of crime, it refers to a range of interventions and programmes designed to facilitate the reintegration of offenders into society, reduce recidivism and promote positive behaviour change. The goal is to address the underlying causes of criminal behaviour, equip offenders with the skills and resources they need to lead law-abiding lives and protect public safety.

Social supply: is the distribution of illegal drugs among friends, acquaintances or peers, often without the intention of making a profit. This practice typically involves sharing or supplying small quantities of drugs for social or recreational use, rather than for commercial gain or large-scale trafficking.

Speedballing: is a term used to describe the simultaneous use of two drugs, typically a stimulant (e.g. cocaine/crack) and a depressant (e.g. heroin)

Stigmatisation/stigma: refers to the social disapproval or discrimination against individuals or groups based on certain characteristics or behaviours, but in the context of drug use, stigma can lead to negative societal attitudes, exclusion and marginalisation of individuals who use drugs. It is largely associated with the work of sociologist Erving Goffman.

Stop and search: is the police practice of stopping individuals in public spaces and searching them for illegal items and/or substances. This practice is used to prevent and detect crime, but it can also raise concerns about civil liberties and potential racial/ethnic profiling that is discriminatory.

Substances: refers to illegal (e.g. cannabis, heroin) and legal substances (e.g. alcohol and tobacco) alongside performance- and image-enhancing drugs (PIEDS)/human enhancement drugs (HEDs)/lifestyle drugs that people consume, which can affect their physical or mental state.

Substitute prescribing: is a treatment strategy used to manage addiction, particularly to opioids, which involves providing patients with a legally prescribed drug (e.g. methadone) that serves as a substitute for the (often illicit) substance they are addicted to (e.g. heroin), aiming to reduce withdrawal symptoms and cravings that will lead towards recovery.

Suspended Sentence Order: is a legal order that allows a court to impose a prison sentence but suspend its execution for a specified period, provided the person complies with certain conditions. If the offender breaches these conditions or commits another offence during the suspended sentence period, they may be required to serve the original prison sentence.

Synthetic drugs: are substances designed to mimic the effects of naturally occurring drugs but are chemically manufactured in laboratories and created to circumvent current drug laws.

Theory/theories: are sets of concepts and relationships that provide a structured way of understanding phenomena, which provide multiple systematic explanations that collectively aim to explain different phenomena like drugs and crime.

Therapeutic Communities (TCs): are structured residential treatment programmes that are often residential and also operate in prisons (e.g. HMP Grendon) and is a community designed for individuals with substance use disorders, which focuses on holistic rehabilitation, incorporating elements of mutual self-help, group therapy, work and community responsibility. Residents support each other through a structured daily routine, aiming for long-term recovery and reintegration into society.

Tough Choices: refers to a UK government initiative aimed at reducing drug-related crime by offering drug-using offenders the choice between treatment and criminal justice sanctions (see Home Office, 2006), the aim being to encourage drug users out of crime and into treatment emphasising the importance of drug treatment as a means of reducing reoffending rates.

Twin track (CJS): involves simultaneously pursuing punitive measures for drug-related offences alongside offering rehabilitative and treatment support to offenders. This can also refer to a bifurcated criminal justice system where drug users are processed differently than non-drug users.

United Nations Single Convention on Narcotic Drugs 1961: is an international treaty aimed at combating drug use through coordinated international control of narcotic drugs by establishing a framework for regulating the production, distribution and use of narcotics for medical and scientific purposes while aiming to limit their availability for non-medical use and abuse.

Utilitarianism: is an ethical theory that suggests the best action is the one that maximises overall happiness or utility – the greatest happiness for the greatest good. In the context of drug policy, a utilitarian approach would prioritise policies and interventions that produce the greatest benefit for the largest number of people, often focusing on harm reduction and public health outcomes.

War on drugs: refers to a government-led initiative aimed at reducing illegal drugs, the production, supply, use and any drug-related crime. The term 'War on Drugs' was popularised by President Nixon in 1971 when he declared drug abuse 'public enemy number one', which is a campaign that employs increased law enforcement measures, such as interdiction and eradication operations, criminal justice policies and to a lesser extent public health strategies to combat the production, distribution and consumption of illegal substances.

REFERENCES

Aaron, P. and Musto, D. (1981) Temperance and prohibition in America In National Research Council (Ed.), *Alcohol and Public Policy: Beyond the Shadow of Prohibition* (pp. 127–180). The National Academies Press. https://doi.org/10.17226/114

ACMD (1988) *AIDS and Drug Misuse*. HMSO.

ACMD (2002) *The classification of Cannabis under the Misuse of Drugs Act 1971 (2022).*

ACMD (2019) *Ageing Cohort of Drug Users*. Available: https://assets.publishing.service.gov.uk/media/5d037c2ee5274a0b8016b395/Ageing_cohort_of_drug_users.pdf

Adda, J., McConnell, B. and Rasul, I. (2014) Crime and the depenalization of cannabis possession. *Journal of Political Economy*, 122(5):1130–1202.

Agnew, R. (1992) Foundation for a general strain theory of crime and delinquency. *Criminology*, 30:47–87.

Agnew, R. (2001) Building on the foundation of general strain theory. *Journal of Research in Crime and Delinquency*, 38:319–61.

Agnew, R. (2006) *Pressured into Crime: An Overview of General Strain Theory*. Oxford University Press.

Aickenhead, D. (2012) Peter Hitchens: 'I don't believe in addiction. People take drugs because they enjoy it'. *The Guardian*, 21st October, 2012. Available: https://www.theguardian.com/books/2012/oct/21/peter-hitchens-addiction-drugs-war

Aitkenhead, D. (2003) The last resort (part one). *The Observer*, Sunday 29th June. Available: https://www.theguardian.com/education/2003/jun/29/schools.uk1

Akers, R. L. and Lee, G. (1996) A longitudinal test of social learning theory. *Journal of Drug Issues*, 26:317–344.

Akers, R.L. and Silverman, A.L. (2004) *Toward a Social Learning Model of Violence and Terrorism in Violence*. Routledge.

Akers, R. L. (2009) *Social Learning and Social Structure*. Routledge.

Albright, J.A., Stevens, S.A. and Beussman, D.J. (2012) Detecting ketamine in beverage residues. *Drug Testing and Analysis*, 4:337–341.

Aldridge, J. and Askew, R. (2017) Delivery dilemmas: How drug cryptomarket users identify and seek to reduce their risk of detection by law enforcement. *International Journal of Drug Policy*, 41:101–109.

Aldridge, J., et al. (2011) *Illegal Leisure Revisited*. Routledge.

Alexander, M. (2010) *The New Jim Crow*. The New Press.

Alexandrescu, L. and Spicer, J. (2023) The stigma-vulnerability nexus and the framing of drug problems. *Drugs: Education, Prevention & Policy*, 30(1):6–16.

Alexandrescu, L. (2018) Ethnobotanicals' and 'Spice zombies'. *Drugs: Education, Prevention & Policy*, 25(4):356–364.

Allen, G. and Kirk-Wade, E. (2020) *Drug Crime: Statistics for England and Wales*. Available: https://www.dsdaily.org.uk/PDF/DrugCrime2020.pdf

Allen, G. and Tunnicliffe, R. (2021) *Drug Crime: Statistics for England and Wales*. Available: https://commonslibrary.parliament.uk/research-briefings/cbp-9039/

Allwright, S., Bradley, F., et al. (2000) Prevalence of antibodies to hepatitis B, hepatitis C, and HIV and risk factors in Irish prisoners. *BMJ*, 321(8).

Amnesty International (2020) *More than 7,000 Killed in the Philippines in Six Months, as President Encourages Murder*.

Andreas, P. and Nadelmann, E. (2006) *Policing the Globe*. OUP.

Andrews, D. and Bonta, J. (2024) *The Psychology of Criminal Conduct*. Routledge.

Anker, J.J. and Carroll, M.E. (2011) Females are more vulnerable to drug abuse than males. *Current Topics in Behavioral Neurosciences*, 8:73–96.

Appleby, L., Kapur, N. and Shaw, J. (2022) *The National Confidential Inquiry into Suicide and Safety in Mental Health*. Annual Report.

Askew, R. and Salinas, M. (2019) Status, stigma and stereotype. *Criminology and Criminal Justice*, 19(3):311–327.

Askew, R., Griffiths, B. and Bone, M. (2022) The importance of PEOPLE who use drugs within drug policy reform debates: Findings from the UK Drug Policy Voices online survey. *International Journal of Drug Policy*, 105:103711.

Atkinson, A. and Sumnall, H. (2020) 'Zombies', 'cannibals', and 'super humans'. *Drugs: Education, Prevention & Policy*, 28(4):299–315.

Ayres, T.C. and Ancrum, C. (2023) *Understanding Drug Dealing and Illicit Drug Markets*. Routledge.

Ayres, T.C. and Jewkes, Y. (2012) The haunting spectacle of crystal meth: A media-created mythology? *Crime, Media, Culture*, 8(3), 315–332.

Ayres, T.C. and Taylor, S. (2020) Media and intoxication. In F. Hutton (Ed.), *Cultures of Intoxication*. Springer.

Ayres, T.C. and Taylor, S. (2022) Cultural competence to cultural obsolescence. In M. Addison, W. McGovern and R. McGovern (Eds.), *Drugs, Identity and Stigma*. Springer.

Ayres, T.C. and Taylor, S. (2023) Drug markets and drug dealing: Time to move on. In T.C. Ayres and C. Ancrum (Eds.), *Understanding Drug Dealing and Illicit Drug Markets*. Routledge.

Ayres, T.C. and Treadwell, J. (2012) Bars, drugs and football thugs: Cocaine use amongst English football firms. *Criminology and Criminal Justice*, 12(1):83–100.

Ayres, T.C., Hatcher, R. and Palmer, E. (2023) *The Drug Recovery Prison*. MoF.

Ayres, T.C., Moss, K. and Cameron, Q. (2024) Substance use in Guyana. *Howard Journal*. https://doi.org/10.1111/hojo.12576

Ayres, T.C. (2019) Substance use in the night-time economy. In O. Smith and T. Raymen (Eds.), *Deviant Leisure and Social Harm*. Springer Nature.

Ayres, T.C. (2020a). Substances. In S. Hall, T. Kuldova and M. Horsley (Eds.), *Crime, Harm and Consumerism*. Routledge.

Ayres, T.C. (2020b). The war on drugs and its invisible collateral damage. In A. Brisman and N. South (Eds.), *Routledge International Handbook of Green Criminology*. Routledge.

Ayres, T. C. (2020c). Childhood trauma, problematic drug use and coping. *Deviant Behavior*, 42(5):578–599.

Ayres, T. C. (2023) Traversing the fantasy of drugs. *Drugs: Education, Prevention & Policy*, 30(1):17–30.

Badrakalimuthu, V.R., Rumball, D. and Wagle, A. (2010) Drug misuse in older people. *Advances in Psychiatric Treatment*, 16(6):421–429.

Baglivio, M. T., Epps, N., et al. (2014) The prevalence of adverse childhood experiences (ACE) in the lives of juvenile offenders. *Journal of Juvenile Justice*, 3(2):1–17.

Bandura, A. (1977) *Social Learning Theory*. Prentice-Hall.

Bandura, A. (1986) *Social Foundations of Thought and Action*. Springer.

Baranyi, G., Fazel, S., et al. (2022) The prevalence of comorbid serious mental illnesses and substance use disorders in prison populations. *The Lancet*, 7(6):E557–E568.

Barratt, M. and Aldridge, J. (2016) Everything you always wanted to know about drug cryptomarkets* (*but were afraid to ask). *International Journal of Drug Policy*, 35:1–6.

Barratt, M.J., Cakic, V. and Lenton, S. (2013) Patterns of synthetic cannabinoid use in Australia. *Drug and Alcohol Review*, 32:141–146.

Barton, A. (2011) *Illicit Drugs*. Routledge.

Barton, A. (2023) Warning after vapes containing Spice drug seized in Selby. *BBC*, 25th October.

BBC (2008) Homes turned into 'drug factories'. *BBC*. Available: http://news.bbc.co.uk/1/hi/england/west_midlands/7257476.stm

BBC (2018) MP Victoria Atkins accused of 'hypocrisy' over legal cannabis farm, *BBC*, 14th May.

BBC (2024) Drugs map of Britain: Cannabis and THC Vapes. *BBC*. Available: https://www.bbc.co.uk/programmes/m001w995

Bean, P. (2014) *Drugs and Crime*. Routledge.

Beard, J. (2019) *Prison Safety in England and Wales*. Available: https://researchbriefings.files.parliament.uk/documents/CBP-7467/CBP-7467.pdf

Beccaria, C. (1986) *On Crimes and Punishment*. Office of Justice Programs.

Becker, H. (1963) *Outsiders*. Nord University.

Beckett Wilson, H. and Metcalf McGrath, L. (2023a) Living in limbo. *Volteface*. Available: https://volteface.me/experiences-of-uk-patients-cannabis/

Beckett Wilson, H. and Metcalf McGrath, L. (2023b) It's a big added stress on top of being so ill. *International Journal of Drug Policy*, 122:104220.

Beckett Wilson, H., Taylor, S., et al. (2017) Propagating the Haze? *International Journal of Drug Policy*, 48:72–80.

Begley, E., McVeigh, J. and Hope, V. (2017) *Image and Performance Enhancing Drugs*. PHI, LJM.

Benard, A.A. (2007) The material roots of Rastafarian Marijuana symbolism. *History and Anthropology*, 18(1):89–99.

Bender, D. and Lösel, F. (2011) Bullying at school as a predictor of delinquency violence and other antisocial behaviour in adulthood. *Criminal Behaviour and Mental Health*, 21(2):99–106.

Bennett, T. and Holloway, K. (2005a) *Understanding Drugs, Alcohol and Crime*. McGraw-Hill Education.

Bennett, T. and Holloway, K. (2005b) The association between multiple drug misuse and crime, *International Journal of Offender Therapy and Comparative Criminology*, 49(1): 63–81.

Bennett, T. and Holloway, K. (2007) *Drug-Crime Connections*. Cambridge University Press.

Bennett, T. and Holloway, K. (2009) The causal connection between drug misuse and crime. *BJC*, 49(4):513–553.

Bennett, T. (1998) *Drugs and Crime: The Results of Research on Drug Testing and Interviewing Arrestees*. Home Office.

Bennett, A. (1999) Subcultures or neo-tribes? *Sociology*, 33(3):599–617.

Bennett, A. (2005) In defence of neo-tribes. *Journal of Youth Studies*, 8(2):255–259.

Bentham, M. (1988) *An Introduction to the Principles of Morals and Legislation*. McMaster University Archive for the History of Economic Thought.

Bentham, M. (1990) *The Politics of Drug Control*. Springer.

BER (2020) *Greened Out: The Bittersweet Impacts of Marijuana Legalization in the United States*.

Berridge, D., Brodie, I. et al. (2001) *The Independent Effects of Permanent Exclusion from School on the Offending Careers of Young People*. Home Office.

Berridge, V. (1996) *AIDS in the UK*. Oxford University Press.

Berridge, V. (1999) *Opium and the People*. Free Association Books.

Berridge, V. (2013) *Demons*. Oxford University Press.

Best, D. and Laudet, A.B. (2010) *The Potential of Recovery Capital*. https://www.thersa.org/globalassets/pdfs/reports/a4-recovery-capital-230710-v5.pdf

Best, D., Walker, D., et al. (2010) Assessing the impact of a high-intensity partnership between the police and drug treatment service in addressing the offending of problematic drug users. *Policing and Society*, 20(3):358–369.

Best, D., Day, E. and Morgan, B. (2006) *Addiction Careers and the Natural History of Change*. National Treatment Agency for Substance Misuse.

Bewley-Taylor, D. (2001) Cracks in the conspiracy. *International Journal of Drug Policy* 12(2):167–180.

Bhaskar, R. (1975) *A Realist Theory of Science*. Routledge.

Björnehed, E. (2004) Narco-Terrorism. *Global Crime*, 6(3–4):305–324.

Black, C. (2020) *Review of Drugs: Executive Summary*. Home Office.

Black, C. (2021) *Review of Drugs Part Two: Prevention, Treatment, and Recovery*. Home Office.

Blackman, S. (1996) Has drug culture become an inevitable part of youth culture? *Educational Review*, 48(2):131–142.

Blackman, S. (2005) Youth subcultural theory. *Journal of Youth Studies*, 8(1):1–20.

Blackman, S. (2007) Hidden ethnography. *Sociology*, 41(4):699–716.

Blakey, D. (2008) *Disrupting the Supply of Illicit Drugs into Prisons*. National Offender Management Service.

Blattman, C., Chaskel, S., et al. (2023) Cognitive behavior therapy reduces crime and violence over 10 years. *American Economic Review Insights*, 5(4):527–545.

Bock, A. (2000) *The Great Drug War*. Macmillan.

Bone, M. (2019) *Human Rights and Drug Control*. Routledge.

Bonello, D. (2023) *Cartels Are Using Pharmacies to Sell Fake Pills Laced with Fentanyl and Meth to Unwitting Tourists*. Vice.

Boness, C.L., Votaw, V.R., et al. (2023) An evaluation of cognitive behavioral therapy for substance use disorders. *Clinical Psychology: Science and Practice*, 30(2): 129–142.

Bonta, J. (2023) *The Risk-Need-Responsivity Model.* Available: https://www.justiceinspectorates.gov.uk/hmiprobation/wp-content/uploads/sites/5/2023/06/Academic-Insight-The-Risk-Need-Responsivity-model-1990-to-the-Present-2.pdf

Bourgois, P. (1995) *In Search of Respect.* Cambridge University Press.

Bourgois, P. (1996) In search of masculinity. *BJC,* 33(3):412–427.

Bourgois, P. (2018) Decolonising drug studies in an era of predatory accumulation. *Third World Quarterly,* 39(2):385–398.

Bovard, J., Bennett, W.J. and Walters, J.P. (1998) D.A.R.E. Programme has been ineffective. In C.P. Cozic (Ed.), *Illegal Drugs.* Office of Justice Programs.

Bovasso, G.B., Alterman, A.I., et al. (2002) The prediction of violent and nonviolent criminal behavior in a methadone maintenance population. *Journal of Personality Disorders,* 16(4):360–373.

Bower, M., Perz, J. and Conroy, E. (2020) What role does substance use play in the social world of Australian people who have experienced homelessness? *Journal of Community & Applied Social Psychology,* 31(3):68–82.

Bowlby, J. (1951) *Maternal Care and Mental Health.* WHO.

Box, S. (1983) *Power, Crime and Mystification.* Routledge.

Boys, A., Farrell, M., et al. (2002) Drug use and initiation in prison. *Addiction,* 97: 1551–1560.

Boys, A., Marsden, J., et al. (1999) What influences young people' use of drugs? *Drugs: Education, Prevention & Policy,* 6(3):373–387.

Boys, A., Marsden, J., et al. (2000) Drug use functions predict cocaine-related problems in young people. *Drug and Alcohol Review,* 19:181–190.

Boys, A., Marsden, J. and Strang, J. (2001) Understanding reasons for drug use amongst young people: A functional perspective. *Health Education Research: Theory and Practice,* 16(4):457–469.

Braga, A.A., Weisburd, D.L., et al. (1999) Problem-oriented policing in violent crime places. *Criminology,* 37(3):541–580.

Broadhurst, K., Duffin, M., et al. (2005) *Research into the Views and Perceptions of Drug Dealers.* Perpetuity.

Broidy, L. and Agnew, R. (1997) Gender and crime. *Journal of Research in Crime and Delinquency,* 34(3):275–306.

Brooke, C. (2010) 'Action pledged on 'Meow Meow' drug after two teen friends die within hours of taking 'legal high'. *Daily Mail,* 17th March.

Brownstein, H. (2013) *Contemporary Drug Policy.* Routledge.

Bruce, R.D. and Schleifer, R.A. (2008) Ethical and human rights imperatives to ensure medication-assisted treatment for opioid dependence in prisons and pre-trial detention. *International Journal of Drug Policy,* 19(1):17–23.

Buchanan, J. and Young, L. (2000) The war on drugs. *Drugs: Education, Prevention & Policy,* 7(4):409–422.

Buchanan, J. (2004) Missing links? *Probation Journal,* 51(4):387–397.

Buchanan, J. (2006) Understanding problematic drug use: A medical matter or a social issue ? *British Journal of Community Justice,* 4(2):387–397.

Buchanan, J. (2015a) Ending prohibition with a hangover. *British Journal of Community Justice,* 13(1):55–74.

Buchanan, J. (2015b) *Will Legalising Cannabis Help End or Extend Prohibition?* Available: https://julianbuchanan.wordpress.com/2015/04/26/will-legalising-cannabis-help-end-or-extend-prohibition/

Buchanan, J. (2015c) *Human Rights: Lost in Legal Regulation?* Available: https://julianbuchanan.wordpress.com/2015/03/14/the-drug-reform-journey-final-destination/

Budd, T., Collier, P., et al. (2005) *Levels of Self-Report Offending and Drug Use Among Offenders*. Home Office.

Bukten, A., Lund, I.O., et al. (2020) Factors associated with drug use in prison. *Health Justice*, 8:10.

Bullock, T. (2003) Changing levels of drug use before, during, and after imprisonment. In M. Ramsay (Ed.), *Prisoners' Drug Use and Treatment*. Home Office. Available: https://bulger.co.uk/prison/Drug%20Research.pdf

Busby, M. (2019) Expert quits Home Office drug panel over 'political vetting'. *The Guardian*, 6th October.

Butler, A. (2010) Killer drug Meow Meow being flown into Britain every day. *The Mirror*, 21st March.

Carr, C., Martins, C.M., et al. (2013) The role of early life stress in adult psychiatric disorders. *The Journal of Nervous and Mental Disease*, 201:1007–1020.

Carson, D.C., Sullivan, C.J., et al. (2009) General strain theory and the relationship between early victimization and drug use. *Deviant Behavior*, 30(1):54–88.

Casey, L. (2023) *Final Report: An Independent Review into the Standards of Behaviour and Internal Culture of the Metropolitan Police Service*. Available: https://www.met.police.uk/SysSiteAssets/media/downloads/met/about-us/baroness-casey-review/update-march-2023/baroness-casey-review-march-2023a.pdf

Čater, M. and Majdič, G. (2022) How early maternal deprivation changes the brain and behavior? *European Journal of Neuroscience*, 55(9):2058–2075.

Caulkins, J.P and Kleiman, M. (2011) Drugs and crime. In M. Tonry (Ed.), *Oxford Handbook of Crime and Criminal Justice*. Oxford University Press.

Chaiken, J. and Chaiken, M. (1990) Drugs and predatory crime. In M. Tonry and J. Wilson (Eds.), *Drugs and Crime*. UCP.

Chambers, M. (2010) Coming Clean. *Policy Exchange*. Available: https://policyexchange.org.uk/wp-content/uploads/2016/09/coming-clean-jun-10.pdf

Christie, B. (2023) UK rejects Scottish government's plan to decriminalise drugs. *BMJ*, 382:1584.

Clarke, R. V. (1995) Situational crime prevention. *Crime and Justice: Review of Research*, 19: 91–150.

Cohen, L.E. and Felson, M. (1979) Social inequality and predatory criminal victimization: An exposition and test of a formal theory. *American Sociological Review*, 44:588–608.

Cohen, A.K. (1955) *Delinquent Boys*. Free Press.

Cohen, S. (1985) *Visions of Social Control*. Polity.

Collins, B., Cuddy, K. and Martin, A. (2017) Assessing the effectiveness and cost-effectiveness of drug intervention programs: UK case study. *Journal of Addictive Diseases*, 36(1):5–13.

Collison, M. (1996) In search of the high-life. *BJC*, 36(3):428–444.

Conroy, E., Degenhardt, L., et al. (2009) Child maltreatment as a risk factor for opioid dependence. *Child Abuse and Neglect*, 33:343–352.

Contreras, R. (2012) *The Stickup Kids*. University of California Press.

Coomber, R., Childs, A., et al. (2023) Social media applications and 'surface web' mediated supply of illicit drugs. In M. Tzanetakis and N. South (Eds.), *Digital Transformations of Illicit Drug Markets*. Emerald Publishing Limited.

Coomber, R. and Moyle, L. (2014) Beyond drug dealing. *Drugs: Education, Prevention & Policy*, 21(2):157–164.

Coomber, R. and Moyle, L. (2018) The changing shape of street-level heroin and crack supply in England. *BJC*, 58(6):1323–1342.

Coomber, R., Moyle, L. and South, N. (2016) The normalisation of drug supply, *Drugs: Education, Prevention & Policy*, 23(3):255–263.

Coomber, R., Moyle, L. and Knox-Mahoney, M. (2019) Symbolic policing. *Policing and Society*, 29(1):1–17.

Coomber, R. (2006) *Pusher Myths*. Free Association Books.

Coomber, R. (2010) Reconceptualising drug markets and drug dealers. *Drugs and Alcohol Today*, 10(1):10–13.

Coomber, R. (2013) Drug treatment and quasi-compulsory treatment. In Coomber, R., McElrath, K., et al. (Eds.), *Key Concepts in Drugs and Society*. Sage.

Cope, N. (2003) 'It's No time or high time': Young offenders' experiences of time and drug use in prison. *Howard Journal*, 42(2):158–175.

Courtwright, D. (2001) *Forces of Habit*. Harvard University Press.

Courtwright, D. (2019) *The Age of Addiction*. Harvard University Press.

Crabtree, A., Mercer, G., et al. (2013) A qualitative study of the perceived effects of blue lights in washrooms on people who use injection drugs. *Harm Reduct Journal*, 8(10):22.

Crewe, B. (2005) Prisoner society in the era of hard drugs. *Punishment and Society*, 7:457–481.

Crocq, M.A. (2007) Historical and cultural aspects of man's relationship with addictive drugs. *Dialogues in Clinical Neuroscience*, 9(4):355–361.

Crowther Dowey, C. (2005) The police and community justice: The Lambeth policing experiment. *British Journal of Community Justice*, 3(3):31–43.

Currie, E. (1985) *Confronting Crime*. Random House.

Cusick, L. and Hickman, M. (2005) 'Trapping' in drug use and sex work careers. *Drugs: Education, Prevention & Policy*, 12(5):369–379.

Cusick, L., Martin, A. and May, T. (2003) *Vulnerability and Involvement in Drug Use and Sex Work*.

Daly, M. (2007) Plant warfare. *Druglink*, 22(2):6–9.

Dasgupta, A. (2019) *Critical Issues in Alcohol and Drugs of Abuse Testing* (2nd edn.). Academic Press.

Dávalosa, L., et al., (2009) Disabusing cocaine. *International Journal of Drug Policy*, 20(5): 381–386.

Davenport-Hines, R.P.T. (2004) *The Pursuit of Oblivion*. Norton.

de Carvalho, S. and Seibel, D. (2009) Crack cocaine use and its relationship with violence and HIV, *Clinics*, 64(9).

De Li, S. (2005) Race, self-control, and drug problems among jail inmates. *Journal of Drug Issues*, 35:645–663.

de Looze, M., Janssen, I., et al. (2015) Neighbourhood crime and adolescent cannabis use in Canadian adolescents. *Drug and Alcohol Dependence*, 146:68–74.

DEA (2023) *One Pill Can Kill*. DEA. Available: https://www.dea.gov/onepill

Debord, G. (1969) *Society of the Spectacle*. Red & Black.

Delavari, F., Sheibani, V., et al. (2016) Maternal separation and the risk of drug abuse in later life. *Addict Health*, 8(2):107–114.

Delgado, R. and Stefancic, J. (2007) Critical race theory and criminal justice. *Humanity and Society*, 31(2–3):133–145.

Demant, J., Munksgaard, R., et al. (2018) Going local on a global platform. *International Criminal Justice Review*, 28(3):255–274.

Denton, B. (2001) *Dealing: Women in the Drug Economy*. UNSW Press.

Derkas, E. (2011) Don't let your pregnancy get in the way of your drug addiction. *Social Justice*, 38(3:125):125–144.

Derkas, E. (2012) The organization formerly known as crack. *Race, Gender and Class*, 19(3/4):179–195.

Dick, D. (2022) *Rutgers Researchers Delve Deep into the Genetics of Addiction*. Available: https://www.rutgers.edu/news/rutgers-researchers-delve-deep-genetics-addiction#:~:text=More%20than%20half%20of%20the,much%20as%2070%20percent%20heritable

Dikötter, F., et al. (2007) China, British imperialism and the myth of the 'Opium Plague'. In J.H. Mills and P. Barton (Eds.), *Drugs and Empire*. Palgrave-Macmillan.

Dishion, T.J. and Tipsord, J.M. (2011) Peer contagion in child and adolescent social and emotional development. *Annual Review of Psychology*, 62:189–214.

Djemil, H. (2008) *Inside Out*. Centre for Policy Studies.

Doherty, E.E., Green, K.M. and Ensminger, M.E. (2008) Investigating the long-term influence of adolescent delinquency on drug use initiation. *Drug and Alcohol Dependence*, 93:72–84.

Dolan, M. and Hamilton, M. (2016) The role of cognitive-behavioral therapy in the UK criminal justice system. *Journal of Forensic Psychiatry and Psychology*, 27(2):228–246.

Dole, V. and Nyswander, M. (1967) Heroin addiction—A metabolic disease. *Archives of Internal Medicine*, 120(1):19–24.

Dorn, N. and South, N. (1987) *A Land Fit for Heroin*. Springer.

Dorn, N., Murji, K. and South, N. (1992) *Traffickers: Drug Markets and Law Enforcement*. Routledge.

Downes, D. (1988) The sociology of crime and social control in Britain 1960–1987. In P. Rock (Ed.), *A History of British Criminology*. Clarendon.

Drug Policy Alliance (2015) *Marijuana Arrests in Colorado after the Passage of Amendment 64*. DPA.

Drug Policy Alliance (2018) *From Prohibition to Progress: A Status Report on Marijuana Legalization*. DPA.

Drug Strategy Unit (2006) *IDTS, the First 28 Days: Psychosocial Support*.

Ducci, F. and Goldman, D. (2012) The genetic basis of addictive disorders. *Psychiatr Clin North America*, 35(2):495–519.

Duncan, R. (2013) The summer of love and protest: Transatlantic counterculture in the 1960s. In G. Kosc (Ed.), *The Transatlantic Sixties*. CUP.

Dunlap, E. and Johnson, B. (1996) Family and Human Resources in the Development of a Female Crack-Seller Career. *Journal of Drug Issues*, 26(1):175–198.

Eastwood, N., Shiner, M. and Bear, D. (2013) *The Numbers in Black and White.* Release. Available: https://www.release.org.uk/sites/default/files/pdf/publications/Release%20-%20Race%20Disparity%20Report%20final%20version.pdf

Edgar, K. and O'Donnell, I. (1998) *Mandatory Drug Testing in Prisons.* Home Office Research and Statistics Directorate.

Edwards, R. and Burton, J. (2021) Young women's recovery from problematic alcohol use, *Journal of Critical Realism,* 20(5):491–507.

Eley, S., Gallop, K., et al. (2002) *Drug treatment and testing orders: Evaluation of the Scottish pilots.* Social Research Scottish Executive. http://www.scotland.gov.uk/Publications/2002/10/15537/11660

EMCDDA (2001) *Study on Assistance to Drug Users in Prisons.*

EMCDDA (2015) *The Internet and Drug Markets.*

EMCDDA (2018) *New Psychoactive Substances in Prison: Results from an EMCDDA Trendspotter Study – June 2018.*

EMCDDA (2019) *EU Drug Markets Report 2019.*

EMCDDA (2020) *European Drug Report 2020: Trends and Developments.*

EMCDDA (2022) *Prison and Drugs in Europe Current and Future Challenges.*

Ennett, S.T., Tobler, N.S., et al. (1994) How effective is drug abuse resistance education? *American Journal of Public Health,* 84:1394–1401.

Europol (2022) *Intellectual Property Crime Threat Assessment 2022.* Available: https://euipo.europa.eu/tunnel-web/secure/webdav/guest/document_library/observatory/documents/reports/2022_IP_Crime_Threat_Assessment/IP_Crime_Threat_Assessment_2022_FullR_en.pdf

Evans, A. and Bosworth, K. (1997) Building effective drug education programs. *International Research Bulletin,* 19.

Evans, G.W., Li, D. and Whipple, S.S. (2013) Cumulative risk and child development. *Psychological Bulletin.* 139:1342–1396.

Evans-Brown, M., McVeigh, J., Perkins, C. and Bellis, M.A. (2012) *Human Enhancement Drugs.* PHI, LJM.

Everett, B. and Gallop, R. (2000) *The Link between Childhood Trauma and Mental Illness.* SAGE.

Eysenck, S.B.G. and Eysenck, H.J. (1977) Personality differences between prisoners and controls. *Psychological Reports,* 40(3-suppl):1023–1028.

Fallu, J.S., Janosz, M., et al. (2010) Preventing disruptive boys from becoming heavy substance users during adolescence. *Addictive Behaviors,* 35(12):1074–1082.

Farabee, D., Joshi, V. and Anglin, M.D. (2001) Addiction careers and criminal specialization. *Crime and Delinquency,* 47(2):196–220.

Farrall, S., Mawby, R.C. and Worrall, A. (2007) 'Prolific/persistent offenders and desistance. In L. Gelsthorpe and R. Morgan (Eds.), *Handbook of Probation.* Taylor and Francis.

Farrell, M. and Marsden, J. (2008) Acute risk of drug-related death among newly released prisoners in England and Wales. *Addiction,* 103(2):251–255.

Farrell, M., Singleton, N. and Strang, J. (2000) *Drugs and Prison: A High Risk and High Burden Environment.* Taylor and Francis.

Farrington, D.P. and Welsh, B.C. (2007) *Saving Children from a Life of Crime.* OUP.

Farrington, D.P., Coid, J.W. and West, D.J. (2009) The development of offending from age 8 to age 50. *Monatsschrift fur Kriminologie und Strafrechtsreform (Journal of Criminology and Penal Reform)*, 92:160–173.

Farrington, D.P. (1986) Age and crime. In M. Tonry and N. Morris (Eds.), *Crime and Justice*. UCP.

Farrington, D.P. (1995) The development of offending and antisocial behaviour in childhood. *Journal of Child Psychology and Psychiatry*, 36:929–964.

Farrington, D.P. (2005) *Integrated Developmental and Life-Course Theories of Offending*. Routledge.

Fergusson, D.M. and Horwood, L.J. (1999) Prospective childhood predictors of deviant peer affiliations in adolescence. *Journal of Child Psychology and Psychiatry*, 40(4): 581–592.

Finney, A. (2004) *Violence in the Night-Time Economy: Key Findings from the Research*. Home Office.

Fisher, H. and Measham, F. (2018) *Night Lives*. Available http://volteface.me/publications/night-lives/

Flacks, S. (2024) Who is the addict-offender? *Social and Legal Studies*, 33(2):149–167.

Fleetwood, J. and Seal, L. (2017) Women, drugs and the death penalty: Sandiford. *The Howard Journal of Criminal Justice*, 56(3):358–381.

Fleetwood, J., Radcliffe, P. and Stevens, A. (2015) Shorter sentences for drug mules: The early impact of the sentencing guidelines in England and Wales. *Drugs: Education, Prevention & Policy*, 22(5):428–436.

Fleetwood, J. (2014) *Drug Mules: Women in the International Cocaine Trade*. Palgrave-Macmillan.

Fleetwood, J. (2015) Mafias, markets, mules. *Sociology Compass*, 9(11):962–976.

Fleming, N. (2010) Mephedrone: The anatomy of a media drug scare. *The Guardian*, 5 April 2020. Available https://www.theguardian.com/media/2010/apr/05/mephedrone-drug-media-scare-newspapers

Ford, J. and Blumenstein, L. (2013) Self-control and substance use among college students. *Journal of Drug Issues*, 43:56–68.

Ford, J. (2008) Social Learning Theory and Nonmedical prescription drug use among adolescents. *Sociological Spectrum*, 28(3):299–316.

Fordham, A. (2024) Reading the 'coca' leaves: Six predictions for global drug policy in 2024. Available https://idpc.net/blog/2024/01/reading-the-coca-leaves-six-predictions-for-global-drug-policy-in-2024

Fornili, K.S. (2018) Racialized mass incarceration and the war on drugs. *Journal of Addictions Nursing*, 29(1):65–72.

Forston, R. (2006) *Harm Reduction and the Law of the United Kingdom*. Available: https://www.neilhunt.org/Reports/2006-JRF-harm-reduction-and-the-law-in-the-UK-fortson.pdf

Fothergill, K.E. and Ensminger, M.E. (2006) Childhood and adolescent antecedents of drug and alcohol problems. *Drug and Alcohol Dependence*, 82:61–76.

Frank, D.A., Augustyn, M., et al. (2001) Growth, development, and behavior in early childhood following prenatal cocaine exposure: A systematic review. *JAMA*, 285(12): 1613–25.

Frary, C., Johnson, R. and Wang, M. (2005) Food sources and intakes of caffeine in the diets of persons in the United States. *Journal of the American Dietetic Association*, 105(1): 110–113.

Friday, P.C., Ren, X., et al., (2005) A Chinese birth cohort: Theoretical implications. *Journal of Research in Crime and Delinquency*, 42(2):123–146.

Fridell, M., Hesse, M. and Johnson, E. (2006) High prognostic specificity of antisocial personality disorder in patients with drug dependence. *American Journal on Addictions*, 15(3):227–232.

Friedman, F., Godvin, M., et al. (2023) Fentanyl, heroin, and methamphetamine-based counterfeit pills sold at tourist-oriented pharmacies in Mexico. *Drug and Alcohol Dependence*, 249:110819.

Friedman, M. and Szasz, T. (1992) *On Liberty and Drugs*. Drug Policy Foundation.

Frood, A. (2008) Drug-fuelled counterculture. *Nature* 455:870.

Gandossy, R.P., Williams, J.R., et al. (1980) *Drugs and Crime: A Survey and Analysis of the Literature*. National Institute of Justice.

Gaudiano, B.A. (2008) Cognitive-behavioural therapies: Achievements and challenges. *Evidence-Based Mental Health*, 11(1):5–7.

Goddard, H. (1912) *The Kallikak Family*. University of Michigan Library.

Goldstein, P.J., Bellucci, P.A., et al. (1991) Volume of cocaine use and violence. *Journal of Drug Issues*, 21(2):345–367.

Goldstein, P.J. (1985) The drugs/violence nexus. *Journal of Drug Issues*, 15(4):493–506.

Golub, A., Johnson, B.D. and Dunlap, E. (2005) Subcultural evolution and illicit drug use. *Addiction Research and Theory*, 13(3):217–229.

Gootenberg, P. (2022) *The Oxford Handbook of Global Drug History*. OUP.

Gore, S.M. and Bird, A.G. (1996) Cost implications of random mandatory drugs tests in prisons. *Lancet*, 348(9035):1124–1127.

Gossop, M., Trakada, K., et al. (2005) Reductions in criminal convictions after addiction treatment. *Drug and Alcohol Dependence*, 79(3):295–302.

Gottfredson, M.R. and Hirschi, T. (1990) *A General Theory of Crime*. Stanford University Press.

Government of Canada (2022) *Taking Stock of Progress*. Available: https://www.canada.ca/content/dam/hc-sc/documents/programs/engaging-cannabis-legalization-regulation-canada-taking-stock-progress/document/pdf-lr-engagement-paper-en.pdf

Grace, S., Lloyd, C. and Perry, A. (2019) The spice trail. *Drugs: Education, Prevention & Policy*, 27(4):271–281.

Green, K.M., Doherty, E.E., et al. (2010) Does heavy adolescent marijuana lead to criminal involvement in adulthood? *Drug and Alcohol Dependence*, 112 (1–2):117–125.

Greenaway, J. (2003) *Drink and British Politics Since 1830*.

Greenberg, J. and Sherman, A. (2021) What is critical race theory, and why are conservatives blocking it? 24th May. Available: https://www.politifact.com/article/2021/may/24/what-critical-race-theory-and-why-are-conservative/

Grella, C.E., Joshi, V. and Hser, Y.I. (2003) Follow-up of cocaine-dependent men and women with antisocial personality disorder. *Journal of Substance Abuse Treatment*, 25(3):155–164.

Grella, C.E., Stein, J.A. and Greenwall, L. (2005) Associations among childhood trauma, adolescent problem behaviors, and adverse adult outcomes in substance-abusing women offenders. *Psychology of Addictive Behaviors*, 19:43–53.

Grothoff, G.E., Kempf-Leonard, K. and Mullins, C. (2014) Gender and juvenile drug abuse, *Women and Criminal Justice*, 24(1):22–43.

Grund, J. and Breeksema, J. (2017) Drug policy in The Netherlands. In R. Colson and H. Bergeron (Eds.), *European Drug Policies: The Ways of Reform*. Taylor and Francis.

Guerra-Doce, E. (2015) Psychoactive substances in prehistoric times. *Time and Mind*, 8(1): 91–112.

Gyngell, K. (2009) *The Phoney War on Drugs*.

Hadfield, E., Sleath, E., et al. (2021) A systematic review into the effectiveness of Integrated Offender Management. *Criminology and Criminal Justice*, 21(5):650–668.

Hadfield, P. (2006) *Bar Wars*. OUP.

Hajar, R. (2012) The air of history (part II) medicine in the middle ages. *Heart Views*, 13(4): 158–162.

Hall, A. and Antonopoulos, G. (2019) The (online) supply of illicit lifestyle medicines: A criminological study. In K. Van de Ven, K. Mulrooney and J. McVeigh (Eds.), *Human Enhancement Drugs*. Routledge.

Hall, S. and Winlow, S. (2006) *Violent Night*. Berg.

Hall, S. and Winlow, S. (2015) *Revitalising Criminological Theory*. Routledge.

Hall, S. and Winlow, S. (2018) Ultra-realism. In W. Dekeseredy et al. (Eds.), *The Routledge companion to criminological theory and concepts*. Routledge Handbook.

Hall, S., Winlow, S. and Ancrum, C. (2008) *Criminal Identities and Consumer Culture*. Willan.

Hamilton, D. (1997) The truth about DARE, *Los Angeles New Times*, March 20th 1997.

Hammer, R., Dingel, M., et al. (2013) Addiction: Current criticism of the brain disease paradigm. *AJOB Neurosci*, 4(3):27–32.

Hammersley, R., Dalgarno, P., et al. (2016) Trauma in childhood. *Addiction Research and Theory*. 24(2):135–151.

Hammersley, R. and Delgarno, P. (2013) *Trauma and Recovery Amongst People Who Have Injected within the Past Five Years*. Scottish Drug Forum.

Hammersley, R., Forsyth, A., et al. (1989) The relationship between crime and opioid use. *British Journal of Addiction*, 84:1029–1043.

Hammersley, R. and Morrison, V. (1987) Effects of Polydrug Use on the criminal activities of heroin users. *British Journal of Addiction*, 82:899–906.

Hammersley, R., Forsyth, A. and Lavelle, T. (1990) The criminality of new drug users in Glasgow. *British Journal of Addiction*, 85:1583–1594.

Hammersley, R. (2001) *Ecstasy and the Rise of the Chemical Generation*. Routledge.

Hammersley, R. (2008) *Drugs and Crime*. Polity.

Hammersley, R. (2011) Pathways through drugs and crime: Desistence, trauma and resilience. *Journal of Criminal Justice*, 39:268–272.

Hands, T. (2018) *Drinking in Victorian and Edwardian Britain*. Palgrave-Macmillan.

Hari, J. (2015) *Chasing the Scream*. Bloomsbury.

Harlow, H.F. and Zimmermann, R.R. (1958) The development of affective responsiveness in infant monkeys. *Proceedings of the American Philosophical Society*, 102:501–509.

Harper and Chitty (2005) *The Impact of Corrections on Re-offending* (p. 291). Home Office research Study.

Hasin, D.S., O'Brien, C.P., et al. (2013) DSM-5 criteria for substance use disorders. *American Journal of Psychiatry*, 170(8):834–851.

Hathaway, A., Mostaghim, A., et al., (2016) A nuanced view of normalisation. *Drugs: Education, Prevention & Policy*, 23(3):238–246.

Hathaway, A.D., Comeau, N. C. and Erickson, P.G. (2011) Cannabis normalization and stigma. *CCJ*, 11(5):451–469.

Hatsis, T. (2015) *The Witches Ointment*. Park Street Press.

Hawkins, J.D., Catalano, R.F. and Miller, J.Y. (1992) Risk and protective factors for alcohol and other drug problems in adolescence and early adulthood. *Psychological Bulletin*, 112(1):64–105.

Hay, G., dos Santos, A.R. and Swithenbank, Z. (2018) *Estimates of the Prevalence of Opiate Use and/or Crack Cocaine Use, 2014/15*. PHI, LJM.

Hayaki, J., Stein, M.D., et al. (2005) Adversity among drug users. *Drug and Alcohol Dependence*, 78(1):65–71.

Hayhurst, K.P., Pierce, M., et al. (2017) Pathways through opiate use and offending. *International Journal of Drug Policy*, 39:1–13.

Hayward, K. J. and Hobbs, D. (2007) Beyond the binge in 'booze Britain'. *BJS*, 58(3):437–456.

Hayward, K.J. and Turner, T. (2019) Be more VIP': illicit drug use, hedonism, and faux luxury culture in Ibiza's party spaces. In O. Smith and T. Raymen (Eds.), *Deviant Leisure*. Routledge.

Hayward, K.J. (2007) Situational crime prevention and its discontents. *Social Policy and Administration*, 41(3):232–250.

Hearnden, I. and Magill, C. (2004) *Decision Making by House Burglars: Offender's Perspectives* (p. 249). Home Office Findings.

Heather, N. (2017) Q:Is addiction a brain disease or a moral failing? A Neither. *Neuroethics*, 10(1):115–124.

Heidensohn, F. (2006) *Gender and Justice*. Willan.

Hendrickson, J.C. and Gerstein, D.R. (2005) Criminal involvement among young male ecstasy users. *Substance Use and Misuse*, 40:1557–1575.

Hernandez-Avila, C.A., Burleson, J.A., et al. (2000) Personality and substance use disorders as predictors of criminality, *Comprehensive Psychiatry*, 41(4):276–283.

Hesmondhalgh, D. (2005) Subcultures, scenes or tribes? *Journal of Youth Studies*, 8(1):21–40.

Higgins, G. and Ricketts, M. (2005) Self-control theory, race, and delinquency. *Journal of Ethnicity in Criminal Justice*, 3:5–22.

Higgins, G. (2004) Gender and self-control theory. *Criminal Justice Studies*, 17:33–55.

Hiller, M.L., Knight, K., Dwayne Simpson, D. (1999) Prison-based substance abuse treatment, residential aftercare and recidivism. *Addiction*, 94(6):833–842.

Hillyard, P. and Tombs, S. (2007) From 'crime' to social harm? *Crime Law Soc Change*, 48:9–25.

Hirschi, T. (1969) *Causes of Delinquency*. Transaction.

Hitchens, P. (2012) *The War We Never Fought*. Bloomsbury.

HMICFRS (2021) *Neurodiversity in the Criminal Justice System*. Available: https://hmicfrs.justiceinspectorates.gov.uk/publications/neurodiversity-in-the-criminal-justice-system/

HMIP (2021) *A Joint Thematic Inspection of Community-Based Drug Treatment and Recovery Work with People on Probation.*

HMIP (2022) *HM Chief Inspector of Prisons Annual Report: 2021 to 2022.*

HMIP (2011) *HM Chief Inspector of Prisons for England and Wales Annual Report 2010–11.*

HMIP (2015) *Changing Patterns of Substance Misuse in Adult Prisons and Service Responses.*

HMIP (2016) *HM Chief Inspector of Prisons for England and Wales Annual Report 2015–16.*

HMIP (2018) *HM Chief Inspector of Prisons Annual Report: 2017 to 2018.*

HMIP (2019a) *The Availability and Delivery of Interventions (Probation Services).*

HMIP (2019b) *HM Chief Inspector of Prisons Annual Report: 2018 to 2019.*

HMIP (2023) *HM Chief Inspector of Prisons Annual Report: 2022 to 2023.*

HMPPS (2019) *Prison Drugs Strategy.*

Hobbs, D. (1995) *Bad Business.* OUP.

Hobbs, D. (2013) *Lush Life.* OUP.

Hoffman, J.P. and Cerbone, F.G. (1999) Stressful life events and delinquency escalation in early adolescence. *Criminology*, 37(2):343–374.

Hoffman, P.T. (2015) *Why Did Europe Conquer the World?* PUP.

Holland, A., Stevens, A., et al. (2022) Analysis of the UK government's 10-year drugs strategy. *Journal of Public Health*, fdac114.

Hollin, C. (1999) Treatment programmes for offenders. *International Journal of Law and Psychiatry*, 22(3–4):361–372.

Hollingworth, M. (2008) An examination of the potential impact of the Drug Rehabilitation Requirement on homeless illicit drug-using offenders. *Probation Journal*, 55(2):127–138.

Holloway, K. and Bennett, T. (2007) Gender differences in drug misuse and related problem behaviors among arrestees in the UK. *Substance Use and Misuse*, 42(6): 899–921.

Holloway, K.R., Bennett, T.H. and Farrington, D.P. (2006) The effectiveness of drug treatment programs in reducing criminal behavior. *Psicothema*, 18(3):620–629.

Holt, M. and Treloar, C. (2008) Pleasure and drugs. *International Journal of Drug Policy*, 19(5):349–352.

Home Office (2010) *Reducing Demand, Restricting Supply, Building Recovery.*

Home Office (1998) *Tackling Drugs to Build a Better Britain.*

Home Office (2006) *Tough Choices.*

Home Office (2006a) *Drug Interventions Programme and Prolific and Other Priority Offender Programme.*

Home Office (2006b) *Experiences and Lessons from Early Implementation Areas Implementing the DIP Condition.*

Home Office (2007) *An Introduction to the Drug Interventions Programme for Prisons and Probation Services.*

Home Office (2008) *Drugs: Protecting Families and Communities.*

Home Office (2014a) *New Psychoactive Substances Review Expert Panel Report.*

Home Office (2014b) *Drugs: International Comparators.*

Home Office (2015) *Integrated Offender Management (IOM).*

Home Office (2017) *2017 Drug Strategy.*

Home Office (2018) *Review of the Psychoactive Substances Act 2016.*

Home Office (2019) *Drug Misuse Declared: Findings from the 2018/19 Crime Survey England and Wales.*

Home Office (2021) *From Harm to Hope.*

Home Office. (2022a) *Seizures of Drugs in England and Wales, Financial Year Ending 2021.*

Home Office (2022b) *Swift, Certain, Tough: New Consequences for Drug Possession.*

Home Office (2022c) *Crime Outcomes in England and Wales 2021 to 2022.*

Home Office (2022d) *Police Powers and Procedures: Stop and Search and Arrests, England and Wales, year ending 31 March 2022.*

Hooks, B. (2004) We Real Cool: Black Men and Masculinity. Routledge

Hope, T. (1994) Problem-oriented policing and drug-market locations. In R.V. Clarke (Ed.), *Crime Prevention Studies*, Vol. 2. Criminal Justice Press/Willow Tree Press.

Hopkins-Burke, R. (2018) *An Introduction to Criminological Theory*. Routledge.

Hough, M., Clancy, A., et al. (2003) *The Impact of Drug Treatment and Testing Orders on Offending: A Two-Year Reconviction Study.*

House of Commons Home Affairs Committee (2013) *Drugs: Breaking the Cycle Ninth Report of Session 2012–13.* Available: http://www.publications.parliament.uk/pa/cm201213/cmselect/cmhaff/184/184.pdf

House of Commons (2021) *General Debate-MDA 1971.* Available: https://researchbriefings.files.parliament.uk/documents/CDP-2021-0090/CDP-2021-0090.pdf

House of Lords and House of Commons (HOL/HOC) (2005) *Deaths in Custody: Third Report of Session 2004-05, Vol. 2.*

HRI (2023) *The Death Penalty for Drug Offences.*

Hser, Y., Huang, D., et al. (2007) Trajectories of heroin addiction. *Evaluation Review*, 31(6): 548–563.

Hughes, C., Ritter, A., et al. (2016) *Decriminalisation of Drug Use and Possession in Australia: A Briefing Note.* Available: https://www.citywide.ie/assets/files/pdf/decriminalisation_briefing_note_feb_2016_final_dpmp.pdf

Hughes, R. (2000) Drug injectors and prison mandatory drug testing. *Howard Journal*, 39(1):1–13.

Humphreys, K., Shover, C., et al. (2022) Responding to the opioid crisis in North America and beyond: Recommendations of the Stanford–Lancet Commission. *The Lancet*, 399: 555–604.

Hutton, F. (2006) *Risky Pleasures? Club Cultures and Feminine Identities*. Taylor and Francis.

Hvozdovich, J.A., Chronister, C.W., et al. (2020) Case report: Synthetic cannabinoid deaths in state of Florida prisoners. *Journal of Analytical Toxicology*, 44(3):298–300.

Hyman, S.E. (2005) Addiction. *American Journal of Psychiatry*, 162(8):1414–1422.

Iglesias, S. (2023) Explaining the pattern of 'war on drugs' violence in the Philippines under Duterte. *Asian Politics and Policy*, 15(2):164–184.

Independent Anti-Slavery Commission (IASC) (2017) *Combating Modern Slavery Experienced by Vietnamese Nationals Enroute to and within the UK.* Available: https://antislaverycommissioner.co.uk/media/r3zpwlef/combating-modern-slavery-experienced-by-vietnamese-nationals-en-route-to-and-within-the-uk.pdf

Institute of Alcohol Studies (IAS) (2014) *Alcohol, Domestic Abuse and Sexual Assault.* Available: https://www.ias.org.uk/uploads/IAS%20report%20Alcohol%20domestic%20abuse%20and%20sexual%20assault.pdf

Jacobson, J., Edgar, K. and Loucks, N. (2007) *There when You Need Them Most: Pact's First Night in Custody Services*. Prison Reform Trust.

Jacobson, J. (1999) *Policing Drug Hot-Spots: Project Report*. Home Office.

Jankowiak, W. and Bradburd, D. (2003) *Drugs, Labor, and Colonial Expansion*. UAP.

Jarvis, G. and Parker, H. (1989) Young Heroin Users and Crime: How do the new users finance their habits? *BJC*, 29(2):175–185.

Jay, M. (2010) *High Society*. Thames & Hudson.

Jewkes, Y. (2007) *Handbook on Prisons*. Willan.

Johnson, B.D. and Golub, A. (2007) The potential for acceleration of heroin use in the United States. *Crime and Justice*, 33:33–76.

Johnson, H. (2004) *Drugs and Crime: A Study of Incarcerated Female Offender*. AIC. Available: https://www.aic.gov.au/sites/default/files/2020-05/rpp063.pdf

Kaplow, J.B., Curran, P.J., et al. (2002) Child, parent, and peer predictors of early-onset substance use: A multisite longitudinal study. *Journal of Abnormal Child Psychology*, 30(3):199–216.

Katz, J. (1988) *Seductions of Crime: Moral and Sensual Attractions in Doing Evil*. Basic Books.

Kaye, S., Darke, S. and Finlay-Jones, R. (1998) The onset of heroin use and criminal behaviour: Does order make a difference? *Drug and Alcohol Dependence*, 53(1): 79–86.

Kedar, Y., Kedar, G. and Barkai, R. (2021) Hypoxia in Paleolithic decorated caves. *Time and Mind*, 14(2):181–216.

Kendler, K.S., Prescott, C.A., et al. (2003) The structure of genetic and environmental risk factors for common psychiatric and substance use disorders in men and women. *Archives of General Psychiatry*, 60(9):929–937.

Kidd, R. (1997) *The Way We Civilise: Aboriginal Affairs*. UQP.

Klötz, F., Petersson, A., et al., (2007) Violent crime and substance abuse. *Forensic Science International*, 173(1):57–63.

Koram, K. (2019) *The War on Drugs and the Global Colour Line*. Pluto Press.

Kranzler, H.R., Tennen, H., et al. (1997) Validity of the longitudinal, expert, all data procedure for psychiatric diagnosis in patients with psychoactive substance use disorders. *Drug and Alcohol Dependence*, 45(1–2):93–104.

Kruis, N.E., Seo, C. and Kim, B. (2020) Revisiting the empirical status of social learning theory on substance use. *Substance Use and Misuse*, 55(4):666–683.

Laing, R.D. (1964) *The Divided Self*. Penguin.

Lammers, S.M., Soe-Agnie, S.E., et al. (2014) Substance use and criminality. *Tijdschr voor Psychiatrie*, 56(1):32–39.

Landenberger, N.A. and Lipsey, M.W. (2005) The positive effects of cognitive–behavioral programs for offenders. *Journal of Experimental Criminology* 1:451–476.

Lansford, J.E., Dodge, K.A., et al. (2010) Does physical abuse in early childhood predict substance use in adolescence and early adulthood? *Child Maltreatment*, 15:190–194.

Laqueur, H., Rivera-Aguirre, A., et al. (2020) The impact of cannabis legalization in Uruguay on adolescent cannabis use. *International Journal of Drug Policy*, 80:102748.

Lawyer, S., Resnick, H., et al. (2010) Forcible, drug-facilitated, and incapacitated rape and sexual assault among undergraduate women, *Journal of American College Health*, 58(5): 453–460.

Lazarus, J., Safreed-Harmon, K., et al. (2018) Health outcomes for clients of needle and syringe programs in prisons. *Epidemiologic Reviews*, 40(1):96–104.

Lea, J. and Young, J. (1984) *What Is to Be Done about Law and Order?* Pluto.

Leban, L. and Gibson, C. L. (2020) The role of gender in the relationship between adverse childhood experiences and delinquency and substance use in adolescence. *Journal of Criminal Justice*, 66.

Lenton, S., Humeniuk, R., et al. (2000) Infringement versus conviction. *Drug and Alcohol Review*, 19(3):257.

Levy, N. (2013) Addiction is not a brain disease (and it matters). *Frontiers in Psychiatry*, 4(24):1–7.

Liebling, A. (2011) Moral performance, inhuman and degrading treatment and prison pain. *Punishment and Society*, 13(5):530–550.

Lilienfeld, S.O. (2007) Psychological treatments that cause harm. *Perspectives on Psychological Science*, 2:53–70.

Lindsay, J. (2022) *Race Marxism: The Truth about Critical Race Theory and Praxis*. Independently Published.

Lines, R., Jürgens, R., et al. (2006) *Prison Needle Exchange*. Prison Policy Initiative.

Lines, R. (2017) *Drug Control and Human Rights in International Law*. CUP.

Linnemann, T. (2016) *Meth Wars: Police, Media, Power*. NYU.

Lipton, D. (1995) *The Effectiveness of Treatment for Drug Abusers under Criminal Justice Supervision*. Office of Justice Programs.

Lissardy, G. (2019) Uruguay: How much the country's drug market has really changed with the legalization of marijuana. *BBC*, 19th December.

Lloyd, C., Page, G., et al. (2014) *Evaluation of the Drug Recovery Wing Pilots*. Available: https://www.york.ac.uk/media/healthsciences/documents/research/mentalhealth research/DRWsFinalPublishedReport.pdf

Lloyd, C., Page, G. and Grace, S. (2018) Policing of cannabis possession is largely accidental – and many officers don't think it makes a difference. *The Conversation*.

Lloyd, C. (2010) *Sinning and Sinned against*. UKDPC.

Loe, M. (2001) Fixing broken masculinity. *Sexuality and Culture*, 5:97–125.

Loose, R. (2002) *Subject of Addiction*. Routledge.

Luck, P., Elifson, K. and Sterk, C. (2004) Female drug users and the welfare system: A qualitative exploration. *Drugs: Education, Prevention & Policy*, 11:113–128.

Lynam, D. R., Milich, R., et al. (2009) Project DARE. In G.A. Marlatt and K. Witkiewitz (Eds.), *Addictive Behaviors*. APA.

Lynch, W.J., Roth, M. and Carroll, M. (2002) Biological basis of sex differences in drug abuse: Preclinical and clinical studies. *Psychopharmacology*, 164:121–137.

Lyng, S. (1990) Edgework. *American Journal of Sociology*, 95(4):851–886.

MacCoun, R. and Reuter, P. (2001) *Drug War Heresies*. CUP.

MacDonald, M. (1997) *Mandatory Drug Testing in Prisons*. University of Central England Centre for Research into Quality.

Maher, L. and Daly, K. (1996) Women in the street-level drug economy: Continuity or change? *Criminology*, 34(4):465–491.

Maher, L. and Hudson, S.L. (2007) Women in the drug economy. *Journal of Drug Issues*, 37(4):805–826.

Maher, L., Dunlap, E. and Johnson, B. (2002) Black women's pathways to involvement in illicit drug distribution and sales. In S. Brochu, et al. (Eds.), *Drugs and Crime Deviant Pathways*. Routledge.

Maher, L. (1997) *Sexed Work*. OUP.

Makarenko, T. (2004) The crime-terror continuum. *Global Crime*, 6(1):129–145.

Makkai, T. and Payne, J. (2003) *Drugs and Crime: A Study of Incarcerated Male Offenders*. AIC. Available: https://www.aic.gov.au/sites/default/files/2020-05/rpp063.pdf

Malloch, M. (2008) *Women, Drugs and Custody*. Waterside.

Mandelbaum, D.G. (1965) Alcohol and culture. *Current Anthropology*, 6(3):281–293.

Mann, R., Howard, F. and Tew, J. (2018) What is a rehabilitative prison culture? *Prison Service Journal*, 235:3–9.

Mansfield, D. and Pain, A. (2007) *Evidence from the Field: Understanding Changing Levels of Opium Poppy Cultivation in Afghanistan*.

Marteau, J. and Stöver, H. (2010) *Introduction of the Integrated Drug Treatment System (IDTS) in English Prisons*. Home Office.

Martin, J. (2014) *Drugs on the Dark Net*. Palgrave.

Matheson, F.I. (2012) Implications of trauma among male and female offenders. *International Journal of Environmental Research and Public Health* 9(1):97–99.

Matthews, R. (2014) *Realist Criminology*. Palgrave.

Matza, D. and Sykes, G. (1961) Juvenile delinquency and subterranean values. *American Sociological Review*, 26(5):712–719.

Matza, D. (1964) *Delinquency and Drift*. Routledge.

Matza, D. (1969) *Becoming Deviant*. Prentice.

May, T. and Hough, M. (2009) Drug markets and distribution systems. *Addiction Research and Theory*, 12(6):549–563.

May, T., Warburton, H., et al. (2002) *Times They Are-A-Changing: Policing of Cannabis*. Joseph Rowntree Foundation.

McBride, A., Pates, R., et al. (2001) Needle fixation, the drug user's perspective. *Addiction*, 96(7):1049–1058.

McCall, H., Adams, N., et al. (2015) What is chemsex and why does it matter? *BMJ*, 351.

McClellan, D., Farabee, D. and Crouch, B. (1997) Early victimization, drug use, and criminality Criminal *Justice and Behavior*, 24:455–476.

McCormack, F., Page, S. and Fedorowicz, S. (2023) *Executive Summary: Research into the Use of the Psychoactive Substance Known as 'Monkey Dust' in Stoke-on-Trent*. Available: https://www.chadresearch.co.uk/wp-content/uploads/2023/07/Research-into-the-use-of-the-psychoactive-substance-known-as-Monkey-dust-in-Stoke-on-Trent-Exec-Summary-July-2023.pdf

McDonald, R. and Marsh, J. (2002) Crossing the Rubicon. *International Journal of Drug Policy*, 13:27–38.

McDonald, R. and Marsh, J. (2005) *Disconnected Youth?* Palgrave.

McGloin, J.M. & Stickle, W.P. (2011) Influence or convenience? *Journal of Research in Crime and Delinquency*, 48:327–363.

McKeganey, N. (2011) *Controversies in Drug Policy and Practice*. OUP.

McLellan, A.T., Lewis, D.C., et al. (2000) Drug dependence: A chronic medical illness. *JAMA*, 284(13):1689–1695.

McMann, T.J., Calac, A., et al. (2022) Synthetic cannabinoids in prisons. *JMIR Infodemiology*, 2(1):e37632.

McSweeney, T., Stevens, A., et al. (2007) Twisting arms or a helping hand? *BJC,* 47: 470–490.

McSweeney, T., Turnbull, P. and Hough, M. (2008) *The Treatment and Supervision of Drug-Dependent Offenders*. UKDPC.

McSweeney, T., Hughes, C. and Ritter, A. (2018) The impact of compliance with a compulsory model of drug diversion on treatment engagement and reoffending. *Drugs: Education, Prevention & Policy*, 25(1):56–66.

McVeigh, J. (2020) *Health and Social Responses to Problems Associated with the Use of Performance- and Image-Enhancing Drugs*. EMCDDA.

Measham, F. and Brain, K. (2005) Binge drinking, British alcohol policy and the new culture of intoxication. *Crime, Media, Culture,* 1(3): 262–283.

Measham, F. and Moore, K. (2008) The criminalisation of intoxication. In P. Squires (Ed.), *ASBO Nation*. BUP.

Measham, F. and Moore, K. (2009) Repertoires of distinction. *Criminology and Criminal Justice,* 9(4):437–464.

Measham, F. and Shiner, M. (2009) The legacy of normalisation. *International Journal of Drug Policy*, 20:502–508.

Measham, F., Aldridge, J. and Parker, H. (2001) *Dancing on Drugs*. Free Association.

Measham, F. (2002) Doing gender-doing drugs. *Contemporary Drug Problems*, 29(2): 335–373.

Measham, F. (2004) Play space. *International Journal of Drug Policy*, 15(5-6):337–345.

Melrose, M. (2004) Fractured transitions. *Probation Journal*, 51(4):327–341.

Melrose, M. (2009) Out on the streets and out of control? In J. Phoenix (Ed.), *Regulating Sex for Sale*. Policy Press.

Meneses, R. A. and Akers, R. L. (2011) A comparison of four general theories of crime and deviance. *International Criminal Justice Review*, 21(4):333–352.

Merton, R.K. (1938) Social structure and anomie. *American Sociological Review,* 3(5): 672–682.

Messina, N., Grell, C., et al. (2007) Childhood adverse events and current traumatic distress. *Criminal Justice and Behavior*, 34:1385–1401.

Metcalf McGrath, L. and Beckett Wilson, H. (2023) *Prescribed but Prohibited. Everyday Society*. British Sociological Association.

Metropolitan Police (2020) *Questions Relating to Cannabis Warnings*. Available: https://www.met.police.uk/foi-ai/metropolitan-police/disclosure-2020/july/Questions-relating-cannabis-warnings/

Mews, A., Hillier, J., et al. (2015) *The Impact of Short Custodial Sentences, Community Orders and Suspended Sentence Orders on Re-offending*. Ministry of Justice.

Miller, A. H. and Damask, N. A. (1996) The dual myths of 'narco-terrorism'. *Terrorism and Political Violence,* 8(1):114–131.

Millings, M., Taylor, S., et al. (2019) Through the gate. *Probation Journal*, 66(1):77–95.

Mill's, J.S. (1910) *On Liberty*. Longman, Roberts and Green Co.

Min, M., Farkas, K., et al. (2007) Impact of childhood abuse and neglect on substance abuse and psychological distress in adulthood. *Journal of Traumatic Stress*, 20:833–844.

Ministry of Justice (MoJ) (2018) *Examining the Educational Background of Young Knife Possession Offenders.*

Ministry of Justice (MoJ) (2020) *A Smarter Approach to Sentencing.*

Ministry of Justice (MoJ) (2013a) *Proven Re-offending Statistics Quarterly Bulletin January to December 2011, England and Wales.*

Ministry of Justice (MoJ) (2013b) *Gender Differences in Substance Misuse and Mental Health Amongst Prisoners.*

Ministry of Justice (MoJ) (2013c) *Transforming Rehabilitation A Strategy for Reform.*

Ministry of Justice (MoJ) (2015) *2010 to 2015 Government Policy: Reoffending and Rehabilitation.*

Ministry of Justice (MoJ) (2019) *Results from the 10 Prisons Project Ad Hoc Statistics.*

Ministry of Justice (MoJ) (2021) *HMPPS Annual Digest: April 2019 to March 2020.*

Ministry of Justice (MoJ) (2022a). *Offender Management Statistics Quarterly, April to June 2022.*

Ministry of Justice (MoJ) (2022b). *Outcomes by Offence Data Tool.*

Ministry of Justice (MoJ) (2022c). *Offender Management Statistics Quarterly: January to March 2022.*

Ministry of Justice (MoJ) (2023a) *Offender Management Statistics Quarterly.*

Ministry of Justice (MoJ) (2023b) *Freedom of Information Reply (230720003). Response to Authors Freedom of Information Request.*

Ministry of Justice (MoJ) (2023c) *Beefed-Up Prison Security Captures Record Level of Contraband.*

Mintz, S. (1985) *Sweetness and Power.*

Moe, A.M. (2006) Women drugs and crime. *Criminal Justice Studies*, 19(4):337–352.

Moffit, T.E. (2003) Life-course persistent and adolescence-limited antisocial behavior. In B.B. Lahey, T.E. Moffit, et al. (Eds.), *Causes of Conduct Disorder and Juvenile Delinquency*. Guilford Press.

Moffit, T.E. (1993) Adolescent-limited and life-course persistent antisocial behaviour. *Psychological Review*, 100(4):674–701.

Mogul, J.L., Ritchie, A.J. and Whitlock, K. (2011) *Queer (In)Justice*. Beacon.

Mohamed, A.R. and Fritsvold, E.D. (2010) *Dorm Room Dealers*. Lynne Rienner Publishers.

Møller, L., Stöver, H., et al. (2007) *Health in Prisons: A Who Guide to the Essentials in Prison Health*. World Health Organization.

Monaghan, M. (2012) The recent evolution of UK drug strategies. *People, Place and Policy*, 6(1):29–40.

Monroe, J. and Alexander, R. (2005) C.R.A.C.K. *Journal of African American Studies*, 9(1):19–31.

Moore, K. and Measham, F. (2008) It's the most fun you can have for twenty quid. *Addiction Research and Theory*, 16(3):231–244.

Morgan, K.A.D. (2013) Rastafari. In P. Sutherland, R. Moodley, & B. Chevannes (Eds.), *Caribbean healing traditions*. Taylor and Francis.

Mott, J. (1986) Opioid use and Burglary. *British Journal of Addiction*, 81:671–677.

Mounteney, J., Evans-Brown, M. and Matias, J. (2018) *The Drug Market on the Dark Net: Implications for Prevention, Research, and Policy*. Public Health Institute, LJM.

Moyle, L., Childs, A., et al. (2019) #Drugsforsale. *International Journal of Drug Policy*, 63: 101–110.

Moyle, L. and Coomber, R. (2015) Earning a score. *BJC*, 55(3):534–555.

Moyle, L., Dymock, A., et al. (2021) Reprint of: Pharmacosex: Reimagining sex, drugs and enhancement. *International Journal of Drug Policy*, 95:103282.

Mugford, S. and O'Malley, P. (1991) Heroin policy and deficit models. *Crime, Law and Social Change*, 15:19–36.

Muggleton, D. and Weinzierl, R. (2003) *The Post-Subcultures Reader*. Berg.

Muggleton, D. (2000) *Inside Subculture*. Berg.

Müller, C.M. and Minger, M. (2011) Which children and adolescents are most susceptible to peer influence? *Empirische Sonderpädagogik*, 2:107–129.

Muller (2011) *Animals getting high: 10 common drunks. Australian Geographic*. Available: https://www.australiangeographic

Mundt, A.P. and Baranyi, G. (2020) The unhappy mental health triad. *Frontiers in Psychiatry*, 11:804.

Muniz, C.N., Fox, B., et al. (2019) The effects of adverse childhood experiences on internalizing versus externalizing outcomes, *Criminal Justice and Behavior*, 46(4):568–589.

Murphy, S., et al. (1990) Drifting into dealing. *Qualitative Sociology*, 13(4):321–343.

Murray, C. (1990) *The Emerging British Underclass*. IEA.

Musto, D.F. (1999) *The American Disease*. OUP.

Nadelmann, E. (1992) *America's Drug Problem*. Springer.

Nagin, D. (1998) Criminal deterrence research at the outset of the twenty-first century. *Crime and Justice*, 23:1–42.

Neale, J., Nettleton, S. and Pickering, L. (2013) Does recovery-oriented treatment prompt heroin users prematurely into detoxification and abstinence programmes? *Drug and Alcohol Dependence*, 127(1–3):163–169.

Nencini, P. (1997) The rules of drug taking. *Substance Use & Misuse*, 32(1):89–96.

NEPTUNE. (2016) *Club Drug Use among Lesbian, Gay, Bisexual and Trans (LGBT) People*. Neptune.

Newcomb, M.D., et al. (2001) The drug–crime nexus in a community sample of adults. *Psychology of Addictive Behaviors*, 15(3):185–193.

NHS (2022) *Smoking, Drinking and Drug Use Among Young People in England, 2021*.

NHS. (2024) *Health Survey for England, 2021*.

Nicholls, J. (2009) *The Politics of Alcohol: A History of the Drink Question in England*. Manchester University Press.

NIDA. (2023) *Drug Overdose Death Rates*.

Niveau, G. and Dang, C. (2003) Cannabis and violent crime. *Medicine, Science & the Law*, 43(2):115–121.

NOMS. (2014) *Supporting Community Order Treatment Requirements*.

Norman, C. (2022) A global review of prison drug smuggling routes and trends in the usage of drugs in prisons. *WIREs Forensic Science*, e1473.

NPCC (2012) *Commercial Cultivation of Cannabis*. Available: https://news.npcc.police.uk/releases/acpo-publishes-uk-national-problem-profile-commercial-cultivation-of-cannabis-2012

Nurco, D.N., Blatchley, R.J., et al. (1999)Early deviance and related risk factors in the children of narcotic addicts. *The American Journal of Drug and Alcohol Abuse*, 25 (1):25–45.

Nurco, D.N., Kinlock, T.W., et al. (1996) Early family adversity as a precursor to narcotic addiction. *Drug and Alcohol Dependence*, 43:103–113.

Nurco, D.N., Balter, M.B. and Kinlock, T.W. (1994) Vulnerability to narcotic addiction. *Journal of Drug Issues*, 24(2):292–313.

Nurco, D.N. (1998) A long-term program of research on drug use and crime. *Substance Use and Misuse*, 33(9):1817–1837.

Nutt, D., King, L. and Blakemore, C. (2007) Development of a rational scale to assess the harm of drugs of potential misuse. *The Lancet*, 369(9566):1047 – 1053.

Nutt, D., King, L. and Phillips, L. (2010) Drug harms in the UK. *Lancet*, 376(9752): 1558–1565.

Nutt, D. (2012) *Drugs without the Hot Air*. Bloomsbury.

O'Gorman, A. (2016) Chillin, buzzin, getting mangled, and coming down. *Drugs: Education, Prevention & Policy*, 23(3):247–254.

O'Hagan, A. and Hardwick, R. (2017) Behind bars. *Forensic Research and Criminology International Journal*, 5(3):158.

OHID (2021) *Adult Substance Misuse Treatment Statistics 2020 to 2021*.

OHID (2022) *Alcohol and Drug Treatment in Secure Settings 2020 to 2021*.

ONS (2013) *Deaths Related to Drug Poisoning in England and Wales: 2012*.

ONS (2018) *Adult Smoking Habits in Great Britain: 2017*.

ONS (2021) *Homicide in England and Wales: Year ending March 2020*.

ONS (2022a) *Drug Misuse in England and Wales: Year Ending June 2022*.

ONS (2022b) *Estimates of the Population for the UK, England, Wales, Scotland and Northern Ireland*.

ONS (2022c) *Regional Ethnic Diversity*.

ONS (2022d) *Homicide in England and Wales: Year Ending March 2023*.

ONS (2023) *Drug-related Deaths and Suicide in Prison Custody in England and Wales: 2008 to 2019*.

ONS (2023a) *Drug Misuse in England and Wales: Year Ending March 2023*.

ONS (2023b) *Police Recorded Crime*.

ONS (2023c) *Crime in England and Wales: Police Force Area Data Tables*.

ONS (2023d) *Adult Smoking Habits in England*.

ONS (2023e) *Deaths Related to Drug Poisoning in England and Wales: 2022 Registrations*.

ONS. (2024a) *Crime in England and Wales: Police Force Area Data Tables: Year Ending December 2023*.

ONS (2024b)

Page, G. (2017) *Rapid Review: Drug Treatment in UK Prisons*. https://www.york.ac.uk/media/spru/EPRA.%20Supporting%20paper%201.%20Review%20of%20Drug%20Treatment%20Need%20and%20Effectiveness%20in%20UK%20Prisons.%209.2.2017.pdf

Paley, D. (2014) *Drug War Capitalism*. AK Press.

Palmer, E., Hatcher, R., et al. (2011) Evaluation of the addressing substance-related offending (ASRO) program for substance-using offenders in the community. *Substance Use & Misuse*, 46(8):1072–1080.

Paoli, L. and Reuter, P. (2008) Drug trafficking and ethnic minorities in Western Europe. *European Journal of Criminology*, 5(1):13–37.

Parker, H. and Newcombe, R. (1987) Heroin use and acquisitive crime in an English community. *BJS*, 3:331–350.

Parker, H., Aldridge, J. and Measham, F. (1998) *Illegal Leisure*. Routledge.

Parker, H. (2005) Normalization as a barometer. *Addiction Research and Theory*, 13(3): 205–215.

Parker, H. (2006) Keeping the lid on. *Criminal Justice Matters*, 63(1):6–38.

Parkin, S. and Coomber, R. (2010) Fluorescent blue lights, injecting drug use and related health risk in public conveniences. *Health & Place*, 16(4):629–637.

Pasquali, S.K., Burstein, D.S., et al. (2010) Globalization of pediatric research. *Pediatrics*, 126(3):e687–e692.

Pates, R.M., McBride, A.J., et al. (2001) Towards an holistic understanding of injecting drug use. *Addiction Research and Theory*, 9(1):3–17.

Payne, A. (2009) Girls, boys and schools. *Criminology*, 47(4):1167–1200.

Pearson, G. and Hobbs, D. (2001) *Middle Market Drug Distribution* (p. 227). Home Office Research Study.

Pearson, F. S. and Lipton, D. S. (1999) A meta-analytic review of the effectiveness of corrections-based treatments for drug abuse. *The Prison Journal*, 79(4):384–410.

Pearson, G. (1987) *The New Heroin Users*. Basil Blackwell.

Pearson, G. (2001) Normal drug use. *Substance Use and Misuse*, 36(1–2):167–200.

Peck, J.H., Childs, K., et al. (2018) General strain theory, depression, and substance use, *Journal of Child & Adolescent Substance Abuse*, 27(1):11–28.

Pedersen, W. and Skardhamar, T. (2009) Cannabis and crime. *Addiction*, 105(1):109–118.

Pennay, A.E. and Measham, F.C. (2016) The normalisation thesis-20 years later, *Drugs: Education, Prevention & Policy*, 23(3):187–189.

Petrosino, A., Turpin-Petrosino, C., et al. (2013) 'Scared Straight' and other juvenile awareness programs for preventing juvenile delinquency. *Cochrane Database of Systematic Reviews* 30(4):CD002796.

PHE (2014) *Turning Evidence into Practice: Optimising Opioid Substitution Treatment*.

PHE (2018) *Young People's Statistics from the National Drug Treatment Monitoring System (NDTMS)*.

Pierce, M., Hayhurst, K., et al. (2017) Insights into the link between drug use and criminality. *Drug and Alcohol Dependence*. 179:309–316.

Pilkington, H. (2006) For us it is normal. *Journal of Communist Studies and Transition Politics*, 22(1): 24–53.

Piquero, N. and Sealock, M.D. (2010) Race, crime, and general strain theory. *Youth Violence and Juvenile Justice*, 8(3):170–186.

Pitts, J. (2020) Black young people and gang involvement in London. *Youth Justice*, 20(1–2):146–158.

Police Foundation (2000) *Drugs and the Law*. Available: https://www.police-foundation.org.uk/wp-content/uploads/2017/06/drugs_and_the_law.pdf

Potter, G. and Chatwin, C. (2018) Not particularly special: Critiquing 'NPS' as a category of drugs. *Drugs: Education, Prevention & Policy*, 25(4), 329–336.

Preble, E. and Casey, J. (1969) Taking care of business. *International Journal of the Addictions*, 4:1–24.

Presdee, M. (2000) *Cultural Criminology and the Carnival of Crime*. Routledge.

PRI (2023) *Global Prison Trends, 2023*. PRI.

Prime Ministers Strategy Unit. (2003) *Strategy Unit Drugs Report Phase One-Understanding the Issues*.

Prisciandaro, J.J., McRae-Clark, A.L., et al. (2011) Psychoticism and neuroticism predict cocaine dependence and future cocaine use via different mechanisms. *Drug and Alcohol Dependence*, 116(1–3):80–85.

Prochaska, J. and DiClemente, C. (1983) Stages and processes of self-change of smoking. *Journal of Consulting and Clinical Psychology*, 51(3):390–395.

PRT (2019) *Bromley Briefings Prison Factfile.*

PRT (2022) *Bromley Briefings Prison Factfile.*

PRT (2023) *Bromley Briefings Prison Factfile.*

PRT (2024) *Bromley Briefings Prison Factfile.*

Pryce, S. (2012) *Fixing Drugs*. Palgrave.

Pudney, S., Badillo, C., et al. (2006) Estimating the size of the UK illicit drug market. In N. Singleton, R. Murray and L. Tinsley (Eds.), *Measuring Different Aspects of Problem Drug Use*. Home Office.

Pudney, S. (2002) The Road to Ruin? *The Economic Journal*, 113(486):C182–C198.

Raden-Keefe, P. (2021) *Empire of Pain*. Picador.

Rahaman, S. (2024) UN criticises Sri Lanka police for arresting thousands in war on drugs. *The Independent*, 15 January 2024.

Ralphs, R., Williams, L., et al. (2017) Adding spice to the porridge. *International Journal of Drug Policy*, 40:57–69.

Ralphs, R., Linnell, M. and Sutcliffe, O. (2023) Adult trend focus: Substances associated with chemsex. In *Greater Manchester: Testing and Research on Emergent and New Drugs (GM TRENDS)*. Research Report. Manchester Metropolitan University.

Ramen, T. and Smith, O. (2019) *Deviant Leisure*. Palgrave.

Rasmussen, N. (2008) *On Speed*. NYU Press.

Raymen, T. (2022) *The Enigma of Social Harm*. Routledge.

Reavis, J. and Looman, K.A. and Rojas, F.B. (2013) Adverse childhood experiences and adult criminality: How long must we live before we possess our own lives? *The Permanente Journal*, 17(2):44.

Rebellon, C.J. (2012) Differential association and substance use. *European Journal of Criminology*, 9(1):73–96.

Redhead, S. (1997) *Subculture to Clubcultures*. Wiley-Blackwell.

Reed, M., Kioumarsi, A., et al. (2020) Marijuana sources in a medical marijuana environment. *Drugs: Education, Prevention & Policy*, 27(1):69–78.

Rego, X., Oliveira, M., et al. (2021) 20 years of Portuguese drug policy. *Substance Abuse Treatment, Prevention, and Policy*, 16(59):1–11.

Reinarman, C. and Duskin, C. (1992) Dominant ideology and drugs in the media. *International Journal on Drugs Policy*, 3(1):6–15.

Reinarman, C. (2004) Between genes and determinism. *Drugs and Alcohol Today*, 4:32–34.

Reinarman, C. (2005) Addiction as accomplishment. *Addiction Research and Theory*, 13(4): 307–320.

Reiner, R. (2016) *Crime, the Mystery of the Common-Sense Concept.*

Release (2016) *A Quiet Revolution: Drug Decriminalisation across the Globe*. Available: https://www.release.org.uk/sites/default/files/pdf/publications/A%20Quiet%20Revolution%20-%20Decriminalisation%20Across%20the%20Globe.pdf

Reuter, P. and Kleiman, M.A. (1986) Risks and prices: An economic analysis of drug enforcement. *Crime Justice*, 7:289–340.

Reuter, P. and Stevens, A. (2008) Assessing UK drug policy from a crime control perspective. *Criminology and Criminal Justice*, 8(4):461–482.

Reuter, P. (2009) Systemic violence in drug markets. *Crime, Law and Social Change* 52(3): 275–284.

Reynolds, S. (1999) *Generation Ecstasy*. Routledge.

Rhodes, D. (2018) NHS accused of fuelling rise in opioid addiction. *BBC*, 15th March. Available: https://www.bbc.co.uk/news/uk-england-43304375

Rodrigues, T.B., Souza, M.P., et al. (2022) Synthetic cannabinoid receptor agonists profile in infused papers seized in Brazilian prisons. *Forensic Toxicology*, 40:119–124.

Rolles, S, and Kushlick, D. (2014) Prohibition is a key driver of the new psychoactive substances (NPS) phenomenon. *Addiction*, 109(10):1589–1590.

Rolles, S. and Measham, F. (2011) Questioning the method and utility of ranking drug harms in drug policy. *International Journal of Drug Policy*, 22(4):243–246.

Rolleston Report/UK Government Report (1926) *Report of the Departmental Committee on Morphine and Heroin Addiction.*

Rosenbaum, D.P. and Hanson, G.S. (1998) Assessing the effects of school-based drug education. *Journal of Research in Crime and Delinquency*, 35(4):381–412.

Rosmarin, A. and Eastwood, N. (2012) *A Quiet Revolution: Drug Decriminalisation Policies in Practice across the Globe*. Available: https://www.release.org.uk/sites/default/files/pdf/publications/A%20Quiet%20Revolution%20-%20Decriminalisation%20Across%20the%20Globe.pdf

Rousseau, J.J. (1978) *On the Social Contract*. St. Martin's Press.

Ruggiero, V. and South, N. (1995) *Eurodrugs*. Taylor and Francis.

Ruiz, P. and Strain, E. (2014) *The Substance Abuse Handbook*. Lippincott Williams and Wilkins.

Runciman, R. (2000) *Drugs and the Law*. Available: https://www.police-foundation.org.uk/wp-content/uploads/2017/06/drugs_and_the_law.pdf

Salinas, M. (2018) The unusual suspects. *International Criminal Justice Review*, 28(3):226–242.

Sandberg, S. and Pederson, W. (2011) *Street Capital: Black Cannabis Dealers in a White Welfare State*. Policy Press.

Saper, A. (1974) The making of policy through myth, fantasy and historical accident. *British Journal of Addiction*, 69(2):183–193.

Sawchuck, S. (2021) What is critical race theory, and why is it under attack? *Education Week*, 18th May. Available: https://www.edweek.org/leadership/what-is-critical-race-theory-and-why-is-it-under-attack/2021/05

Schipper, I. (2008) *SOMO Briefing Paper on Ethics in Clinical Trials: Examples of Unethical Trials*.

Schivelbusch, W. (1992) *Tastes of Paradise*. Pantheon.

Scott, D. and Gosling, H. (2016) Before prison, instead of prison, better than prison. *International Journal for Crime, Justice and Social Democracy*, 5(1):52–66.

Scott, D. and Grosholz, J. (2019) Unpacking the racial disparity in crime from a racialized general strain theory perspective. *Deviant Behavior*, 40(12):1445–1463.

Scottish Government (2021) *International Approaches to Drug Law Reform.*

Scottish Government. (2023a). *A Caring, Compassionate and Human Rights Informed Drug Policy for Scotland.*

Scottish Government (2023b). *Drug Law Reform Proposals.*

Secades-Villa, R., Garcia-Rodríguez, O., et al. (2015) Probability and predictors of the cannabis gateway effect. *International Journal of Drug Policy*, 26(2):135–142.

Seddon, T. (2000) Explaining the drug–crime link. *Journal of Social Policy*, 9(1):95–107.

Seddon, T. (2006) Drugs, crime and social exclusion. *BJC*, 46(4):680–703.

Seddon, T. (2007a). The regulation of heroin. *International Journal of the Sociology of Law*, 35(3):143–156.

Seddon, T. (2007b). The hardest drug? In M. Simpson, T. Shildrick and R. MacDonald (Eds.), *Drugs in Britain: Supply, Consumption and Control.* Bloomsbury Publishing.

Seddon, T. (2016) Inventing drugs. *Journal of Law and Society*, 43(3):393–415.

Selbekk, A., Sagvaag, H. and Fauske, H. (2015) Addiction, families and treatment, *Addiction Research and Theory*, 23(3):196–204.

Senior, P., Wong, K., et al. (2011) *Process Evaluation of Five Integrated Offender Management Pioneer Areas.* Available: https://shura.shu.ac.uk/7046/1/Senior_process_Evaluation_of_five.pdf

Sentencing Council (2012) *Drug Offences.*

Sentencing Council (2019) *Statistical Bulletin Drug Offences.*

Sentencing Council (2021) *Drug Offences: Data Tables.*

Sentencing Council. (2023) *Drug Driving (Guidance Only).*

Shaw, C.R. and McKay, H.D. (1972) *Juvenile Delinquency and Urban Areas.*

Shaw, J. (2015) A review of cognitive-behavioral therapy in the UK prison system. *Criminal Behaviour and Mental Health*, 25(1):1–9.

Sheridan, R.B. (1985) *Doctors and Slaves.* CUP.

Shewan, D. and Dalgarno, P. (2005) Evidence for controlled heroin use? *British Journal of Health Psychology*, 10:33–48.

Shewan, D. (2013) *Drug Use in Prisons.* Taylor and Francis.

Shildrick, T. (2002) Young people, illicit drug use and the question of normalization. *Journal of Youth Studies*, 5(1):35–48.

Shiner, M., Carre, Z., et al. (2018) *The colour of injustice: 'Race', drugs and law enforcement in England and Wales.* Available: https://www.lse.ac.uk/united-states/Assets/Documents/The-Colour-of-Injustice.pdf

Shiner, M. and Newburn, T. (1997) Definitely, maybe not? *Sociology,* 31(3):511–529.

Shiner, M. (2009) *Drug Use and Social Change.* Palgrave.

Shiner, M. (2015) Drug policy reform and the reclassification of cannabis in England and Wales: A cautionary tale. *International Journal of Drug Policy*, 26(7): 696–704.

SIBA (2023) *The SIMA Beer Report 2023.* Available: https://www.siba.co.uk/craft-beer-reports/#:~:text=The%20SIBA%20Craft%20Beer%20Report%202022%20%E2%80%93%20shows%20the%20seismic%20shift,and%20drink%20more%20at%20home

Simangan, D. (2018) Is the Philippine 'war on drugs' an act of genocide? *Journal of Genocide Research*, 20(1):68–89.

Simpson, M. (2003) The relationship between drug use and crime. *International Journal of Drug Policy*, 1(4):307–319.

Singer, M. and Mirhej, G. (2006) High notes. *Journal of Ethnicity in Substance Abuse*, 5(4): 1–38.

Singleton, N., Meltzer, H., et al. (1998) *Psychiatric Morbidity of Prisoners in England and Wales*. ONS.

Singleton, N., Farrell, M. and Meltzer, H. (1999) *Substance misuse among prisoners in England and Wales*. ONS.

Sirdifield, C., Brooker, C. and Marples, R. (2020) Substance misuse and community supervision. *Forensic Science International: Mind and Law*, 1:100031.

Skinner, B.F. (1971) *The Behavior of Organisms*.

Smith, O. (2014) *Contemporary Adulthood and NTE*. Springer.

Smith, M.A. (2021) Social learning and addiction. *Behavioural Brain Research*, 398:112954.

South, N. (1999) *Drugs: Cultures, Controls and Everyday Life*. SAGE.

Spicer, J. (2018) That's their brand, their business. *Policing and Society*, 29(8):873–886.

Spicer, J. (2021) Between gang talk and prohibition. *International Journal of Drug Policy*, 87(1):29–36.

Statistics Canada (2023) *Five Years since Legalization, What Have We Learned about Cannabis in Canada?* Available at: https://www150.statcan.gc.ca/n1/daily-quotidien/231016/dq231016c-eng.htm

Stevens, A. and Measham, F. (2014) The 'drug policy Ratchet'. *Addiction*, 109(8):1226–1232.

Stevens, A. (2007) When two dark figures collide. *Critical Social Policy*, 27(1):77–99.

Stevens, A. (2010) Treatment sentences for drug users. In A. Hucklesby and E. Wincup (Eds.), *Drug Interventions in Criminal Justice*. OUP.

Stevens, A. (2011a) *Drugs Crime and Public Health*. Routledge.

Stevens, A. (2011b) A critical reflection on the conceptual frameworks underpinning the war on drugs. *Criminology and Criminal Justice*, 11(4):423–443.

Stevens, A. (2019) Is policy 'liberalization' associated with higher odds of adolescent cannabis use? *International Journal of Drug Policy*, 66:94–99.

Stevens, A. (2020) Critical realism and the 'ontological politics of drug policy'. *International Journal of Drug Policy*, 84:102723.

Stimson, G. (1990) AIDS and HIV. *British Journal of Addiction*, 85(3):329–339.

Stimson, G. (2000) Blair declares war. *International Journal of Drug Policy*, 11(4):259–264.

Strang, J. and Gossop, M. (2005) *Heroin Addiction and Drug Policy*. OUP.

Surratt, H. L., Kurtz, S. P., et al. (2005) The connections of mental health problems, violent life experiences, and the social milieu of the 'stroll' with the substance use behaviors of female street sex workers. *Journal of Psychology & Human Sexuality*, 17(1–2):23–44.

Sutherland, P., Moodley, R. and Chevannes, B. (2013) *Caribbean Healing Traditions*. Routledge.

Sutherland, E. H. (1947) *Principles of Criminology*. Lippincott.

Sutherland, E.H. (1949) *White Collar Crime*. Dryden.

Swogger, M.T., Conner, K.R., Walsh, Z. and Maisto, S.A. (2011) Childhood abuse and harmful substance use among criminal offenders. *Addictive Behaviors*. 36:1205–1212.

Sykes, G. and Matza, D. (1957) Techniques of neutralisation. *American Sociological Review*, 22:664–670.

Sykes, G. (1958) *The Society of Captives: A Study of a Maximum Security Prison*. Princeton University Press.

Szasz, T. (1961) *Myth of Mental Illness*. SUP.

Szasz, T. (1992) *Our Right to Drugs*. SUP.

Szasz, T.S. (2003) *Ceremonial Chemistry*. SUP.

Tannenbaum, F. (1938) *Crime and the Community*. Columbia University Press.

Taylor, S. and Ayres, T.C. (2024) Are we in a drugs apartheid? *Talking Drugs*. Available: https://www.talkingdrugs.org/are-we-in-a-drugs-apartheid/

Taylor, S., Beckett Wilson, H., et al. (2018) Cannabis use in an English community. *Contemporary Drug Problems*, 45(4):401–424.

Taylor, A. and Bennet, T. (1999) Heroin users in the 1990s. *BJC*, 39(4):575–598.

Taylor, S., Burke, L., et al. (2017) Transforming Rehabilitation during a penal crisis. *European Journal of Probation*, 9(2):115–131.

Taylor, S., Buchanan, J. and Ayres, T.C. (2016) Prohibition, privilege and the drug apartheid. *Criminology and Criminal Justice*, 16(4):452–469.

Taylor, S., Ayres, T.C. and Jones, E. (2020) Enlightened hedonism? *International Journal of Drug Policy*, 83:102869.

Taylor, S. (2008) Outside the outsiders. *Probation Journal*, 55(4):369–388.

Taylor, S. (2011) New Strategy, usual suspects. *Criminal Justice Matters*, 84(1):24-26.

Taylor, S. (2016) Moving beyond the other. *Tijdschrift over Cultuur and Criminaliteit*, 6:100–118.

Teague, R., Mazerolle, P., et al. (2008) Linking childhood exposure to physical abuse and adult offending. *Justice Quarterly*, 25(2):313–348.

The Guardian (2001) The Strong Society: Rights, responsibilities and reform (part two). *The Guardian*, 30 May 2001.

The Lancet (2022) *Managing the Opioid Crisis in North America and beyond*. Available: https://doi.org/10.1016/S0140-6736(22)00200-8

Theobald, D. and Farrington, D.P. (2014) Onset of offending. In G. Bruinsman and D. Weisburd (Eds.), *Encyclopedia of Criminology and Criminal Justice*. Springer.

Thompson, H. (2014) *How Witches' Brews Helped Bring Modern Drugs to Market*. Available: https://www.smithsonianmag.com/science-nature/how-witches-brews-helped-bring-modern-drugs-market-180953202/

Tompkins, C. (2015) There's that many people selling it. *Drugs: Education, Prevention & Policy*, 23(2):144–153.

Tonry, M. and Wilson, J. (1990) *Drugs and Crime*. University of Chicago Press.

Tonry, M. (2004) Racial politics, racial disparities, and the war on crime. *Crime and Delinquency*, 40(4):475–494.

Tonry, M. (2011) *Punishing Race*. Oxford University Press.

Transform (2014) *Drug Decriminalisation in Portugal: Setting the Record Straight*.

Transform (2018) *Cannabis Legalisation in Uruguay: Public Health and Safety over Private Profit*.

Transform (2021) *Drug Decriminalisation in Portugal: Setting the Record Straight*.

Transform (2022) *The Tortured Double Think of the New Drug Strategy*.

Treadwell, J., Ancrum, C. and Kelly, C. (2018) Taxing times. *Deviant Behavior*, 41(1):57–69.

Treadwell, J. (2013) *Criminology*. SAGE.

Turnbull, P. and Skinns, L. (2010) The drug intervention programme. In A. Hucklesby and E. Wincup (Eds.), *Drug Interventions in Criminal Justice*. OUP.

Turnbull, P., Hough, M. and McSweeney, T. (2000) *Drug Treatment and Testing Orders*.

UKDPC (2008) *Reducing Drug Use, Reducing Reoffending*.

UKDPC (2010a) *Drugs and Diversity*.

UKDPC (2010b) *Getting Serious about Stigma.*

UN (1953) *Protocol for Limiting and Regulating the Cultivation of the Poppy Plant, the Production of, International and Wholesale Trade in, and Use of Opium.*

UN (2021) *United Nations System Common Position on Incarceration.* Available at: https://www.unodc.org/res/justice-and-prison-reform/nelsonmandelarules-GoF/UN_System_Common_Position_on_Incarceration.pdf

UNODC (2011) *Estimating Illicit Financial Flows Resulting from Drug Trafficking and Other Transnational Organised Crime Groups.*

UNODC (2015) *The United Nations Standard Minimum Rules for the Treatment of Prisoners (The Nelson Mandela Rules).*

UNODC (2022a) *Afghan Women and the Opiate Trade.*

UNODC (2022b) *World Drug Report 2022. Report 4: Drug Market Trends.*

UNODC (2022c) *Drug Market Trends: Cannabis Opioids.*

UNODC (2023) *Afghanistan Opium Survey 2023.*

User Voice (2016) *Spice: The Bird Killer.* Available: https://www.uservoice.org/wp-content/uploads/2020/07/User-Voice-Spice-The-Bird-Killer-Report-compressed.pdf

Vadivelu, N., Kai, A.M., et al. (2018) The opioid crisis. *Current Pain and Headache Reports,* 22:16.

van Amsterdam, J., Nutt, D., Phillips, L. et al. (2015) European rating of drug harms. *Journal of Psychopharmacology,* 29(6):655–660.

Vannostrand, L. M. and Tewksbury, R. (1999) The motives and mechanics of operating an illegal drug enterprise. *Deviant Behavior,* 20(1):57–83.

Vasilenko, S.A., Evans-Polce, R.J. and Lanza, S.T. (2017) Age trends in rates of substance use disorders across ages 18-90. *Drug and Alcohol Dependence,* 1(180):260–264.

Vaughn, M.G., Qiang, F., et al. (2010) Is crack cocaine use associated with greater violence than powdered cocaine use? *The American Journal of Drug and Alcohol Abuse,* 36(4): 181–186.

Vaughn, M.G., Salas-Wright, C.P., et al. (2015) Crime and violence among MDMA users in the United States. *AIMS Public Health,* 2(1):64–73.

Vazquez, V., Giros, B. and Daugé, V. (2006) Maternal deprivation specifically enhances vulnerability to opiate dependence. *Behavioural Pharmacology,* 17(8):715–724.

Vazsonyi, A., Pickering, L., et al. (2001) An empirical test of a general theory of crime. *Journal of Research in Crime and Delinquency,* 38:91–131.

Verhulst, B., Neale, M.C. and Kendler, K.S. (2015) The heritability of alcohol use disorders. *Psychological Medicine,* 45(5):1061–1072.

Villar, O. (2007) U.S. Narcocolonialism? In P. Zarembka (Ed.), *Transitions in Latin America and in Poland and Syria.* Emerald Group Publishing Limited.

Voeks, R.A. (1997) *Sacred Leaves of candomblé.* University of Texas Press.

Volkow, N.D., Fowler, J.S. and Wang, G.J. (2003) The addicted human brain. *Journal of Clinical Investigation,* 111(10):1444–14451.

Volkow, N.D., Koob, G.F. and McLellan, A.T. (2016) Neurobiologic advances from the brain disease model of addiction. *New England Journal of Medicine,* 374(4):363–371.

Volkow, N.D. (2001) Drug abuse and mental illness. *American Journal of Psychiatry,* 158(8): 1181–1183.

Wacquant, L. (2009) *Punishing the Poor.* Duke.

Wakeling, H. and Lynch, K. (2020) *Exploring Substance Use in Prisons*. Available: https://www.drugsandalcohol.ie/33284/1/HMPPS_Exploring-substance-use-prisons.pdf

Wakeman, S. (2014) No one wins. *Theoretical Criminology*, 18(2):224–240.

Wakeman, S. (2015) Prescribing heroin for addiction. *Criminology and Criminal Justice*, 15: 578–593.

Walklate, S. (2007) *Understanding Criminology*.

Walmsley, I. (2019) Drugs decriminalization: In: S. Wilson (Ed.), *Prohibitions and Psychoactive Substances in History, Culture and Theory*. Routledge.

Walsh, C. (2016) Psychedelics and cognitive liberty: Reimagining drug policy through the prism of human rights. *International Journal of Drug Policy*, 29:80–87.

Wanberg, K. and Milkman, H. (1998) *Criminal Conduct and Substance Abuse Treatment Strategies for Self-Improvement and Change*. SAGE.

Warburton, H., May, T. and Hough, M. (2005) Looking the other way. *BJC*, 45(2):113–128.

Warner, J. (2003) *Craze: Gin and Debauchery in an Age of Reason*. Profile Books.

Webster, R. (2018) *Young People Unable to Access Drug and Alcohol Treatment*. Available: http://www.russellwebster.com/ypndtms18/

Webster, E. (2021) *Drug Driving: The Tip of the Iceberg?* Available: https://www.pacts.org.uk/wp-content/uploads/PACTS-Drug-Driving-The-tip-of-an-iceberg-3.0.pdf

Wechsler, H. and Nelson, T. F. (2001) Binge drinking and the American college student. *Journal of American College Health*, 50(2):101–113.

Weerman, F.M., Harland, P. and van der Laan, P.H. (2007) Misbehavior at school and delinquency elsewhere. *Criminal Justice Review*, 32(4):358–379.

Weil, A. and Ronsen, W. (2004) *From Chocolate to Morphine*. Houghton Mifflin.

Weisburd, D., & Mazerolle, L. G. (2000) Crime and disorder in drug hot spots. *Police Quarterly*, 3(3):331–349.

Weiss, K. and Colyer, C. (2010) Roofies, mickies and cautionary tales. *Deviant Behavior*, 31(4):348–379.

Weissman, M.M., et al. (2006) Long-term effects of cognitive therapy for depression. *Journal of the American Medical Association*, 296(3):263–270.

Wesson, D.R. (2011) Psychedelic drugs, hippie counterculture, speed and phenobarbital treatment of sedative-hypnotic dependence. *Journal of Psychoactive Drugs*, 43(2): 153–164.

Wheatley, M. (2007) Drug Misuse in Prison. In Y. Jewkes, J. Bennett and B. Crewe (Eds.), *Handbook of Prisons* (2nd edn.). Willan.

Whitaker, V., Curtis, P., et al. (2023) Young people's explanations for the decline in youth drinking in England. *BMC Public Health*, 23:402.

White, H.R., Loeber, R., et al. (1999) Developmental associations between substance use and violence. *Development and Psychopathology*, 11:785–803.

WHO (2006) *Intimate Partner Violence and Alcohol*. Available: https://womensaidorkney.org.uk/wp-content/uploads/2014/08/WHO-IPA-and-Alcohol-Fact-sheet.pdf

Widom, C.S., Marmorstein, N.R. and White, H.R. (2006) Childhood victimization and illicit drug use in middle adulthood. *Psychology of Addictive Behaviors*, 20(4):394–403.

Willmot, P. and Jones, L. (2022) *Trauma-Informed Forensic Practice*. Routledge.

Wills, T. A., Pokhrel, P., et al. (2011) Behavioral and emotional regulation and adolescent substance use problems. *Psychology of Addictive Behaviors*, 25(2):279–292.

Wills, T.A., Vaccaro, D. and McNamara, G. (1992) The role of life events family support and competence in adolescent substance use. *American Journal of Community Psychology*, 20(3):349–374.

Wilson, J.Q. and Kelling, G.L. (1982) Broken windows. *Atlantic Monthly*, March 29–38.

Wilson, L. and Stevens, A. (2008) *Understanding Drug Markets and How to Influence Them*. Beckley Foundation.

Wilson, J.Q. (1975) *Thinking about Crime*. Basic Books.

Wilson, A. (2008) *Northern Soul*. Routledge.

Winlow, S. (2014) Trauma, guilt and the unconscious. *The Sociological Review*, 62:32–49.

Winstock, A.R. and Barratt, M.J. (2013) Synthetic cannabis. *Drug and Alcohol Dependence*, 131(1–2):106–111.

Wintour, P. (2014) Drugs legalisation: Cameron stands firm despite Lib Dem pressure. *The Guardian*, 31 October 2014.

Wood, D., Measham, F. and Dargan, P. (2012) Our favourite drug. *Journal of Substance Use*, 17(2):91–97.

Wootson, C. (2017) One politician's solution to the overdose problem: Let addicts die. *Washington Post*, 30 June.

Wright, R. and Decker, S. (1997) *Armed Robbers in Action*. Northeaster University Press.

Wright, R.A. and Miller, J.M. (1998) Taboo until today? *Journal of Criminal Justice*, 26(1): 1–19.

Yochelson, S. and Samenow, S. (1976) *The Criminal Personality*. Rowman and Littlefield.

Young, J. and Matthews, R. (1992) *Rethinking Criminology*. SAGE.

Young, J. (1971) *The Drugtakers*. Paladin.

Yousef, N. (2023) Canadian cannabis market struggles five years after legalisation. *BBC*, 17 October.

Zheng, Z., Fiddes, K. and Yang, L.A. (2021) A narrative review on environmental impacts of cannabis cultivation. *J Cannabis Res*, 3:35.

Ziavrou, K., Noguera, S. and Boumba, V. (2022) Trends in counterfeit drugs and pharmaceuticals before and during COVID-19 pandemic. *Forensic Science International*, 338:111382.

Zinberg, N.E. (1984) *Drug, Set, and Setting*. Yale University Press.

INDEX

Zeitfracht Medien GmbH
Ferdinand-Jühlke-Straße 7
99095 Erfurt, Deutschland
produktsicherheit@kolibri360.de

T u l i p s

Hannah Quinlan & Rosie Hastings
with Christina B. Hanhardt

KONTEXT

Contents

Marsha P. Johnson (left) and Sylvia Rivera (right), captured by amateur photographer Leonard Funk during the Christopher Street Liberation Day March, 1973. Johnson, along with Rivera and other transgender women, were influential in launching the protests surrounding Stonewall in 1969. In 1970, she and Rivera co-founded the activist group Street Transvestite Action Revolutionaries (STAR) to support homeless transgender individuals and drag queens. Since then, she has become a prominent face of the Queer Revolution.

“No pride for some of us without liberation for all of us.”

—Marsha P. Johnson

Editor's Note

Matthias Kliefoth

In this installment of the *Kontext* book series, Christina B. Hanhardt eloquently recounts an overlooked history of gentrification, security, sexuality, and racism. In the essay "Broken Windows at Blue's: A Queer History of Gentrification and Policing," the author takes a look at the history of New York as one center of the American queer movement, spanning from the incisive events of the late 1960s around the Stonewall Inn in Greenwich Village—now one of New York City's 109 official landmarks—to the gentrification and violent repression of the gay, lesbian, and trans communities of Times Square in the 1980s. In her examination of the roles of trans and BIPOC people, sex workers, and gay homeless people, the author shows how these communities were equally as affected by internal power structures as other heteronormative systems in capitalist society. Although the majority of the participants in the Stonewall riots were drag queens or Black and Latina trans women, those who profited most from New York City's subsequent security policies were primarily white homosexual men, who eventually became a key demographic for real estate companies and thus accelerated the process of gentrification.

Hanhardt's account of the violent repression of the LGBTQ+ community, the unequal treatment of individual groups within the community by political directives, and the exercise of power by the police and city administration of New York in the 1970s and 80s offers a variety of parallels to the present: More than thirty years later, the Christopher Street Day parade in Belgrade could only take place under police protection, with only 1,000 people demonstrating for the rights of gays, lesbians, and other members of the LGBTQ+ community. Meanwhile in Istanbul, the Pride parade was banned entirely, and in the summer of 2022, the weekend witnessed over 200 violent arrests. In the same year, the number of trans- and homophobic attacks in Berlin rose to a new high: 456 attacks were recorded, whereas in 2020 the number was at 277 cases, according to a monitoring report compiled by the nonprofit organization Camino and funded by the Senate Department for Justice, Consumer Protection and Anti-Discrimination. The report describes a "double invisibility" in relation to the increase of attacks and the reporting patterns of women* and lesbians within the larger set of queer people. This phenomenon is also likely to apply to homeless people and BIPOC queers who experience "double" violence as a result of their social status, immigrant background, or skin color.

The invitation to Christina B. Hanhardt developed out of intensive exchanges with the artists Hannah Quinlan and Rosie Hastings, who bring Hanhardt's essay into dialogue with works freely arranged throughout this book. The duo uses the traditional medium of fresco painting to depict street scenes with groups of people who represent various power dynamics, class and social relations, as well as positions of authority. Their collaborative work draws on their ongoing research into the relationships between public space, architecture, state infrastructure, gender, and sexual identity. Viewers are invited to question how public space is developed and who controls it today, yesterday, and tomorrow.

BROKEN WINDOWS AT BLUE'S:

Christina B. Hanhardt

A QUEER HISTORY OF GENTRIFICATION AND POLICING

On September 29, 1982, over thirty New York City police officers raided Blue's, a bar in Manhattan's Times Square. The following year, activist James Credle testified at congressional hearings on police misconduct, describing the brutal beatings of the Black and Latino gay men and trans people who made up the bar's main clientele.[1] The event galvanized lesbian, gay, bisexual, and transgender (LGBT) activists for whom police violence was a primary concern. Although one mention of a rally made it into the New York Times, Credle noted in his testimony that the incident itself had been ignored by major media outlets, an insult certainly made worse by the fact that the bar sat across the street from the Times's own headquarters.[2]

Gay activist and journalist Arthur Bell wrote a front-page story about the raid for the alternative weekly the Village Voice. In it, he quoted Inspector John J. Martin, commanding officer of the Midtown South Precinct, who described Blue's as "a very troublesome bar" with "a lot of undesirables" and "a place that transvestites are drawn to ... probably for narcotics use." Bell also noted the striking contrast between the raid and another press-worthy event held that same night: a black tie dinner, $150 a plate, sponsored by the Human Rights Campaign Fund (HRCF), a gay and lesbian political action committee, at the Waldorf Astoria Hotel with a keynote by former vice president Walter Mondale.[3]

Years earlier, Bell had written about a much more famous police raid and response, which had taken place at the Stonewall Inn bar on June 28, 1969. At the time, police raids of gay bars were common, and bar owners often sought protection through payoffs to the police. On June 28, however, the Stonewall patrons and others socializing outside the bar responded to the unexpected raid with a three-day rebellion that is now credited with spurring a more militant and visible LGBT movement. In the decade following the

1 James Credle, "November 28, 1983: Police Brutality: The Continual Erosion of Our Most Basic Rights," in *Speaking for Our Lives: Historical Speeches and Rhetoric for Gay and Lesbian Rights*, ed. Robert Ridinger (Binghamton, NY: Harrington Press, 2004).

2 "Marchers Protest Raid on 43rd Street Bar," New York Times, October 16, 1982. Eric Lerner also noted the lack of major media coverage for the raid in "Militant Blues Rally Draws 1,100," New York Native, November 8–21, 1982, as did Sarah Schulman and Peg Byron in "Who Wants to Drive Blues Out of Business?" *WomaNews*, November 1982, reprinted in Sarah Schulman, *My American History: Lesbian and Gay Life During the Reagan Years* (New York: Routledge, 1994), 54–6.

3 Arthur Bell, "Black Tie and Blood," Village Voice, October 12, 1982, 1.

Stonewall uprising, police abuse remained a problem for many LGBT people, but it was joined by growing concerns about general street safety. In response, many activists attempted to convince the public that gay life was far from "undesirable" and could even be seen as a valuable asset in a city in which the discourses of crime and economic crises had become tightly intertwined. In September 1977, for example, the gay magazine Christopher Street featured a cover story titled "Can Gays Save New York City?" that included a picture of two men embracing a miniaturized image of Lower Manhattan and asked, "How many neighborhoods in Manhattan would be slums by now, had gay singles and couples not moved in and helped maintain and upgrade them?"[4] The magazine often addressed itself to the question of how gay men were reshaping the landscape of New York, regularly featuring New Yorker-style cartoons that poked fun at gay men who were developing niche businesses or at the supposed value of gayness to new forms of industry.[5] In another issue, the editors celebrated urban scholarship highlighting the leadership of gay men in "revitalization" efforts, describing their creativity, adaptability, ego, and openness to risk-taking as key features for achieving success in a speculation-based economy.[6]

For many commentators, new gay investment in the central city was understood to be part of a broader process of middle-class reinvestment in urban areas—what became known as the "back-to-the-city" movement. Often called "gay gentrification," the phenomenon of new, concentrated gay investment was debated not only by gay journalists but also by city boosters and developers, scholars, and activists, many of whom linked the rise of gay social movements with the growth of gay neighborhoods. These gay neighborhoods, they argued, provided a kind of protection for those escaping the presumed anti-gay sentiments of non-urban areas. Cast in such general terms, though, these arguments primarily described a professional class of white gay men, assumed, unlike LGBT people

4 David Rothenberg, "Can Gays Save New York City?" Christopher Street, September 1977, 9.
5 Cartoons include one in which the sign for a toy store has been renamed "Toys 'R' S&M," with the caption "A major firm seeks a market with a higher discretionary income." In another, two men in T-shirts reading "Le Hunk" chat on the street next to a car labeled "Le Car" and a sign that reads "Le Gay Ghetto." In a third, two men tell a professionally dressed woman, "We divide all of the work. I do the dishes and he gentrifies."
6 "Out & Around: Brownstoning," Christopher Street, August 1976, 3.

in general, to be free of the obligations of family, territorial, and suited to the so-called *new* service economy.[7]

But as the raid on Blue's attests, there were many other people —including many white gay men—pursuing same-sex intimacy, non-normative kinship arrangements, and gender expressions that did not conform to mainstream expectations who did not profit from restructuring real estate markets. Liberal and conservative policy makers alike condemned what they saw to be the erosion of traditional family values and gender roles as a sexual zeitgeist gone too far and among the key causes of the "social disorder" that threatened urban cores. They invoked still-popular "culture of poverty" arguments that blamed Black low-income mothers and praised new zoning restrictions that targeted public spaces and businesses in these areas. *Disorder* as a category would be crafted through the very strategies used to contain and curtail it, in policing philosophy as well as models of municipal governance, and in attacks on not only social uprisings but also the daily lives of those increasingly cast as a "permanent underclass."

In fact, at the same time that gay people's affirmative role in real estate was being praised by the mainstream and alternative press, journalists and social scientists were also publicizing theories about the need for police practice to target disorder and the "discovery" of an often amorphously defined sector of the supposedly intractable poor. In 1982, the year of the Blue's raid, criminologists George L. Kelling and James Q. Wilson introduced the ethos of "broken windows" policing to the broader public via the Atlantic magazine, and journalist Ken Auletta published *The Underclass* based on a series of articles from the New Yorker. Broken windows theory emphasizes the problem of disorderliness on residents' sense of safety and in particular the effect of destabilizing, unfamiliar elements, including "loiterers," "rowdy teenagers," "drunks," "prostitutes," and the "mentally disturbed."[8]

Similarly, Auletta explained that the contemporary underclass

7 This argument was most famously elaborated by geographer Manuel Castells, "City and Culture: The San Francisco Experience," in *The City and the Grassroots: A Cross-Cultural Theory of Urban Society Movements* (Berkeley: University of California Press, 1983), 97–172.

8 George L. Kelling and James Q. Wilson, "Broken Windows: The Police and Neighborhood Safety," Atlantic, March 1982.

consisted of the "hard-core unemployed," which he summarized in the pages of the New Yorker as "criminals, drug addicts, or pushers, alcoholics, [and] welfare mothers."[9] The HRCF's event committee for its fundraiser at the Waldorf Astoria included senators Daniel Patrick Moynihan and Edward Kennedy (who did not, however, appear in person). Unlike the politically conservative architects of broken windows theory, Moynihan and Kennedy were liberals. Yet their respective ideas about a culture of poverty and a permanent underclass were easy fits with broken windows theory, insofar as all three revolved around diagnosing cultural pathology and regulating the social norms of the poor.[10]

In these shared contexts, then, disorder functioned as a catchall for poverty in general as well as for specific forms of unregulated street life. It was also a convenient description for those seen as obstructions to the urban improvements promised by a new middle class. Since then, gentrification has proven to be ongoing and global, and policing approaches based on broken windows theory —also known as "order maintenance" policing—have been central to the cycles of devalorization and revalorization that have reshaped New York City and cities around the world.[11] In 1993, William J. Bratton was appointed New York City's police commissioner for the first time. Empowered by a decade of broken windows policing in New York's transit system (including under his own leadership), Bratton quickly crafted a city-wide police strategy of "zero tolerance" for "quality of life" infractions, escalating the enforcement and punishment of misdemeanor crimes, particularly in public spaces.

Bratton's approach was first tested in Greenwich Village, home to the famed Stonewall riots and one of the world's best-known gay enclaves.[12] Among its key targets were nonresident LGBT people

9 Ken Auletta, "The Underclass—I," New Yorker, November 16, 1981, 63. See also Auletta, *The Streets Were Paved with Gold* (New York: Random House, 1979) and *The Underclass* (New York: Random House, 1982).

10 When he was the assistant secretary of labor, Moynihan authored the 1965 report "The Negro Family: The Case for National Action," which explained African American poverty as due to cultural practices passed down though matriarchal families. The term "permanent underclass" was used by Kennedy in 1978 at an NAACP dinner in Detroit to describe persistent poverty and was reported by Ken Auletta in "The Underclass—I" and *The Underclass*.

11 See Neil Smith, *The New Urban Frontier: Gentrification and the Revanchist City* (London: Routledge, 1996).

12 Clifford Krauss, "Efforts on Quality of Life in Village a Success, the Police Say," New York Times, June 24, 1994. Also see Tanya Erzen and Andrea McArdle, eds., *Zero Tolerance: Quality of Life and the New Police Brutality in New York City* (New York: New York University Press, 2001).

of color who enjoyed the neighborhood's abundance of LGBT-oriented services and reputation as a safe haven for LGBT people. As the strategy expanded across the city, it was governed by the logic of its different spatial contexts: taking aim at homeless people and workers in the informal economy in tourist zones (such as Times Square); at unregulated street life in newly gentrified areas; and, in the form of "stop and frisk," at Black and Latino men, especially in parts of the city devalued long enough to become new hot spots for speculative investment.

In this way, it is clear how *queerness*—both as an umbrella term for lesbian, gay, bisexual, and transgender identities and as a lens for examining the operation of power via normalization, stigma, and kinship regulation—offers a helpful analytic for understanding the intersection of gentrification and order maintenance policing. The celebration of gay investment alongside attacks like the one at Blue's demonstrates the often bifurcated function of marginalized identity and social non-normativity in postwar urban development policy. Here certain lesbian and gay claims of vulnerability and calls for safety, especially those paired with or perceived as amenable to redevelopment, are celebrated at the same time that those who stand outside of white, middle-class heterosexuality (including many lesbians and gay men) continue to be targeted by police strategies that pave the way for that selective reinvestment. This framework also allows for a more complex play of identity in urban political economy more generally, refusing to substitute individual choice in the marketplace for a structural critique of capitalism or dismiss the functions of race, gender, or sexuality in ordering the city. Most important, it is an argument that has been developed by a variety of activists, then and now.

Times Square, 1982

The raid on Blue's was violent and destructive. Bell, Credle, and other observers described the scene they encountered the next morning: blood pooled on the floor and streaked across the wall; furniture, liquor bottles, glasses, pinball machines, and mirrors smashed to fragments; and spent bullets scattered on the floor.

Those present reported being beaten with nightsticks and called anti-gay and racist epithets as officers threatened to kill them and stole their money and identification. In turn, the police claimed that the raid was a response to a fight that got out of hand. Yet Bell noted in his coverage that, although the police reported that some officers had been injured, they had arrested none of the bar-goers. Activists and journalists—mostly in the gay and leftist press—suggested that the raid had been part of an ongoing effort to "clean up" Times Square. This effort would have included Operation Crossroads, initiated by Mayor Edward Koch in 1978, which had tripled the police presence in the neighborhood and focused on "hustlers," "prostitutes," "drifters," and "drug sellers." That year, the city also passed a new zoning regulation restricting "adult physical culture" (primarily massage parlors).[13] People familiar with the bar also pointed fingers at New York Times reporters, whom they suspected had called in complaints about patrons of Blue's hanging out on the street.[14] Activist James Credle's observation (described at this chapter's beginning)—that the mainstream press had ignored the raid—can thus be understood as part of a broad indictment; it pointed not only to the paper's failure to recognize the police violence experienced by the gay and trans people of color next door, but also to its literal investment in policing strategies like Operation Crossroads. Writers such as Sarah Schulman and Peg Byron explicitly named gentrification in their coverage of the incident.[15] In fact, police efforts to "clean up" Times Square promised to raise the value not only of the Times headquarters but also, more importantly, of its biggest advertisers and, ultimately, to fuel the city growth machine. As John Logan and Harvey Molotch have shown, major city newspapers often serve as growth boosters across urban regions, advocating for development that will increase subscribers and, in turn, advertiser revenue. The New York Times has long applied this strategy.[16]

13 Selwyn Raab, "Koch Gets Plan for Cleanup of Times Sq. by 1980," New York Times, July 3, 1978; Selwyn Raab, "Police Manpower Tripled in the Times Square Area," New York Times, June 13, 1978.
14 "Midtown Cops Go Berserk in Gay Bar," New York Native, October 11–24, 1982, 1; Bell, "Black Tie and Blood."
15 Sarah Schulman and Peg Byron, "Who Wants to Drive Blues Out of Business?
16 John Logan and Harvey Molotch, *Urban Fortunes: The Political Economy of Place* (Berkeley: University of California Press, 1987), 70–3.

True to form, in 1981, the paper had celebrated Times Square as undergoing a "revival," in which the area was at last to be saved from "sin and decay" with the assistance of private funds, following an (albeit failed) Ford Foundation initiative (whose own offices were further east on 42nd Street).[17] By the time of the Blue's raid, the transformation of Times Square had reached a fevered pitch; no fewer than five theaters were destroyed in 1982 alone to clear the way for luxury hotel development.[18] These projects were facilitated by popular claims about supposed new forms of disruptive, self-chosen poverty. Drawing on a colorful vocabulary and detailed descriptions, journalists and other writers generated categories of people ("bag ladies," for example) and named them as the most difficult denizens of the broader Times Square area: "In the notorious section of midtown surrounding the Port Authority bus terminal, amid throngs of workers, transients, and tourists, lives a compact society of outsiders," feminist Alix Kates Shulman wrote. "Hustlers, hookers, three-card monte players, con men, drug dealers, jack-rollers (thieves who specialize in robbing the poor of their welfare funds) work over their marks between Times Square and the Stroll, that strip of Eighth Avenue serviced by prostitutes and pimps."[19] It is thus no surprise that a policing theory targeting signs of so-called disorder would gain approval in the press, which, in turn, would help build popular consensus in support of it. While broken windows certainly had precedent in other forms of anti-poverty doctrine, racial segregation, and status-based policing, the theory would appeal to a broader political swath than the conservative criminologists who coined it.[20] Developed out of local studies of police foot patrols, based particularly in nearby Newark,

17 Ralph Blumenthal, "A Times Square Revival?" New York Times, December 27, 1981.
18 John Corry, "Broadway Stages a Drama to Save 2 Theaters," New York Times, March 5, 1982.
19 Alix Kates Shulman, "Bag Ladies," New York Times, September 29, 1981. It is worth noting that in her essay Shulman critiques the language of pathology and blame. Samuel R. Delany has written eloquently of life in Times Square during this period, confirming the existence of a cross-class community forged through sexual exchange while noting the often exploitative aspects of the drug economy. He also notes the devastating impact of redevelopment, arguing that it destroyed supportive social networks and replaced the intimacy of "contact" with the depersonalizing structures of profit motives. Samuel R. Delany, *Times Square Red, Times Square Blue* (New York: NYU Press, 1999).
20 For earlier models of policing, see Khalil Gibran Muhammad, *The Condemnation of Blackness: Race, Crime, and the Making of Modern America* (Cambridge: Harvard University Press, 2011) and David Garland, *The Culture of Control: Crime and Social Order in Contemporary Society* (Chicago: University of Chicago Press, 2002).

New Jersey, during the 1970s, the theory focused less on the immediate reduction of crime per se than on the perception of safety, under the assumption that certain environments cultivated future criminal opportunity. As Kelling and Wilson argued, cops working their beats, in collaboration with local residents, were best equipped to identify who belonged and who did not and to quell signs of disorder lest they lead to escalating crime.
Kelling and Wilson drew on the research of Philip Zimbardo to explain this causal relationship. In Zimbardo's famous social psychology experiment, a run-down and seemingly abandoned car led anonymous bystanders to cause it even greater damage. Yet Kelling and Wilson interpreted abuse of the built environment narrowly: quality-of-life policing should target graffiti, per their theory, but not surrounding buildings dilapidated due to landlord neglect. The majority of the theory's examples of disorder, moreover, are not physical but manifest instead in the status and practices of marginalized *individuals*, who are then considered eligible for arrest.
The emphasis on the primacy of an individual's sense of safety or fear, the proposed solution of citizen-police collaboration, and the idea that signs of disorder might lead to bigger threats were, at the time, not only tenets of conservatism but consistent as well with the approach to inequality adopted by postwar liberal politics. The influence of social psychology and faith in the power of rational choice as well as the idea that liberal politics could coexist easily with greater police power bolstered rather than loosened the relationship between the police and the new middle-class communities moving into central city regions abandoned by capital years before.[21] In the case of the new lesbian and gay movement, the social liberalism that celebrated sexual freedom would be understood by some to support place-based land claims, an argument that required separating the terms of sexual/kinship non-normativity from lesbian and gay identity formation. Moreover, gay and lesbian activists held a newly formed belief that individualized, violent threat might be made manifest and promised by the representational signs of the city.

21 See Christopher Lowen Agee, *The Streets of San Francisco: Policing and the Creation of a Cosmopolitan Liberal Politics, 1950–1972* (Chicago: University of Chicago Press, 2014).

Safe in the City

Prior to the late 1960s and early 1970s, the idea of a gay neighborhood as it is commonly held today did not exist, and LGBT people were most associated with areas that housed a range of other social outsiders—such as artists and bohemians, drug users, sex workers, and those made itinerant due to poverty, often in areas considered to be vice districts or skid rows.[22] The risk of street violence was rarely understood as shared by all gay people; instead, police abuse stood at the fore, and activists—in some cases associated with War on Poverty programs—tied the problem of policing to street cleanups intended to facilitate new development. They also fought criminalization and stigma, drawing, as historian Christopher Agee has shown, on the concept of the "harm principle" (arguing that acts that hurt no one should not be considered crimes) and fighting status-based anti-vagrancy laws, both of which disproportionately targeted homosexuals.[23] And, like many participants in the Great Society, they drew on liberal psychology to emphasize the healthiness of prideful identification and increasingly framed "gay" as an affirmative identity rather than simply a stigmatized practice. But in the process of distinguishing homosexuality from categories of harm—those labeled as criminal, sick, or causing psychic damage—the racial and economic associations of those other stigmatized practices were left intact. By the start of the 1970s, popular acceptance of homosexuality had grown, and realtors began marketing gay people as the ideal *tenants* of changing neighborhoods, focusing especially on middle-class white gay men as high-earning, risk-taking, and family-free. But, in an important distinction, the celebration of renters and owners did not include those whose displays of *queerness* primarily took the form of public intimacy, gender non-conformity, or participation in street-based economies. As one journalist explained in late 1969, vice districts that were associated with public

22 The middle sections of this essay draw significantly on research from my book *Safe Space: Gay Neighborhood History and the Politics of Violence* (Durham, NC: Duke University Press, 2013), which provides a longer and more detailed history of LGBT activism and neighborhood politics.
23 For an excellent discussion of the function of the harm principle in gay urban organizing, see Agee, *The Streets of San Francisco;* on gay challenges to vagrancy laws, see Nan Alamilla Boyd, *Wide Open Town: A History of Queer San Francisco to 1965* (Berkeley: University of California Press, 2005).

and commercial sex, such as Times Square, were not considered to be gay neighborhoods since their "gay legions are transient rather than permanent."[24]

Gay neighborhoods emerged alongside a growing movement that had inherited from earlier activism commitments to fighting police abuse and arguing that homosexuality be designated as neither a crime nor an illness. But as the decade continued, vulnerability to violence as a general category was increasingly cast as a unifying gay experience writ large. In turn, on the streets, activism manifested increasingly in campaigns for self-protection (such as safe-streets patrols) that blurred the terms of gay community cohesion and crime control. In other words, in arguing that they were *not* criminals or safe from harm, many gay men and lesbians—in particular those who benefited from the protection of whiteness or class status—aligned themselves with dominant narratives about those who *were*. These assumptions shaped their sense of who did and did not belong in gay neighborhoods: the same determination at the core of Kelling and Wilson's own solution.

And with time, these suppositions achieved the status of common knowledge. Aligned with the popular uptake of urban research—including public familiarity with theories of, for example, the culture of poverty, Black rage, and rational choice criminology—white gay activists turned to cooperative *and* crime of opportunity policing rather than anti-poverty solutions, deeming the latter impossible to realize. Even the very concept of *homophobia* would be ascribed to a uniform culture of racialized poverty. Moynihan's use of the culture of poverty thesis described a Black propensity for violence and attributed it to inequality and emasculation resulting from female-headed households. At the same time, definitions of homophobia outlined a vulnerable masculinity that might take expression in violent behavior. Considered together, Black poverty—rather than the structural constraints upholding the ideals of the normative nuclear family or procreative sex—was seen as a risk to gay identity, which thus functioned, by default, as white, male, and middle-class, even as activists sought to expand the category of gay identity beyond these lines. As a result, the fight against crime was often expressed as a fight against homophobia, itself increasingly

24 Hector Simms, "New York Gay Ghettos," Gay, December 15, 1969, 4–5.

understood as the expression of *disorder* associated with those most targeted by police policy dedicated to normalization and control. And, borrowing from the feminist anti-rape movement, activists often found danger in the signs of *potential* threat—whether in the embodiment of those who seemed to be outsiders or in line with the race and class terms of a "homophobic" diagnosis—which aligned with a broken windows–style fixation on the outsider rather than the violent act itself.[25]

By the end of the 1970s, gay activists were leaders in community-partnership policing models. While some were certainly influenced by the broad law-and-order politics set into motion by Richard Nixon and other conservative politicians of the era, mainstream lesbian and gay ideas of urban crime, safety, and the role of the police continued to borrow from liberal visions.[26] These included the ongoing influence of racialized ideas of psychological injury and the values of self-help from the War on Poverty and other liberal programs of the period, but also from new municipal police policies. The growth of national gay anti-violence politics was anchored in anti-crime models based in New York and San Francisco. As Agee has shown, the emergence of a cosmopolitan liberalism in San Francisco merged the ethos of inclusiveness with a hard-nosed fight against crime. This followed the development of empirically oriented managerial growth politics: the eventual strategies adopted would privilege the localist visions of a professional class that supported stronger police discretion as part of community-based policing—the cornerstone of broken windows theory's participatory, collaborative solutions.[27]

As gay safety activism moved onto a national stage, activists sought partnership with other national—and even international—efforts dedicated to fighting crime. The crime victims' rights movement, for example, had gained prominence in the early 1980s and, along with the Anti-Defamation League (ADL) of

25 I discuss this dynamic in more detail in *Safe Space*, as well as in Christina B. Hanhardt, "Butterflies, Whistles, and Fists: Gay Safe Streets Patrols and the New Gay Ghetto, 1976–1981," Radical History Review 100 (2008): 61–85.

26 For a detailed study of the influence of liberals on postwar prison expansion, see Naomi Murakawa, *The First Civil Right: How Liberals Built Prison America* (New York: Oxford University Press, 2014). Also see Ruth Wilson Gilmore, *Golden Gulag: Prisons, Surplus, Crisis, and Opposition in Globalizing California* (Berkeley: University of California Press, 2007).

27 Agee, *The Streets of San Francisco.*

B'nai B'rith, become leaders in the fight for hate crime statutes (which further penalize crimes found to be motivated by bias). LGBT activists found common ground with the ADL's fight against religious persecution, arguing that lesbians and gay men shared the experience of non-visible marginalized identities and that threats to both groups often manifested in attacks on the built environment or within neighborhoods that *represented* those targeted.

It is also worth noting that among the ADL's leading projects during this period were campaigns combating US student activism against Zionism and supporting US–Israeli police training exchanges. The latter efforts were facilitated by the ADL's affiliated William and Naomi Gorowitz Institute on Terrorism and Extremism. In 2010 the Gorowitz Institute honored William Bratton, noting the connection between his early training in hate crime policy in Boston and his later implementation of broken windows policing in New York.[28] As mentioned above, broken windows theory first formalized in New York quality-of-life policing in the gay enclave of the West Village. Both gay and straight residents collaborated with one of the policy's biggest advocates—the Guardian Angels, a controversial anti-crime vigilante group supported by then New York mayor Rudolph Giuliani—as they targeted loitering, noise, drugs, sex work, and gangs, and took aim at LGBT youth and trans women of color.

"Gay, Straight, Black, White, All United to Fight the Right!"

The activists who mobilized on behalf of Blue's represented a broad range of organizations.[29] This included members of Black and White Men Together (BWMT), Dykes Against Racism Everywhere (DARE), the Coalition against Racism, Anti-Semitism, Sexism, and Heterosexism (CRASH), Salsa Soul Sisters, All-People's Congress, Harlem Metropolitan Community Church, Third

28 "Top Cop William Bratton Honored by ADL for His Vision and Service," Anti-Defamation League press release, October 11, 2010, adl.org.

29 The most detailed academic treatment of the political response to the raid on Blue's can be found in Abram J. Lewis, "'Within the Ashes of Our Survival': Lesbian and Gay Antiracist Organizing in New York City, 1980–1984," Thinking Gender Papers, University of California, Los Angeles, available at escholarship.org.

World Lesbian and Gay Alliance, El Comité Homosexual Latinamericano, Lavender Left, and the New York Prostitutes Collective (which was associated with both Black Women for Wages for Housework and Wages Due Lesbians), among others. Many of these groups also joined the newly founded Coalition Against Police Repression.[30] The raid in late September 1982 was followed by another police raid in early October, considered by activists to be retaliation by the police for the attention they had garnered. With momentum continuing to build, over 1,100 people turned out to the organizers' biggest protest, on October 15, 1982. The issue was covered by the gay press nationwide, and San Francisco activists even held a solidarity rally.[31]

The focus of the protests was twofold: most immediately, activists sought to link the attack on Blue's to other challenges to gay and lesbian bars in the city as well as to new patterns of gentrification and policing. They highlighted, for example, how lesbian bars had been targeted for removal by the city's administrative strategies; both the Duchess and Déjà Vu, the latter of which had a large lesbian of color clientele, had been denied liquor licenses despite a lack of official complaints. Activists also protested police sweeps that profiled trans women of color for suspected prostitution in Greenwich Village, especially near the piers at the end of historic Christopher Street and up the West Side to the meatpacking district.[32] They connected the attacks on gay bars and trans women with the denial of public housing to nontraditional family units, the enforcement of rigid anti-immigration laws, and the criminalization of prostitution, all of which were understood to be

30 "1000 Lesbians, Gays, Supporters March to Hit Cop Attacks on Black Gay Bar," Workers World, October 22, 1982, 6; New York Prostitute's Collective, Press Release, October 12, 1982. Both of these can be found in the International Gay Information Collection at the New York Public Library (hereafter IGIC) under Ephemera—Bars, Blue's Bar. See also Coalition Against Police Repression, "Fightback! Stop the Police," flyer, n/d, IGIC (under Ephemera—Organizations, Coalition Against Police Repression).

31 Ibid; "Bay Area Action Condemns Raid on NYC Black Gay Bar," Workers World, November 5, 1982, 9, IGIC (under Ephemera—Bars, Blue's Bar File).

32 Coalition Against Police Repression, "Stop the Arrests!" Flyer, IGIC (under Ephemera—Organizations, Coalition Against Police Repression); Dykes Against Racism Everywhere, Open Letter/Undated Statement (circa 1983), Lesbian Herstory Archives (hereafter LHA) (under DARE). Consistent with the dominant language of the time, trans women—as an expansive category—were referred to as "transvestites" and "transsexuals." This solidarity with trans women is a striking feature of these campaigns within the history of queer Left and lesbian-feminist organizing.

part and parcel of the gentrification of the city more generally.[33] Activists' second focus was to tie these issues to the risks of an ascendant Right on a local and national scale. They named the threat of Ronald Reagan's proposed Family Protection Act, arguing that the ideal of the normative family was linked to efforts to "clean up" places like Times Square. And many activists, especially those associated with Left/ socialist political parties, put the blame for the attack on Blue's squarely on newly elected mayor Edward Koch. Although a Democrat, Koch won the election with promises to use law-and-order and austerity tactics to facilitate the transformation of places such as Times Square. Like Reagan, his supposedly charismatic charm and populist appeal was part of the rise of neoliberal centrist coalitions in the early 1980s. In 1981, Koch praised Reagan at a press conference at the Waldorf Astoria, aligning himself against Jimmy Carter with his position on Israel and calling Reagan a "man of character." In exchange, the White House approvingly acknowledged Koch's lack of a strong opposition to massive federal cuts to city services.[34]

In later years, Koch would occupy a contradictory place in the political estimations of the gay community: he was unforgivably slow to respond to AIDS but was also an active public supporter of anti-discrimination legislation. In this context, the attack on Blue's and the political response to it presented an opportunity to mobilize those lesbians and gay men who had become complacent about the issues affecting the most marginalized LGBT people, their distance from these issues well represented by the Mondale-headlined fundraiser. Activists emphasized that the attack on Blue's was more violent than the Stonewall raid had been, and that the targets of gentrification and policing who were not always LGBT-identified—such as sex workers, homeless people, and drug users—should also be included in LGBT political coalitions. Their approach contrasted with that of more mainstream gay organizations, who responded to the rise of the Right with

33 See, for example, Dykes Against Racism Everywhere, "How Do We Work?" n.d., LHA (under DARE); Dykes Against Racism Everywhere, public letter on behalf of the Anti-Police Abuse Coalition, 1984, LHA (under DARE).

34 Steven Weisman, "The Reagan–Koch Alliance," New York Times, March 17, 1981. For a personality comparison of Reagan and Koch that also notes their shared status as former liberals, see Norman Podhoretz, "Why Reagan and Koch Are the Most Popular Politicians in America," New York Magazine, April 6, 1981, 30–2.

solutions to reported heightening of street violence based in self-protection and "crime awareness."[35]

In the early 1980s, activists across the country adopted and refuted the merged terms of gay protection and gentrification. In San Francisco, Lesbians Against Police Violence (LAPV) staged a skit about the interaction of lesbian vulnerability, policing, and neighborhood transformation. Titled "Count the Contradictions," it was organized as a sequence of scenes in a gentrifying neighborhood in which the realization of opportunity for some foreclosed it for others: white lesbians calling for police protection from random street harassment that increased violence against working-class Latino men; multiple-adult lesbian households outpricing single mothers; gay men's desires for an affirmative, visible identity manifesting in private property; and gay developers' claims of group identity excluding gay men without the ability to afford the rent. LAPV members performed on street corners and hosted discussions and reading groups that explored changing policing strategies in the context of capitalist development, locating the vexed terms of safety as the key ground for debate.

Years later, the formalization of quality-of-life policing in New York and its application in laws such as "sit/lie" ordinances (which prohibit sitting or lying down in public spaces) in San Francisco and other California cities would also meet creative responses from social movements. In Greenwich Village, for example, where Bratton's new policy affected LGBT youth of color most directly, activists from groups such as Fabulous Independent Educated Radicals for Community Empowerment (FIERCE) fought quality-of-life policing in an attempt to stall the hyper-development of a long-gentrified area. Among their most innovative tactics were protests in which demonstrators simply enacted prohibited acts: eating or playing cards while seated on street corners, drawing graffiti (on disposable objects), listening to music and having fun. Activists also participated in community meetings, despite official regulations stipulating that only those with residential—as opposed to use—claims on the neighborhood could participate.

35 For example, see Gay People's Self-Protection Program, Sponsored by Chelsea Gay Association and Safety and Fitness Exchange, "New York Can Be a *Safe* Place!" IGIC (under Ephemera—Organizations, Chelsea Gay Association).

Conclusion

For decades, those who have engaged in critical debate about gentrification instead of celebrating the process as a natural achievement of the market have been divided into two main camps: those who emphasize the significance of individual consumer choice and those who highlight the global dynamics of uneven economic development. Examining the role of gay men as motors of gentrification has been a key way to explore moral imperatives within a consumer landscape; this has also been the case in discussions of artists and others seen as occupying ambiguous class positions in the urban context. But as Neil Smith once argued, it was capital moving "back to the city" rather than the origins or preferences of individual new residents that most determined people's claims to place.[36]

In this way, LGBT populations should not be understood as the vanguard of gentrification or as uniquely vulnerable to the violence of policing. Such arguments restrict themselves to the framework of consumer choice and distill police violence as motivated by individual responses to singular categories of alterity. These assumptions are central to liberal critiques of gentrification and policing that maintain both as open to remediation. Rather, the correlation between gay identity and gentrification is most secured by those who capitalize on what they claim to be essential characteristics or conditions that are celebrated by the market.

To repeat, mainstream gay political claims in the city emerged by expanding the distance—conceptual *and* spatial—between affirmative gay identity and the broad matrix of so-called deviances often associated with racialized poverty. This was facilitated by the claim that policing should focus on behavior (such as loitering) rather than status (such as homosexual). But that strategy did little to assist those who remained locked within the stronghold of criminalization's categorizations, releasing some without challenging one of their greater purposes—namely, to prime the city for private investment.

36 Neil Smith, "Toward a Theory of Gentrification: A Back to the City Movement by Capital, Not People," Journal of the American Planning Association 45, no. 4 (1979), 538–48.

Here gay identity functions in opposition to *disorder*; the people marked for dispossession in the new economy may be targeted in the name of "gay safety." This is the material of quality-of-life policing: Kelling and Wilson's treatise is in many ways a rejection of the separation of status from behavior. As Allen Feldman writes, "Arrest is the political art of individualizing disorder."[37] These ideas are also in line with social science research and policy that treats poverty as a pathology that harms not only the individual but neighborhoods as well, justifying "cleanups" that provide pro ts to owners rather than resources to residents. Such research and policies underscore the central role liberal psychology has played in neoliberal policing that individualizes ideas of harm and protection. Today the idea of "safe space" so common in classroom and social service contexts can sometimes be, like broken windows theory, more about the perception of safety than anything else.

This analysis of the relationship between policing and gentrification has also been elaborated by activists such as James Credle, with whom I opened this essay and who was a member of Black and White Men Together (BWMT; later, Men of All Colors Together) in the 1980s. In general, radical anti-gentrification groups such as BWMT, DARE, LAPV, and CRASH fought gay participation in gentrification less by targeting individual consumer choice —DARE, for example, recognized the benefits of pooled resources among lesbians while warning against those who would capitalize on that shared identity for profit—and more by dedicating themselves to organizing around issues like policing (such as the raid on Blue's) that facilitated gentrification on the ground. This multi-issue and multi-scale tactic currently characterizes a new generation of activism against order maintenance policing as it has taken form in policies across the United States and the world: whether in heightened ticketing in Ferguson, Missouri; stop and frisk in New York and Baltimore; or police–community partnerships in Chicago and Milwaukee. Political scientist Cathy Cohen recently described some of this activism—notably led by Black youth, and that she groups as part of a broad "black lives movement"—as among the

37 Allen Feldman, *Formations of Violence: The Narrative of the Body and Political Terror in Northern Ireland* (Chicago: University of Chicago Press), 109. I am grateful to Ruth Wilson Gilmore, who first introduced me to this quotation in *Golden Gulag* (235).

most interesting examples of radical queer politics today. Her contention is based not only on the significant proportion of LGBT and queer-identified people in the movement's leadership, but also on the focus of these campaigns on how such policies seek to normalize and discipline kinship, gender, and everyday pleasures in ways inclusive of but not reducible to LGBT identity alone.[38]
In many of these campaigns in recent years, activists have shown how the regulation of behavior deemed to be non-normative can be tightly entwined with real estate interests. For example, in Milwaukee, Dontre Hamilton was shot to death by a police officer who had responded to a call from Starbucks workers who had supposedly followed company protocol and reported Hamilton's behavior as making them feel uncomfortable.[39] Hamilton had been sleeping in Red Arrow Park, and the placement of the café there is an example of the kind of public–private partnerships that Wisconsin governor Scott Walker had so prized when he was Milwaukee County executive.[40] In New York City, police killed Akai Gurley in a stairwell of the Louis H. Pink Houses in East New York, one of Brooklyn's poorest neighborhoods and currently the site of rampant real estate speculation. The police cited the dangerous reputation of the complex, but little if any responsibility was assumed by the New York City Housing Authority, which failed to provide sufficient lighting in its stairwells.[41] And Eric Garner was killed by police in New York after suspicion of selling "loosies" (single cigarettes)—exactly the type of minor violation targeted by quality-of-life laws.[42]

38 Cathy Cohen, "#DoBlackLivesMatter? From Michael Brown to CeCe McDonald on Black Death and LGBTQ Politics," Kessler Lecture, Center for Lesbian and Gay Studies, City University of New York, December 12, 2014. Also see Cathy J. Cohen and Sarah J. Jackson, "Ask a Feminist: A Conversation with Cathy Cohen on Black Lives Matter, Feminism, and Contemporary Activism," forthcoming in the summer 2016 issue of Signs.
39 This claim is based on the testimony of one of the Starbucks workers reported by the organization Occupy Riverwest and repeated by the local press. Her full testimony is available at occupyriverwest.com.
40 Harold A. Perkins, "The Production of Urban Vulnerability through Market-Based Parks Governance," *Cities, Nature, and Development: The Politics and Production of Urban Vulnerabilities*, eds. Sarah Dooling and Gregory Simon (Surrey, England: Ashgate Publishing, 2012).
41 Michael Wilson, "Officer's Errant Shot Kills Unarmed Brooklyn Man," New York Times, November 21, 2014.
42 For a discussion of the NYPD's targeting of the sale of single cigarettes as a way to combat "disorder" and of its role in the arrest of Eric Garner, see Al Baker, J. David Goodman, and Benjamin Mueller, "Beyond the Chokehold: The Path to Eric Garner's Death," New York Times, June 13, 2015.

In all of these cases, radical LGBT and queer activists were among those who organized in response, and they countered the claims of mainstream LGBT organizations that prioritize inclusion in the status quo over broad social and economic transformation. In the words of Cara Page of the Audre Lorde Project and Krystal Portalatin of FIERCE, the real threats are not those individuals whose lives are considered to be at a distance from dominant "norms," but rather:

when banks are allowed to engage in predatory practices that target communities of color and force groups to remain in poverty; when Detroit can declare bankruptcy on a city of mostly black communities and then take away basic rights such as water; when corporations are allowed to abuse other countries and depress US economies; when the US military continues to back and support Israel's oppression of Palestinian people and land.[43]

In this way, activists continue to draw the connections between local and global acts of policing and dispossession, while tracing how the construction of social norms—and how they are made legible through the interplay of, in particular, race, gender, and sexuality—are central to this process. And, finally, they show how the promises of solidarity offer much more than those of safety, and provide a collective alternative to solutions defined within rather than against the market.

43 See "Wake Up, Rise Up!" press release written by Cara Page, executive director of the Audre Lorde Project, and Krystal Portalatin, co-director of FIERCE, and cosigned by the Griot Circle, New York City Anti-Violence Project, Streetwise and Safe, and the Sylvia Rivera Law Project, December 3, 2014, available at fiercenyc.org.

Fred W. McDarrah, *Stonewall Celebrations,* 1969
A group of young people celebrate outside the boarded-up Stonewall Inn (53 Christopher Street) after riots over the weekend of June 27, 1969, that led to the formation of the modern gay rights movement in the United States.

THANSA

Coda

In the spring of 2022, the British Parliament passed the Police, Crime, Sentencing and Courts (PCSC) Act, which criminalized activities that cause "serious annoyance" or "unease" in public space, with the primary intent to restrict forms of protest. Around the same time, the mayor of New York City, Eric Adams, proposed a new policing initiative focused on so-called quality-of-life issues, bringing back to the city the ethos of broken windows policing. Both policies and the resistance each faced from activists are related to each other and to the history told here, and they are also tied to the global impacts of both the COVID-19 pandemic and social movements highlighting antiblack police violence.

As was the case during the years when broken windows policing was first popularized, these contemporary policies cast rising rates of homelessness, inadequate health services, and new collectives organized in response as problems of social order and discomfort rather than as evidence of the need for resources, and mark certain people—be they sex workers, cruising gay men, drug users, trans women, single mothers, unemployed young people, the mentally ill, protesters, or those simply living in public, especially those who are Black and/or assumed migrants—for removal. As in 1982, forty years later the paired projects of state abandonment and state violence (to cite Ruth Wilson Gilmore) continue to target unregulated street life—be that protests or poverty—and *queerness* often figures as a central if unspoken key term. And just as the attack on Blue's and introduction of broken windows policing theory in 1982 was joined by the simultaneous celebration of gay investment in the city, the PCSC Act criminalizes practices outside social norms, as it also pardons some convictions for same-sex sexual activity, and Mayor Adams' proposal for increased funding to police undesirable street life was soon followed by one for LGBT programs and initiatives.

What do we make of this? And what might we do? The violent raid of Blue's occasioned a groundswell of protests that linked different social movements together in response, and so do we today see new coalitions and formations. In the 1980s, activists were innovating visions to respond to Ronald Reagan's and Margaret Thatcher's attacks on social safety nets with, among other strategies, the development of harm reduction practices and collective community care during the height of the HIV/AIDS crisis in the U.S. and U.K. Similarly, in 2020, activists responded to the faux populisms of Donald Trump and Boris Johnson with mutual aid networks in response to COVID-19. In the late 1970s and early 1980s, radical Black activists in London organized in response to the sus (suspected person) law, and, in the years just following, New York activists came together to protest the police killing of Michael Stewart in 1983 and Eleanor Bumpers in 1984. In all these cases, Black feminist organizers demanded that the fight against antiblack police violence include an understanding of gendered violence. #BlackLivesMatter first rose to prominence in 2013, and queer politics was central to its vision; in the almost ten years since, a variety of organizations and collectives committed to Black life and fighting against state violence have grown on a global scale. Although they do not always appear under that name, they often keep queer issues at the top of their agenda. And, of course, many of these struggles and goals have been staged in informal networks and practices that extend much further back and that are not always realized in social movement form. But in most all of these contexts, questions about the state—as both provider of resources and discipline—remain under debate, in particular about how one balances demands that the state provide for the equitable distribution of goods and care with the promise of making something anew.

The frescos of Hannah Quinlan and Rosie Hastings feature many of these same figures and dynamics, without reducing people to categorical types nor making them easy to place—in city space, in social movements, or in our intimate worlds. In these images, public space includes pastoral parks, institutional buildings, and residential areas, but also boxes neither inside nor outside. Authorities appear at first glance clearly delineated, but a close look reveals that identity or style might not be the best way to sort sides. Practices of care are shown as both individual and collective, but they are also revealed as potentially reactive and self-serving. The source of violence is not always clear, nor is the recipient of a pointed look, even as the rhythms of everyday life appear to continue on. Outside of precise time or place, these scenes are our history and our present, but they also distill the contradictions and dialectics of power which might then let us see something new.

Christina B. Hanhardt is an associate professor in the Department of American Studies at the University of Maryland, College Park. She is the author of the book *Safe Space: Gay Neighborhood History and the Politics of Violence* (Duke, 2013).

Hannah Quinlan & Rosie Hastings

T u l i p s

List of Works
Hannah Quinlan & Rosie Hastings

pp. 44—55
A History of Morality, 2022
Fresco on wooden panel, 200 × 200 × 5 cm
Courtesy the artists, Tate Britain, London and Arcadia Missa, London

pp. 56—67
Common Subjects, 2022
Fresco on wooden panel, 200 × 200 × 5 cm
Courtesy the artists, Tate Britain, London and Arcadia Missa, London

pp. 68—79
Expulsion, 2022
Fresco on wooden panel, 200 × 200 × 5 cm
Courtesy the artists, Tate Britain, London and Galerie Isabella Bortolozzi, Berlin

pp. 80—91
Public Decency, 2022
Fresco on wooden panel, 200 × 200 × 5 cm
Courtesy the artists, Tate Britain, London and Galerie Isabella Bortolozzi, Berlin

pp. 92—103
Testimony, 2022
Fresco on wooden panel, 200 × 200 × 5 cm
Courtesy the artists, Tate Britain, London and Arcadia Missa, London

pp. 104—117
The Disinherited, 2022
Fresco on wooden panel, 200 × 200 × 5 cm
Courtesy the artists, Tate Britain, London and Arcadia Missa, London

The series of fresco paintings was created for the exhibition *Tulips* presented at *Art Now* at Tate Britain, London, curated by Amy Emmerson Martin. September 24, 2022 — May 7, 2023.

Available titles of the book series

Disss-co (A Fragment)
Douglas Crimp with Henrik Olesen
English edition

Tumbling Ruins
Henrike Naumann with Angela Schönberger and Andreas Brandolini
German and English edition

Exposing Tears
Lighting The Archive with Mike Sperlinger on Marianne Wex and Chauncey Hare
German and English edition

By The Highway
Ser Serpas with Rafik Greiss and Dora Budor
German and English edition

KONTEXT is a series by DISTANZ

Acknowledgments

Matthias Kliefoth wants to deeply thank Hannah Quinlan & Rosie Hastings and Christina B. Hanhardt.

A special thanks by Hannah Quinlan & Rosie Hastings goes to Arcadia Missa, Galerie Isabella Bortolozzi, Zoe Bromberg-McCarthy, Dr Isabella Maidment, Vaso Papadopoulou, Aristea Rellou, Dominic Lauren, Shaan Bevan, Rozsa Farkas, Fleur Kelly, Jackson Bateman, Amy Emmerson Martin, Tate Britain, London and Christina B. Hanhardt.

Colophon

Editor
Matthias Kliefoth

Design
Manuel Tayarani

Essay
Christina B. Hanhardt

Proofreading
Charlotte Riggert

Photo Credits
Josef Konczak (pp. 44–117)

Image Editing
Reproline mediateam, Munich

Production Management
Charlotte Riggert

Printing and Binding
Druckhaus Sportflieger, Berlin

Distribution
Edel Germany GmbH
international-books@edel.com

ISBN 978-3-95476-517-1
Printed in Germany

Published by
DISTANZ Verlag
www.distanz.de

This book is also published in a German edition.